hair

hair

its power and meaning in asian cultures

edited by

alf hiltebeitel

and

barbara d. miller

foreword by

gananath obeyesekere

STATE UNIVERSITY OF NEW YORK PRESS

Published by
State University of New York Press, Albany

Printed in the United States of America

For information, address State University of New York Press,
State University Plaza, Albany, N.Y., 12246

Production by Marilyn P. Semerad
Marketing by Nancy Farrell

Library of Congress Cataloging-in-Publication Data

Hair : its power and meaning in Asian Cultures / edited by Alf
Hiltebeitel and Barbara D. Miller.
p. cm.
Includes index.
ISBN 0-7914-3741-8 (hc : alk. paper). — ISBN 0-7914-3742-6 (pb :
alk. paper)
1. Hair—Social aspects—Asia. 2. Hair—Erotic aspects—Asia.
3. Hairstyles—Asia—History. 4. Hair-work, Ornamental—Asia–
–History. 5. Asia—Social life and customs. I. Hiltebeitel, Alf.
II. Miller, Barbara D., 1948–
GT2295.A8H35 1998
391.5'095—dc21 97-27147
CIP

10 9 8 7 6 5 4 3 2 1

contents

list of illustrations

Figure 1. A Tamil *sādhu* named Balanand, visiting a festival for the south Indian god Kūttāṇṭavar near Coimbatore, unwinds his matted locks and draws admiration from a festival-goer. Photo by Alf Hiltebeitel, p. 24.

Figure 2. A Tamil *sādhu* shows the length of his matted locks, which, he says, have grown uncut for fifty years since he was age seven. Photo by Alf Hiltebeitel, p. 25.

Figure 3. Illustration of a baboon from a late imperial encyclopedia; in *Gujin tushu jicheng* (Chinese illustrated encyclopedia), 1726, *ce* 522, *juan* 88, *ji* 23, p. 53.

Figure 4. A picture of an Ainu, a population group in Japan alleged to be covered in hair; in Chen Yinghuang, *Renleixue* (Anthropology), Shanghai: Shangwu yinshuguan, 1928 (1st ed. 1918), p. 56.

Figure 5. A boy born with a tail, meant to illustrate the power of degenerative evolutionary forces; in Chen Yinghuang, *Renleixue* (Anthropology), Shanghai: Shangwu yinshuguan, 1928 (1st ed. 1918), p. 58.

Figure 6. Different types of beards in one of the earliest anthropology textbooks in Republican China; in Chen Yinghuang, *Renleixue* (Anthropology), Shanghai: Shingwu yinshuguan, 1928 (1st ed. 1918), p. 59.

Figure 7. A bearded woman, symbol of hermaphroditism in a textbook on sexual differences; in Zhu Xi, *Cixiong zhi bian* (The changes of female and male), Shanghai: Wenhua shenghuo chubanshe, 1945), p. 62.

Figure 8. Hairy man Li Baoshu, put on display in Beijing's zoo during the 1920s; in Liu Mingyu et al. (eds.), *Zhongguo maoren* (Hairy men of China), Shengyang: Liaoning kexue jishu chubanshe, 1982, p. 63.

foreword

gananath obeyesekere

It seems that, though hair has had a perennial fascination for persons in many cultures, the study of hair has never been a popular enterprise for us scholars. It is therefore a pleasure to have this collection of finely nuanced ethnographic studies of the social, personal, and historical meanings of hair in Asian cultures. In dealing with hair this collection also celebrates a feature of contemporary intellectual discourse, namely, the blurring of disciplinary boundaries, such that ethnography no longer is an exclusive preserve of anthropologists. Historians of religions like Hiltebeitel have done extensive field work, while Indologists and historians like Patrick Olivelle and Frank Dikötter have imaginatively ethnographized the past. Such an imaginative procedure requires a detailed cultural and historical contextualization of hair from whence we can deal with issues of larger theoretical interest.

This latter task has been admirably performed by the contributors to this volume. They share with those they study an obsession with hair but hair leads them to more general societal issues. Thus Alf Hiltebeitel's preoccupation with the goddess's mustache leads him to Hindu transvestitism and the crossing of gender boundaries in general; Anne Allison's unusual paper on the Japanese refusal to publicly print female pubic hair and penises leads her to an examination of their censorship laws, the transgression of normative boundaries, and the male anxieties that lie hidden beneath the unprintable; Weikun Cheng and Sarah Nelson refer us to the imperial power structures that use hair to forcibly produce national conformity; while Julia Thompson and Barbara Miller deal with the emancipatory significance of Western hair styles on Nepalese and Indian women. The unexpected pathways into which hair can lead us can be neatly illustrated through Frank Dikötter's study of the deeply entrenched Chinese prejudices that equate hairiness with wildness and, more generally, with otherness. Here we have a fascinating example of "orientalism" in the orient. In this case, conventional labels such as "occidentalism" or "reverse orientalism" won't do because the hairy barbarians held in dread are not only Westerners but also non-Western hairy beings such as Sri Lankans! These and other theoretical and methodological issues dealt with in this volume will surely be debated by scholars in their respective fields.

But why is hair the key signifier or semiotic device used by a variety of Asian cultures for opening up multiple worlds of meaning? In this regard I find Patrick Olivelle's theoretical paper extremely persuasive. As I reread it, hair is by itself not a "natural symbol" but one that provokes the work of culture. Hair is just there as a product of our biological inheritance; but it cannot be just left there. Hair must be dealt with; thus everywhere there is cultural control of hair and this includes those groups who let their hair down or keep it in a culturally defined "natural" state. The question of why hair gets such an affective load brings us to the other dimension of Olivelle's theory. In human beings, in addition to head hair with which one is born, there is hair growth at the onset of puberty and sexual maturity. This key biological condition is the basis, I think, for the opinion that Ebersole shares with several other contributors and which states that "many cultures associate loose hair with sexuality." Moreover, hair that is cut regenerates itself and it can therefore pick up associations with other cultural symbols of regeneration and fertility. Thus, says Olivelle following Victor Turner, hair has a "root meaning" and on this root meaning (or rather a set of root meanings) a culture can erect its own "grammar" or semiotics of hair. I might add that the root symbolism of hair is not static and it can get all sorts of accretions, as for example, when cultures familiar with wild animals might pick hair as a conspicuous feature of wildness and then transfer those associations to human body hair, as in the Chinese case documented by Dikötter and in the medieval European ideas of the "wild man." To borrow another phrase from Victor Turner, what one has here is a "symbolic field" of root meanings. Olivelle himself sketches the outline of the cultural grammar of hair while others examine looser and more open fields of meanings.

Olivelle says, quite rightly, that cultural grammars are themselves "loose," like hair itself. Thus another striking feature of cultural definitions of hair: there seems to be an oppositional dialectic between hair that is tightly groomed or bound and loose hair, illustrated in several of the case studies in this volume. This dialectical relation is not always rigidly structured as binary oppositions either; in some instances those who let their hair down, like those Chinese protesting Manchu tightness, are actively resisting tyrannical impositions of imperial power. Moreover, these case studies invite us to reconsider the neat demarcations with which social theorists structuralize their own theoretical worlds, notions like society and psyche, mind and body. The social and the psychological cannot often be disaggregated; thus control of hair in the Manchu imperial style implies the exercise of power, but I am not convinced that power is not implicated in sexuality, at least obliquely. One can say that the control of hair implies a control of the emotions whereas loose hair shows a loosening of such controls in grief and in love (for surely even Korean and Indian women must let their hair down in bed), in vengeance and the like. But a loosening of control does not mean an absence of cultural control over hair because loose hair is a way to culturally designate (and in some instances design) the loosening of emotions. Thus hirsute and disheveled people are deliberately disheveled, the most notable case being those dropouts from communist and bourgeois culture neatly described by James Watson. Watson's paper brings me to another psychological dimension of hair: anomaly breeds anxiety. Hong Kong destitutes do not see themselves as anomalous; but they, like loose-haired creatures in the other cases, are seen as anomalous beings by *another*, often dominant, segment of the social order. Moreover, loose women and other anomalous ones (even matted-hair ascetics of India) perhaps provoke unconscious anxieties in the beholder, for they can tap hidden and prohibited feelings kept under control among the upright and hair-tight citizenry. Finally one might say that there are instances when neither social nor psychological analysis makes much immediate sense. What happens when women *have* to loosen their hair when they bathe in rivers or in other public places in India, Korea, or wherever hair is tied, braided, or bundled? I suggest that this external situation is not without cultural meaning either, because loosening one's hair, when ordinary conditions demand it, is a cue that selectively activates preexisting cultural associations of loose hair, such that public bathing and similar situations are occasions for gossip, flirting, and relaxed behavior in general.

My final comment is that our descriptions of hair symbolism might suggest a cultural rigidity. But one can after all "unwork" cultural meanings. This unworking is a complex phenomenon but it is clearly highlighted in the case of Kathmandu females and their close cuts. The fact is that there appears to have been no great hue and cry over this stylistic change. It is not only the women protesters who unwork cultural meanings; their parents and others, who might initially oppose it, may end up by giving them their blessings or silently coconspiring with them in bringing about change. I am not suggesting that this happens everywhere; it would not have been possible in Manchu China. But some cultures and subcultures may be more ready for the work of unworking than others, Newari culture perhaps being one example. I am fascinated by the bold Newari woman who shaved her head when her mother died and, horror of horrors, "she even went to the Pashupati [Siva temple] and lit the funeral pyre." But there is a hidden scenario here; why did the temple priests acquiesce in this whole thing, if acquiesce they did? To go back to hair metaphors: the unworking of cultural meanings is a collaborative process in which old structures are "loosened." And while we know little about the cultural conditions and human actions that bring about this process, we do know that some cultures provide greater leeway than others for cultural unworking, while everywhere the historical movement toward modernity is receptive to changing and then recontrolling body behavior. And that applies to hair styles also.

acknowledgments

This volume, like a head of hair in classical Japanese poetry, is a collecting place for powerful spirits, or at least, many helpful people with bright ideas. In the spring of 1992, several Asianists met for dinner following a talk by Charlotte Furth at the University of Pittsburgh—Charlotte Furth, Rubie Watson, Evelyn Rawski, Katy Carlitz, and Barbara Miller. Hair styles, hair meanings, and all kinds of hair became a topic of lively interchange. Alf Hiltebeitel had recently visited the University of Pittsburgh where he had delivered a series of talks for the Asian Studies Program and the Department of Religion. So the topic of hair was in the air. Themes from Hiltebeitel's research on the Hindu goddess Draupadi's hair circled through the conversation. It was suggested that someone should organize a comparative panel on hair at the 1993 meeting of the Association for Asian Studies. Everyone thought the idea was great. Barbara Miller linked up with Alf Hiltebeitel to do the organizing.

That dinner table idea developed into a double panel at the meetings in Los Angeles on "Hair in Asia." The panel included papers by Anne Allison, Frank Dikötter, Alf Hiltebeitel, Barbara D. Miller, Sarah Nelson, Patrick Olivelle, and James Watson. Gananath Obeyesekere served as discussant for the entire set of papers. After the panel, we all met and discussed the possibility of a book. Throughout the following year, additional papers were invited from Weikun Cheng, Gary Ebersole, and Julia Thompson. Gananath Obeyesekere graciously accepted our invitation to write the Foreword.

Along the way, from the initial dinner gathering, through organizing the panel, and final editing of the book, many people have helped us. For their comments and suggestions, we especially thank James Boone, L. Keith Brown, Alison Brooks, Fred Clothey, Liza Dalby, Wendy Doniger, Paul Duff, Shelly Errington, Ian Gilbert, Norman Girardot, Richard Grinker, Robert Goldman, Randy Kloetzli, Dorinne Kondo, Joel Kuipers, Susan MacKinnon, Teresa Murphy, Jonathan Parry, Richard Shweder, Andrew Strathern, Sally Sutherland, Dewey

Wallace, and Harry E. Yeide, Jr. We also thank Nancy Ellegate and Marilyn P. Semerad at the State University of New York Press for their interest in this book and help throughout the publication process. Since the beginning of this project, dozens of people must have said to us: "A book on *what*?" We thank them, too, for their cheerful curiosity and for giving us the chance to keep thinking about why exactly we were doing this.

1 introduction: hair tropes

alf hiltebeitel

Hair seems to be quite ordinary stuff, but it is difficult to discern what is ordinary about it or what sometimes makes it so extraordinary. One might apply Mary Douglas's maxim about impurity, and say that hair, which is often associated with impurity, is matter out of place (1966:35). It would thus have to be ordinary matter when its being out of place can be rectified by setting it in place, until it goes out of place again. From this standpoint, hair would be extraordinary when it appears to have no place at all.

In taking up an invitation to consider hair in Asian cultures, each essayist in this volume can be said to begin by situating her/himself in relation to questions raised by these matters. What is ordinary about hair in Asian population X or tradition X? When is there something extraordinary enough about hair in X to be worth writing about? And how does one write about something so universally ordinary yet sensitive, something that literally gets under one's skin, and takes one under another's?

It is worthwhile to locate the ordinary and the extraordinary in these essays, since each cultural milieu and historical situation has posed different bases for ethnographic description and theoretical reflection. Both Gary Ebersole and Anne Allison, writing about Japan, stress the Japanese perception of hair as "natural," perhaps from its associations in Shinto in which nature is a prominent category. For Ebersole, "the 'natural' symbolism of hair" entails its wildness and links with sexuality, its marking of a person's age. For Allison, although pubic and underarm hair (particularly women's) are "considered natural" in Japan, they are treated otherwise. Each author puts the term in quotes since, as cultural constructionism argues, it is questionable whether human hair, unlike animal hair, ever exists in a natural state. Hair becomes extraordinary when what is "natural" becomes shocking (Allison) or hauntingly beautiful (Ebersole). For Patrick Olivelle, the ordinary has also been natural (though he doesn't use the term) in his treatment of the growth of body hair, and for males' facial hair, with the onset of sexual maturity. He suggests that this trait is uniquely human and one of three factors in the "root meaning" of hair.

But like most of the other essayists in this volume, Olivelle locates the ordinary not in the natural but in the socially and culturally normative. Here the extraordinary is located in breaches of such norms: a woman who shaves her head to perform a funeral rite restricted to males (in Julia Thompson's essay); the disturbing sight of longhaired destitutes (in James Watson's essay); edicts compelling the change of traditional hair styles (Weikun Cheng and Sarah Nelson); the hairiness of barbarians (Frank Dikötter); the transferral of gender codes (Alf Hiltebeitel); varied spectrums of women's hair styles and choices under transcultural negotiation (Barbara Miller).

Emic explanations of hair practices veer between such notions of the ordinary and encounters with the extraordinary, depending on where explanation is attempted. Olivelle, Thompson, Dikötter, Nelson, and Ebersole look to their sources for whatever explanations can be found about hair conventions as they appear, respectively, in lawbooks, hair professions, scientific discourse, sumptuary codes, and poetry. Miller, Cheng, Allison, and Hiltebeitel do the same by looking at family, history, public culture media, and festivals. Most authors bring out varied and competing explanations within their sources. Especially striking is Watson's account of the different explanations for the shocking sight of longhaired destitutes given by Hong Kong urban informants (including police, border patrols, social workers, and diplomats) and villagers still living in their ancestral home areas.

It begins to look as if nothing is ordinary about hair. It gets into everything, but whatever it gets into, it never seems to be explained the same way; rather, it always seems to be used differently to explain something else. Let us consider what is certainly one of Asia's, if not the world's, most sustained meditations on hair. It comes from the Buddhist tradition which, though it is not taken up as a primary focus in any of our essays, is the same tradition that says extraordinary things about the Buddha's hair that are noted by Olivelle and Hiltebeitel, and that, with its practice of head shaving for monks and nuns, has, in the writings of Edmund Leach (1958) and Obeyesekere (1981), probably provoked more theoretical reflection about hair than any other Asian tradition.

In Buddhaghosa's *The Path of Purification*, shaved heads are ordinary and surely in the author's background. Commenting on a passage in which the Buddha directs attention to the "repulsiveness" of the body's thirty-two aspects, Buddhaghosa submits hair to a kind of phenomenological reduction, which he describes as part of "the development of Mindfulness Occupied with the Body as a meditation subject." This is a mindfulness that enables those who savor and find "the deathless" (Nānamoli 1975:259–60). What is first to be noted is the primacy of hair in this meditation. The Buddha's text begins, "Again, bhikkhus, a bhikkhu reviews this body, up from the soles of the feet and down from the top of the hair and contained in the skin as many kinds of filth thus: In this body there are head hairs, body hairs, nails, teeth, skin, flesh, sinews, . . ." etc., down to "urine." Buddhaghosa gives full attention to the rhetorical force of "beginning with head hairs":

> *Head hairs, body hairs:* these things beginning with head hairs are the thirty-two aspects. The construction here should be understood in this way: In this body there are head hairs, in this body there are body hairs.
>
> No one who searches through the whole of this fathom-long carcase, starting upwards from the soles of the feet, starting downward from the top of the head, and starting from the skin all round, ever finds even the minutest atom at all beautiful in it, such as a pearl, or a gem, or beryl, or aloes, or saffron, or camphor, or talcum powder; on the contrary he finds nothing but the very malodorous, offensive, drab-looking sort of filth consisting of head hairs, body hairs, and the rest. Hence it is said: "In this body there are head hairs, body hairs . . . urine." (Nānamoli 1975:261)

Hair—"head hair, body hair"—is thus a synecdoche for the whole body and a metonym for the whole meditation. It is that to which every one of the other thirty-two aspects leads back in a syntagmatic chain. Bhikkhus are enjoined to give attention to the meditation subject through the "sevenfold skill in learning" and the "tenfold skill in giving attention." The first two of the seven ways of learning are verbal and mental recitation. The thirty-two aspects are divided into five pentads and one septad. In both verbal and mental recitation, the first pentad is to be recited forward—"Head hairs, body hairs, nails, teeth, skin"—and then backward, to "head hairs." Likewise, all the remaining sets are recited forward and backward, but the backward recitation continues in each case all the way back to "head hairs." One thus starts with "head hairs, body hairs" only once, but returns to "body hairs, head hairs" six times. And one always ends up the one hundred and forty-nine-part tour where one started: with "head hairs."

> The recitation should be done verbally in this way a hundred times, a thousand times, even a hundred thousand times. For it is through verbal recitation that the meditation subject becomes familiar, and the mind being thus prevented from running here and there, the parts become evident and seem like [the fingers of] a pair of clasped hands, like a row of fence posts. (262)

One notes how the closing image turns from things aggregated to things disaggregated, from things closed in together to things standing separately.

The last five skills of learning then come from attending to the color, shape, direction, location, and delimitation of each of the thirty-two bodily features, beginning with head hair. Delimitation is a technique of identification and differentiation, as in the example, "Head hairs are not body hairs, and body hairs are not head hairs" (Ñānamoli 263). Having "apprehended" the thirty-two features in this five-fold way, the bhikkhu should "define repulsiveness in five ways, that is, by colour, shape, odour, habitat, and location." Here is what makes head hairs repulsive:

> [O]n seeing the colour of head hair in a bowl of inviting rice gruel or cooked rice people are disgusted and say "This has got hairs in it. Take it away." So they are repulsive in *colour*. Also when people are eating at night, they are likewise disgusted by the mere sensation of hair-shaped *akka*-bark or *makaci*-bark fibre. So they are repulsive in *shape*. And the *odour* of head hairs, unless dressed with a smearing of oil, scented with flowers, etc., is most offensive. And it is still worse when they are put in fire. . . . [J]ust as pot herbs that grow on village sewage in a filthy place are disgusting to civilized people and unusable, so also head hairs

> are disgusting since they grow on the sewage of pus, blood, urine, dung, bile, phlegm, and the like. This is the repulsive aspect of the *habitat*. And these head hairs grow on the heap of the [other] thirty-one parts as fungus do on a dung hill. And owing to the filthy place they grow in they are quite as unappetizing as vegetables growing on a charnel ground, on a midden etc., as lotuses or water lilies growing in drains and so on. This is the repulsive aspect of their *location*. (Nānamoli 268–69)

Clearly there is a lot at stake, and quite possibly a good bit of humor, in defining head hairs as repulsive. But once one reaches the last two definitions, the method is clear. Buddhaghosa builds on two features of hair that enter into several discussions in this book. First, hair—or in the strange case of the stringy tree barks felt while eating at night, which by their likeness to hair make us think of hair—can have a certain shock value, and that value can tell us much about hair, and much about ourselves. Second, he draws on a conventional symbolic analogy made widely with hair: that hairs are like plants. But instead of leaving us with the usual mythic decontextualized correspondence, he contextualizes the analogy, as with all the other reductions to the disgusting, to a relatively atypical though certainly not extraordinary situation where disgust at hair is educible. Metaphor becomes metonym. Head hair is contiguous with everything else in the body. Every head hair thus has a disgusting character even when it seems to be in place. But it is when it seems to be out of place that its true ordinariness is seen for what it is. Place being contingent in the Buddhist universe, it is disgusting *everywhere*.

Buddhaghosa is thus troping with hair. That he does so very well is what makes his discussion theoretically interesting, even though he begins with a foregone conclusion: hair is repulsive. What is interesting lies not in this conclusion, which is rather forced, but in his "thick description," his metaphorical lenses, and his further troping through synecdoche, metonymy, and probably irony. What is further instructive is that such troping with hair is rather ordinary. Cultures do it (Turner 1991), and so do scholars (Clifford 1988)—often to support rather foregone conclusions, though, to be sure, the conclusions were not foregone until someone realized that they could explain a great deal. Take the opening of E. E. Sikes's often-cited article in the *Hastings Encyclopedia of Religion and Ethics* as an example of troping in the Frazerian "encyclopaedic" comparative mode (Smith 1982:23):

> In custom, ritual, and superstition, the same ideas underlie the majority of beliefs and ceremonies relating to human hair and nails; and the whole class of observances may conveniently be treated in a single article. . . . [C]ertain practices relating to the hair of the head appear to have originated from the wide-spread belief that the head is particularly sacred. Some races think that a spirit lives in the head, and it is important not to disturb this spirit more than is necessary, or, as among the Greeks, the hair is itself regarded as the seat of life—a belief which is found, in a modified form, among the Omaha. Hence the Burmese shrink from frequent washing of the head; and when the hair of their kings was cut, the operation was attended with great solemnity (Sikes 1912:6, 474).

From this brief example of Asian hair, Sikes's next move is to Samson. The claim that "the majority of beliefs and ceremonies" can be treated in one article is made to support a theory of "connections" grounded on Frazer's concept of sympathetic magic, for which hair practices are indeed often illustrative. The supposed "majority" of hair beliefs and practices is then accounted for by the principle of such connections. A set of practices based on the metonymic principle of contiguity is thus taken as sufficiently representative of hair data as a whole to serve as a synecdoche for that imagined whole, which is explained by and no doubt projected into a metonymic ethnographic style of the most dubious connection making.

Let us note only two further instances in the history of hair theory where tropical enhancement is one of the means of making hair's unruliness manageable: C. R. Hallpike's emphasis on social control (1969) metaphorically makes hair, like society, the subject of "manipulation"; and Gananath Obeyesekere's exploration of unconscious sexual symbolism brings the interpreter and his informants together through the metaphoric image of Medusa (1981:6–7). Olivelle's essay reviews the history of hair theory in order to go to the "roots" of the same subject. And so do nearly all, if not all, of the chapters in this volume make their tropical plays on and with hair. Olivelle "teases out" its social meaning. Thompson traces "the multistranded history of beauty parlors." Miller insists that "the culture of hair is no trivial matter." Cheng finds that hair-cutting and queue-requiring edicts sought "to make Manchus and Hans a unified body." Dikötter and Hiltebeitel play on "missing links"; Nelson on hair as "a life and death matter." Allison signals a tropical alert to the ironies of pubic hair as a "site/sight" for moral arbitration. Olivelle and Ebersole see hair as a "grammar" or "semantic field," with Ebersole in particular concerned with poetic conventions known as "pillow words," one of which puts hair on a cushion. Only Watson makes hair troping hard to spot, but he is respecting a situation in which hair provokes shock and its wearers are silent.

Hair may thus be less finite than at least some theorists have thought. That only God knows the number of the hairs on a human head (to paraphrase Matthew 10.29–30 and Luke 12.6–7) reflects something of the hermeneutical situation. If there is a message in such tropic complicities, it is that hair has had to be richly imagined and contextualized, not only in the histories, cultures, societies, and personal lives described but in the intercultural and interpersonal situations of description; that its messiness and loose ends are resistant to theories that reduce it to manageable proportions; and that theories themselves become entangled in the subject. Olivelle, who is the only one in this book to have proposed a theory of his own, reflects such a situation with his stress on the "dialectical nature of hair symbolism" and his advocacy of a polygenetic approach that traces the root meaning of hair to "a multiplicity of sources," which he works down provisionally to three. His theoretical discussion raises interesting questions, particularly, why are men at the center? It could be argued that the expenditure of effort on hair by men is much less than by women. Men hardly do more than tinker. Women have much more symbolic capital in their hair than men, and men often have more such capital in women's hair than in their own. Perhaps what Olivelle's theory reflects is the way in which marrying men, and often women, may place men at the center in the definition and control of hair norms. Such is indeed what the women do at Thompson's Kathmandu hair salon when they ask, "what kind of woman . . . shaves her head like a man," and does not wait for her brother to perform their mother's cremation? Where such male definition and control do not reach, does the theory still hold? As Obeyesekere notes in his foreword, an uninvested male, like a temple priest, may be supportive to such a woman's determination. Should one theorize from the center or theorize from the boundaries? Olivelle's theoretical position identifies a "central" problem that all are dealing with, and that some might tackle differently. Olivelle's theory serves as a sounding board for the other essays, which tend to be theory selective, theory reflective, or theory resistant rather than theory productive.

The comparative study of hair ripened in formulating south Asia-based paradigms (Leach, Hershman, Obeyesekere, not to mention Buddhaghosa). The catalytic theories developed in these studies are precisely those that are being revised and rethought within different cultural contexts (east Asia for one) and in this book. Studies of hair in south Asia began with a discourse relating psychoanalytic insights primarily to religious data. The combination of south and east Asian studies in this volume contributes to the contemporary shift in theory toward power, politics, and the body that has global relevance. Allison incorporates postmodernist theory, especially French psychoanalytic theory. Thompson finds inspiration in contemporary theorists of globalization, political economy, and the body. Miller's chapter describes three pools of theory: political economy, feminist, and race. Some of these chapters also take up the pros and cons of magical, psychological, and sociological hair theories. Thus Cheng, Ebersole, and Hiltebeitel find points where the magical remains pertinent. Nelson and Cheng find the sociological more useful than the psychological; Hiltebeitel the reverse. Ebersole, Allison, Watson, Miller, Hiltebeitel, and Nelson deal with subjects where muteness or silence—whether politically enforced, culturally tacit, or personally unexpressed—raise questions about what Olivelle calls "exegetical block." These are working premises pertinent to the materials under discussion, strategic to the specificities of hair in certain contexts, and not arguments for the primacy of any of these theories in and of themselves.

What all these chapters have in common is that they are taken up with the politics of hair and the body (Ebersole less here than the rest, but with no lack of attention to the poetics of imperial hair)—and thus hair and the body politic. Indeed, body hair (especially for Dikötter) is, in some cases, given more equal billing with the head-hair/genital-hair axis than theoretical discussions have usually accorded it. If the essays suggest a "master trope," it is boundaries and their control. From this standpoint, the social body is both a bounded construct and a fluid one. Hair norms and policies are defined around civilizational, cultural, racial, caste, and gender boundaries; and around temporal transitions and spatial frontiers. In most of the chapters (Allison, Nelson, Dikötter, Watson, Cheng, Miller) the lines have been overtly if not primarily political. For Thompson, the salon is also a site where cultural styles are negotiated in boundary-breaking conversations. For Olivelle, hair as public marks society's internal boundaries;

for Miller, hair as private marks the family's internal boundaries. For Ebersole, there are permeable boundaries between hair's sacrality and conventionality, its "natural order" (in quotes) and its wildness (out of quotes). For Hiltebeitel, village and festival boundaries are replicated in social and theological distinctions, while present and absent mustaches and phalluses mark gender boundaries under negotiation. To extend Allison's terms from nation to society, culture, religion, and family, one might thus say that in every case there is a "hair debate" that interweaves "the boundaries of nationhood . . . with those of desire and its prohibitions." The rhetoric of such debates would seem to make hair extraordinary where boundaries intersect to open possibilities for reimagining different kinds of power, from the self-discipline of the monk to the goddess's *śakti*, from the policing of borders to what only one's hairdresser knows.

References

Clifford, James. 1988. *The Predicament of Culture: Twentieth-Century Ethnography, Literature, and Art.* Cambridge: Harvard University Press.

Douglas, Mary. 1966. *Purity and Danger: An Analysis of Concepts of Pollution and Taboo.* New York: Frederick A. Praeger

Hallpike, C. R. 1969. "Social Hair." *Man*, n. s., 9, 2:274–98.

Hershman, P. 1974. Hair, "Sex, and Dirt," *Man* 9: 274–98.

Leach, Edmund R. 1958. "Magical Hair," *Journal of the Royal Anthropological Institute* 88:147-64.

Nānamoli, Bhikku, trans. 1975. *The Path of Purification (Visuddhimagga) by Bhadantācariya Buddhaghosa.* Kandy: Buddhist Publication Society

Obeyesekere, Gananath. 1981. *Medusa's Hair: An Essay on Personal Symbols and Religious Experience.* Chicago: University of Chicago Press.

Sikes, E. E. 1912. "Hair and Nails." In James Hastings, ed., *Encyclopaedia of Religion and Ethics.* 12 vols. New York: Charles Scribner's Sons, vol. 6, pp. 474–76.

Smith, Jonathan Z. 1982. "In Comparison a Magic Dwells." In Smith, *Imagining Religion: From Babylon to Jonestown.* Chicago: University of Chicago Press, pp. 19–35.

Turner, Terence. 1991. " 'We Are Parrots,' 'Twins are Birds': Play of Tropes as Operational Structure." In James W. Fernandez, ed., *Beyond Metaphor: The Theory of Tropes in Anthropology.* Stanford: Stanford University Press.

2 hair and society: social significance of hair in south asian traditions

patrick olivelle

The human body has become in recent years the subject of renewed interest across a spectrum of disciplines, from sociology to literary theory. Approaches to its study vary, of course, with each discipline. Since the groundbreaking study "Techniques of the Body" by Marcel Mauss (1935), however, an underlying assumption in the human sciences has been that the human body is not merely a physical and biological reality confronting human consciousness as an external and independent entity, but primarily a cultural construct carrying social and cultural meanings and messages. Attention has also been drawn by many sociologists and social anthropologists to a central dimension of the cultural construction of the body: the human body stands as the primary symbol of the social body, or the body politic (Turner 1984). Mary Douglas posits the interrelationship between the two types of bodies in clear terms:

> The social body constrains the way the physical body is perceived. The physical experience of the body, always modified by the social categories through which it is known, sustains a particular view of society. There is a continual exchange of meanings between the two kinds of bodily experience so that each reinforces the categories of the other. (Douglas 1982:65)

Berger and Luckman (1967), furthermore, have drawn our attention to a central dimension of culture: all cultural creations, including the human body, have a dialectic nature. On the one hand, it is a human product, is nothing but a human product, and is continuously changed and recreated by human activity. On the other hand, culture stands against the individual as a reality that imposes its own logic on individual consciousness, even though cultural grammars, just as those of languages, are very elastic, and individuals continuously change them in the very process of using them.

This chapter deals with just one aspect of the cultural creation of the body—the symbolic use of hair, especially the hair of the head and face—within the cultural history of just one region—South Asia.[1] Yet, attention to the dialectic nature of this symbol is essential to my approach. Just like language, hair symbolism imposes its own grammar on the individuals in a given period of a given society; an individual is unable to produce an entirely new symbolic value of hair from his or her own subjective consciousness and still be able to communicate with the rest of that society. Hence, we can justifiably seek to understand the grammar of this symbol. On the other hand, being a cultural product, the grammar of this symbol is not rigid; it is elastic and subject to diverse individual appropriations and uses. Such individual uses will, over time, change the very grammar of the symbol. We should, therefore, also seek to understand how that grammar may have changed over time.[2] The comparison with language is instructive. Although English imposes itself on my will, and I am not free to use English in any way I want and still expect to be understood, yet my own usage will change the very language that imposes its rules on me. The point I want to make is that searching for the underlying grammar of hair symbolism, as I will do in this chapter, does not imply some form of social determinism.

I will examine some of the ways hair is used as a public symbol to communicate a variety of socially significant meanings—in a special way, to demarcate the interstices within the complex South Asian societies, to mark their internal boundaries. But my interest in hair symbolism goes beyond the merely descriptive. I want to find out some of the reasons why humans, especially South Asians, have placed and continue to place so much value and significance on hair. To twist Lévi-Strauss's expression, why have humans found hair something so good to think and to communicate with? What patterns emerge from this "thinking with hair" and how do they relate to broader issues of individual and social existence?[3]

Symbols, like words, do not operate in isolation but within a web of relations and oppositions to other symbols. This context within which alone a symbol can be adequately understood, is what I would call the "grammar of a symbol." To understand why, for instance, a Sikh male is required to wear his hair long and to cover it with a turban, we need to examine the other customs that demarcate a Sikh male from Sikh females and from non-Sikhs, as well as the historical context in which the custom was created (Uberoi 1967). It is this symbolic grammar—in both its synchronic and diachronic dimensions—of Sikh maleness that will provide us with the context for teasing out the social meanings of Sikh hair.

Our starting point, however, must include (1) as full and accurate a description as possible of the customs, practices, and rituals concerning hair found within South Asian culture and history, (2) an examination of the broader symbolic grammar within which these practices are located, and (3) a study of the explanations and exegeses of these practices offered by native sources, whether they be informants or texts. Given the limits of space and ability, it will be presumptuous of me even to contemplate the completion of such an enormous task. I will therefore limit myself to describing in greater detail some ritual uses of hair and to drawing attention in passing to others, in the hope that we will have sufficient evidence to tease out some broader social meanings of hair symbolism in South Asia.

Hair Practices

With the help of Table 1, I will first explore the broad spectrum of South Asian rites, customs, and institutions involving some form of hair manipulation. This chart clearly does not contain an exhaustive listing; hair manipulation, especially shaving, pops up in the most unexpected of places. Alter (1992:322), for example, has drawn our attention to a rather unusual group, the wrestlers: "Like some *sannyasis*, wrestlers shave their heads completely or at least have their hair cut very short. . . . *Sannyasis* and wrestlers alike are distinguished from other men by their radical attitude toward hair as a symbol of identity."

In India symbolic manipulations of hair appear as variations of three central themes: (1) the groomed control of hair, (2) shaving the hair of the head (in the case of adult males this involves also the shaving of the beard), and (3) the neglect of hair resulting in either

Table 1

PHYSICAL SEPARATION	SOCIETY	RITUAL SEPARATION
Matted Hair and Beard	**Controlled Hair**	**Uncontrolled Hair**
Forest hermit Exile of the ages Political exiles Hair, beard, nails left to grow without any grooming	ADULT MALE Hair groomed: cut or long —arranged close to head and/or covered by turban ADULT FEMALE Hair groomed: always long —arranged either close to head or braided and left hanging; — never covered by turban; but may be covered in other ways	*Pollution Separation* Women in mourning Menstruating women *Vows of Vengence* e.g. Draupadī and Cāṇakya **Shaving** TEMPORARY SEPARATION *Initiatory Separation* First hair cut *(caula)* First beard/hair cut *(gondāna)* Vedic initiation *(upanayana)* Sacrificial consecration Pilgrimage
LONG-HAIR ASCETICS *Avadhūta* Śaivite ascetics Sri Lankan female/male	SIKH MALE Unshaven head and beard hair enclosed in turban	*Reintegration into Society* Outcastes Lepers End of studentship King after consecration Other impure people *Pollution Separation* Mourning son *Penetential Separation* Prior vows and penances
		PERMANENT SEPARATION *Polution Separation* Widows, corpses *Penal Separation* People guilty of major crimes *Ascetic Separation* Hindu/Buddhist/ Jain Ascetic—both male and female [wrestlers]

loose unkempt hair or dirty matted hair, often accompanied by the neglect of nails, and, in the case of males, of the beard. Without denying the possibility of personal meanings—which, after all, are only to be expected, given the dialectic nature of cultural products—all these types of hair manipulation, I hope to show, communicate deeply social meanings, placing the individual whose hair is so manipulated in different relationships both to the broader society and to the segment of that society to which that individual belongs.

Groomed Hair

Groomed and controlled hair is the hallmark of people with publicly recognized roles within society, in a special way of adult males and females (Hallpike 1969). I believe that the "controlled social hair" of such individuals, especially of married males (given the patriarchal nature of traditional South Asian societies), is the point of reference of most—although not necessarily all—other hair manipulations from which they derive their meaning and significance. This is simply to say that society is the ultimate point of reference even in its critique and rejection.

The hair of an adult male in modern India is usually short and combed and his beard and mustache shaved or trimmed. The medical treatise of Suśruta advises a man to keep his hair and nails trimmed, and to oil and comb his hair regularly.[4] The latter advice, as well as trimming the nails,[5] clearly applies to women as well. Customs regarding male hair may have varied according to caste.[6] Brahmin men, for example, were expected to shave their heads but leave a tuft of hair, the topknot, unshaved. This topknot was generally kept tied in a knot when a Brahmin appeared in public.[7]

The hair of an adult female, especially a married woman, is long but restrained by a knot, by one or several braids, or by some other means; some women may even cover their hair, especially when they appear in public. The distinctive ways in which hair is worn by adult males and females clearly symbolize their different gender roles. Even though short hair appears to be distinctive of the male in modern South Asia, the picture is less clear in ancient and medieval periods.[8] Both males and females are depicted in Indian art and sculpture, for example, with long hair but with distinctive coiffures (Padma 1991). It will be an interesting study to detect gender differences in these modes of coiffure, but one distinctive element is the long braided hair of females.[9] What is common to both genders, however, is that their hair is groomed and controlled.

Loose Hair

The groomed control of hair is especially demanded when people present themselves in public. Thus, when a person appears in public with loose and uncontrolled hair, it carries a variety of meanings and messages (see the chapters by Watson and Miller). Untying the hair before a king, for example, is regarded in the legal literature as an insult subject to punishment (Lingat 1973:239). On the other hand, legal authorities uniformly affirm that a thief should run to the king, with his hair loose (*muktakeśa*) and carrying a club on his shoulder, to confess his crime.[10] Here loose hair in the presence of the king appears to indicate the thief's recognition of his status as a sinner and an outlaw removed from the bounds of society.

Loose hair, especially of women, is a sign of domestic informality and even of sexual intimacy. In sculpture, for example, erotic couples are depicted with loose and falling hair (Padma 1991:266–67). In iconography disheveled and flying hair may indicate the demonic and the female outside of male control, as in representations of Kālī.[11] Marglin (1985:54) observes: "The single goddesses are often represented iconographically with loose flowing hair, which signals their celibate state." Indeed, it may signal even more their liminal and dangerous status. An early medieval ascetic text, for example, warns mendicants not to beg from a *muktakeśinī* ("a woman with loose hair"), a term which could indicate either that there is sexual intimacy or, as we shall presently see, that she is having her monthly period.[12]

What is clear, however, is that males and in a special way females are not expected to present themselves in public with loose and ungroomed hair. If they do, their actions carry publicly recognized meanings—they are making a public statement about their social status.

Loose and especially disheveled hair is associated in a special way with temporary ritual separations from society. The most common instance of such a separation is that of women during their menstrual period, when the hair is left unbraided and unwashed. As Hershman (1974:278), in his detailed study of hair among the Punjabis, has shown, the expression "I have to wash my head," is used euphemistically by even contemporary women to indicate the onset of their menstrual period. Their ritual separation makes them untouchables; no social intercourse with them is permitted, including touching. Menstruating women do not cook or even sit with the rest of the household to eat. Loose and disheveled hair of women, but sometimes also of men,[13] is also a sign of mourning, another ritually impure state when normal ritual activities and social relations are suspended.[14] Loose hair on all these occasions of ritual separation tells the world "I cannot be approached."

There are also two prominent cases in Indian literature where the hair is left loose until a vow of vengeance has been fulfilled. Literary sources depict Draupadī, the wife of the Pāṇḍava brothers in the *Mahābhārata*, as leaving her hair loose after she was insulted in public by the Kauravas until their final defeat and death (Hiltebeitel 1981). Her hair was, in fact, already loose when the outrage occurred, because she was then having her period. Cāṇakya, the prime minister of Candragupta Maurya, provides the other example. Viśākhadatta, in his Sanskrit play *Mudrārākṣasa* (Act 1, verse 9), depicts him as keeping his Brahmanical top knot untied until he had fulfilled his vow of placing Candragupta securely on the throne and vanquishing completely the dynasty of the Nandas. In both these cases the vow of vengeance suspends the normal social roles of Draupadī and Cāṇakya until the completion of their vows, a feature such vows share with penitential vows I examine below that require the shaving of the head.

People who display loose and uncontrolled hair in public, therefore, appear to have temporarily suspended—for a variety of reasons and with a variety of consequences—their normally assigned roles in society.

Shaving

Clearly the most common and possibly the most significant manipulation of hair in South Asian societies is the shaving of the head.[15] It occurs so frequently in ritual settings that space does not permit me to fully explore individual instances. Instead, I derive the symbolic grammar of shaving from a brief survey of the broad spectrum and a closer examination of a few of the rituals of shaving. The dominant social meaning of shaving in South Asian traditions that emerges from this examination is the separation of the shaven individual from society, a separation certainly more profound and often more permanent than that signaled by loose hair. For heuristic purposes I distinguish different types of social separation signaled by shaving, both in terms of duration and the type of separation involved.

TEMPORARY SEPARATION

Initiatory Separation: The most common temporary separation occurs in initiation ceremonies. Since van Gennep's (1960) ground-breaking work *Rites de Passage*, initiation rites are commonly recognized as having three moments: separation, liminality, and integration. The initiate is first ritually separated from society and from his or her social role and rank and left in an ill-defined marginal state. The initiatory rite concludes with the reintegration of the initiate into his or her new status within society. In South Asian traditions almost every initiatory separation is accompanied and signaled by the ritual shaving of the initiate.

When a young boy undergoes vedic initiation (*upanayana*), when a sacrificer is consecrated (*dīkṣā*) prior to his performing a vedic sacrifice,[16] when a king is anointed (*abhiṣeka*)—at all these initiatory rites the subject is first shaved. Indeed, these ceremonies are presented expressly as new births of the individuals (Gonda 1965:331). Many explicit statements and symbolic enactments of the initiates' return to the womb are found in these ceremonies:[17] "The sacrificial priests make into an embryo again the man whom they prepare for the sacrificial consecration (*Aitareya Brāhmaṇa* 1.3.1). Shaving of the initiate clearly belongs to the same symbolic grammar. Shaving reduces the individual to the state of an embryo or an infant—the asexual and hairless condition.

The first cutting of a child's hair (*caula* or *cūḍākaraṇa*) is also a rite (*saṃskāra*) that marks a transition. The ceremony is performed generally when the child is about three years old. The mantra accompanying the shaving states that the shaving is intended to assure a long life. The connection with fertility is implicit in the places where the cut hair is buried, for example, in a cow pen or at the foot of an Udumbara tree.[18] Another life-cycle rite is connected with the first shaving of the beard (*keśānta*, also called *godāna*, at which the head is also shaved), performed at age sixteen and associated with sexual maturity (Pandey 1969:143–45).

The final rite of passage in the Hindu liturgy is the funeral. It is regarded by the Brahmanical tradition as the last sacrifice of the deceased at which his own body becomes the victim offered in the cremation fire. Here too the individual is reborn through the sacrifice. Now, according to most ritual texts the head or even the entire body of the corpse is shaved prior to cremation.[19]

I believe that initiatory shaving, especially the shaving of the boy at his vedic initiation and of the sacrificer at his consecration, was paradigmatic and influenced the ritual articulation of most ritual separations in South Asian societies.

Initiatory Reintegration: The other side of the coin of initiatory separation is the reintegration into society of people who have been separated for a considerable period of time due to a variety of factors. Outcasts, the polluted, students at the completion of their period of study, the king after his year-long seclusion following his consecration—all are reintegrated into their respective social ranks through ceremonies that feature the ritual shaving of the head. During the year-long separation the king leaves his hair uncut and ungroomed; he does not bathe and sleeps in the shed where the sacred fire is kept. The student, on the other hand, either lets his hair grow into a matted condition (*jaṭila*) or shaves the head but keeps his topknot unshaved.[20] In these ceremonies of reintegrating people after protracted periods of social separation, shaving appears to mark the conclusion of that period—a kind of separation from their liminal state—and their assimilation into their new social roles.

Noteworthy is the absence of shaving during the marriage rite, which is the most central life-cycle ritual within the Brahmanical system. The reason for this absence is unclear, but it appears that for the adult male the marriage ceremony is the final act of a process that starts at the conclusion of his vedic studies. The final bath and the other ceremonies associated with his return from his teacher's house remove him from the ascetic, celibate, and mendicant life of a student. Such an individual, technically called *snātaka* ("bathed"), is then decorated with garlands, ornaments, and finery. His status is said to be higher than that of a king. It is significant that in the legal literature the provisions for a *snātaka* often overlap those for a married householder, who is also often referred to as *snātaka*. The interval between the completion of studies and marriage is supposed to be relatively short. We may thus view the shaving prior to the ritual bath at the conclusion of his studentship as the first step and the marriage itself as the final chapter of the reintegration of the student into his new social role and status.

Pollution Separation: Social intercourse is forbidden with people who are tainted with ritual pollution. Such people are ritually separated during the period of impurity. Some of these temporary periods of separation, such as those created by the death of a close relative, can also be marked by shaving. A son, for example, is expected to shave his head at the death of his father or mother.[21]

Penitential Separation: A person undergoing a penance or vow (*vrata*) also is separated from society, and many of the major penitential practices of Hinduism are preceded by the shaving of the penitent. Some sources give a reason for this practice: sins become lodged in the hair. Thus a person who wishes to expiate sins should shave the hair.[22] People also shave when they go to a place of pilgrimage (*tīrtha*), an act which may be regarded as either an initiatory or a penitential separation from society.[23]

PERMANENT SEPARATION

Pollution Separation: A permanent ritual separation from society occurs in the case of a widow. The social position of a widow has undergone repeated changes in Indian history. There is at least one period when the ritually impure, inauspicious, and unmarriageable state of a widow was signaled by the shaving of her head. A frequently cited verse states: "The long hair of a widow's head grows in order to bind her husband. A widow should, therefore, always keep her head shaved."[24] The permanence of this condition, moreover, required that she keep her head permanently shaven, and in this and other customs a widow often resembled an ascetic.[25]

Penal Separation: Major crimes, such as murder, were punished by death, but when the capital punishment was not meted out, as when the criminal happened to be a Brahmin, the criminal was shaved and lived the life of a beggar outside of society.[26]

Ascetic Separation: The best known ritual shaving associated with permanent separation from society is that of the Hindu *saṃnyāsin* or renouncer, the Buddhist and Jain monk, and their female counterparts. A central feature of the rites of initiation into the ascetic life in all these traditions is the removal of head and facial hair. Throughout their life these ascetics keep their head and face clear of hair by periodic shaving.[27]

Even though, as I will argue, the central social meaning of ascetic shaving, just as the shaving of students, sacrificers, and widows, is that of separation from society, sexual symbolism is not lacking. Not just ascetics, but all people ritually shaven are forbidden to engage in sex. For most this is a temporary condition required by a rite of passage or necessitated by ritual pollution, but for the ascetic (and often also for the widow) it is permanent, and therein lies the difference between ascetic and other forms of ritual shaving. Social control, after all, is primarily sexual control, and the controlled hair of social individuals symbolizes their participation in the socially sanctioned structures for sexual expression, especially marriage (Hallpike 1969). Removal of hair separates the individual from that structure and from the legitimate exercise of sexual activity. Shaving for the ascetic, I believe, indicates his or her removal from socially sanctioned sexual structures, and, a fortiori, also from other types of social structures and roles.[28] In the Indian context, this implies loss of caste, inability to own property, and lack of legal standing in a court of law for most purposes (Olivelle 1984:140–51).

Elements of the ascetic initiatory ritual also indicate that shaving symbolizes the return to the sexually and socially undifferentiated status of an infant. During the Hindu ritual, for example, the shaven ascetic takes off all his clothes. The naked renouncer is significantly called *jātarūpadhara*, which literally means "one who bears the form he had at birth." The ascetic is not just naked; he is reduced to the condition in which he was born, to the state of a new-born infant. I believe that shaving is part of the symbolic complex that signifies his return to "the form he had at birth." The absence of hair, just as much as nakedness, takes the initiate back to the prepubertal state of infancy.

The sexual symbolism of hair also helps explain some interesting features of ascetic behavior toward hair. It is well known that Jain monks at their initiation and periodically throughout their life remove their head hair by tearing them by the roots, a painful procedure I believe. That this custom was not limited to the Jains is demonstrated by its presence in a somewhat abbreviated form in the Hindu ritual of ascetic initiation. Here the ascetic's hair is first shaved, but five or seven hairs at the crown are left uncut.[29] At the conclusion of the rite, the ascetic plucks these few hairs from the roots. Although one may attribute these practices to the common ascetic propensity to bodily torture and pain, this literal eradication of hair, especially viewed in the light of the broader grammar of ascetic bodily symbols, can be seen as a symbolic and ritual uprooting of sexual drives and attachments.

That shaving is the opposite of sexual engagement is also brought out in the head-shaving rites of Hindu ascetics during the annual liturgical cycle. They are not allowed to shave any time they may want. Rather the prescribed time for shaving is at the junctures between the five Indian seasons: spring, summer, rains, autumn, and winter. Now the Sanskrit term for season is *ṛtu*, the same term that is used to indicate the monthly menstrual cycle of a woman. Brahmanical law and ethics require a husband to engage in sexual intercourse with his wife in her *ṛtu*, that is, soon after the end of her period when a new "season," a new fertile period, begins for his wife (*Manusmṛti* 3.45). I think it is not farfetched to see a correspondence between the husband approaching his wife at the beginning of her fertile season (*ṛtugamana*), and the ascetic shaving his head at the beginning of each calendrical season (*ṛtuvapana*). The *ṛtugamana* is thus transformed into *ṛtuvapana*. This shaving appears to symbolize an ascetic's renunciation of sex precisely at the time—at least in a terminological sense—when the ethics of society requires a married man to engage in it. Significantly, it is this very need for periodic shaving that is denied in the case of the Buddha. According to a Jātaka account, the Buddha cut his hair with his sword to the length of two fingers-breath. His hair remained the same length for the rest of his life, signifying, it would seem, the total extinguishing (*nirvāṇa*) of his sexual fires.[30]

A closer examination of the three institutions involving either permanent or extended periods of separation from society marked by head-hair shaving—the vedic student, the widow, and the world renouncer—indicates their structural similarity. Indeed, the Brahmanical legal literature frequently brackets these three institutions together because many legal provisions are common to all three.[31] They share similar characteristics: all are shaven-headed, all are forbidden to have sexual relations, all receive their food from others, all are expected not to adorn themselves or to participate in amusements, and all have a marginal legal status—they do not own property, for example, and are not permitted to enter into contracts or to take part in legal proceedings, such as being a witness or a surety in a court of law. They lead a penitential life, sleeping on the floor, not chewing betel, not anointing their bodies, and eating little. Students are reduced to the level of servants of their teachers. Both students and ascetics move out of their homes and are reduced to the status of beggars; neither is affected by pollution at the death of a relative.[32]

Indeed, when we look at the other prolonged states of separation signaled by shaving, we detect many of these same features. I want to focus here especially on food. People who are either in a permanent or a prolonged state of ritual separation, including ascetics, vedic students, widows, and criminals, do not own food; they have to obtain their food from people in society.[33] During shorter periods of separation, people either fast or eat food cooked and given to them by people within society. There is a parallel between the restrictions with regard to food and sex, both being derived from their removal from social structures and roles. I want, however, to highlight one aspect of the food habits of shaven individuals.

Apart from caste endogamy, the most distinctive feature of Hindu society consists of dietary restrictions that limit the exchange of food across caste boundaries. The purest food is your own food. Those who are ritually separated from society, however, live in a liminal state defined by the absence of boundaries. This absence is symbolized, I believe, by their acceptance of food from others—in the case of ritual beggars, from people whose level of purity cannot be easily determined; hence the legal fiction that begged food (*bhikṣā*) is always pure. Begging is the paradigmatic opposite of the restrictive laws of food exchange. The one establishes and reinforces social boundaries; the other symbolizes the lack, or, as in the case of ascetic ideology, the transcendence, of such boundaries. Significantly, Hindu law forbids householders from accepting cooked food from other people.[34] The food of shaven people, likewise, becomes unfit for others: people are instructed, as we have noted, not to touch the food of ascetics and people consecrated for a sacrifice (*dīkṣita*).

Shaven individuals of widely different sorts, from ascetics to criminals, are excluded from the two central institutional spheres of society: the sexual and the economic. Celibacy and mendicancy are the results of the separation of shaven individuals from social structures, whatever the cause and motive of that separation.

Neglected Hair

Finally, we have a unique manipulation of hair by refusing to manipulate it at all—that is, the utter neglect of hair. The most common instance of neglected hair is the so-called matted hair (*jaṭā*) associated with forest hermits.[35] At least in its early history, neglected and matted hair symbolized ideally and typically an individual's physical separation from society and civilized living, even though there are instances when the *jaṭā* is recommended for other individuals separated from social living but not necessarily from social geography, such as vedic students (see above n.20).

To understand the symbolism of matted hair it is necessary to locate it within the larger grammar of the symbols associated with physical withdrawal from society in ancient India. Besides long and matted hair, bodily symbols of forest living included a long and uncut beard in the case of males, long and uncut nails, eating only uncultivated forest produce, clothes of tree bark or animal skin, and frequently also bodily uncleanliness.[36] People with matted hair are required to live in the forest or wilderness; they are repeatedly

Figure 1. A Tamil *sādhu* named Balanand, visiting a festival for the south Indian god Kūttāṇṭavar near Coimbatore, unwinds his matted locks and draws admiration from a festival-goer. Photo by Alf Hiltebeitel.

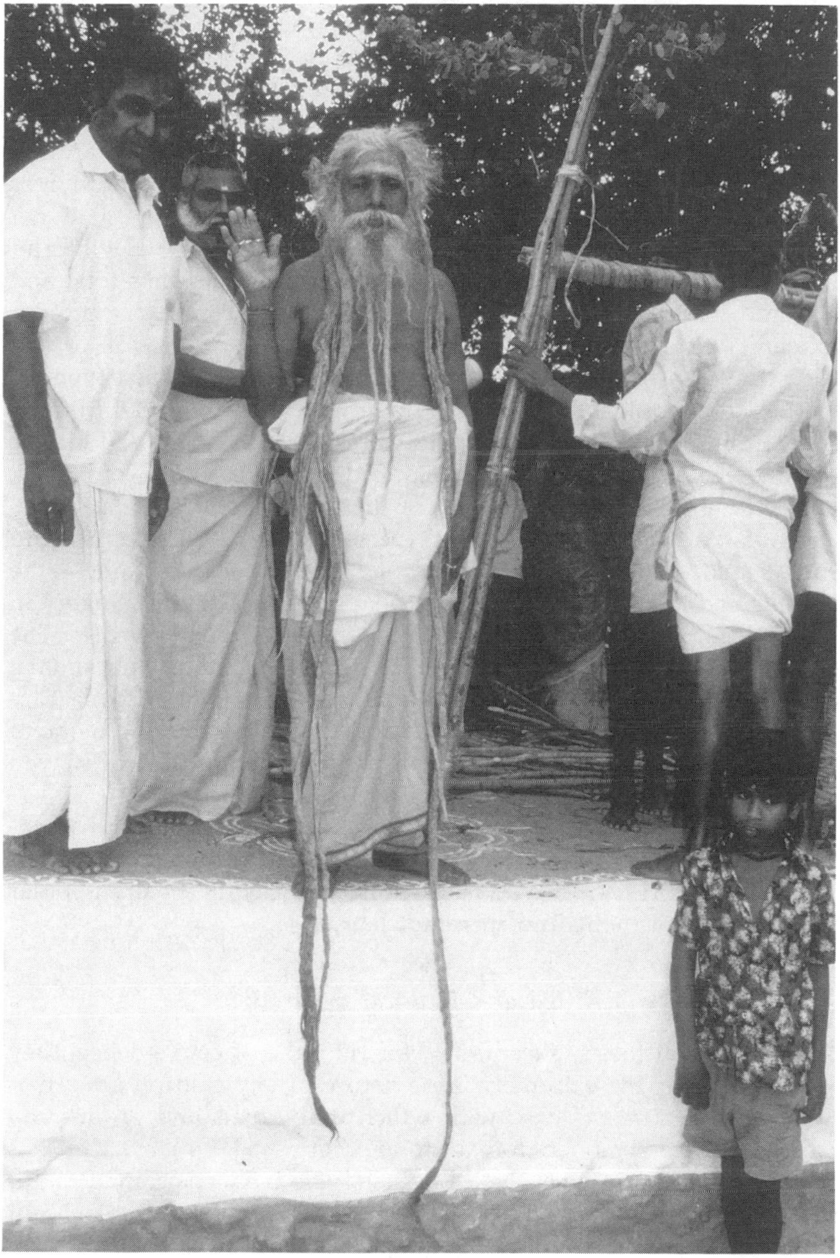

Figure 2. A Tamil *sādhu* shows the length of his matted locks, which, he says, have grown uncut for fifty years since he was age seven. Photo by Alf Hiltebeitel.

admonished "not to step on plowed land," the prime symbol of civilized geography.[37] They are often said to imitate the habits of wild animals. One can decipher from this symbolic grammar the following statement: a matted-hair individual withdraws from all culturally mediated products and institutions and from all culturally demarcated geographical areas and returns to the state of nature, the condition of the wild, to the way of life of animals. Not grooming the hair, not controlling it in any way, letting it grow naturally into a wild and matted condition—all this appears to symbolize a person's total and absolute withdrawal from social structures and controls and from human culture as such.[38]

In Indian history we can identify at least three distinct types of matted-hair people who have withdrawn or have been forced to withdraw from society. First, there are the forest hermits called Vaikhānasa or Vānaprastha, and second, the aged. Old people, especially old kings, both within the Hindu institution of the four orders of life (*āśrama*s) and outside that structure, were expected to leave their family and society and assume a forest mode of life.[39] These two classes—the hermits and the retirees—are often collapsed into a single category in Indian legal literature. The third class consists of political exiles. The epic heroes of the *Mahābhārata* and the *Rāmāyaṇa,* the five Pāṇḍava brothers and Rāma, for example, are all sent into political exile. Significantly, political exiles assume the bodily symbols and the mode of life of forest hermits just as criminals assume the life style of shaven ascetics.

People and groups viewed by the mainstream of society as standing outside social boundaries, such as the tribal and forest peoples of India and the Sri Lankan Veddas, are also depicted in art and popular imagination with long and unkempt hair.

Exceptions to Ritual and Physical Separation

Although I call these "exceptions" for the sake of convenience, they illustrate rather the extremely loose nature of any cultural grammar. They demonstrate the ease with which individuals and groups can cross from one symbolic domain to another.

The first example is the Sikh male.[40] He is not permitted to cut any of his hair—head hair or beard—from birth until death. An adult Sikh male is distinguished by his long hair and beard. He is, however, married and part of the social fabric. To understand the hair symbolism of Sikh males we have to locate it within the historical context—

North India between the fifteenth and the eighteenth century—that gave birth to the Sikh tradition. Coming from the background of devotional religion (*bhakti*) and saints (*sant*) of northern India, the early Sikh gurus deliberately drew a contrast between the Sikh bodily symbols and those of both the traditional Hindu renouncer with his shaven head and the Moslem with his circumcised penis. The Sikh holy man, by contrast, has long hair, is married, and is uncircumcised. There is a structural inversion between Hindu renouncers and Sikhs. The Sikh householder, the representative of a new form of holiness, stands, in structural opposition to two Hindu institutions: the ordinary householder because the Sikh is a holy man, and the renouncer because the Sikh affirms holiness within marriage and society. This dual opposition is symbolized on the one hand by the Sikh long hair and on the other by the turban that encloses and controls the hair and by the well-groomed and waxed beard. An interesting historical point is that the Sikh long hair is itself a symbol borrowed from another and by then obsolete form of separation from society, the uncut hair and beard of the forest hermit. Yet, as part of the social fabric, the uncut hair of the Sikh is not neglected; it is washed, oiled, combed, and enclosed within a turban—a traditional way of hair control in India. As Uberoi (1967:96) has pointed out, the symbolism of the five *k's* expresses power and its control. The comb controls the power of the hair, the steel bangle controls the power of the sword, and the underwear (*kach*) the power of the uncircumcised penis.

As the Sikh male crosses the boundary between society and ritual separation from it, so the long matted hair of certain types of Hindu ascetics living within society stands at the boundary between ritual and physical separation from society. There were and are a variety of such ascetics, including those of some Śaivaite sects and those known in the ascetic literature as Avadhūtas. We must include within this class the Sri Lankan male and female matted-hair ascetics described by Gananath Obeyesekere (1981) in his *Medusa's Hair*. The literature makes it clear that the Avadhūtas, and possibly also other Śaivaite ascetics, let their hair grow and become matted to symbolize their liberated status and freedom from normal ascetic rules. Thus they let their hair grow to show their transcendence of the shaven-headed state of the ordinary ascetic. They, like the Buddha, have no need to periodically shave their head. The Avadhūta symbol of matted hair, therefore, should be understood not in relation to the adult male in society but in relation to the mainstream asceticism of shaven monks, an institution these ascetics claim to have transcended.

A Search for Meanings

The Native Exegesis

It would be equally naive to limit scholarly investigations to the meanings assigned to rites by the actors themselves or by the native tradition and to ignore the meanings and interpretations offered by that tradition. Both the rites and the indigenous interpretations of the rites constitute the data that the scholar must take into account.

As with most condensed and central symbols of a society, indigenous exegesis of hair is neither extensive nor frequent. The ascetic literature, for example, never tells us why an ascetic must shave his head. This block in native exegesis, which generally waxes eloquent in most other areas of ritual practice, suggests some level of discomfort in dealing explicitly with this symbol.[41]

One aspect of hair that stands out clearly in native exegesis, however, is its impurity.[42] Most ancient Indian sources require that people throw away any food contaminated by hair.[43] Hair in this sense is equal to excrement. Seneviratne (1992:181) refers to a Sinhala belief that hair and nails are made from the impure waste produced in the process of digesting food, and that cutting hair and nails is similar to voiding excrement.

Ancient vedic texts share this belief; the reason for shaving before a ritual is to remove the impurity of hair and nails from the body. The *Śatapatha Brāhmaṇa* (3.1.2.2), for example, explains why a sacrificer must shave before his consecration:

> He [the sacrificer] then shaves his hair and beard, and cuts his nails. For impure, indeed, is that part of man where water does not reach him. Now at the hair and beard, and at the nails the water does not reach him: hence when he shaves his hair and beard, and cuts his nails, he does so in order that he may become pure before he is consecrated.[44]

According to this interpretation, hair and nails are impure because they do not absorb water, the ultimate means of purification, whereas according to the *Taittirīya Saṃhitā* (6.1.1.1–2) they are impure because they are dead skin.

A significant and informative contradiction within the native tradition occurs, however, when what is said to be equivalent to feces is offered ceremonially to gods and goddesses (Hershman 1974). This happens, as we have seen, especially when young children are shaved for the first time. How can the same substance be regarded as excrement in one ritual setting and as a substance fit for the gods in another?

The sexual symbolism of hair that I discuss below may provide one clue. If at some level of its symbolic complex hair represents the fertile sexuality of its owner, then we can see how it can be at the same time both a sacred offering and excrement. Indeed, sexual fluids, especially male semen, are at one time said to be the most refined part of the body and of food, even the carrier of personality from one birth to the next,[45] and at other times bracketed with urine and feces as impure substances. A common way to indicate the depravity of a particular act, for example, is to say that if a man does it "he, in fact, offers to his ancestors semen, urine and excrement."[46]

Another element of the native exegesis of hair is its frequent connection in both myth and ritual to grass and plants, emphasizing thereby its relationship to fertility. A couple of Ṛgvedic verses (8.91.5–6) connects three areas of hair/grass growth: head, pubic region, and fields. In this hymn Apālā, a young girl, prays to Indra to make the hair grow on her father's head, on her own pubic region, and in her father's fields.[47] The connection between hair and grass/plants is well established in the vedic literature (Gonda 1985). The *Taittirīya Saṃhitā* (7.5.25.1) states quite simply that "vegetation is hair." Another text records the myth that the hair that fell from the creator god Prajāpati's body turned into vegetation (*Śatapatha Brāhmaṇa*, 7.4.2.11). Other myths connect the creation of grasses and plants to the hair of Viṣṇu incarnate as a boar (Gonda 1985:63–64). This correlation is brought out nicely in the Upaniṣadic verse:

> As a spider spins out a thread, then draws it in;
> as plants sprout out from the earth;
> as on body and head hair grows from a living man;
> So from the imperishable all things here spring.[48]

Gonda (1981) has objected to Lincoln's (1977) claim that haircutting rituals of Brahmins establish a clear association between hair and vegetation. Even though Gonda is right that there was no fixed rule regarding the disposal of ritually cut hair as suggested by Lincoln,[49] it is nevertheless clear that shaving the head is related to prolongation of an individual's life span and that many elements of the rite, including grass, sesame seed, ghee, and the burial of the hair in a place covered with herbs, posit a clear relationship of hair cutting with fertility. Indeed, Gonda (1956) himself has suggested a similar correlation in another hair ritual, the parting of a pregnant wife's hair (*sīmantonnayana*).

This correlation is brought out clearly in two riddles and their solutions recorded in the *Śatapatha Brāhmaṇa* (11.4.1.6–7, 14–15). The riddles ask how one knows from an analysis of the full-moon and new-moon sacrifices (1) why people are born with hair, why hair grows a second time on the face, armpits, and other parts of the body, and why in old age the hair of the head first turns gray and finally one becomes gray all over; and (2) why the semen of a boy is not fertile, that of a man in midlife is fertile, and that of an old man is again infertile. Here are the solutions:

> Inasmuch as he spreads a cover of sacrificial grass (on the altar), therefore, creatures here are born with hair; and inasmuch as he for the second time, as it were, spreads the Prastara-bunch of grass, therefore, for the second time, as it were, the hair of the beard and the armpits, and other parts of the body grow; and inasmuch as at first he only throws the Prastara-bunch after (the oblations into the fire), therefore it is on the head that one first becomes gray; and inasmuch as he then throws after it all the sacrificial grass of the altar, therefore, in the last stage of life, one again becomes gray all over.
>
> And inasmuch as the fore-offerings have ghee for their offering-material, a boy's seed is not productive, but is like water, for ghee is like water; and inasmuch as, in the middle of the sacrifice, they sacrifice with sour curds and with cake, therefore it is productive in the middle stage of life, for thick-flowing, as it were, is that offering, and thick-flowing, as it were, is seed; and inasmuch as the after-offerings have ghee for their offering-material, it again is not productive in his last stage of life, and is like water, for ghee, indeed, is like water. (Eggeling's trans. slightly modified)

Here is an interesting and informative juxtaposition of hair growth, ritual use of grass, and fertility of semen. Hair on the head of children produces weak and infertile sexuality. The second birth of hair on the face and body produces fertile semen. The graying of hair produces a second childhood when semen becomes weak and infertile.[50]

The Social Meanings of Hair Manipulations

There is no single and unique meaning to be discovered within this vast range of hair rituals. Further, as we have seen in the case of Sikhs and Sri Lankan ascetics, historical contexts and individual decisions can give new meanings to traditional symbols.[51] It is in the very nature of the dialectic character of a cultural product, moreover, that the same fact or act may carry different meanings to different individuals or groups of individuals, creating what Obeyesekere (1981) calls "personal symbols."

Nevertheless, a set of related symbols of a society—in this case the ritual manipulations of hair—cannot exist in total isolation. Just as a word in a language, so a symbol operates within a broader grammar within which alone it becomes meaningful. And just as it is heuristically profitable to search for the root meaning or the etymology of a linguistic symbol, not because it will exhaust the meanings available in actual usage but because such a meaning permits us to discover the relationships among those operational meanings and thereby further our understanding of those very meanings, so also is it useful to search for a root meaning, or a cluster of such meanings, of a symbol such as hair. Such a root meaning will not exhaust the multiplicity and the variety of operational meanings, but it may allow a deeper understanding of those meanings and their interrelationships and of the enormous power of this ubiquitous symbol. The validity and usefulness of such a search is also indicated by the relative uniformity of the modes of life signaled by shaving and the neglect of hair in South Asian traditions. Why, for example, are all shaven people, whether they are ascetics or criminals, forbidden to engage in sex or to eat their own food?

Much of the theoretical work on the symbolism of hair has been carried out thus far by scholars in the fields of anthropology and psychoanalysis. It may be useful here to review briefly some of the major contributions. James Frazer in *The Golden Bough* (1913:II, 252–87) was one of the earliest to pay systematic attention to the customs relating to hair. Although his focus is on the reasons for the methods various peoples use to dispose of cut hair and nails, Frazer also deals with the significance of the head, head hair, and hair cutting. The reason why people of widely different cultures consider the head and head hair sacred and taboo, Frazer (1913:II, 252–53) argues, is because they believe that various spirits or divinities reside in the head and hair. "When the head was considered so sacred," Frazer concludes, "it is obvious that the cutting of the hair must have been a delicate and difficult operation" (258). A fascinating, though no doubt extreme, example of the precautions taken at cutting one's hair is that of the chief of Namosi in Fiji, who, according to a letter Frazer received from a Christian missionary, "always ate a man by way of precaution when he had his hair cut. There was a certain clan that had to provide the victim, and they used to sit in solemn council among themselves to choose him" (264).

There are two major problems with Frazer's analysis. The first, common among early anthropologists, is that he cites examples of hair customs from around the world without regard either to the accuracy of description or to the social and cultural context within which those customs are located. He cites indiscriminately from travellers' diaries, from the writings and letters of Christian missionaries, and from ethnographies of varying degrees of reliability. He makes little attempt, moreover, to understand the customs he mentions within their contexts. The meanings of symbols, like those of words, can be studied adequately only if they are located within the broader grammar of the society. In the case of the Fijian chief, for example, we do not know whether he ate the man because he wanted to shave, or whether he shaved in order to eat the man, or, what is more likely, whether both acts were part of a larger ritual undertaking and liturgical calendar within which alone the two acts may reveal their significance.

This brings us to the second problem: what Frazer offers as a theory is in fact merely a generalized account of the native exegesis. Hair is sacred because a god dwells in it. A theory, if it is to have cross-cultural validity and usefulness, has to go beyond the native exegesis, which is part of our data and not a substitute for a theory.

Moving beyond Frazer, theories of hair symbolism fall broadly into two categories: psychological and sociological. The psychological, or, more accurately, the psychoanalytic theory sees hair symbolism among humans as derived from the workings of the unconscious. Clinical observations reveal that through the mechanism of displacement the head often stands for the penis. The phallic symbolism of the head, it is argued, is transferred to the hair, where hair itself may stand for semen or the phallus. Cutting of hair or shaving is thus viewed by proponents of the psychoanalytic theory as equivalent to castration.[52]

Edmund Leach (1958) in his influential essay "Magical Hair" examines the psychoanalytic theory and finds that the ethnographic evidence by and large corroborates the sexual symbolism of hair. He concludes that "an astonishingly high proportion of the ethnographic evidence fits the following pattern in a quite obvious way. In ritual situations: long hair = unrestrained sexuality; short hair or partially shaved hair or tightly bound hair = restricted sexuality; close shaven hair = celibacy" (1958:154). Leach, however, wants to keep the psychoanalytic and the anthropological fields separate, the former dealing with individual motives and the latter with social meaning. He does so by neatly dividing symbols into private and public. A private symbol "reflects the *actual* psychological state of the actor" (1958:153, original italics), whereas a public symbol is merely a means of communication with publicly recognized meanings and does not necessarily correspond to the "psychological state of the actor."

Hallpike rejects even the somewhat circumspect acceptance of the unconscious association of hair and sexuality of Leach in his response to Leach, appropriately entitled "Social Hair" (1969). He rejects the association of shaving with castration for the simple and obvious reason that it is inapplicable in the case of women, whose heads may also be shaved in ritual contexts such as mourning. He also asks why, if head hair equals male genitals, so little regard is paid to beards, the symbol par excellence of masculinity, in ritual contexts. The hair of the beard, after all, is physically more similar to pubic hair than the hair of the head. Finally, he finds it very strange that, if long hair equals unrestrained sexuality, celibate ascetics wear long hair. Not surprisingly, Hallpike rejects the psychoanalytic theory and offers instead a thoroughly sociological one. His own theory boils down to this: "Long hair is associated with being outside society and . . . the cutting of hair symbolizes re-entering society, or living under a particular disciplinary regime within society" (1969:260). He accepts dressing the hair as a ritual equivalent of cutting. Thus we have the equation: cutting or dressing the hair places a person within society and social control, while long and loose hair places one outside such control.[53] Hallpike appears to include within one category both the cutting of hair by ordinary people in society and the close shaving of the head associated with monks and ascetics. "Thus the cropped head or tonsure in all three cases of monk, soldier and convict," Hallpike (1969:261) argues, "signifies that they are under discipline."

The manipulative potential of hair makes it suitable for use in ritual,[54] but Hallpike never shows why hair and only hair has become almost universally a powerful symbol of the relationship between individuals and society. The psychoanalytic theory provides a reason for this association, and if we are to reject that theory then we must be prepared to offer an alternative. Further, Hallpike's identification of the shaven head and the ordinary cutting of hair and grouping them together under the category of social control and discipline are unconvincing; the evidence points in a different direction.

Two anthropologists, Hershman (1974) in his excellent essay "Hair, Sex and Dirt" on hair symbolism among the Hindu and Sikh Punjabis and Gananath Obeyesekere (1981, 1990) in two of his recent works, *Medusa's Hair* on modern Sri Lankan matted-hair ascetics and the more theoretical *The Work of Culture*, have attempted to bridge the divide between the psychoanalytic and the sociological viewpoints.

Hershman (1974:274) does so by establishing "a connexion between the symbolism of the individual subconscious and that of the collective consciousness." "It is my contention," he argues,

> that this connexion lies in the fact that bodily symbols gain their emotive power through being subconsciously associated with the anal-genital organs and processes, but that they are then used to spell out cultural messages, where the message is something quite separate and apart from the symbols which are transmitting it. It follows that a message becomes empowered by the subconscious associations of the symbols in whose terms it is expressed, but that its communication content remains something entirely different.

I agree that there is a distinction between the emotive power of a symbol and its social message; but the two, surely, cannot be "entirely different." A theory of hair must address the problem of their connection: how is the socially accepted message related to the original unconscious symbolism of hair?

A way toward a solution is pointed out by some important concepts put forward by Obeyesekere, who objects both to Leach's watertight division between private and public symbols and to the psychoanalytical assumption that all symbols must have deep motivational significance. He suggests a distinction between personal symbols, where deep motivational significance is involved, and "psychogenetic symbols."

> Psychogenetic symbols *originate* in the unconscious or are derived from the dream repertoire; but the origin of the symbols must be analytically separated from its ongoing operational significance. This is often the case in myths and rituals: symbols originating from unconscious sources are

> used to give expression to meanings that have nothing to do with their origin. (1981:13–14; original italics)

Obeyesekere's distinction between the genesis and the operational significance of symbols is similar to, but expresses more clearly, Hershman's distinction between emotional power and cultural message. But is it possible that the operational significance of a symbol could "have nothing to do with their origin?"

In his later book, *The Work of Culture,* Obeyesekere presents a more systematic and theoretical discussion of the phenomenon that he earlier referred to simply as the distinction between a symbol's unconscious genesis and its operational significance. He calls this distinction "symbolic remove." A symbol may operate at different levels of symbolic remove from its genesis in deep motivation "producing different levels of symbolization, some closer to, some more distant from the motivations that initially (psychogenetically) triggered the symbolic formation" (1990:57). The theory of symbolic remove, I believe, is an important contribution to our understanding of the formation and function of symbols, and in what follows I will examine the symbolic remove that takes place in the case of hair symbolism of South Asia.

Let us make some preliminary observations. Although Obeyesekere's theory of "symbolic remove" is a rich heuristic device, at least implicitly he appears to acknowledge only a single source—namely, the unconscious—for the origin of a symbol. Such a position could be called the "monogenesis" of symbols. But I think we should posit that at least some symbols, including hair, are polygenetic—they originate from a multiplicity of sources. This suggests at least two consequences. First, polygenesis may create the polysemy of a symbol; that is, the same symbol either simultaneously or in different contexts may contain more than one meaning.[55] Second, not all the meanings of a symbol may be reducible to a single root meaning or to the same source.

An adequate theory, moreover, should offer a root meaning (or a cluster of such meanings) of a symbol—that is the meaning least removed from its genesis—and should delineate the process of symbolic remove that gives rise to its operational meanings. Now a root meaning of a symbol, like the root form of a verb, is ultimately a fiction; it is abstracted or extrapolated from observed meanings and forms. Yet, as in the case of words, it helps us establish the various symbolic removes that occur in actual practice and understand the relationship between various operational meanings of the same symbol that may appear on the surface to have little in common. A root meaning, in other words, helps us formulate the grammar of a symbol.

As a fiction, the root meaning is neither true nor false, but more or less adequate or useful. The adequacy and usefulness of the root meaning we ascribe to a symbol can be validated only by comparing it with the actual and operational meanings available through ethnographic and historical study. This may appear to be a vicious circle, the root meaning being abstracted from operational meanings and the root meaning in turn validating the operational meanings. Just as in philology, however, this circle can be converted from a vicious to a hermeneutical circle (Obeyesekere 1990:93). The concrete uses of a symbol yield its root meaning; the root meaning will reveal further levels of meaning of the symbol; as more operational meanings from the same culture (and from other cultures, if one is engaged in a cross-cultural study) are analyzed, they will help us further refine the root meaning.

In explicating my theory, I first examine the sources from which the symbolism of hair is derived and then proceed to analyze the root meaning and the levels of symbolic remove. At least three sources are significant for the development of the symbolic meanings of hair.

First, in humans there is a clear and visible association between the growth of body hair—especially axillary, pubic, and, among males, facial hair—and the onset of puberty and sexual maturity. As far as I know, this is a developmental feature unique to human beings; at least it is absent in animals likely to influence the human creation of symbols. This curious biological fact is also the likely foundation of the second source,[56] namely the unconscious association between head hair and sexuality; this association has been sufficiently demonstrated both clinically and ethnographically. One may observe, however, that this association can stand on its own and apart from the related unconscious association of the head with the penis suggested by psychoanalysts. This dissociation of head and hair symbolism is also necessitated by the fact noted by Hallpike that female hair is treated in ways very similar to male hair. The third source is the biological fact that hair and nails are unique among body parts in that they grow continuously and they grow back when cut. On the one hand, they can be trimmed, shaved, and otherwise manipulated in ways that are impossible with other bodily parts. On the other hand, they may be viewed as imbued with extraordinary vitality. Hair on the human body, as we have seen, bears a striking parallel to grass on earth; both grow again when they are cut, and both testify to the vitality and the fertility of their respective hosts. Hair and grass even show a certain physical resemblance.

All three sources contribute to the complex of hair's symbolic meanings. There may be others. Some symbolic uses of hair that consider it as excrement may derive that meaning from the fact that hair resembles dead matter, without blood or sensation, and often falls from the body on its own. The South Asian materials we have examined, however, point to the association of hair with puberty and sexual maturity as the primary source of the root meaning of hair symbolism at least within the South Asian context.

Now to the root meaning. I posit that the root meaning from which most, though not necessarily all, operational meanings of hair is derived is a multifaceted complex consisting of sexual maturity, drive, potency, and fertility. For the sake of brevity, I shall henceforth refer to the root meaning simply as sexual maturity. The adequacy of this root meaning can only be gauged by examining how the operational meanings can be derived from or related to it, and how it enhances our understanding of those operational meanings.

The root meaning I have assigned to hair is significantly different from the one proposed by the psychoanalytic school. In some contexts, as in neurotics, in the dream repertoire, and when hair is used as what Obeyesekere calls "a personal symbol" by an individual, hair may stand for the sex organ in general or the phallus in particular. That psychoanalytic meaning, however, cannot explain the variety of socially established and ritually enacted forms of hair symbolism we have encountered in South Asia; indeed, even apart from female shaving, in many cases the equation of shaving with castration is simply inadmissible. But at least one portion of the psychoanalytic theory is essential for explaining the process of symbol formation in the case of hair, and that is the theory of displacement. Simply stated, displacement occurs when the unconscious substitutes the entity X for the entity Y, thus permitting individuals at the conscious level to speak about and to manipulate X which at a deeper level are statements about and the manipulation of Y.

The need for displacement arises because of a block at the conscious level that prevents individuals from dealing with Y directly. In the case of hair, it is not the pubic, axillary, or even facial hair—that is, hair associated with sexual maturation—that is the focus of attention in most rituals but the hair on the head. This hair at the source level is unrelated to puberty, appearing as it does at birth or soon thereafter. In ritual contexts the root meaning of hair as sexual maturity appears to be displaced from hair with clearer sexual connotations to the hair on the head without such connotations.[57]

The root meaning of hair as such, however, does not occur in actual ritual or social settings. A basic symbolic remove intervenes between the root and operational meanings. This symbolic remove consists in the transformation of the root meaning of sexual maturity into its operational meanings relating to the status and role of an adult within the structures of society. This transformation of meaning is a fairly simple operation, because the central social structure within which adults are co-opted into and operate within society is marriage, the structure that controls the adult sex drive. This assumption is validated by, among others, the fact that, as we have observed, the ritual separation from society associated with shaving the head invariably entails the suspension of sexual activity.

Having isolated the root meaning and its main operational derivative, we must nevertheless recognize that the meaning of a symbol, by its very nature, is rich, nuanced, and multifaceted, that several meanings normally inhere simultaneously, and that individuals participating in a ritual performance or social custom may be aware of or place emphasis on different aspects of that complex of meanings.

Using this basic operational meaning, let me now delineate what I consider to be the main features of hair symbolism manifested within the broad spectrum of hair rituals in Indian religious history that we have examined. Hair in ritual has no inherent or absolute meaning; its meaning or meanings are derived always from its relationship or opposition to other ritual functions of hair existing within the same society. Thus, to understand the meaning of shaving the head or letting the hair fall loose and uncontrolled we must locate them in relationship to others in society who do not shave their head or who keep their hair braided or under control.

Now, it is not necessary that all hair rituals obtain their meanings in relationship to a single point of reference. Thus, as we have seen, the long hair and beard of Sikh males derive their primary meaning in relation to the shaven head of a Hindu ascetic, whereas the clean and trimmed hair of an adult in society may be the point of reference for the long matted hair of hermits. Nevertheless, I believe that the most significant and central person with reference to whom most other hair rituals within the South Asian social context, and probably in most other societies, derive their meaning is the adult male, and to a lesser degree the adult female living within society. Their status and role within the social structure, their submission to and participation in the structures of social control, including structures for sexual control, are symbolized by the public control of their hair, a control that can be exercised in a variety of ways and not just by cutting, as supposed by Hallpike.[58] There are cultural and historical variations in the methods of hair control, but the most common method, at least in contemporary South Asia,[59] is for an adult male to trim and dress the hair and to shave or at least to trim the beard and for an adult female to braid or to tie the hair in a knot. Thus we arrive at our first principle: *control of hair by cutting, grooming, braiding, enclosing in a turban, or other means indicates an individual's participation in social structures within a publicly defined role and that individual's submission to social control.* Such a submission assigns the subject clear social roles and grants him or her rights and privileges.

We have seen that the most significant and widespread ritual use of hair in India is shaving, most frequently the shaving of the head and face, but sometimes also of the entire body. If we return to our root meaning of hair as sexual maturity, removal of hair would mean the denial or suspension of sexual maturity. The shaven individual is ritually reduced to the level of an infant, that is, to a sexually, and therefore socially, undifferentiated status. At a level symbolically removed from this, the primary meaning of shaving, I posit, is that the shaven individual is placed outside the social structures and denied a social status and role; hence, the almost universal association of shaving with rites of passage. Since permitted sexual activity is restricted to precisely such a social structure, namely marriage, shaven separation from society invariably involves celibacy. Thus we arrive at our second principle: *shaving the head amounts to the ritual separation of an individual from society either for a temporary period or permanently.* Shaving relating to reintegrating into society of persons who have been separated for a relatively long period of time shows an inversion of that process. Here the separation is not from society but from a liminal condition; the individual is released from that condition to assume his or her new social role.

Variant forms of ritual separation from society are expressed not through shaving but through lack of control of hair. We have seen that periods of separation resulting from pollution such as menstruation and death are often marked by women leaving their hair unbraided, uncombed, and unwashed. Shaving and leaving hair uncontrolled, therefore, in their own way oppose the controlled public hair of people in society. In both cases there is some form of interdiction of social intercourse between people in society and those ritually separated from it.

Related to such lack of control over hair is the third type of ritual use of hair in India: the neglect of hair associated with the physical separation of an individual from society. When an individual is ritually separated from society, he or she continues to live within the geographical boundaries of society and often in close relationship with people in society, whereas in physical separation the rite of separation culminates in the individual's departure from the social geography into the uncivilized realm of the forest or the wilderness. In India this type of separation is symbolized by long and uncontrolled hair that is left unkempt and unattended. The meaning of matted hair must be seen in its relation to the controlled hair of the adult within society. The total lack of hair control and the resultant long, ugly, matted hair (accompanied by long nails) indicates an individual's utter separation from civilized structures and controls and his or her integration to the uncivilized realm of the wild and the beast. The third principle, therefore, is: *matted hair indicates an individual's physical separation from society and civilized structures.* In medieval and modern South Asia, however, such physical separation has not been a lived reality. Thus, we have seen the diverse operational meanings given to matted hair in South Asian traditions. The case of the Sri Lankan male and female ascetics studied by Obeyesekere falls into the latter category. When the institution of forest hermits disappeared, it was easier to give new operational meanings to this practice.[60]

Conclusion

Once a particular social meaning has been assigned to a form of hair manipulation within a specific institutional or ritual setting—shaving as ascetic separation, for example—that same symbol may acquire new meanings for the participants, meanings that may go beyond, and thereby transform the earlier meaning. Thus ascetic shaving has acquired the meaning of "belonging" to a particular community as opposed to separation from society, in a way similar to that of the Sikh hair. In this way hair becomes a symbol that demarcates new boundaries—the monastic community or the Sikh community. Its new conventional meanings may thus hide to a large degree some of the basic meanings that I have attempted to uncover.

In the new conventional settings a particular type of hair manipulation may become a "condensed symbol," that is a symbol so powerful that it encapsulates all the diverse aspects of the symbolized, which under normal circumstances would require separate symbolic expressions. A flag or a national anthem may become such a condensed symbol; the rule against pork for the Jews and Friday abstinence from meat for traditional Catholics are similar condensed symbols that signify the essence of being a Jew or a Catholic. I think that the shaven head for the Buddhist monk and the uncut hair enclosed in a turban for the Sikh are such condensed symbols. This is nicely illustrated by an ethnographic observation of H. L. Seneviratne,[61] who found that one way contemporary Buddhist monks in Sri Lanka display their independence from monastic authority and their modernist outlook is to let their hair grow, now only to the length of a crew-cut, but who knows what is in store for the future? Hair thus remains both a means of strong institutional control and an instrument of liberation from and critique of social and institutional controls.

Notes

1. My principal focus will be on traditional India, although I will comment on some modern practices in several South Asian societies.

2. This diachronic and historical aspect of hair symbolism is often ignored by anthropologists and psychoanalysts. Obeyesekere (1990:39) notes the need for uncovering the historical/genetic etymology of a symbol. Truly diachronic study of a symbol within a given culture can advance the study of its etymology, just as much as psychoanalytic investigations. Such a historical study (with a keen sense of humor) of the beard in Europe has been done by Reynolds (1949).

3. I am not searching for a single and universally applicable reason because the reasons are multiple even within the same culture. Further, I am not searching for a single meaning of all hair practices or even of a single practice. I am convinced that this is a complex symbol with a spectrum of meanings and significances both public and private, both conscious and, often, unconscious (Obeyesekere 1981).

4. *Suśruta Saṃhitā*, Cikitsāsthāna, Ch. 24. 29, 73–75, 89. Manu (*Manusmṛti* 4.35), likewise, advises a young adult who has completed his vedic studies and is about to get married (*snātaka*) to keep his hair, beard, and nails trimmed (*kḷptakeśanakhaśmaśruḥ*).

5. Most sources regard hair and nails as a pair. When hair is cut, as we shall see, so are the nails, and when hair is left unattended, nails are also left to grow.

6. The *Vasiṣṭha Dharmasūtra* (2.21), for example, states that people should wear their hair according to the custom of their castes.

7. An ancient text states: "He shall not untie his topknot on a road"—*na pathi śikhāṃ visṛjet*. Hārīta quoted in Aparāditya's commentary on the

Yājñavalkyasmṛti (Ānandāśrama Edition), p. 225. On the practice of keeping a certain number of topknots to indicate one's lineage, see Kane II, 263–64.

8. Even in modern times long haired men were a common sight in Sri Lankan villages until quite recently; the practice has not completely disappeared even today. Sikh men, of course, do not cut their hair or beard. The length of male and female hair is subject to cultural determination. In Tikopia, for example, women's hair is short, while men's hair is long (Firth 1973:272). It is thus not possible to make a universal symbol out of the customs of modern South Asia and Europe, as Hallpike (1969) appears to do. Nevertheless, within each society gender difference is expressed in the prescription of gender specific coiffure.

9. On the distinctive patterns of braiding called *ekaveṇi* (single braid or clasping all the hair once in the back and letting the rest fall loose), *triveṇi* (triple braid), and the like, see Hiltebeitel 1981:184–86. On the way hair is worn by contemporary women in Punjab, see Hershman 1974.

10. See *Manusmṛti*, 8.314; *Āpastamba Dharmasūtra*, 1.25.4; *Gautama Dharmasūtra*, 12.43; *Baudhāyana Dharmasūtra*, 2.1.16; *Vasiṣṭha Dharmasūtra*, 20.41. The king beats the thief over the head with the club. Whether he dies or survives the blow, the thief is freed from his crime and sin.

11. See Kinsley 1975:81–159; Hiltebeitel 1981:206.

12. Yādavaprakāśa, *Yatidharmasamuccaya*, ed. P. Olivelle (Albany: State University of New York Press, 1994), 6.145.

13. The loose topknot of a Brahmin, for example, may be a sign of mourning: *Āśvalāyana Gṛhyasūtra*, 4.2.9; *Śrautakośa*, English Section, ed. R. N. Dandekar (Poona: Vaidika Saṃśodhana Maṇḍala, 1958–73), I.2, p. 1079. The disheveled hair of a woman in mourning is recorded already in the *Atharvaveda*, 9.9.7. Some sources instruct the mourners to ruffle their hair and to put dust on it: *Āpastamba Dharmasūtra*, 2.15.7; *Śrautakośa*, I.2, p. 1052.

14. The relatives of a person excommunicated from the caste are also expected to let their hair hang loose during the rite: *Vasiṣṭha Dharmasūtra*, 15.13.

15. For a study of cross-cultural symbolism of shaving, see Firth 1973:287–91.

16. The *Taittirīya Brāhmaṇa* (1.5.6.1–2) provides the interesting detail that at a sacrifice the shaving should be done the "divine" way: one first shaves the hair of the armpits, then the beard, and then the head. The demons (Asuras), on the other hand, did it the opposite way, which was the reason for their defeat at the hands of the gods. The *Śatapatha Brāhmaṇa* (3.1.2.3) alludes to a custom of shaving the entire body of a man at his sacrificial consecration.

17. For a detailed examination of the symbols of rebirth, see Gonda 1965:284–462, especially 337.

18. For a study of the connection between hair and fertility, see Lincoln 1977. At least in modern times, the hair is often offered to the goddess or put in a river: see Hershman 1974; Freed and Freed 1980:396–97.

19. For primary sources from the Gṛhyasūtras, see the *Śrautakośa*, I.2, pp. 1033, 1039, 1070, 1071, 1074, 1080, 1083. See the *Āśvalāyana Gṛhyasūtra*, 4.2.9, for shaving the whole body.

20. See *Manusmṛti* 2.219; *Āpastamba Dharmasūtra*, 1.2.31–32; *Gautama Dharmasūtra*, 1.27; *Vasiṣṭha Dharmasūtra*, 7.11.

21. For the general behavior expected of people in mourning, see Kane IV, 238ff. See also above, n.13.

22. See Kane IV, 122 for sources of this belief and for other customs involving shaving when a person performs a vow or a penance.

23. Some sources, such as the *Padma Purāṇa* and the *Skanda Purāṇa*, make shaving obligatory prior to a pilgrimage. See Kane IV, 573–76 for further details and sources of this practice. A frequently quoted verse states: "One should shave one's hair at Prayāga, before a pilgrimage, and at the death of the father or mother; one should not shave without cause" (Kane IV, 574, n. 1300). Kane (IV, 575) notes that some texts make a distinction between the technical terms *kṣaura* and *muṇḍana*, the former referring to the shaving of the head and the beard, and the latter indicating the shaving of only the head. Val Daniel (1984:245–87), in describing the pilgrimage to the shrine of Ayyappan, notes the initiation rite prior to departure, a rite that amounted to the ascetic renunciation of the pilgrims. He does not mention shaving explicitly, but the context strongly suggests it.

24. The *Kāśīkhaṇḍa* (4.75) of the *Skanda Purāṇa*. See Vāsudevāśrama, *Yatidharmaprakāśa* (ed. P. Olivelle; Vienna: 1976–77), 71.96–97; Kane IV, 585.

25. See Kane II, 583–98 for the customs and duties relating to a widow.

26. For further details see Kane III, 396–97. Other punishments subject to shaving include adultery and incest with the wife of one's teacher. Shaving associated with punishment and reduction to slavery is a widespread practice cross-culturally: Firth 1973:289–90; Hallpike 1987:155.

27. Hindu renouncers shave at the beginning of each of the five Indian seasons, thus shaving approximately every two months. Periodic shaving (or uprooting) of head hair is a feature also of Buddhist and Jain monks. One rule permits Buddhist monks to keep only one and a half inches of hair on their head: see *Cullavagga*, 5.2.2–3.

28. This is the opposite of what Eilberg-Schwartz (1990:145) points out in the case of circumcision: "Since circumcision exposes a boy's sexual organ, it is also a natural symbol of his readiness for social intercourse. Sexual intercourse, after all, is one of the most powerful symbols of social intercourse." As Eilberg-Schwartz (1990:145) himself notes, "when a person is outside or in transition between recognized social positions, sexual intercourse is prohibited."

29. These hairs represent the Brahmanical topknot. Its uprooting may thus also indicate the ascetic's abandonment of the ritual religion represented by the topknot and the sacrificial string, both of which are abandoned by some types of Brahmanical ascetics. See the *Yatidharmaprakāśa*, ed. cit., 21.39, 104.

30. See Zimmer 1962:160. See H. C. Warren, *Buddhism in Translations* (New York: Atheneum, 1962), p. 66. The belief that the hair and nails of a liberated individual (*kevalin*) do not grow is found also in the Jain tradition (Dundas 1985:179 and n.142).

31. One source, for example, states: "Ascetics, vedic students, and widows should abstain from chewing betel leaves, from anointing their bodies with oil, and from eating out of brass plates." Yādava Prakāśa, *Yatidharma-samuccaya*, ed. cit., 7.140. For the legal status of a renouncer, see Olivelle 1984, and for a discussion of the similarities and differences between a widow and an ascetic, see Leslie 1991.

32. See Kane IV, 298, where other instances are given where ascetics and students are treated alike with reference to periods of impurity. With regard to food, the ascetic resembles a man consecrated for a vedic sacrifice (*dīkṣita*): the food of both causes impurity and are not to be eaten by others. On the ascribed purity of begged food, see Yādavaprakāśa, *Yatidharma-samuccaya*, ed. cit., 6.95, 109–10.

33. On the symbolism of food in the ascetic traditions, see Olivelle 1991.

34. "By giving cooked food to a householder one goes to the Raurava hell." Vāsudevāśrama, *Yatidharmaprakāśa*, ed. P. Olivelle (Vienna, 1976–77), 68.62–63.

35. Matted hair is generally caused by the neglect of hair. I have found one instance, however, where the matted coiffure is artificially created using the juice of a banyan tree: *Rāmāyaṇa*, 2.46.55–56. For a study of modern examples from Sri Lanka, see Obeyesekere 1981; the subjects of his study uniformly viewed the appearance of matted locks as sudden and interpreted it as a divine gift.

36. See *Gautama Dharmasūtra* 3.26–35; *Āpastamba Dharmasūtra*, 2.22.1–11; *Baudhāyana Dharmasūtra*, 2.11.5; 3.3.1–22; *Vasiṣṭha Dharmasūtra*, 9.1–12. A significant incident in the epic story of the *Mahābhārata* relates to the ugliness and smell of an ascetic. While accepting the invitation to father a son for his deceased brother, Vyāsa tells his brother's widow that she should "bear with my ugliness. If she bears with my smell, my looks, my garb, and my body, Kauśalyā shall straightway conceive a superior child" (MBh 1.99.42–43; trans. of van Buitenen). His odor and sight are so overwhelming, however, that the woman is forced to close her eyes when he comes to her bed, resulting in the blindness of her son, Dhṛtarāṣṭra.

37. See *Gautama Dharmasūtra*, 3.26–35; *Baudhāyana Dharmasūtra*, 2.11.15.

38. A man with matted hair (*jaṭila*) is among those forbidden at a funerary offering (*śrāddha*): *Manusmṛti* 3.151. There is nothing in this symbolic structure to suggest the unrestrained sexuality proposed by Leach 1958:154. The operational meaning of neglected and long hair in this context is far removed from what I call its "root" meaning (see below). It is, however, clear that even though the operational meaning is about withdrawal from society, the rules of life of hermits are very ambivalent regarding their sexuality, some prescribing celibacy and others suggesting a noncelibate life style. Celibacy is not a hallmark of matted-hair ascetics in quite the same way as it is of shaven-headed ascetics.

39. See Olivelle 1993; Sprockhoff 1979, 1981, 1984, 1991. Both the *Rāmāyaṇa* (2.20.21) and the *Mahābhārata* (3.186.2–3) ascribe the institution of this practice to ancient seers or to the very first king. Buddhist sources ascribe its foundation to the universal emperor Daḷhanemi (*Dīgha Nikāya*, III, 60–64) or to King Makhādeva of Mithilā, who was the Buddha in one of his former births (*Majjhima Nikāya*, II, 75–82).

40. For extensive studies of hair among the Sikhs, see Uberoi 1967 and Hershman 1974.

41. On the possible reasons for such blocks in native reflections on rites and symbols, see Obeyesekere 1990, 43.

42. For an examination of this attitude toward cut or fallen hair cross culturally, see Leach 1969:156–57, and Firth 1973:287. Hershman (1974:292–94) objects, I think wrongly, to Leach's and Douglas's (1966) cross-cultural study of "dirt" as applied to hair.

43. *Āpastamba Dharmasūtra*, 1.16.23. Yādavaprakāśa (*Yatidharmasamuccaya*, ed. cit., 10.74) tells an ascetic to discard both his bowl and the food in it when water from the hair or beard falls into it. In a significant juxtaposition, he immediately goes on to say what an ascetic should do if he happens to purge, to vomit, or to void urine or excrement while he is begging. The *Mahābhārata* (1.3.126) records the story of one Utaṅka, who curses King Pauṣya because the king gave him food with a hair in it.

44. The block in native exegesis that I referred to earlier is borne out by the contradictory reasons given in the *Śatapatha Brāhmaṇa* itself. In giving the reason why a king after his consecration remains unshaved for a year, it says: "The reason why he does not shave his hair (is this): that collected essence of waters wherewith he is then sprinkled (anointed) is vigor, and it is the hair (of his head) that it reaches first when he is sprinkled; hence were he to shave his hair, he would cause that glory to fall off from him and would sweep it away: therefore he does not shave his hair" (5.5.3.1; Eggeling's trans.). So one shaves because the water does not reach the hair, and one refrains from shaving because the water reaches it first!

45. The *Bṛhadāraṇyaka Upaniṣad*, 6.4.1, states: "Earth is the essence of these beings; water is the essence of earth; plants are the essence of water; flowers are the essence of plants; fruits are the essence of flowers; man is the essence of fruits; and semen is the essence of man." See also *Praśna Upaniṣad*, 1.14. For the semen as the carrier of personality, see *Bṛhadāraṇyaka Upaniṣad*, 6.2.9–16; *Chāndogya Upaniṣad*, 5.4–10.

46. See, for example, Varada's *Yatiliṅgasamarthana* (ed. in P. Olivelle, *Renunciation in Hinduism: A Medieval Debate*, vol. 2; Vienna, 1987) III.43.

47. For an examination of this text, see Schmidt 1987; Vajracharya 1988.

48. *Muṇḍaka*, 1.1.7. The *Aitareya Upaniṣad* (1.1.4) makes following sequence in the way the original being (man) gave rise to the creation: first the skin; from skin, the body hairs; and from the hairs, the plants and trees.

49. The list of places cited by Kane (II, 263)—near water, under an Udumbara tree, in a bunch of *darbha* grass, in a wooded area—indicate a clear association with fertility.

50. In this context it may also be worthwhile to note that bald-headed men were considered ritually handicapped and bracketed with others with similar disabilities, such as eunuchs, lepers, cripples, and the blind. The *Gautama Dharmasūtra* (15.18) forbids the feeding of a bald man at a *śrāddha*. Bald men also, along with eunuchs, are among those not permitted to become Brahmanical ascetics: *Nāradaparivrājaka Upaniṣad*, 136; *Bṛhat-Saṃnyāsa Upaniṣad*, 251–52 (both in *Saṃnyāsa Upaniṣads*, trans. P. Olivelle; New York: Oxford University Press, 1992). A person who is *keśava*, probably meaning a man with long hair, is said in the *Śatapatha Brāhmaṇa* (5.1.2.14) to be neither a woman, because he is a man, nor a man, because he has long hair. The reference may be to a eunuch. On the relation between hair and sex within the Indian context, see also Hara 1986.

51. We see a similar profusion of significations in modern fads and practices. There have been and are actors and athletes who have shaved their heads. And there is the motley group of young men called "skin heads." It is difficult to see a uniform social meaning or message underlying all these practices.

52. See Berg 1951; Leach 1958; Obeyesekere 1981 and 1990; Hershman 1974.

53. Mary Douglas (1982:72, 85, 89) also supports such a distinction, where the smooth stands for control and the shaggy, for the informal, the antisocial, and the prophetic.

54. Hallpike's (1969:257) analysis of hair symbolism is based on nine special characteristics of hair that he isolates: "1. Like the nails it grows constantly. 2. It can be cut painlessly, again like the nails. 3. It grows in great quantity, such that individual hairs are almost numberless. 4. Head hair is apparent on infants of both sexes at birth. 5. Genital/anal hair appears at puberty in both sexes. 6. In some races, males develop facial hair after puberty, and also body hair. 7. Hair on different parts of the body is of different texture, e.g. eyelashes, pubic hair, head hair. 8. In old age hair often turns white and/or falls out. 9. Hair is a prominent feature of animals, especially monkeys, man's analogue in the animal kingdom." At least some of these features, as I shall point out, clearly played a role in the genesis of hair symbolism.

55. Indeed, polysemy of symbols is at the very heart of Obeyesekere's (1990:56) theory. Although polysemy is possible in the context of symbolic remove even within a monogenetic scheme, I think the parallel notion of polygenesis will strengthen the case for polysemy.

56. I say the foundation, because the unconscious after all must receive the grist for its mill from the conscious and the sensory spheres.

57. This displacement is clear in the case of Brahmanical ascetics who are not only enjoined to shave their heads but also positively forbidden from shaving their armpits and the pubic regions; appropriate penances are prescribed for those who do (see Yādava Prakāśa, *Yatidharmasamuccaya*, ed. cit., 8.9–11).

58. The Sikh males are a good example from India. Rivière (1969) has shown how the hair tube is used by the tribes in the northern Rupununi

district of Guyana to enclose and control the long hair of adult males. Cf. n. 8 on the Tikopia.

59. As I have noted above, the picture is much less clear in ancient times.

60. I wonder, however, whether within the mainland of India, where the legends of matted-hair ascetics and seers are still alive, an ascetic would be able to publicly claim that his or her matted hair was the gift of a god, as the Sri Lankan ascetics regularly claim. In Sri Lanka where the matted hair tradition and legends are less frequent, it is evidently easier to ascribe deeply personal meanings to this symbol because it lacks an articulated public meaning.

61. Personal communication.

References

Alter, J. 1992. "The Sannyasi and the Indian Wrestler: The Anatomy of a Relationship." *American Ethnologist* 19:317–36.

Berg, C. 1951. *The Unconscious Significance of Hair*. London: George Allen and Unwin.

Berger, P., and Luckmann, T. 1967. *The Social Construction of Reality*. Garden City, N.Y.: Doubleday.

Cooper, W. 1971. *Hair: Sex Society Symbolism*. New York: Stein and Day.

Daniel, V. 1984. *Fluid Signs: Being a Person the Tamil Way*. Berkeley: University of California Press.

Derrett, J. D. M. 1973. "Religious Hair." *Man* (N.S.) 8:100–103.

Douglas, M. 1966. *Purity and Danger: An Analysis of the Concepts of Pollution and Taboo*. London: Routledge & Kegan Paul.

———. 1982. *Natural Symbols: Explorations in Cosmology*. 2nd ed. New York: Pantheon Books.

Dundas, P. 1985. "Food and Freedom: The Jaina Sectarian Debate on the Nature of the Kevalin," *Religion* 15:161–98,

Eilberg-Schwartz, H. 1990. *The Savage in Judaism: An Anthropology of Israelite Religion and Ancient Judaism*. Bloomington: Indiana University Press.

Firth, R. 1973. *Symbols: Public and Private*. London: George Allen and Unwin.

Freed, R. S., and Freed, S. A. 1980. *Rites of Passage in Shanti Nagar*. Anthropological Papers of the American Museum of Natural History, vol. 56, pt. 3. New York.

Frazer, J. G. 1913. *The Golden Bough: A Study in Magic and Religion*. 3rd ed. London: Macmillan, part 2, 252–87.

Gennep, Arnold van. 1960. *The Rites of Passage*. Trans. M. B. Vizedom and G. L. Caffee. Chicago: University of Chicago Press.

Gonda, J. 1956. "The Sīmantonnayana as Described in the Gṛhyasūtras," *East and West* 7:12–31.

———. 1965. *Change and Continuity in Indian Religon*. Disputationes Rheno-Trajectinae, 9. The Hague: Mouton.

———. 1981. "The Treatment of Hair Cuttings in the Gṛhyasūtras," *Ṛtam* (Akhila Bhāratīya Saṃskṛta Pariṣad, Lucknow) 10 (1–2):37–40.

———. 1985. *The Ritual Functions and Significance of Grasses in the Religion of the Veda*. Amsterdam: North-Holland Publishing Company.

Hallpike, Christopher R. 1969. "Social Hair," *Man* (N.S.) 4:256–64.

———. 1987. "Hair." *The Encyclopedia of Religion*. Ed. M. Eliade et al., 6:154–57.

Hara, M. 1986. "The Holding of the Hair (*Keśa-grahaṇa*)," *Acta Orientalia* 47:67–92.

Heesterman, J. C. 1968. "The Return of the Veda Scholar." In *Pratidānam*, ed. J. C. Heesterman et al., The Hague: Mouton, pp. 436–47.

Hershman, P. 1974. "Hair, Sex and Dirt," *Man* (N.S.) 9:274–98.

Hiltebeitel, A. 1981. "Draupadī's Hair." In *Autour de la déesse hindoue*, ed. M. Biardeau. Paris: Éditions de l'École des Hautes Études en Sciences Sociales, pp. 179–214.

Kane, P. V. 1962–75. *History of Dharmaśāstra*. I.1 (1968), I.2 (1975), II.1–2 (1974), III (1973), V.1 (1974), V.2 (1962). Poona: Bhandarkar Oriental Research Institute.

Kinsley, D. 1975. *The Sword and the Flute: Kālī and Kṛṣṇa, Dark Visions of the Terrible and the Sublime in Hindu Mythology*. Berkeley: University of California Press.

Leach, E. R. 1958. "Magical Hair," *Journal of the Royal Anthropological Institute* 88:147–64.

Lingat, R. 1973. *The Classical Law of India*. Trans. J. D. M. Derrett. Berkeley: University of California Press.

Leslie, I. J. 1991. "A Problem of Choice: The Heroic *Satī* or the Widow-Ascetic." In *Problems of Dharma: Rules and Remedies in Classical Indian Law*, ed. I. J. Leslie. Panels of the 7th World Sanskrit Conference, ed. J. Bronkhorst. Vol. 9. Leiden: E. J. Brill, pp. 46–61.

Lincoln, B. 1977. "Treatment of Hair and Fingernails Among the Indo-Europeans," *History of Religions* 16:351–62.

Marglin, F. A. 1985. "Female Sexuality in the Hindu World." In *Immaculate and Powerful: The Female in Sacred Image and Social Reality*, ed. C. W. Atkinson, C. H. Buchanan, and M. R. Miles. Boston: Beacon Press, pp. 39–59.

Mauss, Marcel. 1935 (original). "Techniques of the Body," trans. Ben Brewster, *Economy and Society* 2.1 (1973):70–88.

Obeyesekere, G. 1981. *Medusa's Hair: An Essay on Personal Symbols and Religious Experience*. Chicago: University of Chicago Press.

———. 1990. *The Work of Culture: Symbolic Transformation in Psychoanalysis and Anthropology*. Chicago: University of Chicago Press.

Olivelle, P. 1984. "Renouncer and Renunciation in the Dharmaśāstras." In *Studies in Dharmaśāstra*, ed. R. W. Lariviere. Calcutta: Firma KLM, pp. 81–152.

———. 1991. "From Feast to Fast: Food and the Indian Ascetic. In *Problems of Dharma: Rules and Remedies in Classical Indian Law*, ed. I. J. Leslie. Panels of the 7th World Sanskrit Conference, ed. J. Bronkhorst. Vol. 9. Leiden: E. J. Brill, pp. 17–36.

———. 1993. *The Āśrama System: The History and Hermeneutics of a Religious Institution*. New York: Oxford University Press.

Padma, B. 1991. *Costume, Coiffure and Ornaments in the Temple Sculpture of Northern Andhra*. Delhi: Agam Kala Prakashan.

Pandey, R. B. 1969. *Hindu Saṃskāras (Socio-Religious Study of the Hindu Sacraments)*. 2nd ed. Delhi: Motilal Banarsidass.

Reynolds, R. 1949. *Beards: Their Social Standing, Religious Involvements, and Decorative Possibilities, and Value in Offence and Defence through the Ages*. New York: Harcourt Brace Jovanovich.

Rivière, P. G. 1969. "Myth and Material Culture: Some Symbolic Interrelations." In *Forms of Symbolic Action*. Ed. R. F. Spencer. Seattle: American Ethnological Society, pp. 151–66.

Schmidt, H. P. 1987. *Some Women's Rites and Rights in the Veda*. Poona: Bhandarkar Oriental Research Institute.

Seneviratne, H. L. 1992. "Food Essence and the Essence of Experience." In *The Eternal Food: Gastronomic Ideas and Experiences of Hindus and Buddhists*, ed. R. S. Khare. Albany: State University of New York Press, pp. 179–200.

Sprockhoff, J. F. 1979. "Die Alten im alten Indien: Ein Versuch nach brahmanischen Quellen," *Saeculum* 30:374–433.

———. 1981. "Āraṇyaka und Vānaprastha in der vedischen Literatur: Neue Erwägungen zu einer alten Legende und ihren Problemen," pt. 1, *Wiener Zeitschrift für die Kunde Südasiens* 25:19–90.

———. 1984. "Āraṇyaka und Vānaprastha in der vedischen Literatur: Neue Erwägungen zu einer alten Legende und ihren Problemen," pt. 2, *Wiener Zeitschrift für die Kunde Südasiens* 28:5–43.

———. 1991. "Āraṇyaka und Vānaprastha in der vedischen Literatur: Neue Erwägungen zu einer alten Legende und ihren Problemen," pt. 3, *Wiener Zeitschrift für die Kunde Südasiens* 35:5–46.

Turner, B. S. 1984. *The Body and Society*. Oxford: Basil Blackwell.

Uberoi, J. P. S. 1967. "On Being Unshorn." In *Sikhism and Indian Society*. Transactions of the Institute of Advanced Study, vol. 4. Simla, pp. 87–100.

Vajracharya, G. 1988. "Apala Versus Romasa: The Vedic View About the Hair and Fertility." Paper presented at the American Oriental Society Meeting, Chicago, March 1988. Unpublished draft.

Van Gennep, Arnold. 1960. *The Rites of Passage*. Chicago: University of Chicago Press.

Zimmer, H. 1962. *Myths and Symbols in Indian Art and Civilization*. Ed. J. Campbell. New York: Harper.

3 hairy barbarians, furry primates, and wild men: medical science and cultural representations of hair in china

frank dikötter

This chapter is about the emergence of medical science and its impact on cultural representations of hair in China during the twentieth century. Although some mention is made of hair on top of the head,[1] the main concern is with body hair. Most of the primary sources on which this research is based are confined to higher registers of scientific discourse, but other levels of culture are occasionally explored.[2] From late imperial China to the People's Republic, body hair was used to symbolically represent boundaries of "sex," "race" and "civilization." Despite some historical continuities, cultural representations shifted from an emphasis on the spatial dimension (body hair as a symbol of the geographically remote barbarian) to an increased focus on the temporal dimension (body hair as a symbol of the historically distant primate).

Late Imperial China (1600–1911)

Wild Men

If a plurality of ambiguous and often contradictory meanings was ascribed to hair in late imperial China, body hair most commonly symbolized the fragile border separating the human from the beast. As in Christian countries up to the beginning of the nineteenth century,[3] boundaries between man and ape were blurred in imperial China: learned literature compared "red-bearded" Europeans to "macaques" (*mihou*) (Zhang Xinglang 1928:180), and "curly-haired" Africans were seen as devil-slaves (*guinu*). Similar to the beasts, black slaves were not thought to understand human speech (Zhu Yu 1935–1936.2:2b). Some animals living within the realm of the empire, on the other hand, were described as wild men with a long tail: although orangutans (*xingxing*) and baboons (*feifei*) were covered in black hair (figure 3), they were sometimes held to speak human language (Li Shizhen 1981.4:2912 and 2920). "Hairy men" (*maoren*) were also reported in the imperial annals. From 1555 onward, the local gazetteer of Fang county in Hubei province repeatedly mentioned people from the mountains covered in long hair (*Fangxianzhi ce* 12); these reports inspired several vernacular stories by the poet Yuan Mei (1987:1716–1797). Where earlier versions in the Daoist tradition presented the acquisition of body hair as a step toward immortality,[4] most of Yuan Mei's accounts presented excessive hair growth as a transformation away from "civilization."[5] Comparable to the myth of the wild man in Europe,[6] the hairy man was located beyond the limits of the cultivated field, in the wilderness, the mountains, and the forests: the border of human society, he hovered on the edge of bestiality. Body hair indicated physical regression, generated by the absence of cooked food, decent clothing, and proper behavior. Hair as a symbol of excessive sexuality was encapsulated in stories about the abduction of humans by hairy men, a theme also prominent in some medieval ape tales. Some of these tales included pictorial representations of women with simian hands clutching baby apes (Wu Hung 1987).

If hairy men could be found within the realms of imperial space, stubbly barbarians were strictly confined to the edges of civilization. Official cosmologies located otherness at the periphery of the civilized world, where the degree of remoteness from the imperial center corresponded to levels of cultural savagery and physical coarseness. Although ancient works of geographical mythology populated the edges of the world with imaginary spirits and monstrous beasts that were often hirsute, hair only became a dominant symbol of otherness with the arrival of Europeans after the sixteenth century.

Hairy Barbarians

Many Chinese were struck by the hairy appearance of Europeans, and the bearded missionaries seem to have made a durable impression during the seventeenth century. Giulio Aleni, for instance, was described as a

Figure 3. Illustration of a baboon from a late imperial encyclopedia; in *Gujin tusha jicheng* (Chinese illustrated encyclopedia), 1726, *ce* 522, *juan* 88, *ji* 23.

"man with blue eyes and the beard of a dragon" during his first visit to Fujian province between 1625 and 1639 (Gernet 1985:250). The Dutch were commonly referred to as "red-haired barbarians,"[7] whereas the Portuguese were described as "seven feet tall, eyes like a cat, a mouth like an oriole, an ash-white face, thick and curly beards like black gauze, and almost red hair" (Zhang Xie 1981:93). Cultural representations of barbarian hair became more pervasive after the Opium War (1839–1842), as is indicated by the diary of Lin Zexu (1785–1850), the imperial commissioner appointed to suppress the opium trade: "They have heavy beards, much of which they shave, leaving one curly tuft, which at first sight creates a surprising effect. Indeed, they do really look like devils; and when the people of these parts call them 'devils' it is no mere empty term of abuse" (Waley 1958:68–69). Zhigang, head of the first diplomatic mission to the West from 1866 to 1870, confided in his journal that he was shocked by the natives of Ceylon, whose "black hair, about four centimetres long, covers their chest and all of their back" (Zhigang 1985:374). Fixation on hair transcended the private realm of the diary. In 1848, Xu Jiyu (1795–1873), governor of Fujian province, published an influential work on world geography, in which Europeans were described as follows: "Europeans are tall and fair-skinned. They have high noses, recessed sockets and yellow eyes (some have black eyes). Their hair is often left on the temples or coiled around the cheeks. Some have it straight like Chinese, some have curly whiskers, some are entirely shaven, some leave it long, some separate the whiskers and the moustache like the Chinese. Young and old alike, the hair is worn about a decimetre long; it is cut when it is longer. Hair and beards are often yellow or red" (Xu Jiyu 1861.4:7b).

Explorers of the West brought home more exotic descriptions of barbarian hair growth. Zhang Deyi (1847–1919) reported from Europe that "when about twenty years old, the moustache and beard of foreign men start to grow. As a rule, they do not cut or shave them, allowing them to develop. At the age of fifty or sixty, either they start to trim the moustache, or they cut both moustache and beard, as it is said that when men become older and weaker, there is no further need to wear them, as they hinder whilst drinking or eating" (Zhang Deyi 1985:450). Boundaries of age seemed to be transgressed in the Far West, since the long beard was a symbol of seniority in the Confucian universe. Confusion of gender borders was also thought to exist in Europe, and some observers even discerned male hair on female bodies: Zhang Deyi, for instance, noticed that in France "many women have long beards and moustaches" (Zhang Deyi 1985:395, 424). Yuan

Zuzhi, a grandson of the poet Yuan Mei mentioned above, observed that women in the West had "beards and moustaches all over their face" (Yuan Zuzhi no date:2b).

The pictorial world of late imperial China, situated at the privileged juncture of high culture and folk beliefs, also teemed with furry bogymen. Picture-story books for popular consumption started representing foreigners from the sixteenth century onward (see A Ying 1984). A booklet on Macao, popular in the south during the eighteenth century, included ten drawings of the "various barbarians" (Yin and Zhang 1751 *juan* 2). Bearded, moustached, and whiskered, tall like a vision, with a conchlike nose and squinting eyes, the Westerner loomed regularly in the Chinese iconography of exotic countries during the late Qing.[8]

Republican China (1911–1949)

Furry Primates

Evolutionism had an enormous impact in China from the last decade of the nineteenth century onward. Many leading intellectuals, however, proposed evolutionary theories that were much closer to neo-Lamarckism than to Darwinism.[9] Neo-Darwinists imagined evolution to be an open-ended process governed by natural selection, adaptation, and random mutation. Growth and development represented a process of specialization, leading to new branches on the evolutionary tree. Neo-Lamarckists, on the other hand, viewed evolution as an inevitable ascent through a preordained hierarchy of developmental stages on a ladder. Design and progress guided the neo-Lamarckist theory: from invertebrates to fish, reptiles, mammals, and man, the embryo was thought to develop in a purposeful way toward maturity. Unilinear models of evolution infused meaning and order in a shifting universe; they legitimized the cult of progress and the need for hierarchy. Progressivism dominated the writings of social reformers in China, in which time was articulated as an axis with one direction only: forward. *Jinhua*, or "evolution," meant "transformation forward," whereas its antipode *tuihua*, or "devolution," meant "transformation backward." Devolution faced evolution: both concepts rapidly infiltrated the public debate, particularly during the first decades of the twentieth century, marked by the loss of prestige of Confucianism and the disintegration of the imperial system.

Anthropologists and sociologists in Republican China started dividing mankind into different stages of "civilization." The "raw"

Figure 4. A picture of an Ainu, a population group in Japan alleged to be covered in hair; in Chen Yinghuang, *Renleixue* (Anthropology), Shanghai: Shangwu yinshuguan, 1928 (1st ed. 1918).

barbarian (*shengfan*), coated with thick hair and inhabitant of the dark forests of the mountains, became a symbol for the lowest stage of evolution. A development away from the lower furry species, "half-civilized races" (*ban kaiming minzu*) were thought to have attained the second level of evolution. In anthropological discourse, the "civilized races" (*kaiming minzu*) were confined to the English and Chinese, spear-heads of the evolutionary process: authors frequently noted that both "races" had patches of body hair only on the chest and on the legs (Gong Tingzhang 1926:11; Zhu Weiji 1948:72). Chen Yinghuang, the first professor of physical anthropology at Beijing University, gave examples of "races" that had never evolved beyond the ape-man stage: the overdeveloped hair system of the Ainu, a minority from the Hokkaido region, became a common illustration of racial regression. A line drawing in Chen Yinghuang's book represented a naked Ainu, heavily bearded and covered with hair from top to toe (figure 4). Other authors compared the Ainu to Europeans, as both were imagined to suffer from excessive body hair (Liu Min 1932:209).

The concept of recapitulation was central to neo-Lamarckism: embryological growth was imagined to pass through the earlier stages of evolution, starting with the amoeba and ascending to the level of fish, reptile, and finally mammal. In its ascent to mankind, the human fetus gradually lost its hair (called lanugo) after the first seven months. Racial atavism highlighted the fragile nature of the delineation between human and animal: furry beasts were always lurking behind a thin veil of "humanity" and "civilization." You Jiade's *Origins of Mankind* (1929), like many other books on human biology in the 1920s and 30s, drew extensively on the theory of recapitulation. The "fine and long hair" covering the fetus was compared to that of a monkey and was thought to fall out at the moment of birth (You Jiade 1929:7).

Further proof of man's descent from the monkey was thought to reside in his atrophied tail. If the human was no more than an evolved anthropoid, the "sons of the Yellow Emperor" (*huangdi zisun*) were merely the "descendants of apes" (*yuanhou zisun*). The ancestors of the sage Confucius had lived in trees, clutched to branches with their tails, eating raw meat and drinking blood, with no clothes to protect them from the elements. "Most people do not wish to hear that man has a tail. But if we dissect the human body we will immediately find proof for the existence of a tail, which consists of three, four or even five coccyxal vertebras merged together in the lower part of the spine. The human foetus has a tail which is longer than a limb and also has a muscle to wag it. In the grown-up person this muscle survives in the form of a filamentous joint" (Zhang Ziping 1930:46). In Germany, Liu Piji even reported in his *Misinterpretations in Everyday Biology*, a boy had been born with a tail thirty centimeters long (figure 5): "This is clear proof that civilized people also have a tail!" (Liu Piji 1928:80). "Inferior races," however, were said to be much closer to primitive man, and Africans were sometimes considered to have a hairy tail. Periodicals regularly reported about newly discovered "races" with tails (You wei 1929), and daily newspapers titled "Apes have tail; man has tail too" (Houzi 1936; Sheng 1936); reversions of man to ape were also reported (Ren 1935).

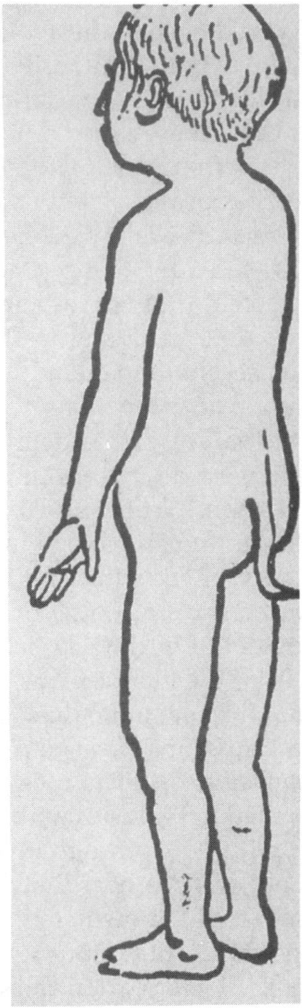

Figure 5. A boy born with a tail, meant to illustrate the power of degenerative evolutionary forces; in Chen Yinghuang, *Renleixue* (Anthropology), Shanghai: Shangwu yinshuguan, 1928 (1st ed. 1918).

Anthropologists commonly isolated hair as a significant marker of "race." Chen Yinghuang's survey of mankind began with a detailed analysis of hair. Three pages were devoted to the classification of different types of beards, whiskers, and moustaches (Chen Yinghuang 1918:66–69), a system replicated by primers of geography for middle schools (figure 6) (Liu Huru 1931:33–35). Zhang Ziping, a popular writer of textbooks, also selected hair as the most reliable criterion for racial taxonomies. He produced a drawing of different hair textures that corresponded to his fivefold classification of mankind. Six years later, Zhang listed the straight-haired races (i.e., Chinese) and the curly-haired races as two distinct branches in the genealogy of organisms.

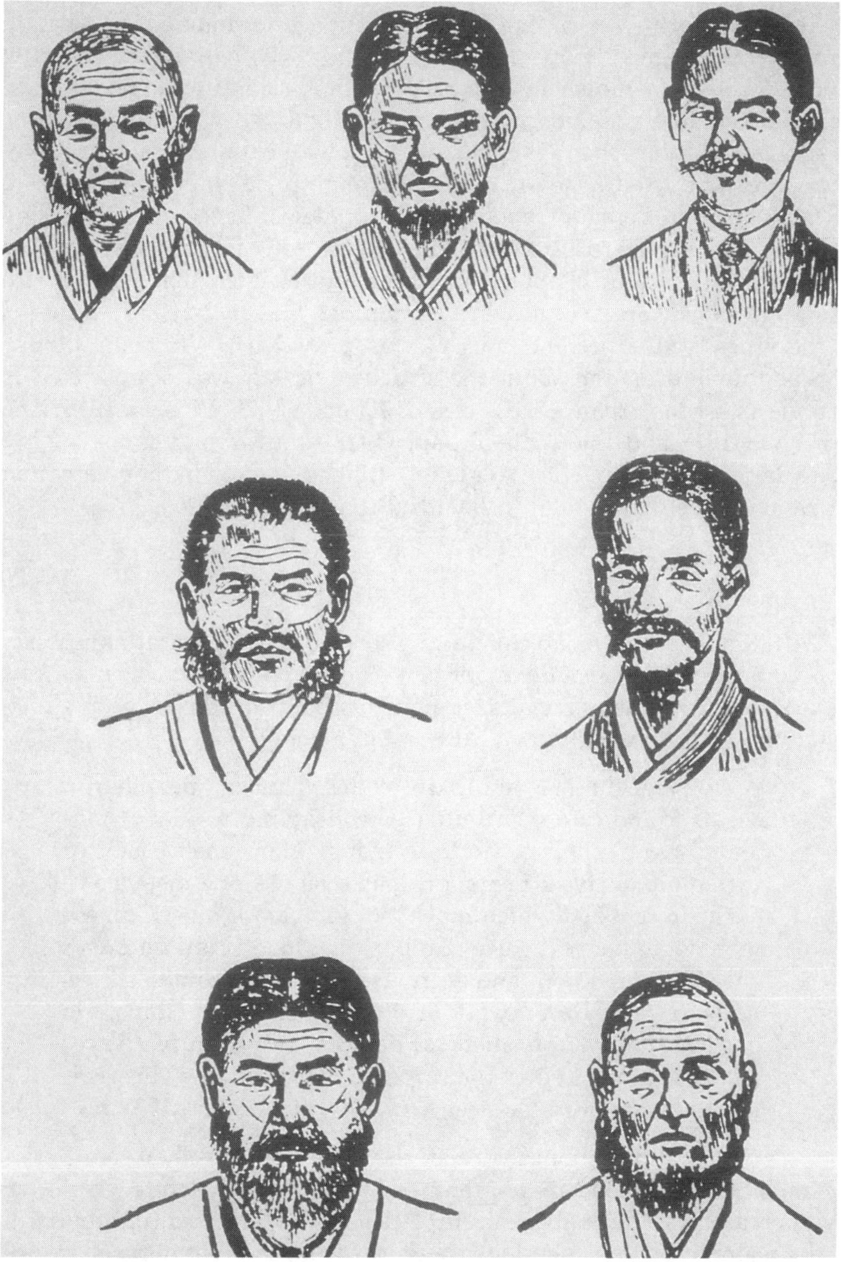

Figure 6. Different types of beards in one of the earliest anthropology textbooks in Republican China; in Chen Yinghuang, *Renleixue* (Anthropology), Shanghai: Shangwu yinshuguan, 1928 (1st ed. 1918).

Aesthetic norms and scientific observation intermingled, as straight hair was judged "more beautiful" than curly hair (Zhang Ziping 1930:74, 84). In nineteenth-century Europe, scientists sometimes divided hair into a "leiotrichous" type (straight and wavy, i.e., Europeans) and a "ulotrichous" type (crisp, woolly, or tufted): each group of people conducted its own taxonomic enterprise under the guise of "science." Wu Zelin, a respected anthropologist in search of a foreign authority, referred to "Professor Huntington" of Yale University, whose book included four chapters on China and claimed that people with straight hair were evolutionarily the most "advanced" (an "index of roundness" for different "races" was provided) (Wu Zelin 1932).[10] Scientific information about the structure of hair was popularized in reviews for the urban middle class (Shaoying 1925, Yi Luan 1916, Zhu Tiehua 1917 and Shou Zhenhuang 1922), but as late as as 1989, a textbook of "physiological hygiene" still had to explain that wavy hair could not be detrimental to health (Su and Lu 1989:17).

Bearded Women

With the theory of recapitulation, absence of hair from face and body became a sign of racial development. Female bodies in particular were searched for signs of racial specificity, as indicates the following quotation from the well-known author Lin Yutang:

> A study of the hair and skin of the [Chinese] people also seems to indicate what must be considered results of millenniums of civilized indoor living. The general lack or extreme paucity of beard on man's face is one instance of such effect, a fact which makes it possible for most Chinese men not to know the use of a personal razor. Hair on men's chests is unknown, and a moustache on a woman's face, not so rare in Europe, is out of the question in China. On good authority from medical doctors, and from references in writing, one knows that a perfectly bare mons veneris is not uncommon in Chinese women. (Lin Yutang 1935:26)

Observations about the relative absence of pubic hair in different "races" were echoed in popular sex handbooks (Dikötter 1995). As much as racial discourses attempted to locate cultural differences in the realm of biology, gender differences were thought to be grounded in nature. Degrees of hairiness were imagined to reflect features of the mind; excessive bodily excrescences were signs of deregulation. A lowbrow *Secrets of the Bedchamber* (1938), for instance, noted how lewd women generally developed an abundant tuft of hair at the site of vice, which would decrease after menopause. Erratic growth of pubic hair was also thought to be common during pregnancy, considered a dangerous period of female instability (Xu Zheshen 1938:58–59).

The most fearful collapse of gender distinctions, however, was embodied in the hermaphrodite (Dikötter forthcoming). As in nineteenth-century Europe (Moscucci 1991), hermaphrodism became a source of fascination within the medical sciences in China. Zhu Xi, a professor at Sun Yatsen University in Canton and an authority in the field of reproductive biology, devoted much attention to this phenomenon in his book entitled *The Changes of Female and Male* (1945) (figure 7). Prominently displayed after the title page of the book was a representation of a bearded female with a hairy chest; the impact of this illustration was enhanced by a long beard, a reflective appearance and a mandarinal posture (a straight back, both hands on the lap and the legs evenly spread) (Zhu Xi 1945:309–12). Hermaphrodism was thought to demonstrate the biological continuity that existed between male and female reproductive organs; beyond the narrow circles of scientific research, however, the bearded woman became a symbol of the fragility of gender boundaries.

Hairy Monsters

Atavisms, or racial reversions to ancestral traits, were part of the theory of recapitulation. An arrested development of the fetus during the seventh month, the hairy monster was thought to retain his lanugo after birth: he regressed back to a previous level of evolution. Zhang Zuoren, a professor of zoology at Sun Yatsen University in Canton, reprinted a picture of a hirsute man "born in Russia" in his book on the history of human evolution.[11] Chinese examples were also provided: in 1921, a certain Miss Wang had given birth to a hairy baby, later exhibited in the Agricultural Experimental Ground of Beijing (Zhang Zuoren 1930:51–52). The same year, photographs of Chinese "hairy man" Li Baoshu were put on display in the capital's zoo (figure 8).[12] The scientific discourse on hypertrichosis, as aberrant hair growth is called, was echoed in the popular press: in an age spellbound by the implications of evolution, reports about "monsters" covered with hair appeared regularly for the amazement of the public (Jinghainong 1934; Kuangzhong 1935). As in modern Europe (Bogdan 1988), malformations and freaks had a popular

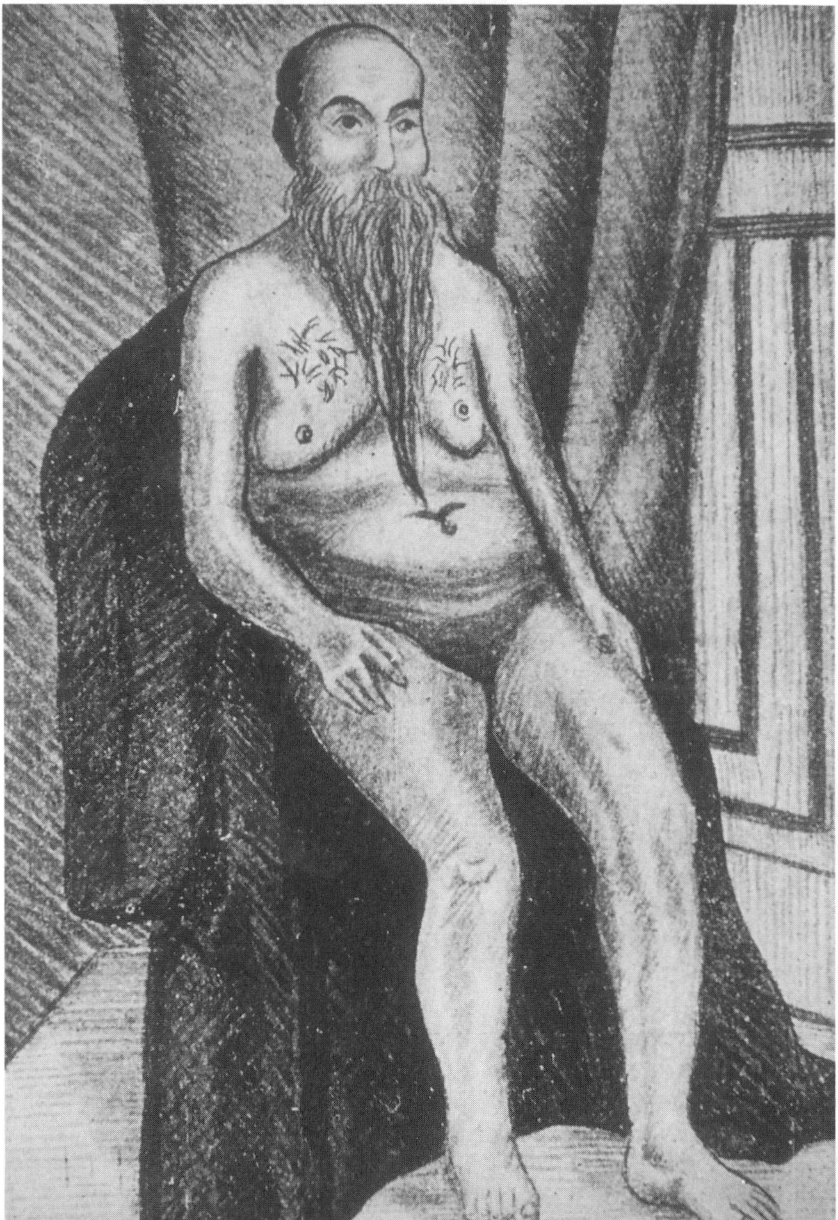

Figure 7. A bearded woman, symbol of hermaphrodism in a textbook on sexual differences; in Zhu Xi, *Cixiong zhi bian* (The change of female and male), Shanghai: Wenhua shenghuo chubanshe, 1945.

Figure 8. Hairy man Li Baoshu, put on display in Beijing's zoo during the 1920s; in Liu Mingyu et al. (eds.), *Zhongguo maoren* (Hairy men of China), Shenyang: Liaoning kexue jishu chubanshe, 1982.

appeal that was shared by different levels of society. Teratological products were exhibited on fairground stalls and offered to the public gape. From the imperial reports about hairy men to the popular exhibitions in Republican China, the fascination with the abnormal was localized and domesticated in the construction of the "monster." Representations of the "hairy monster" came to most clearly express the fear of physical disintegration and racial reversion back into the darkness of time.

Shaggy Imperialists

Hairiness as a symbol of barbarism also became a major feature of anti-Japanese caricatures during the 1930s (Dikötter 1985). The midget's kimono concealed a coat of bristles and hair, embodiment of the beastlike attributes of the invader. In many caricatures, the stubbly and furry dwarf was a molester of virginal Chinese girls, personifying the rape of civilization by barbarism. The clog and the furry leg, trampling on Chinese sovereignty, became a widely used symbol of Japanese imperialism during the 1930s. Women in kimonos used international treaties to wipe their hairy bottoms, revealing both the island nation's disdain for law and the subhuman features of the female sex. Where claws, fangs, and horns emerged, the unregenerate dwarf receded from bestiality into the darkness of devilry. In the pictorial world of wartime China, ghoulish hobbits roamed lands laid waste by the forces of evil. Westerners also partook in the iconography of malevolence. Drunken, debauched, brutish, and loathsome, crouching among moneybags and armaments, the unshaven capitalist became a popular stereotype of Chinese socialist caricature in the 1930s. The political use of hair was also prominent in the anti-imperialist mass movements under the communists during the 1950s. From the xenophobic drawings of the late empire to the anti-imperialist cartoons of the People's Republic, otherness was often dominated by the stigma of hair.

Communist China (1949 to the present)

Hairy Children

During the late nineteenth century, hypertrichosis inspired a mass of literature in Europe that was entirely out of proportion to the number of actual cases reported (for instance Geyl 1890; see also Cockayne 1933:245). Scientists devised different taxonomies to impose structure and meaning upon the variety of growth disorders that had been observed (in particular Bartels 1876; Chiari 1890). "Hypertrichosis universalis" or "hypertrichosis lanuginosa" was considered the most extreme case of aberrant hair growth, in which the patient's face and body were covered with a thick coat of long soft hair. Called "dog-men" or "ape-men," such cases of extreme hypertrichosis were exhibited for amusement until the end of World War II. Rudolph Virchow in 1873 was the first natural scientist to suggest that aberrant hair growth was a form of arrested development: the persistence of embryonic conditions in the lanugo was thought to be associated with the normal development of the rest of the organism (Virchow 1873). The reincarnation of man's primitive ancestry, it was believed to be an atavistic manifestation of the original hairiness of mankind. The idea of racial reversion was favorably received by some researchers, but came increasingly under attack during the 1920s and 30s (Danforth 1925; see also Savill 1935). While the atavistic hypothesis no longer receives much support (Rook and Dawber 1982:233), the theory of recapitulation is unanimously rejected.[13] In the People's Republic, however, the theory of racial reversion has become an institutionalized myth supported by scientific literature and mass publications.

"Hairy men" in particular became objects of marvel during the 1970s and 80s.[14] Constructed as a medical category with finite borders, "hairy men" (*maoren*) became the exclusive object of investigation of a special unit set up by the department of biology of Liaoning University in 1978. Four years later, the unit published the results of its investigation with a collection of photographs of thirty-two cases from China (Liu Mingyu 1982). The first sentence of the book summarized the conclusion reached by the team in a concise manner: "hairy men are racial atavisms." The greatest part of the book focused on Yu Zhenhuan, a stunning case of hypertrichosis whose development had been closely charted by the Liaoning University team. Covered with long hair on most parts of the body, Yu Zhenhuan was taken as the most pristine example of a "racial reversion" (figure 9). Three other cases of hairy children, born in the same year as Yu Zhenhuan, were also brought to the attention of the public. Similar to explanations popular in Europe during the 1920s, the hereditary aspect of hypertrichosis was highlighted by the pedigree of four families in which aberrant hair growth had occurred over two to three generations. If the myth of racial atavism dated from the late nineteenth century, the only scientific reference of the authors was to a sentence from Charles Darwin's *Descent of Man*: "Three or four cases have been recorded of persons born with their whole bodies and faces thickly covered with fine long hairs; and this strange condition is strongly inherited and is correlated with an abnormal condition of the teeth" (Darwin 1881).[15] Cast in the language of medical science, stereotypical imagery sustained the myth of the "missing link": a hairy child from

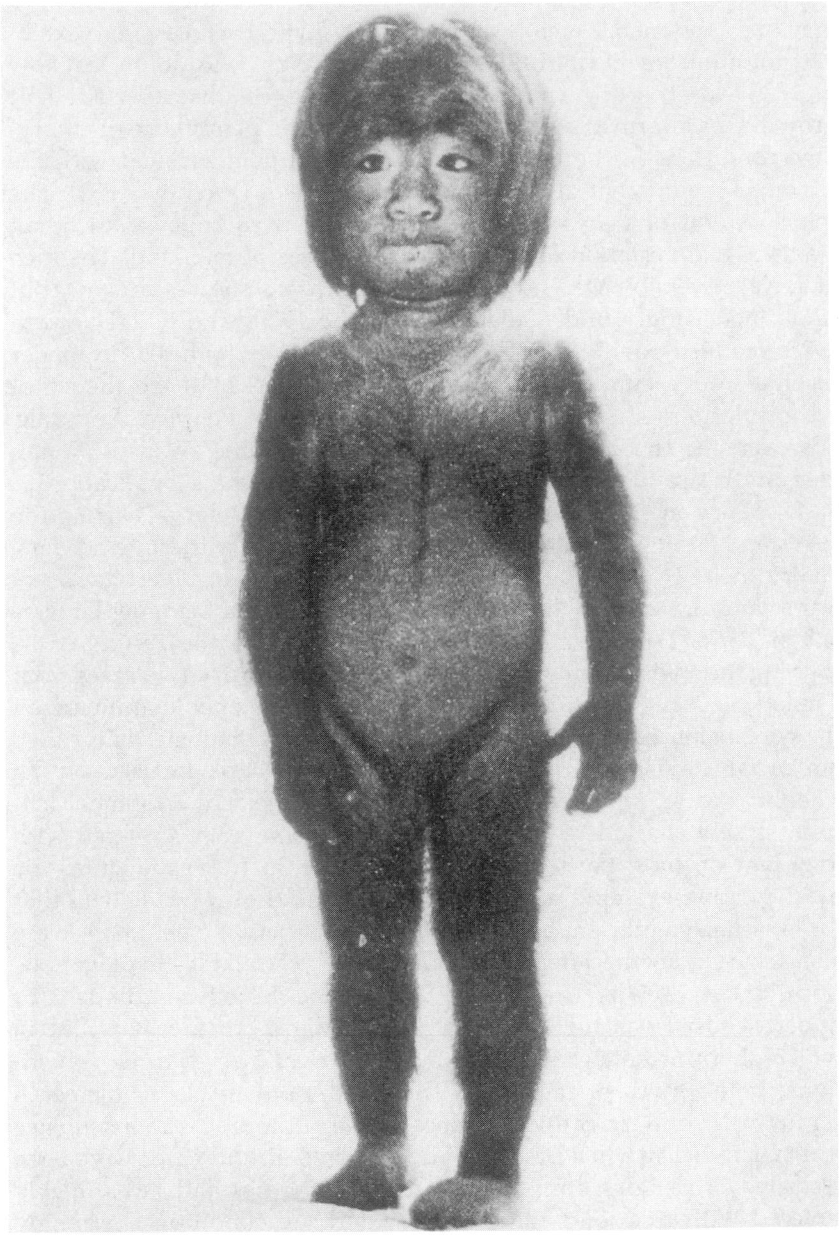

Figure 9. The hairy child Yu Zhenhuan, national symbol of "racial" reversion; in Liu Mingyu et al. (eds), *Zhongguo maoren* (Hairy men of China), Shenyang: Liaoning kexue jishu chubanshe, 1982.

Kaifeng was said to have a "simian face," the "flat nose and thick lips" of a hairy girl from Shazhou were described as "typical of hairy people." Narratives of "humanity" and "civilization" were also promoted with the reification of "otherness": some photographs showed Yu Zhenhuan in "natural" conditions that could touch the sensibility of the reader: little Yu playing doctor, little Yu chasing chickens in the courtyard. The fear of dissolution and the desire to control was most evident in the suggestion that "positive and effective measures" be implemented to prevent the spread of hypertrichosis to the rest of the population.

Yu Zhenhuan rapidly became an object of marvel and wonder: news on television, reports in the official press, feature articles in more popular magazines brought images of the "hairy child" to the general public. A widely distributed *Mysteries of the Human Body* (1989), to take but one instance, had an entire paragraph devoted to "hairy people" and reported in compelling detail the story of Yu Zhenhuan (Zou Guangzhong 1989:53–56). Excessive body hair had become a national symbol of racial reversion.

The Return of the Wild Man

Although the myth of the wild man had been explored in Republican China (Cui Daiyang 1928), it only gained widespread currency after the advent of the communists. Officially sponsored research into the "mystery of the wild man" became particularly prominent after the reforms initiated by Deng Xiaoping in 1978. Most noticed were reports about the "wild man" (*yeren*) from Shennongjia in Fang county, Hubei province, a place where hairy creatures had been sighted since the Ming dynasty. Where scattered mentions to otherness had sufficed in imperial ideology, however, materialist philosophy demanded a full investigation. A China "Wild Man" Research Society was founded in August 1981 with the support of highly regarded scientists such as anthropologist Wu Dingliang (Fudan University), paleontologist Jia Lanpo (Chinese Academy of Science), biologist Qian Guozhen (Huadong Normal University) and medical expert Fang Zhongyou (Guangxi Hospital).[16] If the hairy barbarian of imperial knowledge had been a spatial notion projected onto the periphery of civilization, modern versions presented the wild man as the repository of a lost phylogeny, the "missing link" between the ape and the human: hair had become a symbol of borders in time.[17] Represented as the vessel of evolutionary traits that had disappeared with civilization, the scientific analysis of the wild man's hair was thought to reveal prehistoric conditions of life. The findings of a tuft of brown hair in 1980 and remains of more than three thousand "red hairs" of the "wild man" from Shennongjia were scrutinized (Liu Minzhuang 1988). A book entitled *On the Trail of the "Wild Man"* provided detailed comparisons between hair of apes and that of the wild man (Jiang and Yun 1983:91–94), whereas the Research Unit for Forensic Medicine of the Wuhan Hospital concluded that the wild man's hair was structurally comparable to that of humans: "We infer that the hair from these 'wild men' could belong to an as yet unknown higher primate" (Zhongguo 1986:125).

Reports about the wild man became rife during the 1980s, such as a daily newspaper's article about a girl abducted by a wild man who later escaped back to "civilization" with her two shaggy children (*Yangcheng wanbao* 1984); in 1986, the *Science Evening Paper* even brought to the attention of the public a "wild boy" coated with hair recently discovered near the Himalaya mountains and kept hidden in a military hospital of Shaanxi province as a living fossil (*Kexue wanbao* 1986). Illustrations of the "wild man," based on "scientific data," seemed to have become an intrinsic part of popular urban culture by the end of the 1980s (figure 10): from images of barbarians to myths of regression, the modern transformation of hair as a symbol of otherness was completed.

Conclusion

The research presented in this chapter is of an impressionistic nature and only tentative hypotheses may be offered as a conclusion. Firstly, historical continuities in the cultural realm cannot be exaggerated; representations of hair underwent important changes in China over the past hundred years, from an emphasis on the spatial dimension (body hair as a symbol of the geographically remote barbarian) to an increased focus on the temporal dimension (body hair as a symbol of the historically distant primate). Second, the impact of "the West" on representations of body hair in China should not be given undue emphasis: although the rise of medical science affected discursive practices in a significant manner, intellectuals in China remained relatively independent agents of change who critically interacted with foreign thought systems. Third, representations of hair in China would not appear to be significantly different from those elaborated in other complex societies. The time of appearance of certain symbols, the meanings invested into them and their configuration, on the other hand, are all factors that have undergone considerable variation.

第 二 部 分
当代人对"野人"的目击和考察
科学家根据资料描绘的神农架"野人"图

Figure 10. Artist's impression of the wild man from Shennongjia; in *Zhongguo "yeren" zhi mi* (The mystery of China's "wild man"), Guangdong: Huacheng chubanshe, 1986.

Notes

1. Philip A. Kuhn (1990) has explored the semiotics of hair on the head in late imperial China.

2. For an introduction to the meanings of hair in popular culture in China, see Jiang Shaoyuan (1937).

3. As late as 1831, a work was published in which the orangutan was classified as human in the "great chain of beings" (Curtin 1964:368).

4. The "hairy woman" (*maonü*) was thought to be an immortal creature who lived in the forests covered in hair; when captured and fed on cooked cereals, she lost her natural coat, aged and died (Kaltenmark 1953:159–60); the "wild woman" (*yenü*) mentioned by Li Shizhen is described as a disheveled creature with no particular body hair (Li Shizhen 1981.4:2920).

5. See for instance Yuan Mei, "Guandong maoren yi ren wei er" (The hairy men from Guandong use humans as bait), "Qin maoren" (The hairy men from Qin), "Da maoren qu nü" (A big hairy man abducts a girl), "Lümaoguai" (The green-haired freak) in Yuan Mei (1987:22, 97, 123 and 175).

6. For a classic introduction to the topic, see Dudley and Novak (1972); more relevant to the themes of this chapter is Zanco (1983); see also Zapperi (1987).

7. In Singapore, foreigners are still called *angmo* or *angmogao*, Hokkien dialect for "red-haired ape."

8. See for instance the *Dianshizhai huabao*, a pictorial published by the highly popular *Shenbao* in Shanghai from 1884 to 1898.

9. See Frank Dikötter (1992) for a detailed discussion.

10. Huntington's book, *The Character of Races*, was partially translated by the eugenist Pan Guangdan as *Natural Selection and the Character of the Chinese Race* (Pan Guangdan 1928).

11. The picture probably represented Stephen Bilgraski, alias "Lionel the lion-man," an artist who appeared in freak shows for many years with Barnum and Bailey at the beginning of this century; compare with Mannix (1990:87).

12. The case of Li Baoshu from Hebei province was investigated by anthropologist Liu Xian of Fudan University in Shanghai.

13. Some forms of hypertrichosis are currently explained as an exclusively inherited condition, caused by an autosomal dominant gene, but it still remains unclear whether all cases are the expression of a single genotype; dermatological textbooks, moreover, also stress acquired factors such as endocrine disorders (hyperthyroidism), developmental defects (Hurler's syndrome) and biochemical imbalances (tumors and drugs).

14. Although gender distinctions are not necessarily implied by the terms *maoren* and *yeren*, I have used "hairy man" and "wild man" in my translations. *Ren* generally refers to "human being" or "person"; in the absence of gender distinctions, however, it implicitly refers to the male only. The terms *maonü* and *yenü* are expressly used when a female is meant. See also note 4 above.

15. The authors also refer to a certain Professor Alex Brandt, who is alleged to have informed them that he had discovered how the hair from the face of a man suffering from hypertrychosis was structurally similar to the lanugo of the fetus; far from having entered into an academic exchange with a foreign expert, the authors have in fact taken out of context a sentence of Charles Darwin: "Prof. Alex. Brandt informs me that . . ." (Darwin 1881:19).

16. The "Wild Man" Research Society is currently one of the three branches of the China Anthropology Society.

17. A popular book on evolutionary materialism, Engels's work on the historical role of labor was translated as *From Ape to Man* (Engels 1937).

References

A Ying. 1984. *Zhongguo lianhuan tuhua shihua* (History of the picture-story book). Beijing: Renmin meishu chubanshe.

Bartels, Max. 1876. "Über abnorme Behaarung beim Menschen,"*Zeitschrift für Ethnologie* 8:110–29.

Bogdan, Robert. 1988. *Freak Show: Presenting Human Oddities for Amusement and Profit*. Chicago: University of Chicago Press.

Chen Yinghuang. 1918. *Renleixue* (Anthropology). Shanghai: Shangwu yinshuguan. Reprint Taipei: Xueren yuekan zazhi she, 1971.

Chiari, Hans. 1890. "Über Hypertrichosis des Menschen," *Prager Medizinische Wochenschrift* 15:495–97, 512–15.

Cockayne, A. E. 1933. *Inherited Abnormalities of the Skin and Its Appendages.* Oxford: Oxford University Press.

Cui Daiyang. 1928. "Yeren geti de yuansuo yu jiexian" (Facts about the wild man), *Minsu* (Ethnology) 23–24:1–11.

Curtin, P. D. 1964. *The Image of Africa: British Ideas and Action, 1780–1850.* Madison: University of Wisconsin Press.

Danforth, C. H. 1925. *Hair: With Special Reference to Hypertrichosis*. Chicago: American Medical Association.

Darwin, Charles. 1881. *The Descent of Man and Selection in Relation to Sex.* London: Murray.

Dikötter, Frank. 1985. "La représentation du Japon et des Japonais dans la caricature chinoise (1923–1937)." MA thesis. University of Geneva.

———. 1992. *The Discourse of Race in Modern China*. London: Hurst; Stanford: Stanford University Press; Hong Kong: Hong Kong University Press.

———. 1995. *Sex, Culture and Modernity in China: Medical Science and the Construction of Sexual Identities in the Early Republican Period*. London: Hurst; Honolulu: Hawaii University Press.

———. Forthcoming. "The Intermediate Sex: Hermaphroditism, Medical Science and Gender Boundaries in China." In Frank Dikötter and Leslie Hall, eds., *The Body and Beyond: The Creation and Violation of Bodily Boundaries.*

Dudley, Edward and Maximillian E. Novak, eds. 1972. *The Wild Man Within: An Image in Western Thought from the Renaissance to Romanticism.* Pittsburgh: University of Pittsburgh Press.

Engels, F. 1937. *Cong hou dao ren* (*Role of labor in the process of the humanizing of the apes*). Shanghai: Taidong shuju. Many reprints in the PRC.

Fangxianzhi (Local gazeteer of Fang county). "Zaji" (Miscellanea). *ce* 12.

Gernet, Jacques. 1985. *China and the Christian Impact: A Conflict of Cultures.* Cambridge: Cambridge University Press.

Geyl, Arie. 1890. *Beobachtungen und Ideen über Hypertrichose.* Hamburg: Dermatologische Studien.

Gong Tingzhang. 1926. *Renlei yu wenhua jinbu shi* (History of the progress of culture and mankind). Shanghai: Shangwu yinshuguan.

"Houzi you weiba renlei ye you weiba" (Apes have tail; man has tail too). *Dagongbao.* 9 January 1936.

Jiang Shaoyuan. 1937. *Fa xu zhua: guanyu tamen de mixin* (Superstitions about hair, beards and nails). Shanghai: Kaiming shudian.

Jiang Yan'an and Yun Zhonglong. 1983. *"Yeren" xunzong ji* (On the trail of the "wild man"). Xi'an: Shaanxi renmin chubanshe.

"Jinghainong chan guai'er bianti sheng baimao" (Monster child covered with white hair born in village of Jinghai). *Xianggang gongshang.* 8 November 1934.

Kaltenmark, Max. 1953. *Lie sien tchouan.* Beijing: Bali daxue Beijing Hanxue yanjiusuo.

Kexue wanbao, 19 June 1986.

"Kuangzhong mou shouliu bianti changmao guai xiaohai" (Small monster child covered with long hair found in Kuangzhong). *Shenbao,* 20 September 1935.

Kuhn, Philip A. 1990. *Soulstealers: The Chinese Sorcery Scare of 1768.* Cambridge, Mass: Harvard University Press.

Li Shizhen. 1981. *Bencao gangmu* (Compendium of materia medica). Beijing: Renmin weisheng chubanshe.

Lin Yutang. 1935. *My Country and My People.* New York: John Ray.

Liu Huru. 1931. *Rensheng dili gaiyao* (General principles of human geography). Shanghai: Shangwu yinshuguan.

Liu Min. 1932. *Renleixue tixi* (Anthropological systems). Shanghai: Xinken shudian.

Liu Minzhuang. 1988. *Jiekai "yeren" zhi mi* (Clues to the mystery of the "wild man"). Nanchang: Jiangxi renmin chubanshe.

Liu Mingyu et al., eds. 1982. *Zhongguo maoren* (Hairy men of China). Shenyang: Liaoning kexue jishu chubanshe.

Liu Piji. 1928. *Renjian wujie de shengwu* (Misinterpretations in everyday biology). Shanghai: Shangwu yinshuguan.

Mannix, Daniel P. 1990. *Freaks: We Who Are Not As Others. With Rare and Amazing Photos from the Author's Personal Scrapbook.* San Francisco: Research Publications.

Moscucci, Ornella. 1991. "Hermaphroditism and Sex Difference: The Construction of Gender in Victorian England." In Marina Benjamin, ed., *Science and Sensibility: Gender and Scientific Enquiry, 1780–1945*. London: Blackwell.

Pan Guangdan. 1928. *Ziran taotai yu zhonghua minzuxing* (Natural selection and the character of the Chinese race). Shanghai: Xinyue shudian.

"Ren bian hou zhi qiwen" (Strange news about a man changing into an ape). *Beiping chenbao*, 6 June 1935.

Rook, Arthur, and Rodney Dawber. 1982. *Diseases of the Hair and the Scalp*. London: Blackwell.

Savill, A. 1935. *The Hair and the Scalp: A Clinical Study with a Chapter on Hirsuties*. London: Arnold.

Shaoying. 1925. "Guanyu maofa zhi xin zhishi" (New knowledge about hair). *Funü zazhi* 11.11:1771–73.

"Sheng yi liangzhou zhi daiwei nühai" (Girl with tail already two weeks old). *Zhongyang ribao*, 29 April 1936.

Shou Zhenhuang. 1922. "Maofa zhi jiegou" (The structure of hair). *Kexue* 7.7:707–10.

Su Liwen and Lu Qiyi, eds. 1989. *Shengli weisheng zhishi* (Knowledge about physiological hygiene). Beijing: Xinhua shudian.

Virchow, Rudolph. 1873. "Die russischen Haarmenschen," *Berliner Klinische Wochenschrift* 10:337–9.

Waley, Arthur. 1958. *The Opium War through Chinese Eyes*. London: Allen and Unwin.

Wu Hung. 1987. "The Earliest Pictorial Representations of Ape-tales," *T'oung Pao* 73.1–3:86–112.

Wu Zelin. 1932. *Xiandai zhongzu* (Contemporary races). Shanghai: Xinyue shudian.

Xu Jiyu. 1861. *Yinghuan zhilüe* (A brief survey of the maritime circuit). Osaka: Kanbun.

Xu Zheshen. 1938. *Xingfang mijue* (Secrets of the bedchamber). Shanghai: Xinxin shudian.

Yangcheng wanbao, 17 to 22 October 1984.

Yi Luan. 1916. "Shuo fa" (About hair), *Funü zazhi* 2.6:17–20.

Yin Guangren and Zhang Rulin. 1751. *Aomen jilüe* (Notes on Macao).

You Jiade. 1929. *Renlei qiyuan* (Origins of mankind). Shanghai: Shijie shuju.

"You wei renzhong yu shiren renzhong de fajian" (Discovery of a race of men with tails and a race of cannibals), *Dongfang zazhi* 26.5:99–101. March 1929.

Yuan Mei. 1987. *Zibuyu quanji* (Complete short stories). Shijiazhuang: Hebei renmin chubanshe.

Yuan Zuzhi. no date. *Tanyinglu* (Travels).

Zanca, Attilio. 1983. "In tema di hypertrichosis universalis congenita: Contributo storico-medico," *Physis* 25.1:41–66.

Zapperi, Roberto. 1987. "Arrigo le velu, Pietro le fou, Amon le nain et autres bêtes: Autour d'un tableau d'Agostino Carrache," *Annales: Économies, Sociétés, Civilisations* 40.2:307–27.

Zhang Deyi. 1985. *Suishi Faguo ji* (Notes on following the mission to France). Beijing: Yuelu shushe.

Zhang Xie. 1981. *Dong Xi yang kao* (Geography of south-east Asia). Beijing: Zhonghua shuju.

Zhang Xinglang. 1928. "Zhongguo renzhong Yindu-Riermanzhong fenzi" (Indo-Germanic elements in the Chinese race), *Furen xuezhi* 1:179–94.

Zhang Ziping. 1930. *Renlei jinhualun* (The theory of human evolution). Shanghai: Shangwu yinshuguan.

Zhang Zuoren. 1930. *Renlei tianyan shi* (History of human evolution). Shanghai: Shangwu yinshuguan.

Zhigang. 1985. *Chushi Taixiji* (Notes on the first mission to the West). Beijing: Yuelu shushe.

Zhongguo "Yeren" Kaocha Yanjiuhui. 1986. *Zhongguo "yeren" zhi mi* (The mystery of China's "wild man"). Guangdong: Huacheng chubanshe. Republished in 1987 in Hong Kong by the Xiangjiang chuban gongsi.

Zhu Tiehua. 1917. "Guang shuo fa" (General facts about hair), *Funü zazhi* 3.2:32–35.

Zhu Weiji. 1948 (1st ed. 1945). *Shengwu de jinhua* (Evolution of organisms). Shanghai: Yongxiang yinshuguan.

Zhu Xi. 1945. *Cixiong zhi bian* (The changes of female and male). Shanghai: Wenhua shenghuo chubanshe.

Zhu Yu. 1935–1936. *Pingzhou ketan* (Anecdotes and stories). Changsha: Shangwu yinshuguan.

Zou Guangzhong, ed. 1989. *Renti zhi mi* (Mysteries of the human body). Beijing: Xinhua chubanshe.

4 "long black hair like a seat cushion": hair symbolism in japanese popular religion

gary l. ebersole

Hair symbolism in Japanese religion is not as prominent as it is in, for example, the religions of South Asia (see Olivelle's chapter in this volume). This is not to say that hair symbolism is nonexistent but rather to note that in general the human body is treated less explicitly in Japanese myths, rituals, and other forms of symbolic activity than in some other cultures. This chapter will explore the "natural" symbolism of hair insofar as it is associated with life force and the normal human aging process. I draw upon myths, popular legends and folktales, historical chronicles, and works of literature in order to sketch the broader symbolic complex surrounding hair in ancient (sixth–ninth centuries) and medieval Japan (tenth to seventeenth centuries). My focus is limited to popular nonsectarian Japanese religion and does not include hair symbolism in Japanese Buddhism.

Proverbs and Practices

Let us begin with a few examples of popular sayings (*kotowaza*) and ritual practices concerning hair from the nineteenth and twentieth centuries. I will then delineate the symbolic complex surrounding hair, which underlies or informs these sayings and practices.

Selected sayings:

People with thinning hair have bad luck.

People with thick hair will suffer in life.

If a crow (or a bird) carries a strand of a person's hair in its beak, that person will go crazy.

If you cut some hair and bury it at the roots of a bamboo tree, your hair will turn black.

If you burn your hair, you will go crazy.

If someone steps on a strand of your facial hair, you will come down with a facial disease.

It is unlucky to part your hair on the left and then have your parents see it.

[For a woman] long hair hides seven defects.

Selected folk beliefs and ritual practices:

In the ritual raising of the ridgepole (*jōtō shiki*), human hair is tied to a bow in order to ward off demons.

Burning human hair will ward off dangerous animals.

The *kamioki* rite was widely observed for boys and girls three years of age from the Heian period down to the Edo period, and is still observed in a few areas even today. Generally held on the 15th day of the 11th lunar month, it marked the first time that the children's hair, which until then had been cut, was allowed to grow. The participants wore wigs woven of white hair and covered their faces with white powder, while prayers were offered to Ubusuna-gami, the god of good fortune.[1]

In the Edo period, it was believed that the *kami* of the plague was especially attracted to the coiffure of geisha and prostitutes.[2]

In the *Hōsō majinai hiden-shu*, a nineteenth-century text, among the prohibitions listed for families where the plague was present is an injunction against burning human hair.

Another Edo text, the *E'iri hashika yoke majinai*, warns against speaking about the plague in the presence of a woman fixing her hair.

In many areas of Japan, following childbirth, women were prohibited from tying up their hair.

In Aomori Prefecture, seamen who encountered dangerous storms at sea would cut their hair and offer it to the *kami* of the sea with prayers.

During the wars of the twentieth century, many Japanese wives and girlfriends offered locks of their hair to shrines and temples for the safe return of a soldier.

A number of temples in Japan contain ropes, sometimes of gigantic size, made of human hair donated by women.

In Okinawa, priestesses often give their brothers protective amulets containing locks of their hair.

The sumo wrestlers of the top rank all wear their hair long and tied up in a special knot. When a Grand Champion retires, his hair is shorn in a special public ritual.

What is one to make of this diverse list of popular sayings, folk beliefs, and ritual practices? Taken alone, this Frazerian hodgepodge of folkloric or ethnographic information offers little immediate insight into the Japanese religious or symbolic worlds of meaning, other than a vague sense that human hair is somehow powerful and can be both beneficial and dangerous. Yet, I will demonstrate that each item here (and many others not included) participates in a very old magicoreligious symbolic complex surrounding hair. In an effort to suggest the outlines of this symbolic complex and to demonstrate both its age and remarkable staying power, a few selected examples of hair symbolism from some of the oldest extant texts in Japan will be introduced. We will find that hair was used in ancient Japan to signal both normality and abnormality, wildness and enculturation. Moreover, hair was associated with sexuality, female reproductive power, and ritual communication with divinities (*kami*) and the dead.

In many cultures hair styles or other treatments of hair mark one's sex, age, social and religious status, and so forth; Japan was (and is) no exception to this. Hair styles have changed dramatically over the centuries, but my interest in this chapter is less in these changes in hair styles per se than in the deeper symbolic resonances hair (of various sorts) has had in Japan. To begin with, the ancient Japanese seem to have been struck by the fact that even after the rest of one's body had ceased to grow, one's hair,[3] like fingernails and toenails, continued to grow by itself, outside one's conscious control. This may be one reason why hair was associated positively with life force and energy, but at the same time had the negative valence of wild or untamed energy. Thus, for example, we find that *kaminaga* or "the long-haired one(s)" was a taboo word used in early Japan to refer (ironically) to both Buddhist priests (cf., Morrell 1985:73) and (more literally) women. Hair was at once attractive and frightening, desirable and potentially dangerous. Like sexuality, with which it is often associated, hair is linked to the individual person, yet almost inevitably it quickly falls under social controls and regulations.

Both sexuality and hair are in one sense "natural"—that is, they are simply givens, a part of the human condition. Yet, once each of these is understood to be a site or source of power, it becomes something that needs to be treated with care; wild nature needs to be transformed into domesticated or controlled culture. The very naturalness of sexuality and hair is finally unacceptable to many persons precisely because *as such* they apparently fall outside of human control. (One recalls here Baudelaire's statement, which while referring to only one sex, is more generalizable: "La femme est naturelle, c'est à dire abominable.") Human beings have rarely been satisfied with the natural order of things, no matter how that order was imagined. As a result, they have frequently attempted to intervene in this "natural order" in some way in order to alter it, control it, or to deny its absolute hold over them. To this end, human beings in many societies and in different historical ages have developed a variety of means—physical, social, psychological, and ritual—to control sexuality and hair, as the other chapters in this volume demonstrate.

The widespread ritual practice of shaving one's head as part of an initiation is an instance of this sort of intervention, which seeks to deny, transcend, invert, or otherwise control the natural wildness that inheres in both sexuality and hair. In sum, hair-related ritual activities generally represent an attempt on the part of human beings to *control* the power (however it is imagined) that is symbolized by hair or that is believed to be contained in it. Alternatively, the ritual handling of hair may signal that such control has already been achieved.

Hair also naturally marks a person's age, insofar as white hair (Jap. *shiraga*), thinning hair, or baldness generally come with age. In Japan a full head of pure black hair is associated with youth and sexual vigor, while white hair or hair streaked with gray is associated with age and a loss of vigor. Two verses from the *Man'yōshū*, a late-eighth-century anthology of Japanese poetry, illustrate this. The first verse, MYS IV:627 (NKBT 4:282–83), was sent by a young maiden to a courtier, named Saeki Akamaro, who had made sexual advances to her. The latter (#628) is his response to her verse:

waga tamoto	Great man
makamu to omowamu	who thinks to pillow
masurao wa	on my sleeves,
ochimizu motome	search for the water of youth,
shiraga oi ni tari	for your hair has grown white.

shiraga ōru	I do not think about
koto wa omowazu	white hair growing on my head,
ochimizu wa	but I will search all over
ka ni mo kaku ni mo	for the water of youth,
motomete yukamu	then go to you.

As a natural symbol of sorts, hair—both black and white—was often used by the Japanese to represent normal human developmental or aging processes, as in these verses. Cases of premature graying and balding were not unknown in Japan, of course, but these tended to be understood and reacted to in light of the normal pattern of human development and of societal expectations of how a human life cycle should unfold (as the English term *premature* also implies). When the natural aging process or life cycle was interrupted by premature death, the Japanese often turned to the natural symbolism of hair in order to express the pain and longing occasioned by the death of a beloved young person. MYS III:481 (NKBT 4:224–25) is an example of this usage. The poem is a *banka* or funeral lament in which a husband laments the fact that his young wife has died, depriving him of her companionship as he ages. The opening lines read:

shirotae no	Side by side,
sode sashi kaete	our white sleeves crossed,
nabikinuru	swaying together,
waga kurokami no	my wife and I vowed
mashiraga ni	to live together,
narinamu kiwami	our bonds unbroken,
aratayo ni	like a string of beads,
tomo ni aramu to	until our black hair
tama no o no . . .	turned pure white . . .

The lament goes on to rehearse how the wife's death had frustrated the couple's expectation that they would grow old together. The image of an unbroken love and conjugal life as being like an unbroken string or cord of beads is common in the poetry of early

Japan, as is the converse metaphor of the scattering of the beads from a bracelet or necklace that has broken, which was used to express the breaking of a romantic union or death. These metaphors are based on the magicoreligious belief, generated by a homonym,[4] that a person's soul or spirit (*tama;* mod. Jap., *tamashii*) could be captured or contained in a bead or jewel (*tama*). As we will see below, these sorts of beads are immediately associated with hair. MYS III:436 illustrates the association of beads with the animating spirit:

hitogoto no
shigeki kono koro
tama naraba
te ni makimochite
koizu aramashi o
(NKBT 4:206–207)

These days, when the gossip
flies so thick,
if you were a jewel
I would wrap you round my wrist,
and cease my painful longing.
(Levy 1981:221)[5]

MYS III:424 presents an example of a verse employing the opposite metaphor where a broken bracelet stands for death. It is a lament on the death of an imperial prince:

komoriku no
Hatsuse otome ga
te ni makeru
tama wa midarete
ari to iwazu yamo
(NKBT 4:202–203)

Do they not say
the *tama* wrapped round the wrist
of the maiden of Hatsuse,
the hidden land,
are scattered?

In "The Wormwood Patch" chapter of the *Genji monogatari* (*The Tale of Genji*, c. 1000), one finds the symbolism of hair and scattered beads or jewels used to telling effect (Seidensticker 1976:297). There the Safflower Princess, who had briefly been Genji's lover when he had been exiled to Suma, now lives alone, save for the presence of one longtime maid named Jijū, in a dilapidated house in a deserted area. When her spiteful aunt comes to take even Jijū away, the princess has nothing of value to give her companion as a parting gift, so she gives her some of her ten-foot-long hair she had saved and an old jar of incense. On parting, the Safflower Princess rebukes Jijū with a verse, protesting that she had thought their bond was as strong as her hair or "jeweled strands," which now are to be scattered. Here the tensile strength of hair is used to refer to the durability of the bond between two people. At the same time, hair represents the essence of the person from whose head it came. Thus, the Princess' long hair is a sign of intimacy between these women and, as it is carried away, a symbol of her decline, both physically and in terms of social standing.

I will return to the central importance of the *tama*-based religious beliefs in ancient Japan. First, though, let us look at a different type of use of the natural symbolism of black and white hair. MYS III:430 is a funeral lament attributed to Hitomaro, a famous oral poet associated with the palace of the Crown Prince Kusakabe in the late eighth century. The poem was recited before the funeral pyre of a young unidentified female drowning victim. The ancient Japanese believed that the spirits of those who had died in an accident, in an unnatural manner, or in an agitated state of great emotion (e.g., passion, anger, jealousy) remained in this world, rather than going to the land of the dead. Such spirits were dangerous, haunting the living, and causing illness and even death. So, too, the spirits of the dead for whom funeral rites had not been performed were believed to be potentially dangerous.

The ancient Japanese developed a number of rituals, known as *tama-shizume* or *chinkon-sai*, to pacify (*shizumeru*) such spirits. Many *banka* or funeral laments, including this one, come out of such ritual contexts. In this lament, Hitomaro uses an apparent poetic conceit identifying the smoke from a funeral pyre as the white hair of the young woman who had drowned. For Hitomaro and his contemporaries, though, this was more than just a poetic conceit, for, by implicitly equating the smoke from the cremation with her white hair and clouds, the poet was attempting to pacify the spirit of the deceased by suggesting that the drowning victim had indeed passed through the natural life cycle. One might see this as simply a form of verbal trickery or sleight of hand, but I suggest that Hitomaro was evoking a full set of symbolic associations in an effort to deny that the maiden's death had finally terminated the power of fertility identified with her as a young woman and with her long black hair. The poem reads:

yakumo sasu Izumo no kora ga kurokami wa Yoshino no gawa no oki ni nazusō (NKBT 4:204–205)	The black hair of the girl of Izumo, where rise the eightfold clouds, floats out over the depths of the Yoshino River. (Levy 1981:219)

The first word of this verse, *yakumo,* literally means "eight-fold clouds" or "many clouds," but "yaku" is also homonymous with "to burn," so that there is an implicit aural reference to the funeral pyre and the smoke from it. The mythological associations of Izumo and the "pillow word" associated with the place name—"where rise the eightfold clouds"—are also important. According to a myth preserved in both the *Kojiki* (NKBT 1:88–89) and the *Nihonshoki* (NKBT 67:122–23; Aston I 1972:53–54), the god Susano-o first came to Izumo, where he built his palace and consummated his marriage with Kushi-nada-hime ("The Comb Princess of Inada") and began procreation between heavenly and earthly *kami* in this world. The song he sang, moreover, was traditionally cited as the first Japanese poetic verse (*uta*). In a number of ways, then, the allusion to this myth brings into play several elements of primordial creativity or cultural "firsts." The relevant passage reads in the *Kojiki* version:

> Hereupon Haya-Susano-o-no-mikoto sought for a place in the land of Izumo to build his palace. Arriving at Suga, he said: "Coming here, my heart is refreshed [*suga-sugashi*]." Therefore that place is still called Suga. When this great deity first built the palace of Suga, clouds rose from that place.
>
> He made a song, which said:

yakumo tatsu[6]	The eight-fold fenced palace of Izumo,
Izumo yahegaki	where rise the eight-fold clouds,
tsumagomi ni	I build the eight-fold fences
yahegaki tsukuru	to dwell there with my wife.
sono yahegaki o	Oh! Those eight-fold fences!
	(Philippi 1968:91, adapted)

The site mentioned here, Izumo, is associated with refreshment or reenergizing oneself and with purification through a famous myth telling how the deity Susano-o was expelled from heaven and had to undergo a purification or expiation rite. Izumo is also associated with marriage and the power of reproduction through the myth, as are the manifold clouds. Turning to Hitomaro's verse, the prose headnote identifies the female drowning victim as a young woman from Izumo. This further strengthens the associations with the elements of the Susano-o/Izumo myth already mentioned. In addition, the site of the cremation, Yoshino, was itself well known as a place filled with life-energy, where people could find rejuvenation from the magical waters that granted youth and vigor (Ebersole 1989:30–39).

At first glance, this verse appears deceptively simple and seems to be merely descriptive. Yet, starting with the symbolic associations of black female hair and working out from them, we have found that the verse is remarkably complex, while its deep meaning comes from the broader symbolic associations that are evoked. In this ritual verse, Hitomaro has skillfully employed several symbolic resources in order to relocate this death in a larger transformative context.

When alive, the young maiden embodied the potential power of reproduction, which would have been symbolized by her long black hair. When her life was cut short by her accidental drowning (or, perhaps, her suicide), this potential was seemingly thwarted. The natural expectations of both the young woman and of society that she would marry, have a family, and pass through the normal aging process were frustrated. As a result, this maiden's unnatural death produced not only a corpse but also the potential danger that, precisely because her hopes and desires had been frustrated, she might turn into a haunting spirit. Significantly, such haunting spirits, especially female ghosts, were imagined as having wild and disheveled hair (see Watson, this volume). Moreover, it was widely believed that the hair of the corpse of such a person would not fall off during the natural process of decomposition but would instead remain attached to the skull. Thus, in the popular imagination, the hair of a person who had met a "bad" death was seen as having the power to somehow vivify the corpse so that it could still "live" and move about in this world.[7]

In this light, the fact that the maiden's corpse was cremated, rather than buried, takes on added significance, for prior to the eighth century, burial was the normal funerary practice in Japan. Perhaps in cases of abnormal death such as this, cremation was found to have the advantage of destroying (and/or transforming) the hair of the deceased. In the face of the potentially dangerous situation posed by the presence of the corpse of this drowning victim, Hitomaro had no doubt been called on in his capacity as a religious specialist to perform a *tama-shizume* ritual, from which the *banka* cited above came.

The symbolic associations Hitomaro invokes in the verse are central to the scenario of transformation that he offered to both his live audience and to the spirit of the deceased. While the maiden's life had been taken, and with it apparently her power of fertility (= long black hair), leaving only a corpse, the cremation fire transformed her black hair into smoke (= white hair), which then rose and blended with the eight-fold clouds, floating over the Yoshino area and the Yoshino River. This much is fairly explicit in the verse. But we can also assume the following further implicit or unspoken steps of transformation to have been posited. Clouds produce rain, which falls to earth and, in so doing, promotes growth and fertility and sustains life there.[8] Thus, the deceased is portrayed as regaining the power of giving life through the transformation effected by the cremation, even as she moves through the natural life cycle, symbolized by black hair turning white.

The poet of the verse we have just looked at employs the symbolism of hair, in conjunction with other symbolic elements, to deny that the natural aging process has been broken. MYS IV:573 concerns the contravening of a different sort of social expectation. The Buddhist priest Mansei sent this verse to a close friend who had been sent to be the commander of the imperial troops in Dazaifu. Manzei's sense of loneliness and longing is somewhat unexpected and, given his status as a Buddhist priest, perhaps to some people's minds at least, inappropriate. Ideally Manzei should have already cast off the world and all attachments to it.

nubatama no	Though my jet-black
kurokami kawari	hair has turned
shirakete mo	white,
itaki koi ni wa	at times I still know
au toki arikeri	the pain of longing.
(NKBT 4:270–71)	

In MYS IV:563 we can see the natural symbolism of gray hair turned to positive effect in a related way. Here a female poet uses her age to emphasize the strength of the love and longing she feels:

kurokami ni	I never knew
shirakami majiri	such a painful longing
oyuru made	before now
kakaru koi ni wa	when my long black hair
imada awanaku ni	is streaked with white.
(NKBT 4:266–67)	

Even when the natural symbolism of hair is employed in cases such as these, broader symbolic associations or additional material elements are often brought into the semantic field of play and, as a result, a more complex meaning emerges. In such cases, it would be misleading to read references to white hair, for example, as merely referring to the aging process. The deeper or more complex meaning can be recovered by paying careful attention to the broader symbolic complex surrounding hair in Japan and, more specifically, to the way this complex informed the religious lives of the Japanese and, indeed, continues to function in popular Japanese culture today.

MYS II:87 & 89 (NKBT 4:62–63) employ the natural symbolism of black hair turning white to indicate the passage of time, but the deeper meaning of the songs (*uta*) is based on a broader, largely unspoken, symbolic and ritual complex. These verses are from a set designated as "exchange poems" (*sōmon*), a genre defined as poems exchanged between two persons or which otherwise served as a means of communication between two persons. A prose headnote further reports MYS II:85–88 to be "four songs by the Empress Iwanohime, thinking of the Emperor [Nintoku]." These songs were probably orally generated and performed and only later committed to writing.[9] The two verses which concern us read:

#87	aritsutsumo kimi oba matamu uchitabiku waga kurokami ni shimo no oku made ni	I shall wait for you like this as long as I live, until the frost cakes my trailing black hair. (Levy 1981:81)
#89	iakashite kimi oba tatamu nubatama no here, waga kurokami ni shimo wa furedomo	Until dawn breaks I shall wait for you unsleeping, although the frost falls on my bejeweled black hair.[10]

At first glance, these verses seem to employ natural elements (frost, hair, dawn) to express readily recognizable feelings of sadness, anxiety, love, and longing when one is separated from a loved one. While this reading, as far as it goes, is not wrong, it is severely limited, even impoverished, insofar as it ignores the specific religious symbolic complex informing these constituent elements and the significance the temporal-spatial locus of the verses would have had for the ancient Japanese. It is this informing (and, thus, unspoken) symbolic complex that we must explicate if we are to understand the probable meaning these verses had for the early Japanese.[11] This will require a preliminary excursus into the wider symbolic world of meaning of the ancient Japanese before we return to these verses.

In many cultures hair is frequently associated with sexuality. In Japan this association obtains especially in the case of female hair—especially long black hair—which is associated with life force, sexual energy, growth, and fertility. In addition, the long hair of young women was believed to have the power to attract *kami* or divinities, who would descend into it and temporarily reside there. This latter belief is immediately relevant to several of the folk beliefs mentioned in the list above. This power of hair was especially identified with female mediums, who served as intermediaries between the divine and human realms, although all women possessed this power to some extent. This power was not exclusively positive, for it was believed that female hair could also attract malevolent *kami*, such as the *kami* of the plague, as well as benevolent deities.

A series of entries in the *Nihonshoki* (720) testify to the importance attached to the long flowing hair of female mediums or *miko*. In 682 the Emperor Temmu promulgated a decree ordering all men and women in the court to tie up their hair. Two years later, however, under pressure from unidentified sources, the following exemptions were granted: "Women of forty years of age or upwards are allowed to tie up their hair or not . . . as they please. An exception is made for ritual mediums [*kamunaki-hafuri*] who are exempted from the requirement to tie up their hair" (NKBT 68:462–463). The first exemption for women over forty, considered to be past child-bearing age, suggests the association of female hair and reproductive power, which was both powerful and potentially dangerous. The second exemption suggests that the long flowing hair of female mediums was essential to the effective performance of their ritual roles.[12]

In Japan, human hair was employed in purification rituals, but it was also a potential source of pollution and danger. The hair of women had the power to attract back the spirits or souls (*tama*) of absent lovers, as well as the *tama* of the dead. Thus, in certain ritual contexts, involving either deceased individuals or absent loved ones, female hair (to a lesser extent, male hair) functioned as *goshintai*, literally "the kami's body," just as mirrors, swords, and other objects did.[13] Hair could serve as a *katami*, an object in which the *tama* of the individual resided. At times, the spirits of the dead or *kami* would be attracted by women's hair and possess them outside any ritual context.

MYS II:149 is an example of a verse referring to this *tama*-based ritual practice of calling back the spirit of the dead. A death lament attributed to the Empress after the Emperor Tenji (r. 661–71) had passed away, the verse mentions a ritual object known as *tamakazura*. This was a wreath or headdress decorated with *magatama*, crescent-shaped beads, which also helped to attract back the *tama* of the dead, so that the deceased could be seen and communication between the living and the dead continued. Such headdresses have been found in archaeological sites from the ancient Korean kingdoms, as well (see chapter by Nelson, this volume).

hito wa yoshi	People say, "Enough,
omoi yamu to mo	stop thinking of him,"
tamakazura	yet I cannot forget
kao ni mietsutsu	while I see your face
wasuraenu kamo	in the *tamakazura*.
(NKBT 4:88–89)	(Levy 1981:107, adapted)

Several *haniwa* or clay figurines of *miko* from the Jomon period link the hair of such women with their ritual powers. In addition to the presence of other ritual objects (round beads, jewels, a mirror, a bow and quiver of arrows, a flat hat[14] or headdress), which the *miko* either wears on her body or carries, the presence of *tama* (beads or jewels) and *magatama* on many of these figurines call for attention. Such beads have been found in tombs and other excavated sites. While the precise symbolic significance of the *magatama*, which resemble either bear claws or the crescent moon, is unknown, their more general association with magical powers of reproduction is clear. As we have already noted *tama* (bead, ball, jewel) is homophonous with another term, written with a different Chinese character, which refers to the animating spirit of the human body. *Magatama* and other beads were worn as arm and ankle bracelets, but also in women's hair; in addition, they were found on sacred items including ritual bows, mirrors, swords, and wands. It is likely that *magatama* were used for more than decorative purposes; they were a source or repository of spiritual power.

Immediate confirmation of the symbolic association of hair, *magatama*, and the power of reproduction is found in the famous episode of the myth of Amaterasu, the Sun Goddess, and her brother, Susano-o, preserved in both the *Kojiki* (712) and the *Nihonshoki* (720) [Ebersole 1989:86–101]. In this myth, which survives in a number of different versions, Izanagi-no-mikoto, the male *kami* who created the world along with the female, Izanami-no-mikoto, has given birth to a number of *kami* through the act of ritually purifying himself after he has visited the land of the dead. Among these newly created *kami* are Amaterasu and Susano-o, whom he has assigned to rule the heavens and the underworld respectively. When he sends Amaterasu off to assume her realm, he does so by ritually presenting her with a necklace of *magatama*. Susano-o, however, seeks to contravene the orders he has received and attempts to usurp power over the heavens. He refuses to assume his assigned position, instead excessively weeping and lamenting the death of Izanami "until his beard eight hands long extend[s] down over his chest" (Philippi 1968:72; NKBT 1:72–73).[15]

(When Susano-o is finally forced to stop mourning and is exiled, his hair and nails are cut. While the texts are silent on this, his beard would, no doubt, also have been shaved off or at least trimmed.)

In exasperation, Izanagi finally uses a ritual spell to expell Susano-o, who then asks to be allowed to take formal leave of his sister, Amaterasu, before he goes into exile. I turn here to the *Kojiki* version of the myth to note the description of Amaterasu as she prepared for Susano-o's arrival and to draw attention to the similarities between this description and the representations of *miko* introduced above:

> Then, undoing her hair, she wrapped it in hair-bunches. In the hair-bunches on the left and right [sides of her head], on the vine securing her hair, as well as on her left and right arms, she wrapped long strings of myriad *magatama* beads. On her back she bore a thousand-arrow quiver; on the side of her chest she attached a five-hundred-arrow quiver. Also she put on an awesome high arm-guard; and shaking the upper tip of her bow, stamping her legs up to her very thighs into the hard earth, and kicking [the earth] about as if it were light snow, she shouted with an awesome fury, she shouted stamping her feet. (NKBT 1:74–75; Philippi 1968:74–75)

Kami in Japan generally have at least two forms—a "soft" or benevolent aspect (*nigitama*) and a fearsome, wild, or "rough" aspect (*aratama*). The passage above is a description of Amaterasu transforming herself from her gentle to her fearsome aspect. Significantly, this is done in large part by, first, undoing her hair, then redoing it in a martial style, and, finally, by securing a large number of *magatama* in her hair and on her arms. Clearly, these *magatama* are a source of power and strength.

When Susano-o arrives, he challenges Amaterasu to a ritual contest that will prove whether his intentions toward her are pure or evil. The contest involves magically bearing children; the one who bears male children is to be declared the winner. Amaterasu takes a jeweled sword borne by Susano-o, breaks it into pieces, rinses these in the heavenly well, chews the pieces and, finally, spits out a misty spray from which three female *kami* are produced. For his part, Susano-o asks for *magatama* from the left and right hair-bunches of Amaterasu,[16] from the vine that binds these up, and from the bracelets on her left and right arms. After chewing the *magatama*, he spits out five male *kami*, and declares himself to be the winner.

Magatama were not the only things woven into the hair of women in early Japan. In the mythic episode, following that above, Amaterasu, the Sun Goddess, secludes herself in a cave, thus plunging the world into darkness; she is drawn out in large part by the lewd dance performance of Ame-no-Uzume-no-mikoto. This performance is widely regarded as a mythic prototype of the ritual practice of *miko* in ancient Japan as they sought to induce a trance state. According to the *Nihonshoki*, Ame-no-Uzume "took [a branch of] the sacred *sasaki* tree of Heavenly Mount Kagu and decorated her hair with it" (NKBT 67:112–13). Mount Kagu (Kagu-yama) is said to have come down from heaven, becoming a sacred site where the heavenly *kami* descend from heaven. Thus, by placing a branch of the *sasaki* tree from this mountain in her hair, Ame-no-Uzume is further transforming her hair into a "landing site" or resting place for *kami*, as she invites divine possession. Significantly, in the *Nihonshoki* the Chinese character used for "uzu" in the name Ame-no-Uzume means "headdress" or "crown."

A number of *Man'yōshū* verses describe women with flower blossoms or autumn leaves woven in their hair. At least in some cases such references should not be taken to be merely expressions of pastoralism, since these poems were oral performative ritual songs. Rather, the symbolic and ritual complex surrounding female hair needs to be taken into consideration when interpreting these verses. Two examples must suffice. MYS I:38 is a "long verse" or *chōka* recited at the time of an imperial procession to the detached palace at Yoshino, which as already noted was a sacred area especially known for its powers of rejuvenation. The song is a typical praise poem, extolling the Empress as a living *kami*.

yasumishishi	Our Lord
wago ōkimi	who rules in peace,
kamunagara	a very god,
kamusabisesu to	manifests her divine will
Yoshino gawa	and raises towering halls
tagitsu kōchi ni	above the Yoshino riverland
takadono o	where waters surge,
takashirimashite	and climbs to the top
noboritachi	to view the land.
kunimi o seseba	On the mountains
tatanazuku	folding upward around her
aokaki yama	like a sheer hedge of green,
yamatsumi no	the mountain gods
matsuru mi-tsuki to	present their offerings.

harube wa	They bring her blossoms
hana kazashimochi	in spring time
akitateba	to decorate her hair
momichi kazaseri	and, when autumn comes
yukisou	they garland her
kawa no kami mo	with yellow leaves.
ōmi-ke ni	The *kami* of the river
tsukaematsuru to	that runs alongside, too, makes offering for her imperial feast.
(NKBT 4:30–31)	(Levy 1981:57–58, adapted)

In this verse, in weaving blossoms and leaves into her hair, the Empress seeks to absorb the power of the *kami* of the Yoshino River and of Mt. Yoshino into herself. Thus, the reference to the Empress's hair is not incidental, nor is it trivial. It is the larger symbolic complex surrounding hair, which would have been well known to all of the early Japanese, that generates the full meaning of this ritual activity and the public declamation of the Empress's divine status. This interpretation is strengthened by the reference to the Empress performing a land-viewing (*kunimi*) ritual, which was intended to guarantee the fertility and prosperity of the land she surveys (Ebersole 1989).

In MYS II:196, a funeral lament for an imperial princess, Hitomaro uses the image of blossoms and leaves in her hair to recall her youth and vitality, now cut short by death. The verse reads in part:

utsusomi to	While in this world,
omoishi toki	in the spring
harube wa	she would decorate her hair
hana orikazeri	with blossoms,
aki tateba	when autumn came,
momiji kazashi	decorate it with yellow leaves
(NKBT 4:104–105)	

Hair and Embodied Spirits

Having established, in outline form at least, a symbolic complex including, among other things, female hair, *magatama*, *tama*, and fertility, we are now ready to return to the two verses introduced above, MYS I:87, 89. Other verses in the set (#s 85–89) indicate that the Emperor has gone into the mountains, while the Empress asks if she should go there to meet him. Even though the Emperor is absent (indeed, dead), the Empress addresses him directly. In ancient Japan (and in some rural areas today), the land of the dead was believed to be in the mountains. Thus, the spatial context suggests strongly that the Emperor has died or "gone into the mountains." If this is so, then it is likely these verses were a part of a ritual, called *tama-furi*, performed to attract back the spirit of the deceased. All-night vigils were often held for this purpose. Moreover, the crack of dawn, the temporal point betwixt and between night and day, was considered to be a time when such communication was most readily realized. Thus, the Empress's declaration that she will await her husband until her black hair turns white with the frost must be understood in a double sense: it is to be taken both literally (she will wait up all night) and metaphorically (she will faithfully come into the mountains to perform *tama-furi* rites, even until her hair turns white with age, in the hope that she might see her husband again). The sexual allure of the Empress's long black hair is employed in the effort to attract back her husband's *tama*.

Additional evidence of the belief that spirits could reside in hair is easy to find. For instance, in another mythic episode involving Susano-o, he discovers three persons—a male earthly *kami*, his wife, and a daughter—weeping (see NKBT 1:84–89; Philippi 1968:88–90). He learns from them that an eight-tailed dragon (in some versions, a serpent) has come to their home once every year for eight years and eaten one of their daughters each time. They fear that he is about to come for their last daughter, named Kushi-nada-hime ("The Comb Princess of Inada").[17] Susano-o offers to slay the dragon if they will give him their daughter as his wife. When they agree, he transforms the daughter into a comb, which he inserts into his hair-bunch. Through this, Susano-o gains magical power and goes on to trick and slay the dragon. In addition, he discovers the famous Kusanagi sword, which would become one of the imperial regalia, in the dragon's stomach.[18]

Combs often possess magical powers in Japanese myths and are an important additional element of the symbolic complex surrounding hair. For instance, when Izanagi is trying to flee from the underworld after having viewed the decomposing corpse of Izanami, he is pursued by horrible hags. In order to escape them, he removes a comb from his hair-bunch and throws it down behind him. The comb is magically transformed into bamboo shoots, which the pursuing demons pause to eat, allowing Izanagi to escape (Philippi 1968:64–65; Aston I, 1972:24–25).

The same symbolic complex linking a comb, bamboo, and rejuvenating power is found in the "Congratulatory Words of the Nakatomi," one of *norito* or sacred prayers preserved in the tenth-century *Engi-shiki*. This prayer recalls the myth of how a *kami* was given a heavenly jeweled comb (*ama no tamagushi*) and sent down from the High Heavens to serve the Emperor a mixture of heavenly and earthly water in order to guarantee his longevity. The instructions he received from the myriad heavenly *kami* read in part: "Stand this jeweled comb up, and from the time that the waning sun goes down until the morning sun shines recite the heavenly ritual, the solemn ritual words. If you thus recite, as a sign, sacred manifold bamboo shoots will sprout forth like young water plants, and from underneath many heavenly springs will gush forth" (NKBT 1:460–61; Philippi 1990:77).

Recall one of the popular sayings cited above—"If you cut some hair and bury it at the roots of a bamboo tree, your hair will turn black." Hair, combs, and bamboo are all related to fertility, reproductive power, and life force or energy. The bamboo tree, for instance, is known for its ability to shoot up several inches over night. In the myth involving Izanagi, the pursuing hag demons from the world of the dead stop to consume a foodstuff (in this case, produced from a comb, as in the *norito*) identified with the power of life. The symbolic logic behind the practice of burying a lock of one's gray hair at the roots of a bamboo tree suggests that the life power or vitality of the bamboo would be transferred to the person the hair belongs to. Once that happened, his or her hair would turn black again.

No doubt because of their inherent association with hair, combs were also often considered to be *katami*, at once a memento of a dead person and, more importantly, an object which, through ritual means, could become the repository of a person's *tama*. In one myth, when Yamato-takeru is seeking to cross a sea, his progress is blocked by the *kami* of the crossing. His wife, Ototachibana-hime, offers to sacrifice herself in order to pacify the deity. She steps from their boat onto carpets laid on the water and sinks into the sea, drowning herself. "Seven days later, the empress's comb was washed ashore. Taking this comb, they made her tomb and placed it within" (NKBT 1:214–15; Philippi 1968:241–42). Here the wife's comb "embodies" the deceased princess and serves as a substitute for her corpse. She is present in the comb and in that form receives the ritual honors due her.

Combs and other hair accessories also served as symbols of sexual intimacy in early Japan. The phrase "jewelled comb box" (*tamakushige*) referred to both the toiletry article and, metaphorically, to both sexual secrets and female genitals. "To open one's comb box," for instance, was a poetic metaphor for a woman's giving her body to a man. MYS

IV:591 employs this image. Knowing that "the world is thick with the eyes of others," this female poet fears that a dream she has just had means that a secret affair she has been having has been discovered and that this is the reason why her lover has not visited her for so long.

waga omoi o	Have my thoughts
hito ni shirure ya	been revealed to others?
tamakushige	My jeweled comb box
hiraki aketsu to	was opened to the light
ime nishi miyuru	in the dream I had.
(NKBT 4:274–75)	

The same sexual imagery informs the following poem, MYS IV:635, by Prince Yuhara, which he sent to a lover left behind in the capital:

kusamakura	Although I have brought
tabi ni wa tsuma wa	my wife on this journey,
itaredomo	with grass for pillow,
kushige no uchi no	my thoughts are only on
tama o koso omoe[19]	the jewel inside the comb box.
(NKBT 4:284–85)	

A final example must suffice. The following verse, MYS I:93, was sent by a princess to one of the most powerful men in the country, who had been secretly seeing her:

tamakushige	The jewelled comb box
ohou o yasumi	is easily opened,
akete ikaba	yet if you go after dawn,
kimi ga na aredo	you have your name,
waga na shi oshimo	but I will rue mine.[20]
(NKBT 4:66–67)	

Through these associations, the ancient Japanese alluded erotically to the jewel-*tama*, the source of human fertility, hidden by pubic hair, without having to resort to explicit language or crudity. Hair is associated with both pleasure and anxiety; it is wild and unruly and at once attractive and frightening. The function of combs, of course, is precisely to control, order, and style hair. Hair is a primary symbol, while a comb is a secondary symbol, whose meanings flow from the primary symbol. Combs are to hair as culture is to nature.

The symbolic associations of hair informed the import of combs in Japan. If hair suggests sexuality, then combs, which are manufactured objects designed to control and style hair, will have an extended, correlate symbolic import. Hair that is well groomed or coiffured suggests controlled sexuality and, more generally, a self-controlled person. At the same time, long hair that is tied up nevertheless suggests the possibility (attractive and yet dangerous) that it could let down. For a woman, to let her hair down in the presence of a man was a sign of intimacy. It is in this sense that verses such as MYS III:493 must be understood:

okite ikaba	When I go, leaving her,
tsuma koimu kamo	my wife will fall into longing,
shikitae no	spreading her long black hair,
kurokami shikite	like a seat cushion,
nagaki kono yo o	this long night through.
(NKBT 4:244–45)	

The poet here was being sent out of the capital to take up a government post, but his wife would remain behind. He imagines her longing for him in his absence. "Shikitae no" is a "pillow word" (*makurakotoba*, a term in Japanese poetics for an adjectival epithet) which modifies "kurokami" ("[long] black hair"). "Shikitae no" is literally "sitting pillow" or "seat cushion," but "shiki" is also homonymous with another word designating a demarcated sacred space found in some shrine grounds (including the Grand Shrine of Ise). It is covered with white pebbles and bounded by sacred ropes and *kami* are believed to descend and reside within this space. The pillow-word *shikitae no*, when used in association with the symbolic charge of long black female hair, allows one to "hear" an implicit reference to the wife's hair as a sacred site/"seat cushion" where the *kami* or, in this case, the spirit of the absent husband, might come to rest. In letting her hair down and spreading it out as she retires at night, the wife would not only have remembered (in our modern sense of the term) the times she had slept with her husband, she would have experienced at times a more "real" presence. That is, I take the phrase *shikitae no kurokami* to be an allusion to her ability to call her husband's (or lover's) spirit back in the night, perhaps in the form of a dream or a vision. This interpretation fits the larger symbolic complex described above. This *makurakotoba* remains inexplicable without some such informing symbolic complex.[21]

The belief that hair could serve as a *katami* survived through the centuries in Japan as the following passage, from *Nozarashi kikō*, a poetic travel journal by Matsuo Bashō (1644–1694) illustrates. Bashō had returned to his hometown after many years, only to find that his mother had died in his absence:

> Nothing was the same as it had been in the past—the sideburns of my brothers were white, their faces wrinkled. We rejoiced to see each other alive, but said no more. My eldest brother brought out an amulet bag and opened it, saying, "Here, look, Mother's white hair. You're like Urashima opening the jewelled treasure box, what with you, too, now an old man." We wept for a while . . .

te ni toraba kienu namida zo atsuki aki no shimo (NKBT 46:38)	When I take it in my hand, it melts like autumn frost through my hot tears.

From well-groomed and tied-up hair, we turn to the opposite case. In Japan, as in many societies, disheveled hair is a sign of psychic or spiritual turmoil. In Japanese poetry, in prose literature, on the kabuki and nō stages, in works of art, and in cinema, wild or unkemp hair represents a breakdown of psychic and social order. In the *Man'yōshū*, for instance, disheveled hair is commonly used to suggest a woman crazed with love and longing for an absent lover. MYS II:118 (NKBT 4:74–75) and IV:724 (NKBT 4:304–305) are representative:

nagekitsutsu masurao no ko no koure koso waga yūkami no hijite nurekere	It is precisely because a distinguished man like you longs for me that my hair is drenched and come undone.
asagami no omoi midarete kaku bakari nane ga koureso ime ni miekeru	Did I see you in my dreams, my love, because you long all day for me, your thoughts disheveled like your morning hair?

Unbound and disheveled hair indicates an uncontrollable passion, a frustrated love, or great psychic or physical distress. Two further verses illustrate this. MYS II:123, 124 (NKBT 4:76–77) are part of a set of poems purportedly exchanged by newlyweds, after the husband had fallen seriously ill and was confined to his sickbed. The first verse is by the husband; the second is his bride's response.

takeba nureta kaneba nagaki imo ga kami kono goro minu ni kakiretsuramu ka	Put up, it fell back down. Left down, it's too long. I have not seen my wife's hair these days. Has she combed it, I wonder?
hito wa mina ima wa nagashi to take to iedo kimi ga mishi kami midaretari tomo	Though everyone says, "It's too long now, put it up," so what if the hair you saw is disheveled?

Here the young wife's disheveled hair expresses her distress over her husband's illness. She argues that given the situation, her appearance is appropriate since it accurately represents her inner turmoil to the world.

One final example must suffice. In "The Cypress Pillar" chapter of the *Genji monogatari*, General Higekuro, who has been seeing a young woman named Tamakazura, has been having a fight with his wife, who is jealous. Finally, even though a heavy snow is falling, he decides to go out to visit Tamakazura and his wife dutifully helps to prepare his robes. The wife is apparently calm and resigned to her husband's leaving. But suddenly she stands up, takes a container filled with the ashes of burned incense, and pours the contents over her husband's head (Seidensticker 1976:497–98). The husband and others in the household assume that the wife has been possessed by a demon. Not surprisingly, the *Genji monogatari ekotoba*, a sixteenth-century guide for painters on the proper iconography for Genji illustrations, explicitly states that the wife in this scene "should be in her casual, somewhat rumpled and faded robes and *her hair should be in disarray*" (Murase 1983:175, emphasis added).

Modern Japanese Proverbs and Practices Reconsidered

My purpose will have been served if the reader, aware of the symbolic complex surrounding hair from ancient and medieval Japan, is now better able to understand many other popular religious beliefs and practices found over the centuries in Japanese cultural history. Let us return briefly to the list of contemporary popular or folk beliefs and practices given at the beginning of this chapter.

We have seen that hair represents life force and vitality. Thus, we can readily recognize why thinning hair would bode ill for an individual—it indicates an ebbing of vitality. But especially full or bushy hair is also dangerous or undesirable insofar as it indicates an excess of sexual energy. Such hair might, moreover, attract the attention of malevolent *kami* or evil spirits. Thus, the prohibition against speaking about the plague in the presence of a woman combing or fixing her hair comes from the belief that *kami* and other spirits are attracted to the long hair of women. Similarly, the hair of geisha or prostitutes (i.e., women who are excessively active sexually) is especially attractive to the *kami* of disease, who bring death, disfigurement, or infertility. The popular saying "Long hair hides seven defects" suggests that vitality, sexual energy, and reproductive power are more important when selecting a bride than mere beauty.

The belief that a person's hair contains the life essence or *tama* of that individual informs a number of popular beliefs, including those that indicate anxiety and concern over the possibility that other persons or animals might come to possess a strand or clipping of one's hair.[22] Some individuals fear they would face the wrath of the *kami* if a bird used strands of their hair to build a nest in a sacred tree in a shrine complex. Similarly, while burned hair can keep dangerous animals at bay because it gives off the stench of death, at the same time burning one's hair can be dangerous since in doing so one might be destroying one's life essence. Then, too, the noxious odor of burning hair might attract malevolent spirits, who are drawn to disgusting things and who linger around sites of death. For similar reasons, those already in a state of pollution, such as menstruating women or women who have just given birth, are especially vulnerable to having their hair attract malevolent spirits.

On the other hand, human hair—most especially female hair—has positive powers. As a repository of the powers of life and fertility, it can ward off demons and other spirits that might bring illness, death, or infertility into a house. Incorporated into an amulet, female hair can protect the health and welfare of the individual carrying it. It can also serve as a substitute for an individual or as a *katami*. When fishermen or seamen caught in a storm throw tufts of their hair into the sea, they are making a substitute sacrifice to the *kami* of the sea in lieu of their own lives.

The offerings of female hair made to temples and shrines to protect men who have been sent to war were based on the belief that hair had the power to attract back the spirit of absent loved ones. The ropes made of human hair found in temples had a practical purpose, of course, given the great tensile strength of hair, since such ropes could be used to lift large beams into place without breaking. But the more important religious purpose was to contribute the life essence of these women to the good works of these religious institutions and to build good karma. For Buddhist adherents, moreover, such offerings could also serve as a symbolic taking of the tonsure.

Mention might also be made of the ritual significance of the hair of sumo wrestlers. Sumo began many centuries ago as a ritual contest held on shrine grounds, although today the tournaments are usually held in indoor arenas. The wrestler's long hair, like Samson's, represents power and life force, but it also may serve to attract the *kami.* Traditionally it was believed that it was the *kami* who decided the sumo matches. Today wrestlers continue to participate in a series of rituals before each tournament and before each match. There is an opening rite where the *kami* are invited down, as well as a concluding rite sending them off. Before each match, the contestants stamp their feet and clap their hands to announce their presence to the *kami.* When a sumo wrestler retires, his topknot is cut in a special ritual marking this change in status; he no longer needs to invite the *kami* to his matches.

The ambivalence attached to hair can be witnessed in the *kamioki* rite in which the hair of small children, who had survived infancy, was allowed to grow long for the first time, representing their growing life force. A certain anxiety was associated with this rite of passage, since long hair was sexually charged and could attract all kinds of spirits. Dressing the children up as elderly men and women with white hair, while prayers were offered for their good fortune, was done in the hope that the children might live to pass through the natural aging process to reach old age.

Conclusion

In this chapter I have briefly surveyed the religious symbolism of hair in Japan over twelve hundred years. The remarkable continuity in this symbolism over the centuries, in spite of the great vississitudes in Japanese religious history, suggests the presence of a deep and fundamental complex. Whether this represents a fundamental psychological complex or a historically transmitted symbolic and ritual complex remains a subject for debate. As the evidence marshalled here has shown, the association of hair with sexuality is undeniable, but this is not the only association found in the Japanese data. More generally, hair is associated with the power of fertility or vitality (and its inverse, disease or death).

In Japan, the association of the phenomenological or "natural" symbolism of hair with the broader symbolic and ritual *tama* complex, found from the earliest historical period down to the present, was the key to its longevity and sustained power. Yet the fact that specific ritual practices changed over time and found diverse forms of expression in different religious traditions suggests the existence of a deeper source. This, I want to claim, was—and is—the *tama*-based religious anthropology, which not only survived the rise and eventual dominance of Buddhism but fundamentally informed the history and structure of Japanese Buddhism. This religious anthropology posits that human life is based on the presence of the *tama* or animating spirit residing in the body. But this spirit can leave the body and wander elsewhere, causing illness, unconsciousness, and death. This religious anthropology has remained the dynamic core of popular Japanese religion, where possession and curing are often based on the *tama* beliefs. The religious symbolism of hair in Japan cannot be understood without appreciating its deep association with this religious anthropology.

Notes

1. The fifteenth day of the eleventh month was also the traditional time the *niiname-sai* or harvest festival was held in the imperial court. Thus, this time was associated with fertility, as well as the sacral kingship.

2. See, for example, a song performed in a ritual dance designed to ease the effects of the plague in Rotermund 1991:44.

3. The Japanese generally have very little bodily hair. Thus, "hair" generally refers to hair on the head, as well as facial hair for men. There is, however, at least one myth where the bodily hairs from different parts of the body of a deity (Susano-o) are transformed into the first examples of various sorts of trees. See NKBT 67, *Nihonshoki, jō*:127–28; Aston I, 1972:58.

Pubic hair is rarely referred to and rarely represented in Japan, except in Edo period works of erotic art. Even today, there are legal prohibitions against picturing pubic hair in magazines or films. In general, the Japanese have not found bodily hair to be aesthetically pleasing. The famous twentieth-century novelist Tanizaki Junichiro is representative in this respect, writing in an essay entitled "Ai to Shikijō" ("Love and Sexual Passion") that, while Western women are better proportioned than their Japanese counterparts, they are best viewed from a distance, for "they are disappointing when one gets too close and sees how coarse and hairy their skin is." See also the chapter by Allison, this volume.

4. In a different context, Victor Turner referred to the widespread fascination with and use of homonyms in the rituals of the Ndembu in Africa as "serious punning" (Turner 1977). The same may be said for ancient and medieval Japan.

5. See also MYS II:150. All translations are my own unless otherwise noted, as here.

6. The verb *tatsu* ("to rise") here is the same as *sasu* in Hitomaro's verse. See NKBT 4:205, n. 430.

7. For an example of this belief, see the twelfth-century *Konjaku monogatari-shū*, Book 24, Tale 20. This is a tale of a man who divorced his wife of many years and abandoned her. She was so deeply hurt that she cried and cried until she finally passed away. Because she had no relatives, her corpse lay in the house. Strangely enough, though the flesh decayed, the skeletal remains did not fall apart, nor did the hair fall from the skull. Neighbors also reported seeing an eerie green light continually coming from the house, which also frequently rattled, frightening them. When news of the strange goings on reached the ex-husband, he feared that he had caused his wife's death and that, as a haunting spirit, she would now seek to injure or kill him. He consulted a diviner, who assured him that he could help him. The husband would have to sit on the skeleton all night, grasping its hair firmly in his hand, never letting go no matter what happened. Because he feared for his life, the husband agreed. About midnight, the corpse stirred and got up, saying, "Let's go hunt for him." The poor man hung on for dear life as the skeleton departed, returning just before dawn, when it lay down again as before. When the man reported to the priest that he had followed his directions, the priest said everything would be all right. Then, he faced the skeleton and recited a magical formula. The compiler of the *Konjaku monogatari* declared that this tale was true and that the children of the husband and of the diviner were still living.

8. For an Indian myth that parallels this, see O'Flaherty 1973:41–42 and O'Flaherty 1976:28. There the smoke from a funeral pyre rises as smoke, turns into clouds, which produce rain. The rain produces vegetables, which, when eaten, produce semen, which leads to new human life.

9. Verse #89 is listed as a variant of #87, but we should not understand this to indicate a textual variant. More probably such songs were orally performed on multiple occasions and, as is often the case in oral traditions, were achieved in slightly different form in each performance. Thus, the now textual variants point to an earlier fluidity of the performative verse, since oral songs were not characterized by fixity. Such songs were subject to innovation on the part of any given performer, as well as to being adapted to different occasions and needs specific to those occasions.

10. Levy 1981:81 mistranslates *shimo* here as "dew" rather than "frost."

11. My working assumption is that it is possible to recover the probable meaning of such verses as it was mediated in the oral performative context(s) of the songs and, later, in their reception in textual form by later readers, who

still shared the same symbolic world of meaning as the oral performer and her audience.

12. For the initial decree, see NKBT 68:452–53; Aston II, 1972:355. Cf. Nelson, in this volume, on Korean women shamans.

13. It is worthwhile recalling that the three imperial regalia in Japan are a mirror, a sword, and *magatama* (curved or cresent-shaped *tama*).

14. The use of this hat in the *miko*'s costume did not survive past the Jomon period.

15. This reference to hair seems to be a metaphorical way of indicating the passage of a long period of time; it may also reflect a prohibition for men in mourning against cutting or shaving their beard. From other sources we know that in ancient Japan some mourners were not allowed to cut their fingernails or toenails either.

16. In the *Lotus Sutra* one finds a reference to "the single jewel on the crown of hair." In Buddhism this jewel in the hair of a Buddha referred to the highest enlightenment. Here, though, we are dealing with a pre- or at least non-Buddhist practice, involving multiple *magatama*. Of course, these two symbolic meanings coaelesced at some points later in history. For a metaphorical allusion to the Buddhist sense, see MYS III:412 in NKBT 4:198–99; Levy 1981:210.

17. The term *kushi* in the daughter's name means "comb," but also "wondrous."

18. For the *Nihonshoki* versions of this myth, see Aston I, 1972:52–53, 55–57. Only the first version contains the element of Kushi-nada-hime being transformed into a comb and worn in Susano-o's hair.

19. The following verse, which accompanies #635, is one of innummerable indications that articles of clothing could also serve as *katami*:

waga koromo	I send you
katami ni matsuru	my robe as a *katami*.
shikitae no	Do not keep it far
makura o sakezu	from your well-woven pillow;
makite sanemase	sleep wrapped in it.

20. This verse is extremely hard to translate because it is filled with double entendres. Levy has attempted to capture these in his translation:

> The jewelled box is easily opened, and the night, opening into
> dawn, saw you leave. What of your name if this be known?
> My regrets are for my own.
>
> (Levy 1981:84)

The prose headnote to this verse gives its generative context as: "When Lord Fujiwara, the Great Minister of the Center, asked Princess Kaga to wed him, she sent him this poem." Given the content of the poem, though, it seems more likely that the woman was challenging the minister to legitimate their relationship, rather than responding to a marriage proposal.

In yet another *Man'yōshū* verse, MYS III:522, a man compares himself and his inability to meet a lover for a long time to old combs that remain unused in jewelled comb boxes. Here the sexual imagery suggests a prolonged intimacy that has been broken. The longing for the loved one is increased by the memories of past trysts.

otomera ga	I have become like
tamakushige naru	the well-worn combs of maidens,
tamakushi no	in jewelled comb boxes . . .
kamusabikemu mo	unable to meet
imo ni awazu areba	my lover.
(NKBT 4:252–53)	

21. The NKBT, for instance, merely notes that this is a pillow word without attempting to discern its possible symbolic meaning(s). See NKBT 4:245, n. 493.

22. There are many Japanese folktales concerning how some individual or spirit (usually female) comes under the control of another when that person discovers three strands of her hair. In such tales, hair functions much as the robe of the heavenly maiden does in the famous Tanabata tale (cf. Mayer 1984:24–26).

References

Aston, William G., trans. 1972. *Nihongi: Chronicles of Japan from the Earliest Times to A.D. 697*. Rutland, Vt. and Tokyo: Charles E. Tuttle.

Blacker, Carmen. 1975. *The Catalpa Bow: A Study of Shamanistic Practices in Japan*. London: George Allen and Unwin.

Ebersole, Gary L. 1989. *Ritual Poetry and the Politics of Death in Early Japan*. Princeton, N.J.: Princeton University Press.

Koji zokushin kotowaza daijiten. 1984. Tokyo: Shōgakkan.

Levy, Ian Hideo, trans. 1981. *The Ten Thousand Leaves*, vol. 1. Princeton, N.J.: Princeton University Press.

Mayer, Fanny Hagin. 1984. *Ancient Tales in Modern Japan: An Anthology of Japanese Talk Tales*. Bloomington: Indiana University Press.

Miyata Noboru. 1987. *Hime no minzokugaku*. Tokyo: Seidōsha.

Morrell, Robert E., trans. 1985. *Sand and Pebbles (Shasekishū): The Tales of Mujū Ichien, A Voice for Pluralism in Kamakura Buddhism*. Albany: State University of New York Press.

Murase Miyeko. 1983. *Iconography of The Tale of Genji: Genji Monogatari Ekotoba*. New York and Tokyo: Weatherhill.

NKBT. *Nihon koten bungaku taikei*, ed. Takagi Ichinosuke et al. 1957. Vols. 1, 4, 5, 46, 67 & 68. Tokyo: Iwanami Shoten.

Nihonshi daijiten, vol. 2. 1993. Tokyo: Heibonsha.

Obeyesekere, Gananath. 1990. *The Work of Culture: Symbolic Transformation in Psychoanalysis and Anthropology*. Chicago: University of Chicago Press.

O'Flaherty, Wendy Doniger. 1973. *Asceticism and Eroticism in the Mythology of Siva*. London: Oxford University Press.

———. 1976. *The Origins of Evil in Hindu Mythology*. Berkeley: University of California Press.

Philippi, Donald L., trans. 1968. *Kojiki*. Tokyo: University of Tokyo Press.

———. 1990. *Norito: A Translation of the Ancient Japanese Ritual Prayers*. Princeton, N.J.: Princeton University Press.

Rotermund, Hartmut O. 1991. *Hōsōgami ou la petite vérole aisément*. Paris: Maisonneuve et Larose.

Seki Keigo, ed. 1963. *Folktales of Japan*. London: Routledge and Kegan Paul.

Seidensticker, Edward G., trans. 1976. Murasaki Shikibu, *The Tale of Genji*. New York: Alfred A. Knopf.

Turner, Victor. 1977. *The Ritual Process: Structure and Anti-Structure*. Ithaca, N.Y.: Cornell University Press.

5 bound hair and confucianism in korea

sarah m. nelson

Skinned-back hair frames stern faces in portraits of Korean women of the late nineteenth century. These unsmiling visages and controlled hair give rise to questions about the relationship of women's severe hairstyles to the controlled society advocated within Korean Confucianism, particularly since the prescribed rigid social order was one in which women were invariably subordinate to men. The portraits represent upper-class women, and while that group may have been the most repressed, photographs of village women show the same hair style—parted in the middle and knotted at the nape of the neck, without softening fringes, bangs, or curls.

Men's hairstyles are invisible in the portraits and photographs of that time, for hats or caps were worn by men but not women, at least in photographs. Women covered their heads on "outings" with a kind of bonnet (Kim 1977:150). But there are many dimensions to hair styles in Korea. Men's hair, although covered, was not loose. Under caps and hats, men's obligatory topknots also restricted their hair, and a tight band prevented any stray strands from escaping. And while hair was styled according to age and gender but not class, class was made visible on the head by means of hats that revealed rank or occupation for men, and hairpins differing in size and costliness for women.

This chapter explores some strands of hair-style meanings in Korea. To what extent did the severity of Late Yi dynasty (1392–1910) hair styles reflect the strictures of Confucianism as it was practiced in

Korea at the time? How were attitudes toward hair expressed? Can a connection betweeen tightly bound hair and a tightly organized society be established? If bound hair is congruent with Confucianism and the repression of women, why are women's heads allowed to go uncovered? Is hair not associated with sexuality, so that covering women's hair is of no concern? What considerations might override a need to cover a feature considered sensual in many societies?

The focus of this chapter is social rather than psychological. I will show that the condition of the hair in Korea was important enough to fight and die for in the late 19th century, yet whatever psychological states may have been necessary to produce violence over hair, it was the social meaning of hair that caused the turmoil.

It is also important to note that ecstatic religion still exists in Korea, but it is unrelated to loose hair. Thus hair meanings are quite different from those discussed in *Medusa's Hair* (Obeyeskere 1981) or "Magical Hair" (Leach 1958). Korea's female shamans, *mudang*, do not loosen their hair when they go into trances. Loose, wild, or matted hair is not relevant to achieving contact with Korean spirits, in spite of the fact that vigorous dancing leading to trance is a necessary feature of the rituals.

Methods and Sources

In order to establish the connection between hair styles and Confucianism, it is important first to describe both the hair styles and the Korean manifestation of Confucianism. The truism that association does not imply causality applies here, however. To indicate that the association is more than accidental, I will show that although the basic features of Korean hair styles remained static for more than two thousand years, the severity of women's hair style increased in the Yi dynasty, becoming tighter and ultimately completely controlled.

The slow Confucianization of Korea during the course of the Yi dynasty (1392–1910) (see table 2) has been described by Martina Deutchler (1992). She demonstrates that women gradually lost their ability to control their own lives under the influence of Confucianism during the course of the Yi dynasty. Thus, a connection between increasing Confucianism and tighter hair might be established with reference to historical trends. I will provide evidence that during the Three Kingdoms period (57 BC–AD 668) when women had freedom to ride horses independently and were eligible to be rulers (Nelson 1993),

Table 2. Korean and Chinese Dynasties Mentioned in the Text

Korea	**China**
Yi dynasty 1392–1910	Qing dynasty 1644–1912
Koryo dynasty 918–1392	Ming dynasty 1368–1644
United Silla 668–935	•
Three Kingdoms	•
Old Silla 57 BC–668	•
Paekche 18 BC–660	•
Koguryo 37 BC–668	•
Lelang Commandery 108 BC–313	Han dynasty 206 BC–220
Wiman Choson 193–108 BC	Qin dynasty 221–206 BC

hair styles for women were looser, athough similar to those of the late Yi dynasty. It appears that men's hair styles changed less over the course of centuries, athough the evidence is less secure for men's hair than for women's, because men are usually depicted wearing hats.

These problems are only partly approachable with written records, for in the rare instance where hair styles are mentioned, the description is brief, usually only a word or two. Nevertheless, Chinese written documents provide a few useful references to hair in Korea, as do the Korean histories (*Samguk Sagi* and *Samguk Yusa*) in their tales, myths, and legends. Another documentary source, focusing on artifacts, concerns the sumptuary laws of the Silla kingdom. Permitted and forbidden hair ornaments for different classes of women, and head coverings for men of different ranks, are described in detail in this document.

Likewise, archaeological data occasionally throw light on hair styles. Depictions of men and women in tomb murals and funerary statuary offer some direction, along with hats and hairpins that remain undecayed long after the hair, and even the skull it was attached to, has vanished.

Thus a sketchy and gappy record using pictorial and written sources, from China as well as Korea, and from protohistory to the present, can be used in exploring earlier hair styles in Korea. In some cases the appearance of the hair is depicted, from others the meanings of those hair styles can be gleaned. These varied sources allow a composite picture of the meanings and messages of Three Kingdoms hair in Korea to be compiled, and to be compared with Confucian Korea.

Confucian Korea

The essence of Confucianism as practiced in Korea is the maintenance of a social structure in which relationships are inherently unequal. According to this social theory, society runs smoothly only when the members of society adhere to their appointed places. The five Confucian relationships include king to subject, father to son, older brother to younger brother, man to woman, and friend to friend. While the last category may seem to imply equality, in practice relative status is established on the basis of social standing, job category, or age. The Korean language itself reflects status differences. To utter grammatical sentences in Korean requires "speaking down" or "speaking up" in both sentence construction and choice of words. Without establishing relative status, it is impossible to speak modern Korean.

It appears to be a paradox that, although the hair was always under control, not allowed to flow freely and dressed severely, the meanings attached to particular hair styles, especially the topknot of adult men, were so emotionally laden that both murder and suicide occurred in defense of topknots. Life itself was considered less important than preservation of this hair style. The hair, expressing the Confucian principle that members of society should know their proper places and behave accordingly, could thus be the cause of un-Confucian violence. This circumstance suggests that Confucianism was "skin deep" in some ways and did not affect all parts of the culture equally.

Hair styles in Confucian Korea were based on uncut hair. All of a son's body belonged to his parents, and it was disgraceful for a person to harm himself, including by cutting his hair. Uncut hair was thus a visible sign of filial piety. James Scarth Gale recounts a tale of a man who, in 1894, committed suicide rather than cut his hair. "As a lad this young prince had been taught to count every hair of his head as precious, a link that bound him to his father and mother" (Rutt 1972:117). The hair was so inalienable from a person that combings were collected and kept, to be included in the coffin with the corpse at burial (Bishop 1898:265).

Uncut, however, does not imply unruly. The long hair was never allowed to hang freely. It was controlled: knotted or braided in particular ways, each style specifying aspects of the wearer's social position. Children's hair was parted in the middle and braided, the long braids hanging down their backs, boys with one braid and girls with one or two (Bishop 1898:127, Rutt 1972:25). On attaining adulthood (defined by marriage no matter what the actual age of the bride or groom), the hair style was changed in one of the major life-cycle ceremonies conducted for both men and women (Griffis 1885:139; Bishop 1898:114). Ceremonies for tying up girls' hair at puberty were similar to those of boys (Landis 1898).

To construct the adult male topknot, the bridegroom's hair was secured with a band, twisted tightly into a knot that leaned slightly forward from the top of the head and covered with a close-fitting cap. The cap was henceforth worn night and day, in the house as well as in public. For outside wear, the *yangban,* members of the upper class, donned a large, broad-brimmed, horsehair hat with a high crown to cover the inner cap. The *yangban* were the only men able to afford this expensive and fragile hat (it became soggy in the rain and was easily crushed), and therefore it functioned as a highly visible status symbol (Bishop 1898). Male farmers wore sturdier hats of straw to protect their heads and topknots from sun and rain, or sometimes simply wrapped their heads in cloth. Members of the court were distinguished by black hats with wings, and the military wore distinctive hats as part of their uniforms. Thus occupation as well as class was made manifest on men's heads.

For daily wear, women parted their hair severely in the middle, pulled it back tightly, twisted a bun on the nape of the neck, and secured the bun with a hairpin. On formal occasions (Figure 11), women of the nobility might add loops of artificial hair (Bishop 1898:258), although wigs had been discouraged in the mid-Yi dynasty (Kim 1977:149–50). Women's headgear was more likely to be a small crown for ceremonies or a bonnet for outings, with the exception of *kisaeng* (courtesans) and *mudangs* (shamans), the only occupations open to women. Conspicuous hairpins functioned to demonstrate women's social class, for they varied significantly in size and ornateness.

Thus, although hair was uncut, everyone, even children, wore controlled hair. The braids of children turned into the even more restricted topknot or chignon when the wearers were ready to take on the burdens of adulthood. The form of hair binding differed according to age and sex, but no one was allowed loose hair. Braided or knotted hair was a sign of a proper citizen, a person who knew the Confucian relationships and how to apply them.

Ethnicity

We have seen that the topknot for men and the knot of hair on women's necks were symbols of gender, of adulthood, of proper behavior, and of filial piety. In the late nineteenth century the topknot also became

Figure 11. A palace woman in full regalia. From *The Passing of Korea,* by H. B. Hurlbert (1906).

a symbol of Korean ethnicity, for it differed from the queue required in China by the ruling Manchus of the Qing dynasty, as well as from hair in contemporary Japan. In Japan, older styles included shaving part of the head, but Western shorter hair for men was gradually adopted (Saito 1939). In Korea, short hair was associated with the shaved tonsure of Buddhist monks. This made short hair particularly unappealing, for Buddhism was denigrated by Confucians and monks were not held in high repute.

In 1895, pressed by the Japanese to modernize, the Korean king and men of his court cut off their topknots to set an example to lesser men. This was accompanied by an edict from the king that all other men should follow suit. This edict caused rioting. Some officials in the countryside who did cut off their topknots were murdered by the horrified peasants (Bishop 1898:359–70). A few men even committed suicide rather than have their topknot shorn. Violence occurred on both sides of the issue. Police in Seoul cut off the hair of resisting peasants who haplessly came to the capital with their topknots intact. Eventually the situation became so desperate that the king fled to the Russian legation for safety and issued a new proclamation rescinding his topknot edict.

Binding, Morality, and Sexuality

People with loose hair had loose morals and were outside the proper order of things. Stories from earlier times were used as parables to demonstrate this connection. For example a beggar in an ancient tale was identifiable as disreputable by his disheveled hair (Rutt 1972:152 [*Samguk Sagi* chapter 45]). Only people without family would allow their hair to be unkempt (see Watson, this volume). The hair was released from its topknot to be combed at death, and the hair of the corpse was retied, but loosely (Hulbert 1906:448), perhaps signifying the release from earthly relationships.

In paintings of the eighteenth and nineteenth centuries, a woman with loose fluffy hair designates a *kisaeng*, a kind of courtesan, suggesting a sexual dimension to uncontrolled hair, as well as a lack of connection to the proper world. Japanese styles for women in which the hair, although quite controlled, curves out away from the head (Saito 1939), were not considered proper in Korea. Moreover, the telling detail used to describe the exceptionally beautiful Queen Kwanna of Koguryo (37 B.C.–A.D. 668) is her hair, said to have been nine feet long (Rutt 1972:138). She was bad as well as beautiful, and perhaps the long hair stands for both her wickedness and her beauty. Another example of long loose hair representing sexuality is found in part of a fertility ritual in a special *kut* performed for women hoping for conception. The *kut* tells the story of a semidivine princess, Tangum Agassi, who is pulled by her long hair, which is described as "messed up like seaweed." Her behavior is "embarrassing and shameful" (Kinsler 1983:75). Not only had she become pregnant with triplets, but the conception is said to have occurred as a result of a monk "stroking her hair three times" (73), clearly connecting her loose hair with sexuality.

Figure 12. Fluffy *kisaeng* hairstyles of the eighteenth and nineteenth centuries.

Origins

In spite of the fervor with which the topknot was defended, its antiquity is disputed. One author claims that the "styles of hats and hair dressing became fixed in their present condition" in 1392, at the beginning of the Yi dynasty (Griffis 1885:29). He does not suggest how these hairdos may have differed from previous styles. Gale, citing a sixteenth-century Korean author, believes that the *mang-kun*, or headband, dates only to 1380, early in the Chinese Ming dynasty, when it was brought to Korea by a Daoist priest (Rutt 1972:228). We cannot be sure about the headband, but other evidence makes it seem likely that the topknot existed in some form for at least two-thousand years. The *Weizhi*, a Chinese chronicle from the third century A.D., reports that Mahan men of southwestern Korea wore their hair on top of their heads (128), thus they wore a topknot of some description.

A further leap into the distant past, back to the third century B.C., when the first intimation of Korean hair is found in the *Houhan Shu,* also suggests the Korean topknot. The Chaoxian (Korea) chapter of this Chinese history describes the origin of the first recorded Korean state, called in Korean "Wiman Choson." Wiman, the founder of the new state, had lived in the northeastern Chinese state of Yan but fled to Korea due to shifting political alliances. Apparently he escaped in disguise, for he "gathered together a band of a thousand or more followers and, adopting the mallet-shaped hairdo of the barbarians, escaped over the eastern border" (Watson 1961:258). There is no further description of this "mallet-shaped" hairdo, but Korean writers assume it is a topknot.

Wiman's flight to Korea occurred not long after the Qin emperor of China created and buried his famous pottery army (Qian, Chen, and Ru 1981) in the third century B.C. The statues are useful as a baseline for hair styles of both Chinese and border peoples in the Qin emperor's army, perhaps including some from the Korean peninsula. The Qin emperor caused to be buried thousands of life-sized statues of soldiers, depicting many details, including varied and intricate hair styles. It is impossible to say which of these, if any, might represent a Korean version of the topknot, but it is clear that soldiers in the Qin army wore their hair uncut and elaborately dressed with braids, knots, and other devices. Combining the details of the pottery army and the Chinese documents, it is obvious that topknots were worn by soldiers and that the Korean male hairstyle was distinctive and indicative of non-Chinese ethnicity.

The earliest artifactual evidence of hair styles in Korea is found in excavations of tombs near near Pyongyang, North Korea. These tombs are associated with the Lelang commandery, which was established by the Han dynasty of China, successor to the Qin. Han generals conquered the armies of Wiman's grandson Ugo and established control over the northern part of the Korean peninsula. The earth mounds of the burials covered wooden or brick chamber tombs, most of them long since looted, but all probably attributable to the ruling class (Kayamoto 1962). In a few excavated burials some ordinarily perishable artifacts were preserved in water-logged conditions. These artifacts include hairpins of various materials, stiff silk hats, and wooden combs. For example, in the Tomb of Wang Kang (Tomb 219 at Sogamni), a silk gauze hat and some beads were found in the west coffin, along with a sword and a seal. The silk hat had room to cover a topknot. In the east coffin, jade beads were found under the woman's neck, as if they had been attached to a net covering a hair knot (114). This tomb was a two-room wooden structure beneath a mound of earth, a style of tomb building derived from China. It is difficult to know whether the burial is that of native Koreans, Chinese colonists, or sinicized Koreans (Pearson 1978), but it is interesting that both the man's topknot and the woman's hairknot are implied, suggesting that the tomb inhabitants were native Koreans.

Other burials of the Han commandery suggest similar hair dressing. The tomb of Wang Guang contained a hat with a chin strap in the man's coffin and hairpins in the woman's. Many of the artifacts in this tomb have inscriptions indicating that they are imports from Han China (Umehara 1952), and perhaps this tomb is more likely to be that of a Chinese posted to this faraway place than a local dignitary (Pai 1989). Did this couple "go native" and adopt Korean hairstyles? In the Tomb of Wang Xu, tortoise shell hairpins were found in two of the coffins and lacquered hairpins in another, all assumed to be female burials, and a tortoise shell "hair ornament" (perhaps a comb) in the fourth one, belonging to a male. An incised date on a lacquer bowl translates to 45 A.D. (Hamada 1936), placing the burial in the early period of the Han commandery.

Lacquered wooden hair ornaments and hairpins of tortoise shell likewise were found in the Tomb of the Painted Basket, Tomb 116 at Namsuri (Hamada and Koisumi 1934). A silk gauze cap discovered in the casket probably belonged to an adult male. A bundle of hair stuck with hairpins of silver, bamboo, and tortoise shell were found in another coffin along with a "circular comb-like hair ornament" (5). Hair and hairpins were also found in the third coffin. It seems that knotted hair was required even at this early date in Korea, but it is not clear whether it was a Chinese or a Korean custom. The evidence of hats and hairpins in Lelang graves suggests topknots and chignons as customary hair styles of the nobility, at least.

Growing up on the northern border of the Chinese commandary, eventually to become its conqueror, was the Koguryo kingdom. The rulers were buried in large, above-ground, stone chambers, constructed to be reentered for ancestral ceremonies and further interments. As such they were both visible on the landscape and highly accessible, allowing the tombs to be easily robbed. Tombs near the early capital in Jian (north of the Yalu river, now part of China) were plundered in antiquity, and little is left of the tomb contents. However, even though tomb contents are rare and fragmentary, painted murals with scenes of daily life as well as depictions of the noble couple themselves have left a stunning legacy, with views of the people and their activities (Kim 1982).

Daily life was depicted in some detail. Representations of men and women, elites and servants, cover the interior walls. The main tomb occupants, usually a noble married pair, often were painted the same size, sitting side by side on a covered dais. Around them servants, warriors, wrestlers, dancers, and court attendants are shown occupied in various ways. Imaginary beings in human form such as angels and tomb guardians also display their hair styles (Kim 1986; McCune 1962).

In the Koguryo tombs, men are almost always depicted with their hair covered. Exceptions are tomb guardians, wrestlers, dancers, and angels. The major male personage in the tomb wears a hat, and other men's heads are covered with one of a variety of hats, sometimes rather strange. For example, one tomb features men with headdresses that include animal heads—a cow and a horse are among the clearer paintings. Hunting scenes show men with long pheasant feathers in their caps, and men in armor wear feathers in their hats as well. It is clear that headgear for men was significant. The nobleman in the central painting usually wears a hat with some height but otherwise seems quite simple for a dignitary buried in such an elaborate tomb. Presumably the hat revealed his status in some important way.

Fifth- and sixth-century Koguryo tombs are found in the vicinity of Pyongyang, which became the Koguryo capital after the conquest of Lelang. These tombs were also robbed, but wall paintings again depict people and their hair styles. At Chinp'ari, the Twin Pillar tomb is particularly interesting (Rutt 1972:144–46). The dancers and wrestlers have hair that is expectedly controlled, but the floating angels, both male and female, have floating hair. Does the loose hair suggest that they are released from earthly constraints? In one case the central woman wears a style characterized by large loops of hair emanating from the top of her head or behind it, and her ladies in waiting have similar hair styles. This hair style appears to have been continuous into the end of the Yi dynasty, for at the time the photograph of the Yi dynasty looped style was made, the tomb paintings had not yet been rediscovered. Thus this elaborate style must have been continuous, and not an archaism introduced in the Yi dynasty.

Takamatsuzuka, an excavated tomb from the Nara period in Japan, has tomb murals that are said to reflect styles from the Paekche kingdom (Hong 1994). Thus it is important to note that the noble women painted on the tomb wall have softer-looking hair, with locks that escape from their chignons and cascade over their shoulders. A Chinese chronicle describes the hair of Paekche women as similar to the styles in the Takamatsu tomb painting. Married women wore their hair in two pinned-up braids, while the unmarried had braids that hung down their backs (Hong 1994:156).

From the contemporaneous Silla kingdom, wall paintings are rare and those that exist have for the most part, geometric patterns. However, written sumptuary laws imply something of the rules for hair styles. These laws can be further contextualized by contemporaneous archaeological finds. The construction of Silla tombs made them much harder to rob than those of the other Korean kingdoms, so that when excavated their contents are usually unlooted and relatively undisturbed. Unfortunately, few of these tombs have produced perishable artifacts, and even bones are rarely preserved in the acidic southern soil. Therefore, direct evidence of hair styles has not survived. However, many metal crowns and hats have been unearthed, made of sheet gold, gilt bronze, silver, or bronze (Yun 1980). The crowns, earrings, necklaces, and other jewelry do not appear to be gender marked, since all may appear with or without a sword, which is argued to be the only indication of a male burial (Ito 1971).

The Silla sumptuary laws controlled the use of various materials and kept everyone from rising above the rank into which they were born. The populace was divided into *kolpum*, or bone ranks. These included the *Songgol*, or Holy Bone, the *Chingol*, or True Bone, the Sixth-, Fifth-, and Fourth-Head ranks, and commoners. Each person belonged to a castelike rank and was visibly marked by the size and value of various accouterments. The sumptuary laws were broad, covering clothing, houses, carts and carriages, and riding equipment. Of particular interest here is the list of permitted and forbidden clothing, which begins in every case with what might or might not be worn on the head. The allowable materials for men's hats or head coverings are enumerated. The Holy Bone are not mentioned, presumably because no restrictions were placed upon the highest class (Kim 1977).

Some examples of headgear specifications give the flavor of the rules. True Bone men were permitted to wear hats, which may indicate that Holy Bone men wore crowns instead of hats. Members of the Sixth-Head class were allowed hats of soft but coarsely woven wool and stiff but finely woven silk and cotton cloth; the Fifth-Head class could wear a hat of raw silk or stiff but finely woven material and thin silk, while the commoners could wear only thin silk and cotton.

Women's restrictions on head gear apply to hairpins. Commoners were allowed only hairpins made of brass, stone, or lesser materials. The Fourth-Head class could use combs made of ivory, antler, and wood but were prohibited from using hairpins engraved or inlaid with gems and gold. Fifth-Head class women were allowed to use silver or lesser materials but were prohibited from wearing crowns, while the Sixth Head women are enjoined from using combs with gold decorations or hairpins inlaid with pure gold and silver with decorations of gems and jades. Head coverings had to be made of fine but sparsely woven materials such as raw silk, gauze, and thin silk. Finally, the True Bone women could not use hairpins inlaid with gems and jade, colored combs made of tortoise shells, or a crown with gold decorations simulating flowers. This last restriction suggests the crowns buried with the king and queen of Paekche in 523 (National Museum of Korea 1971), but crowns of this type have not been found in Silla graves. The tortoise shell combs hark back to Lelang tombs.

Quite aside from rank, the women's hairpins imply chignons. It is not clear whether men wore the topknot, but their hats obviously marked status. Certainly the hair and its adornments were important in the Silla kingdom. Thus, it is possible to conclude that hairstyles similar to those of the Late Yi dynasty were worn in Korea for at least two millennia and that hair styles and head coverings have long been an important marker of status. Braided hair down the back marked children and the unmarried, while hair twisted up marked adult men and hair twisted back marked adult women. It can be argued, however, that the binding became tighter as Confucianism was embraced by the upper class, although the chronological gap between the tomb murals and the Yi dynasty is a long one.

Gender Differences

For people who mattered, hair was always controlled. Wild hair was a sign of sexuality or fringe status of some sort. It is interesting, however, that simply binding the hair was enough to control its sexuality. So women in portraits and photographs are shown with uncovered heads, unlike South and Southwest Asian traditions of headcovering. It was men who covered their hair, not women. Upper-class men covered their hair completely, visibly expressing their social standing with hats rather than hair, although the topknot in traditional Korea could be seen through the loosely woven horsehair hat.

Women's social status was expressed in the elaboration of the hair as well as the richness of the hairpins, but we have no evidence that cutting a woman's hair was a life-or-death matter. The topknot riots were over men's hair, not women's. The fact that hair went uncut with the understanding that all parts of the body belonged to one's parents is relevant here. Under the Confucian scheme, the son's filial piety was more important than the daughter's, who left to join another family and bear male offspring for them. Women's hair was less relevant to the social order than that of men.

Modern Korea

The present, in terms of hair, is largely severed from the past. Hair styles in South Korea today could be found anywhere in the modern world. Haircuts stylish in New York or Paris may be found on Koreans in the streets of Seoul. Men commonly wear short to medium hair, while short, artificially curled hair is worn by adult women. Age differences in haircuts reflect those of the industrialized world. Therefore it is interesting that hair makes a statement separate from clothing. Middle-aged and older women may still be seen wearing *hanbok* for women, the *chima* and *chogori*, the long skirt and short jacket in pastel colors that is the current version of Korean women's traditional clothing. However, most women who habitually wear the *hanbok* do not style their hair as in the Yi dynasty, with the hair parted in the middle and drawn back severely into a bun at the nape of the neck. Men are still less likely to wear the national costume. Following the Korean War few men wore *hanbok* in South Korea, and then only elderly men in the countryside. Even these men probably never wore the man's topknot. Thus, while the national costume is still worn, Yi dynasty hair styles are not.

The violent emotions that accompanied the cutting of topknots is forgotten, but hair is still emotionally charged. In 1970, when the musical *Hair* was running on Broadway, and loose, shoulder-length hair on boys and young men in the United States had become a symbol of rebellion, the newspapers in Seoul frequently carried stories of police arresting young men with long hair and shearing their offensive long locks on the spot. The length of male hair was considered to be a proper concern of the state, or at least of its sanctioned police force. The meaning of long male hair was obvious in that time and context, and rebellion was not to be tolerated. Thus, shifting meanings of long hair are reflected not only in different hair styles, but in reactions to them.

Conclusion

Comparing portraits and photographs of the late Yi dynasty of Korea with earlier tomb paintings, written history, and artifacts found in burials, cases can be made for both continuity and change in Korean hair styles. On the one hand, hair gathered on the top of the head for men and on the back of the head for women seems to be continuous through time. On the other hand, women's hair knots become tighter through time, until in the late nineteenth century they are utterly severe.

The relationship of tightly bound hair to Confucianism is inferential, yet the end result of the tightened hair coincides with the late Yi dynasty, when Confucian values were at their zenith. Modernizing in South Korea suggests a loosening of Confucian controls, as well as looser hair.

In attempting to understand the differences between men's and women's hair, it is important to note that gender hierarchy is an important element of Confucianism. Because women's hair is less associated with filial piety, it is therefore less emotionally laden. Women's hair showed marital status and class—the differences among women that counted—but these categories could also be shown in other ways.

Finally, it may be that hats were considered a male privilege. As such, it was not only not important for women to cover their hair, but by doing so they would be arrogating to themselves the rights of males.

Hair, thus, was laden with meanings in Korea. Some are similar to meanings elsewhere, some are related to Confucianism, and some are uniquely Korean. This mix produced the tightly bound hair of all members of the society that characterized Korea in the late nineteenth century.

References

Bishop, Isabella Bird. 1898 [1970]. *Korea and Her Neighbours.* London: John Murray. Reprinted by Yonsei University Press, Seoul.

Deutchler, Martina. 1992. *The Confucian Transformation of Korea, A Study of Society and Ideology.* Cambridge, Mass.: Council on East Asian Studies, Harvard University.

Griffis, William Elliot. 1885. *Corea Without and Within.* Philadelphia: Presbyterian Board of Publication.

Hamada Kosaku. 1936. *On the Painting of the Han Period: Memoirs of the Research Department.* Tokyo: Toyo Bunko.

Hamada Kosaku, and Koisumi Akio. 1934. *The Tomb of the Painted Basket of Lo-lang*. Archaeological Research, vol. 1. Seoul: The Society for the Study of Korean Antiquity.

Hong, Lady. 1985. *Memoirs of a Korean Queen*. Ed. and trans. Yang-hi Choe-Wall. London: KPI.

Hong, Wontack. 1994. *Paekche of Korea and the Origin of Yamato Japan*. Seoul: Kudara International.

Hulbert, Homer B.. 1906 [1969]. *The Passing of Korea*. Reprinted, Seoul: Yonsei University Press.

Ito Akio. 1971. *Zur Chronologie der frühsillazeitlichen Gräber in Südkorea*. Bayerische Akademie der Wissenschaften, Philosophische—Historische Klasse: Munich.

Kayamoto Kamejiro. 1961. "On the Excavation of the Tomb of Wangkeng in Nangnang." *Misul Charyo* 4:17–30. (in Korean).

Kayamoto Tojin. 1962. *Han Tombs of Lo-lang: Their Studies by Japanese Scholars*. Tokyo: Memoirs of the Toyo Bunko No. 21 (in Japanese with English Summary).

Kim Chong-sun. 1977. "The Kolpum System: Basis for Sillan Social Stratification." *Journal of Korean Studies* 1(2):43–69.

Kim Ki-ung. 1982. *Tomb Paintings in Korea*. Seoul: Dong-ho (in Korean).

Kim Pu-sik. 1145 [1983]. *Samguk Sagi*. Trans. and annotated by Yi Pyong-do. Seoul: Il-yu Munhwasa.

Kim Won-yong. 1986. *Art and Archaeology of Ancient Korea*. Seoul: Taekwang Publishing Company.

Kim Yung-Chung. (ed. and trans.) 1977. *Women of Korea, A History from Ancient Times to 1945*. Seoul: Ehwa Women's University Press.

Kinsler, Arthur W. 1983. "Korean Fertility Cult for Children in Shaman Ritual and Myth." In *Korean Folklore*, Korean National Commission for UNESCO, eds, Seoul: Si-sa-yong-o-sa Publishers.

Landis, E. B. 1898. "The Capping Ceremony of Korea," *Journal of the Anthropological Institute of Great Britain and Ireland* 27:525–31.

Leach, E. R. 1958. "Magical Hair," *Journal of the Royal Anthropological Institute* 88:147–64.

McCune, Evelyn. 1962. *The Arts of Korea: An Illustrated History*. Rutland, Vt.: Charles E. Tuttle.

National Museum of Korea. 1971. *Treasures from the Tomb of King Munyong of the Paekche Dynasty*. Seoul, National Museum.

Nelson, Sarah M. 1993. "Gender Hierarchy and the Queens of Silla," In Barbara D. Miller, ed. *Sex and Gender Hierarchies*. Pp. 297–315. New York. Cambridge University Press.

Obeyeskere, Gananath. 1981. *Medusa's Hair, An Essay on Personal Symbols and Religious Experience*. Chicago: University of Chicago Press.

Pai, Hyung-il. 1989. *Lelang and the Interaction Sphere in Korean Prehistory*. PhD Dissertation, Harvard.

Parker, E. H. 1890. "On Race Struggles in Korea," *Transactions of the Asiatic Society of Japan* 23:137–228.

Pearson, Richard J. 1978. "Lolang and the Rise of Korean States and Chiefdoms." *Journal of the Hong Kong Archaeological Society* 8 (1976–1978):77–90.

Qian Hao, Chen Heyi, and Ru Suichu. 1981. *Out of China's Earth.* New York: Harry N. Abrams.

Rutt, Richard. 1972. *A Biography of James Scarth Gale and a New Edition of His History of the Korean People.* Seoul: Taewon Publishing.

Saito, R. 1939. "Japanese Coiffure," trans. M. G. Mori. Tourist Library, Board of Tourist Industry, Japanese Government Railways.

Umehara Sueji. 1926. "Deux grandes découvertes archéologiques en Corée," *Revue des Art Asiatiques* 3:24–33.

———. 1952. "Newly Discovered Tombs with Wall Paintings of the Kao-kou-li Dynasty," *Archives of the Chinese Art Society of America* 6:8–9.

Watson, Burton. 1961. *Records of the Grand Historian of China,* vol. 2. New York: Columbia University Press.

Yi Kon-mu, Lee Yong-hun, Yun Kwang-jin, and Shin Dae-gon. 1989. "Excavation of the Proto-Three Kingdoms site at Dahori, Uichang-gun," *Kogo Hakchi* 1:5–174 (in Korean).

Yun Se-young. 1980. "On the Study of Old Korean Crowns and Hats—Mainly the Crowns and Hats of the Three Kingdoms Period," *Hanguk Kogohak* 9:23–44.

6 politics of the queue: agitation and resistance in the beginning and end of qing china

weikun cheng

Anthropologists have analyzed the roles of head hair in society from several perspectives. Leach (1958) and Obeyesekere (1981) emphasize the association between hair and sexuality, although the former stresses psychological theory and the latter personal emotion and social context. Having examined individual attitudes toward social authorities, Hallpike suggests that "cutting the hair equals social control" (1969:263). I examine historical materials to explore the role of men's hair as a political symbol in China during the Qing (1644–1911) and early Republic periods (1912–1920). I find Hallpike's viewpoint the most informative since the changes in hair style were a form of social control. Political elites determined hair styles during the Qing period, and they were motivated by administrative and military forces rather than religious, social, or conventional drives. Due to the intimate relationship between hair and political control, variation of political conditions led to changing symbolic meanings of hair. In this chapter I analyze why and how changes in hair style occurred during the transition periods at the beginning and end of the Qing. I explore what hair styles symbolized under different social circumstances, and how hair styles induced ethnic and cultural conflict.

The Manchus and Han Hair Style Change

The Qing government was not the first to regulate people's hair styles. Some religions, such as Buddhism, Hinduism, and Christianity, have rules on tonsure. Soldiers and convicts provide other examples of hair cutting or shaving under discipline (Firth 1973:283; Hallpike 1969). The Manchu rulers, however, were probably unique in the stress they placed on the political significance of men's hair dressing, and in their willingness to compel by force so huge a population to adopt an alien headdress.

Cross-cultural evidence demonstrates that hair has social and personal significance. Hair styles can indicate not only an individual's aesthetic preference but also social differences, varying according to age, sex, marital, and other status (Firth 1973:271). The Qing queue style reduced both of these functions of hair to a minimum. Under the Qing regime, it was difficult for a male to make a personal statement symbolically with his hair or to express his aesthetic taste in hair fashion. A foreigner once noticed that queues were incompatible with the colorful fashions of people's clothes:

> The full costume of both sexes is, in general terms commodious and graceful, combining all the purposes of warmth, beauty, and ease, which could be desired; excepting always the shaven crown and braided queue of the men, and the crippled stumps of the women, in both of which fashions they have not less outraged nature than deformed themselves. (Williams 1848. 2:29).

Like a woman's bound feet, which embodied the physical and moral restrictions of women by men's power, a Han male's queue reflected the Manchus drive to submit Hans to the minority's political and cultural hegemonies and its symbolic standardization of the people's political ideology.

Long before the Manchu conquest, Han males had become accustomed to the practice of binding up their long hair on the top of their heads. This custom is inferred by such idioms as "to bind hair when starting school" (*sufa shoushu*), or "to bind hair while being a soldier" (*Jiefa congrong*). When a student was twenty years old, he ought to have a "capping ceremony" (*guanli*) in which he changed his child's headdress to an adult's, demonstrating his entrance into the mature world. This tradition can be traced back to the Zhou dynasty (1100–256 B.C.) (SSJZS 1:945). Under the Ming regime, the ceremony was adopted by more social categories than the scholar-official class (Zhang 3:1377–87). Ming men, once capped, let their hair grow long, and wore it in elaborate fashion under horsehair caps (Ricci 1953:78).

The change of the traditional headdress started before the Manchus had entered the Great Wall, when some Chinese denoted their submission to the new rulers through taking the queue style (Kuhn 1990:53). The regent Dorgon, uncle of the young emperor Fulin, first announced the hair-cutting policy on June 5, 1644 (Wakeman 1985. 1:420). Objections of Han collaborators and peasants' rebellions near Beijing shook his determination on the tonsure (Xie Guozhen 1956:50, 61–62). Upon occupying Nanjing, however, he issued a decree formally requiring all Chinese to shave their foreheads and plait their hair in a queue like the Manchus. Chinese men had to conform to the new rulers' hair style. Disobedience would be "equivalent to a rebel's defying the Mandate (of Heaven)" (*ni-ming*) (SZSL 17:7b–8). Having accepted the Confucian notion that the ruler was like a father and the subjects like his sons, Dorgon emphasized the physical resemblance between the Manchus and the conquered Chinese. The affirmed purpose was to make Manchus and Hans a unified body. Being afraid of inspiring any anti-Manchu imaginations and actions, the Qing rulers enforced the hair cutting policy and persecuted hair growers without mercy.

A slogan of the tonsure operators was "Keep your head, lose your hair; keep your hair, lose your head" (Wakeman 1975a:58), which epitomized the ruthlessness of the Manchu's hair cutting. In those days, local governments sent armed barbers to search for people who had kept their long hair. If the latter refused to accept the tonsure, they were killed immediately and their heads were hanged on the barbers' poles (Li 1955:11). Kuhn provides two cases in which a military licentiate of Gansu Province and a peasant of Hubei Province were executed because they had retained frontal hair (1990:56–58).

The tonsure command was reminiscent of the infamous edict of 1129, when the Jin decided to shave the heads of the "southern people" (*nan min*) after the fall of Kaifeng (Trauzettel 1975:206). Lack of cultural confidence and an interest in establishing an awe-inspiring image might account for the Manchus' enthusiasm in the hair-shaving campaign. Originating from frontier tribes, Manchu rulers were sensitive to the sneers of Han officials and literati who preferred the "System of Rites and Music" of the defeated Ming Dynasty. "If officials say that people should not respect our Rites and Music but rather follow those of the Ming," Dorgon asked, "what can be their true intentions?" (Shan 1979: 4:260). The queue style, plus Manchu clothes and caps, would physically remind the Han scholar-official class of the new political masters, as well as undermine their sense of cultural superiority.[1]

The breakdown of the Ming regime perhaps provoked the Han people's resistance less than the order of tonsure, which offended their cultural self-respect. The harsh execution of the hair-cutting rules further exacerbated the resentment of the local communities. In the lower Yangzi cities local gentry, along with merchants, craftsmen, and peasants, organized militia units to protect their communities and their bodily integrity. They expelled or killed local collaborators, claimed to be Ming loyalists, and withstood the Manchus' military suppressions, which usually caused heavy loss of lives and properties (Li 1955:10–32; Wakeman 1985. 1:651–80; Yang 1912. 3:8–16). After the pacification of the rebellions, many scholars attempted to avoid the hair-cutting orders by hiding behind their villa walls, sheltered from public view by friends and servants (Gu *Tinglin yuji*, 24a; Ji 283; Yang 1912:3:10).

The Hans' stubborn resistance to the tonsure might be explained by their belief in hair's magical power. Some anthropologists such as Frazer argue that "ritual hair symbolizes some kind of metaphysical abstraction—fertility, soul-stuff, personal power." Leach suggests that people unconsciously connect hair with genitalia (1958). This might be true in Chinese popular culture, in which hair is believed to absorb and store spiritual power. In Cantonese funerals, women rub their hair against the coffin to enhance fertility and lineage continuity (Watson 1982:173). In his research on soul stealing, Kuhn explores the Chinese assumption that hair could be used to extract soul force and strengthen one's power (1990:1–29, 71–118). Chinese faith in the power of human hair led them to emphasize the healthy function of hair. In their view, the function of hair was to protect the brain. If hair was shaved, the scalp would be exposed to the air, which would cause illness. A widespread rumor in the late Ming connected the tonsure to brain injury and death (Yang 1912.3:8–16; SLXS 1:747).

The Chinese tendency to maintain their hair uncut was also a result of the Confucian fear of bodily mutilation. Hair cutting contravened Mencian injunctions to preserve one's parents' progeny intact (Wakeman 1985.1:648). According to the *Xiaojing* (*Classic of Filial Piety*), which appeared in the East Han period (A.D. 25–220), a son was able to accomplish great filial piety through honoring his parents in two ways: preserving his bodily integrity and achieving high social status and prestige. Since hair, like other parts of the human body, was inherited from one's parents, to abuse hair meant to humiliate the older generation or to offend the spirits of one's ancestors (SSJZS 2:2545). For instance, Hua Yuncheng, a member of the Donglin faction in the Late Ming, was arrested by the Qing government because he refused to wear the queue. Before his execution, he addressed his "departed parents, generations of ancestors, and spirits in Heaven," saying, "Yuncheng's hair cannot be cut, nor will his body surrender" (Wen 1830:228–29).

Additionally, Hans rejected the Manchu headdress partly because hair shaving had been a traditional form of penalty and made the shaved shameful. In the penal code of the Qin Dynasty (221–206 B.C.), shaving (of head hair and beard), together with tattooing and mutilation, was cataloged as a humiliation to be inflicted on slaves and convicts (Kuhn 1990:58–59). The punishment consisting of an iron collar and a shaven head was also employed during the Han Dynasty (206 B.C.–A.D. 220) (Hulsewe 1955.1:129). This shameful punishment may have been retained for centuries.[2]

In contrast, caring for and protecting hair was a component of Confucian rites. According to the *Liji* (*Book of Rites*), a man's hair should be neat and be protected by a cap. Only upon the death of his parents could he publicly unbind his hair and unbuckle his clothes to exhibit his sorrow (SSJZS 1:1301). Down to the Ming Dynasty, carefully preserved long hair was a necessary element of the scholar-official image. Foreign missionaries in China during the late Ming provide vivid depictions of hair styles of the scholar-official class. Father Martin de Rada wrote: "They are proud to have a great head of hair. They let it grow long and coil it up in a knot on the crown of the head. They then put it in a hairnet parted in the center to hold and fix the hair in position, wearing on top of it a bonnet made of horsehair. This is their ordinary headgear, although their captains' bonnets are of another kind made of finest thread and underneath a hairnet of gold thread. They take a good time each morning in combing and dressing their hair" (Boxer 1953:282).

The Han hair style was treasured by Confucian literati as distinguishing Chinese culture from that of "barbarians." The identification of barbarism with strange dress and hair styles goes back to the *Analects*, where Confucius, praising Guan Zhong for having kept out the barbarians, said: "But for Guan Zhong, we should now be wearing our hair unbound, and the lappets of our coats would button on the left side" (SSJZS 2:2512). Civilizing the barbarians by teaching them the Chinese rites, rather than adopting the customs of barbarians, was one of Mencius's doctrines (2:2706). Long and bound-up hair was the symbol of Chinese civilization. It was also an institutional component of the Great Ming, for both the emperor and his subjects shared the same hair style. This belief accounted for many Ming loyalists' disobedience of the tonsure orders, at the expense of their career prospects or even their lives (Yang 1912.3:10–16). According to the common folk, the Manchu tonsure would undermine their manhood. Some peasant mobs became involved in the anti-Manchu riots because they were convinced that hair cutting would make them lose their wives (Wakeman 1985.1:650).

The Manchu rulers' success in subjecting the vast population to their control was symbolized by the universal acceptance of the queue-style headdress. To shave the head and wear a queue became a measure of a person's loyalty toward the Qing throne. Hair growing was a sign of political resistance. Rebels, such as the Taiping Army, would grow their hair to show their opposition to the Qing rule. For the Han Chinese, the queue hair style embodied the alien conquest, the power of autocracy, and the downfall of traditional rites and cultural pride.[3]

The Queue-Cutting Campaign

If the Hans' acceptance of the queue style at the beginning of Qing signified their obedience to the Manchu court, then queue cutting at the end of the dynasty denoted their attempt to get rid of Manchu autocratic dominance. The change did not mean the restoration of the Han empire and the traditional culture but rather the establishment of a modern nation-state with a Westernized life style.

The nineteenth century witnessed the decline of imperial China in the face of outside imperialistic forces. Although the Manchu administration had tried different approaches to overcome the national crisis, its incompetent and corrupt image was too firmly established to be altered. In the early twentieth century, radical intellectuals, believing in the necessity of establishing a Western-style government that could build an industrialized society and obtain equal status in the world, launched the anti-Manchu movement. They used the headdress issue to arouse the Han population, since it reminded them of their humiliation and oppression by the Manchu conquerors.

The anti-Manchu agitation was based on the premise that the Manchus to a certain extent were still estranged from the Han mainstream. Manchu rulers maintained their cultural identity by living apart from Han Chinese in garrison cities, They outlawed intermarriage between Manchus and Chinese. Maintaining a homeland base in Manchuria, they retained their skills in archery and horsemanship, the use of their native language, and customs (Crossley 1990:13–30). In spite of the increasing accommodation between Manchus and Hans during the late Qing period, Manchus never ceased to discriminate against Hans in the bureaucracy. Manchus enjoyed hereditary aristocratic status, preferential treatment, and privileges in official recruitment and promotion.[4]

The revolutionaries disputed with the pro-Manchu reformers, such as Kang Yuwei, who asserted that the Manchu headdress and clothes were proper to retain because Manchu and Han had been already assimilated (SLXJ 1:213). The revolutionaries insisted on the oppressive nature of the tonsure (SLXJ 1:662; QKJS 2:483). Wang Jingwei, an editor of *The People's Journal* (*Minbao*), emphasized the headdress as an important "ethnic symbol" (SLXJ 2:92). In his opinion, the Manchu tonsure, barbarized Hans and eliminated their cultural identity. Along with Cheng Qubing and other revolutionary writers, Wang condemned the cruelty and bloodiness of the Manchu tonsure, and praised the loyalty and integrity of Ming scholars and officials who refused to collaborate with the Manchu rulers by preserving their traditional headdress (QKJS 2:363–64; SLXJ 1:747–48, 2:92–93).

To arouse Hans' anti-Manchu sentiments did not mean that the revolutionaries intended to reestablish a new dynasty with the "impressive and dignified manner of the Han bureaucrats" (*hanguan weiyi*). In their view, the change of hair style was associated with the political transformation. In the Meiji Restoration, the Japanese imitated Western-style headdress and clothes, thus furthering the process of modernization. The Chinese also needed a series of changes, from hair style and clothing to political behavior on the Western model (SLXJ 1:472–75). "The Manchu hedge cannot be destroyed unless its symbol is abolished," an anonymous writer affirmed. Once the "burdensome, foul, and repugnant stuff" was abandoned, the Qing's despotic system could be transformed (SLXJ 1:748).

Support for queue cutting reflected the growing nationalism. In the late Qing, nationalism included two aspects: one involved overthrowing the Manchu government and establishing a new republic ruled by Hans; the other was withstanding the incursions of imperialism and building up an independent and strong China. The queue style, a source of foreign ridicule and insults, such as "pigtail," "the tailed lackey," and "half-shaved monk," was apparently detrimental to China's international prestige (QKJS 2:483, 3:275). The author of "Lun bianfa yuanyu" ("On the reasons of changing hair style") remarked: "A Chinese male has his forehead shaved and wears a queue on his back, looking like a rope, a chain, or an animal tail. In so doing, he inevitably has a sense of inferiority, leaving aside how he looks to others" (SLXJ 1:746). Another writer satirized some overseas students who maintained queues to "make the motherland humiliated and themselves derided" (QKJS 2:488). The change of hair style would renovate the national image, on the one hand, depriving foreigners of an excuse to attack China. On the other hand, it would symbolize Chinese aspirations to construct a new country.

The proposal to change the Manchu headdress was also justified by social Darwinism (see Dikötter, this volume). Introduced into China at the turn of the century, the theories of Darwin and Spencer, especially their notions of grouping and progress, had become the ideological foundation of Chinese intellectuals. The humiliating experience of contact with the foreign powers, and the infusion of Western technological inventions, humanistic and scientific knowledge, and institutions, impressed the Chinese with the strength of the industrialized West. The radical students were thus convinced that the only way for China to survive in global competition was to learn from the West. For them, Western headdress and clothing style were more hygienic, aesthetic, and practical, representing a higher level of cultural progress. By comparison, the Chinese headdress, impeding the people's physical mobility and hampering their work, could not keep abreast of the times and bring any advantages to the nation (SLXJ 1:472–73). The author of "Lun bianfa yuanyu" even generalized that the hair binding of the ancient Chinese, the queue wearing of Manchus, and the short hair of Westerners were three stages in the evolutionary process of Chinese headdress (SLXJ 1:474, 748). Some writers asserted that only when Chinese adopted the Western hair style and clothing could they develop an independent character. A suitable headdress and clothes style could promote Chinese access to foreigners and make it convenient for them to study Western politics, laws, technology, and marketing systems (SLXJ 1:748, 1:474). The queue cutting hence was highlighted as a medium of learning from the West and a pathway to China's modernization.

In spite of the queue cutting propaganda, only a small group of intellectuals were dauntless enough to discard their queues and change their hair and clothes to the Western style in the late Qing. In most cases, this action meant a break with the Manchu government.[5] Those who changed their headdress, including overseas Chinese, new students, and Christians, were mocked by the majority (NCCTBJ 1, n.p.). Sometimes they wore artificial queues to avoid the sneers of others, to conceal their revolutionary inclinations, or to be able to hold office (Mao 1936, 20:18–23; HYL 1:612; DGB 10/16/1903).

Meanwhile, a few reformers in officialdom started to consider the beneficial effects of altering the queue style, hoping to improve the image of the government in the world and to inspire people's fervor for the project of nation making. It was reported that Zaize and Dai Hongci, members of the Constitutional Studies' Commission sent abroad by the court in 1905, attempted to persuade the Empress Dowager, Cixi, to adopt a queue-cutting policy after they returned home (DGB 9/10/1906). The suggestion was echoed occasionally by other officials as well. But the court, afraid of losing its political mastery, firmly rejected the proposal (DGB 11/28/1911). It was not until after the Wuchang Uprising in October 1911 that the court finally approved the queue-cutting bill passed by the Central Assembly (XWXTK 2:9296).

After the Uprising of 1911, queue cutting, like the Manchu tonsure over two hundred years earlier, became the critical mark of changing political positions. The governments of the independent provinces, such as Hubei and Jiangsu, soon ordered a change of headdress (MLB 10/29/1911, SEB 1/10/1912). Sun Yat-sen, the provisional president of the Nanjing government, promulgated a decree requiring people to abandon their queues within twenty days on March 5, 1912.

The queue-cutting campaign was supported by many social reform societies and the public media controlled by the new intellectuals. A variety of queue cutting societies surfaced throughout the country (SEB 12/7/1911, 1/1, 1/3, 1/10, 2/8/1912; MLB 12/12/1911). Mass rallies involving queue-cutting were also held periodically in cities and towns (MLB 11/23/1911). The momentum was reinforced by the Westernized literati who published uncountable editorials, commentaries, poems, and essays on the subject. The column of "Free Talk" in *Shenbao*, for instance, was a major base of attacking the Manchus' style of hair and dress.

The administrative decrees, the societies' activities, and the Republican propaganda together mobilized the populace to do away with queues, especially in the urban areas of the south. Although we lack statistical data to indicate the percentage of the population who cut their queues, scattered records suggest that the common people zealously participated in the campaign. In Guangdong 200,000 men cut their queues on the day provincial independence was declared (Dahan rexinren 456). Students of Changsha at Hunan Province scissored all the queues they could find in school and on the street (HYL 2:194). Even in Japanese-administered Taiwan "the mood of queue-cutting began to be popular in the urban areas, finally spreading into the countryside" (HYL 4:510).

Many elements accounted for the people's support of the queue-cutting policy. The New Policies Reform in the late Qing resulted in an increase of taxation, reinforcing popular dissatisfaction with the Qing government. Its failure to protect the nation's sovereignty and rights made the court a common target of different social groups. The widely circulated newspapers and journals of the late Qing made anti-Qing arguments more accessible to the commoners. When the Republican revolution occurred, people expected an efficient administration, a democratic system, lighter taxation, and higher international status for the nation. They changed their headdress to show their conversion to the new regime.

Since the lower classes were less subject to Western influence and continued to hold traditional beliefs in the magical power of hair, they treated the queue cutting more seriously and ritualistically than the new intellectuals. A contemporary of the revolution described the situation:

> When the Qing court was overthrown, innumerable Han people happily had their queues—the marks of servitude—cut. Some superstitious people chose the auspicious date in advance, and then, having held a memorial ceremony for their ancestors, solemnly cut and burned their queues. Some persons preferred to scissor their queues on the same day with others. When the ritual was finished, they set off firecrackers and held parties to celebrate. (Xu and Xu 1956:16)

A similar procedure for queue cutting was observed by Liang Ruosheng's father, a farmer of Guangdong Province. The only difference was that the latter offered sacrifices to the gods he worshiped at home in order to exorcise evil spirits before the change of hair style (HYL 2:363–64). These signs of popular superstition reflected the length of time the population had worn the Manchu headdress, the norm of nonmutilation that had survived the early Qing tonsure and blocked further hair cutting, and concerns about the instability of the political situation.

Hair style was closely associated with mode of dress. After the unfolding of the queue-cutting campaign, a parallel clothes-changing movement took place. Commoners detested the clothes and the personal adornment of the Qing dynasty because they embodied hierarchical ritual institutions and values. As the revolution transformed the polity, the feather hats, official uniforms, mandarin jackets, and ornaments that masked imperial prerogative and ethnic oppression were discarded (Hu 1923:3 Jingzhao, 27). The dress reform simulated the West. People were so attracted by Western-style clothes and hats that their demands for imported goods and related raw materials shot up (SEB 4/3/1912).

Resistance to Queue Cutting

Although queue cutting became a political requirement for the new government, many Han people, especially in the hinterland or in the north where the new concepts had not reached, still insisted on the Qing headwear. Even in the south, where the new government endeavored to carry out the hair style-changing policy, a proportion of the population withstood the tendency.

An important section of queue-wearing people were from the lower classes. The main reason for their retention of queues was probably custom. As Firth argues, hair styles could be strongly conventionalized, given moral approval, and used as instruments of social expression and social control (1973:271). In the north and in some peripheral areas, laborers in urban areas and peasants in the countryside tended to maintain queues, ignoring the changed political situation. For example, in Beijing, two months after the establishment of the Republic, laborers and servants still had their long queues and wore the old-style hats (SEB 4/15/1912). A similar phenomenon could be found in Jinan, Shandong Province, where most of the coolies wore queues (Hu 1923:3 Shandong, 15). Huang Danlu, a contemporary legislator of Jiangsu Province, once pointed out that peasants of his province had no political concerns. "They view the queue-style headdress as an unalterable custom only because it is a 268-year-old practice. Offspring take over the queue-wearing convention from their ancestors and never think about its ethnic or political meanings" (SIB 3/16/1912). There is much evidence of strong social discrimination against persons who turned to short hair in undeveloped regions. Isolation or illiteracy may also have contributed to the lower classes' continued practice of the Qing headdress.

In contrast to the lower classes, many members of the scholar-official class firmly resisted queue cutting. Some diehards preserved queues to demonstrate their political devotion to the former dynasty and their abhorrence of Republican authority. For instance, when the Republic was set up, Zhao Erxun, governor-general of Manchuria, together with Qi Yaoling, governor of Henan Province, had many persons arrested and executed for the "crime" of not having queues (SEB 2/15/1912). Another famous opponent was Liang Dinfen, an editor of the Imperial Academy, who declared at the end of 1912 that "I would rather have my head cut off than have my queue lost" (SIB 12/25/1912). Shengyong, governor-general of Shanxi and Gansu provinces, went so far as to kill his son because he changed his headdress (SIB 5/5/1912). Records of Xinghua, Songyang, Lingpuo, and Tianjin show that officials and degree holders in these areas hoped for the restoration of the Qing dynasty and preserved their queues as evidence of their political commitment (HYL 8:111, 4:203; Hu 1923:3, Zhili, 75; MLB 12/28/1911).

Some members of local elites, while working in the new government for personal purposes, were concerned that the Qing dynasty might be revived and left their options open by keeping queues. For example, Wang Hesheng, vice chairman of the assembly of Haifeng County, Shandong Province, tried to organize opposition to the queue-cutting proposal made by the assembly's chairman (SIB, 1/9/1913). Gu Qiulan, the head of the assembly of Shanyi County, Jiangsu Province, took advantage of his influence to block the queue-cutting act (SEB 1/12/1912). Gentry members in many areas invented diverse methods to protect queues or leave the possibility of returning to the queue style. They simulated the dress mode of the Han dynasty in which a person covered his coiled queue with a square scarf and wore a large robe, or mimicked the Taoist hair style in which a person ceased to shave his forehead and wore all his hair gathered into a high bun on the top of his head (MLB 12/28/1911; SEB 11/18/1912). Sometimes they simply hid their queues in clothes or went out by a sedan (SEB 1/14/1912). The local elite's efforts to protect their queues made the hair fashions of the early Republic diverse and colorful, mirroring specific patterns of the transitional society.

Confucian concepts of filial piety that once justified the traditional hair style gradually turned into the cornerstone of the queue style. Examples of this shift can be found in Jiangsu, Zhejing, and Xinjiang provinces, where elements of the gentry took the norms of loyalty and filiality as weapons to withstand the queue-cutting movement (HYL 4:203–204, 8:111; SIB 9/15/1912). According to Xu Ke's *Ke Yian* (*Frankly Talking*), even ten years after the collapse of the Qing court, queue wearers could still be seen everywhere in the country. They argued that since the queue was a part of the Qing institutions, to cut it meant to forget the retired monarch. The queue was also inherited from one's parents and to scissor it meant that one could no longer be a filial son (Xu Ke 1923.3:23). Some queue bearers even defended queue keeping as the Chinese cultural tradition. A typical tone can be heard in an anonymous letter received by the Assembly of Tianjin city after the Wuchang Uprising. The writer attributed the queue-wearing custom to the filial rules of the ancient Chinese sages, while condemning short hair, together with newspapers, new schools, and new women, as Western evils (DGB 12/23/1911). Clearly, the Manchu tonsure did not destroy the deeply rooted beliefs underlying the traditional hair style. The hair that remained after shaving the forehead was as valued as before by Chinese. The norm of antimutilation implied rejection of cutting the queue.

Along with the notion of filial piety, political loyalty was another pillar of the queue style maintained by the official gentry members. The establishment of the Qing dynasty was a process in which the Manchu ruling group and the Han intellectuals altered their relationship from conflict to collaboration. At the beginning, many Han official-gentry members refused to recognize the legitimacy of the Manchu regime, so they excluded the queue-wearing style from the Confucian cultural repertoire. This situation, however, soon changed. On the one hand, the Manchu throne played the role of the Chinese Son of Heaven, adopted Confucian doctrines and the Ming institutions,[6] and spared no pains to draw Han intellectuals into the bureaucracy (Naquin and Rawski 1987:3–21). On the other hand, Han scholar-officials, apart from their personal ambitions, also wished to contribute to social order and welfare. Consequently the two parties rallied together to rule the country. The Han gentry's commitment to the Qing might be marked by the success of the special examination (*buoxue hongci*), arranged by Kangxi in 1679. Even Ming loyalists appreciated the emperor's deference in their direction and encouraged friends and relatives to enroll for the examination (Wakeman 1975b:92). Inasmuch as the Han intellectuals recognized Qing legitimacy, they accepted Manchu queues and clothes as the marks of their political allegiance to the Qing throne.

Unrest Over the Queue-Cutting Issue

As the queue cutting issue was related to the conflict between the new and old forces and ideologies, it gave rise to many disturbances and incidents of unrest around the country. On the one hand, the new government saw queue-cutting as a political task, and pursued a hardline policy to accomplish it, which invited popular resentment. On the other hand, those who were discontented with the Republic or the reforms usually took advantage of the queue-cutting issue to agitate against them. Therefore, the clash over queue cutting became more acute.

The revolutionary leaders depended on administrative means to eliminate queues, and demonstrated both impatience and brutality. They expected people to give up the long-established custom in a short time. The allotted time of the Nanjing Provisional Government was twenty days. In Hubei, Zhejiang, and Yunnan, the deadlines were even stricter (SEB 2/8, 11/1/1912).

For those who refused to discard their queues, the punishments were extreme. Many local governments treated queue wearers as enemies. In 1912 a few senators in Beijing even put forward a proposal to deprive queue wearers of the franchise (DGB 11/20/1912). More terrible was the use of coercive methods. When the deadline was reached, local officials often sent soldiers or policemen to cut queues on the road, which caused widespread panic and upset the social order. In Shanghai, soldiers angered local people by cutting their queues on the street, and civilian activists followed their example. Peasants in the suburbs were afraid of going downtown (MLB 12/31/1911). The same molestations occurred in Hangzhou, Zhengjiang, Nanjing, and Kunming, where compulsory queue cutting aroused popular indignation (SEB 1/29, 2/3/1912).

The government's policy of queue cutting was responsible for some mutinies and riots. For instance, a company of soldiers in Huangxian County, Shandong Province, rebelled against the queue-cutting order issued by the magistrate, and bandits seized the opportunity to rob and burn (SEB 11/1/1912). Wang Gengyian, the magistrate of Guangxing District, Jiangxi Province, was murdered by somebody who hated his harsh supervision of queue cutting (SEB 2/10/1912). The hair-changing campaign provoked a shopkeepers' strike in Yantai, Shandong Province. A group of merchants who treasured their queues shut down their businesses to protest the official enforcement of the alteration of headdress (SEB 7/24/1912).

Opposition to queue cutting was still more complicated. Besides the miscalculations of the government that brought about turmoil, some conservative forces also exploited the queue issue to rebel against the Republic. In these efforts, secret societies took the lead. Some secret organizations, such as the Elder-Brother Society in the Yangzi region, participated in the anti-Qing revolution. But they were distinguished from the Republicans by their backward-looking political purposes, xenophobic inclinations, and destructiveness. Revolutionary control of society restrained their banditlike behavior. Since political and social reforms after 1911 represented an attempt to Westernize China, they opposed the new regime and most of its reforms. In particular, they expressed their distate for short hair.

In the case of the Queue-Protection Society (Baobianhui) of Chuzhou, Zhejiang Province, agitators made use of the people's dislike of the queue-cutting policy to serve their own interests. Tang Yuguang, head of a secret society, collected a thousand people and organized a Militarist Society. Allied with the Queue-Protection Society, he broke into the local government office and demanded the return of a fine. His group violated the prohibition on opium and gambling, and seized money and grain collected as taxes by the government (SEB 5/1/1912).

A second incident included the Society for Restoring Ancient Ways (Fuguhui) in the border area of Hubei and Sichuan Provinces, where the Elder-Brother Society and the White Lotus sect were active. When local officials ordered people to discard queues, the secret societies spread rumors that queue cutting meant becoming like foreigners. Then they established the Society for Restoring Ancient Ways, in which many gentry members joined, coiling their hair on top of their heads and adopting the Taoist dress mode. Besides the queue-protection activities, they also grew opium, and prepared munitions for rebellion (SEB 5/17/1912). The behavior of the anti-queue-cutting group here is obviously related to its antiforeign and reactionary attitude.

The Elder-Brother Society of Wudang Mountain is the third case. Cao Xongfei, head of the society, led his followers in an occupation of Wudang Mountain, with the aim of resisting the queue-cutting movement. He proclaimed himself the Protecting Emperor's General and declared publicly:

> Recently I went to Beijing and had an audience with Pu Yi, the retired monarch. He looked like a real Son of Heaven and might regain his position after five year's adversity. By that time, all the pro-Western parties and the lackeys of foreign masters will be eliminated naturally. So now I am going to train a 100,000 man army to protect the emperor. (SEB 5/31/1912)

The group aimed at rejuvenating the Qing's dominance, but they regarded the Qing emperor as a representative of Chinese tradition rather than a minority ruler.

Except for the first case, in which the main motive was personal avarice rather than the hair conflict, societies defended queues as the symbol of the Chinese autocracy and traditional institutions vis-a-vis Western cultural invasions. This phenomenon indicated that the queue-cutting issue embodied more the confrontation between the new, Westernized trend and the old, Chinese tradition than it did any Man-Han racial conflict.

Hair Politics

This case shows how hair became a means of social control and a focus of cultural and political conflict. In traditional China men's long and bound-up hair epitomized the Confucian norm of filial piety, Han culturalism, and magical power. During the Qing dynasty, the shaved forehead and queue symbolized Manchu autocratic authority and its cultural dominance, though Han Chinese still held a moral and respectful attitude toward their hair. After the fall of the Qing court, short hair replaced the queue style, embodying nationalism and Westernization. In Chinese consciousness of hair, moral discipline is more perceivable than sexual restraint. Cutting hair is more critical than the change of hair style. In the periods under consideration, hair cutting meant social control, not only supported by the conventionalized and morally approved fashions, but also regulated and supervised by the political authorities.

This control, however, does not conform to Hallpike's simple formulation: long hair=being outside society; cutting hair=reentering society (1969). The form of social control varied with the changing historical context. In the Ming and before, long hair=S.C.; cutting hair=anti-S.C. During the Qing Dynasty, tonsure head (and queue)=S.C.; full hair and short hair=anti-S.C. After the Revolution of 1911, short hair=S.C.; tonsured head (and queue)=anti-S.C.

Why was the hair issue so important in modern China that both political rulers and the ruled ardently fought over it? The notable position of hair in Confucian rites and philosophy enhanced the significance of hair style in the Qing and early Republican periods. Chinese respect for their elders and pride in their cultural legacy strengthened the stability of hair fashions and their function as a medium of political and social transformation. The Man-Han ethnic conflict probably dramatized the significance of hair style and made it possible to use hair as a tool in political and cultural contests.

Notes

*I thank Professors William T. Rowe and Emily Martin for their guidance and help.

1. The regulations on costumes in the Qing dynasty were enforced through oppressive orders promulgated by the Manchu court. Costumes of the Qing dynasty were influenced by the nomadic clothes of the Manchus. The lower part of a man's gown was cut into four vertical sections to facilitate horse riding. The gown was always covered by a short overcoat covering the upper part of the body. The sleeves were long and narrow so that a rider could pull down his sleeves to keep his hands warm when riding in cold weather.

2. In many societies, enforced cutting or shaving of hair may convey contempt and degradation, and extreme reduction in status. For example, in some countries that had been occupied by the Germans during World War II, after the liberation, some women accused of collaboration with the invaders, especially those who gave sexual favors, had their heads forcibly shaved (Firth 1973:289).

3. An eighth-century European analogy of hair cutting, though on a smaller scale, is Pippin's shearing of the heads of Merovingian chieftains in order to establish political hegemony over the Franks (Wallace-Hadrill 1982:156–58, 244–47).

4. Whether or not the Manchus maintained their cultural identity is a controversial question. There are basically two opinions. One is represented by Wright (1957) who asserts that the Manchus had been gradually sinicized and that, after the Taiping Rebellion, the Man-Han ethnic conflict became insignificant. The other has been advanced by Crossley (1990) and Elliot (1990) who stress the Manchus' cultural alienation from the Han Chinese mainstream.

5. Zhang Taiyan cut his queue in 1900, demonstrating his determination to rebel against the Qing court (QKJS 1:42–43).

6. Due to their minority origins, the Manchu rulers made even more strenuous efforts to indoctrinate Confucian norms in order to consolidate their dominance, such as reading the Sacred Edict at public performances, establishing the new rape law, praising chastity of women, emphasizing the Confucian teachings in the examination system, and encouraging the patriarchal system of lineage building.

References

Boxer, C. R., ed. 1953. *South China in the Sixteenth Century: Being the Narratives of Galeote Pereira; Fr. Gaspar da Cruz, O.P.; Fr. Martin de Rada.* O.E.S.A. (1550–1575). London: Hakluyt Society.

Crossley, Pamela K. 1990. *Orphan Warriors: Three Manchu Generations and the End of the Qing World.* Princeton, N.J.: Princeton University Press.

Dahan rexinren. 1961. "Guangdong duli ji" (Record of Guangdong Independence). In Zhongguo kexueyuan jindai shisuo, ed., *Xinhai geming ziliao* (Materials on the Revolution of 1911). Beijing: Zhonghua shuju. 1:435–71.

DGB *Dagong bao* (Great public). Tianjin, 1902–? Microfilms. Beijing: Zhongguo guojia tushuguan. 1978.

Elliot, Mark. 1990. "Bannermen and Townsmen: Ethnic Tension in Nineteenth-Century Jiangnan," *Late Imperial China* 11(1):36–74.

Firth, Raymond W. 1973. *Symbols: Public and Private*. Ithaca, N.Y.: Cornell University Press.

Gu Yanwu. 1966. *Tinglin shiwen ji* (A collection of the prose and poetry of Tinglin). Sibu beiyao ed. Taibei: Zhonghua shuju. This ed. includes *Tinglin shiji*, 5 juan; *Tinglin wenji*, 6 juan; *Tinglin yuji*, 26 pp.

Hallpike, C. D. 1969. "Social Hair," *Man* 4(2):256–64.

Hu Puan. 1923. *Zhonghua quanguo fengsu zhi* (Popular culture in China). 4 ce. Shanghai: Guangyi shudian.

Hulsewe, A. F. P. 1955. *Remnants of Han Law*. 2 vols. Leiden: E. J. Brill.

HYL. 1981–1982. *Xinhai geming huiyilu* (Reminiscences of the Revolution of 1911). Ed. Zhongguo renmin zhengzhi xieshang huiyi quanguo weiyuanhui, wenshi ziliao yanju weiyuanhui. 8 vols. Beijing: Wenshi ziliao chubanshe.

Ji liuqi. 1671. *Mingji nanlue* (An outline of the southern *regime* of Ming dynasty). Taiwan wenxian congkan no. 148. 3 vols. Taibei: Bank of Taiwan, 1963.

Kuhn, Philip A. 1990. *Soulstealers: The Chinese Sorcery Scare of 1768*. Cambridge, Mass.: Harvard University Press.

Leach, Edmund R. 1958. "Magical Hair," *Journal of the Royal Anthropological Institute* 88:147–64.

Li Tianyou. 1955. *Mingmo Jiangyin Jiading renminde kangqing douzheng* (The anti-Qing struggles of Jiangyin and Jiading people in the late Ming). Shanghai: Xuexi shenghuo chubanshe.

Mao, Dun. 1936. "Xinhai niande guangtou jiaoyuan yu jianbian yundong" (Bald teachers and the queue-cutting movement in 1911). In *Yefeng* (Wind of the south) (semimonthly, Shanghai) 20:18–23.

MLB *Minli bao* (By the people). Shanghai, 1910–13. Microfilms in Beijing Library.

Naquin, Susan, and Evelyn S. Rawski. 1987. *Chinese Society in the Eighteenth Century*. New Haven, Conn.: Yale University Press.

NCCTBJ *Nancun caotang biji* (Notes of Nancun cottage). Privately printed, N. A. D. P.

Obeyesekere, Gananath. 1981. *Medusa's Hair: An Essay on Personal Symbols and Religious Experience*. Chicago: University of Chicago Press.

QKJS. 1982–1986. *Xinhai geming shiqi qikan jieshao* (Introductions on the periodicals in the Revolution of 1911). Ed. Ding Shouhe. 4 vols. Beijing: Renmin chubanshe.

Ren Xu. 1936. "Xinhai geming zai guiyang" (The Revolution of 1911 in Guiyang), *Yefeng*. 20:24–8.

Ricci, Matteo. 1953. *China in the Sixteenth Century: The Journals of Matthew Ricci: 1583–1610*. Trans. Louis J. Gallagher. New York: Random House.

SEB *Shenbao* (Shanghai news). Shanghai, 1872–1949. 400 ce. Reprint by Shanghai shudian.

Shan Shih-yuan. 1979. "Qingdai *Qiju zhu*" (Records of the Emperors' Life during the Qing Dynasty).[56] In *Qingdai dangan shiliao congbian* (Collections of Qing archival materials). Beijing: Zhongua shuju, 4:259–71.

SIB *Shibao* (Eastern times). Shanghai, 1904–? Microfilms in Beijing Library.

SLXJ. 1977. *Xihai geming qian shinianjian shilun xuanji* (The collection of selected essays, 1901–1911). Ed. Zhang Nan and Wang Renzhi. 3 vols. Shanghai: Sanlian chubanshe.

SSJZS. 1978. *Shisanjing zhushu* (Thirteen classics with notes and commentaries). Reprinted. 2 vols. Beijing: Zhonghua shuju.

SZSL. 1964. *Daqing shizu zhang (Shunzhi) huangdi shilu* (The veritable records of the Qing Emperor Shizu Zhang *Shunzhi*). 144 juan. Reprint. 3 vols. Taibei: Huawen shuju, 1964.

Trauzettel, Rolf. 1975. "Sung Patriotism as a First Step Toward Chinese Nationalism." In John Winthrop Haeger, ed., *Crisis and Prosperity in Sung China*. Tucson: University of Arizona Press, pp. 199–213.

Wallace-Hadrill, J. M. 1982. *The Long-Haired Kings*. Toronto: University of Toronto Press.

Wakeman, Frederick E., Jr. 1975a. "Localism and Loyalism During the Ch'ing Conquest of Kiangnan." In Frederick Wakeman, Jr., and Carolyn Grant, eds., *Conflict and Control in Late Imperial China*. Berkeley: University of California Press, pp. 43–85.

———. 1975b. *The Fall of Imperial China*. New York: Free Press.

———. 1985. *The Great Enterprise: The Manchu Reconstruction of Imperial Order in Seventeenth-Century China*. 2 vols. Berkeley: University of California Press.

Watson, James L. 1982. "Of Flesh and Bones: The Management of Death Pollution in Cantonese Society." In M. Bloch and J. Parry, ed., *Death and the Regeneration of Life*. New York: Cambridge University Press.

Wen Ruilin, ed. 1830. *Nanjiang yishi* (Neglected history of the southern regions). 6 ce. Reprinted. Taiwan wenxian congkan. no. 132. Taibei: Bank of Taiwan, 1959.

Williams, Wells S. 1848. *Middle Kingdom: A Survey of the Geography, Government, Education, Social Life, Arts, Religion, and C., of the Chinese Empire and Its Inhabitants*. 2 vols. New York: Wiley and Putnam.

Wright, Mary C. 1957. *The Last Stand of Chinese Conservatism*. Stanford: Stanford University Press.

Xie Guozhen, ed. 1956. ed., *Qingchu nongmin qiyi ziliao jilu* (Collected records of peasant uprisings in the early Qing dynasty). Shanghai: Xin zhishi chubanshe.

Xu Ke. 1923. *Keyian* (Frankly talking). In *Tiansuge congkan* (Collection of Tiansu attic). 6 ce. Hangxian xushi qianyin ben.

Xu Shaoji and Xu Jincheng. 1956. *Minguo yeshi* (Unofficial history of the Republic of China). Hongkong: Lili chubanshe.

XWXTK. 1964. *Qingchao xuwenxian tongkao* (Continuation of the complete examination on the Qing documents). Ed. Liu Jingzao. Reprint. 4 vols. Taibei: Xinxing shuju.

Yang Shengmin. 1912. *Manyi huaxia shimoji* (The history of Manchu's dominance in China). Shanghai: Xinzhonghua tushuguan.

Zhang Tingyu et al., comps. 1974. *Mingshi* (History of the Ming). 28 vols. Beijing: Zhonghua shuju.

7 hair like snakes and mustached brides: crossed gender in an indian folk cult

alf hiltebeitel

Two Tamil folk cults rooted in the Indian epic mythology of the *Mahābhārata* may be contrasted in their treatments of hair. One is the cult of Draupadī, the epic's chief heroine and wife of the five Pāṇḍava brothers, the epic's main heroes. The Kūttāṇṭavar cult—this essay's main focus—is that of a minor epic figure named Aravāṉ (in Tamil) or Irāvat (in Sanskrit), and called Kūttāṇṭavar by his worshipers: the son of the middle Pāṇḍava Arjuna and a snake princess named Ulūpī or Nāgakkaṉṉī ("Serpent maiden"), with whom Arjuna has a brief affair sealed by an estranged marriage. Each is worshiped as an adjunct figure in the other's cult. Draupadī temples are found throughout Tamilnadu and up into southern Andhra Pradesh and western Karnataka; Kūttāṇṭavar temples only in a belt across north-central Tamilnadu from South Arcot to Coimbatore.[1] But both cults are concentrated in the districts of South and North Arcot.

The Draupadī cult builds upon a pan-Indian "popular" tradition that is not explicit in the Sanskrit *Mahābhārata*, but already alluded to there (Hiltebeitel 1981:186–201): the menstruating Draupadī vowed after she was abused at the pivotal epic dice match by the Pāṇḍavas' rivals, the Kauravas, that she would keep her hair disheveled until she could dress it with blood from the Kaurava king Duryodhana's thigh.[2] These images are all traceable to a classical-medieval-"folk" continuum within the public culture of India, and decipherable in the context of a code of women's hair styles. Loose hair or dishevelment is for widows and menstruating women; the triple braid (*triveṇī*) and chignon (Tamil *kūntal* or *koṇṭai*) are for auspicious married women; the "single braid" (*ekaveṇī*), a kind of pony tail, is for women separated from their husbands (*virahiṇī*s). These conventions can be reconstructed from classical Sanskrit and Tamil texts (Hiltebeitel 1981:184–85; 1980–81; 1985). Even Draupadī's gruesome demands for a rib comb and a garland or hair ribbon of guts have counterparts in public rituals like Dasarā, the fall festival for Durgā, or the iconography of Kālī (Hiltebeitel 1991a:388, 436). The deep motivations that shape Draupadī's hair rituals—the thirteen-year extension of her menstrual purification terminated by her use of womblike blood from a male thigh (1991a:396–98)—do not seem to require elaborate interpretative routes through psychoanalytic theory. When I observed that no one in the night-long dramas performed at Draupadī festivals ever mentions that Draupadī is menstruating when she makes her vow, and asked my chief actor informants why not, suspecting I'd found a suppressed or unconscious theme, I was told that there was no need to mention it: "Everybody knows that" (1988:234–35). When women and men identify with Draupadī in rituals of possession and vow taking, even where it includes loosening, letting fly, and binding of hair, there is thus no reason to think that the hair symbol is personally motivated. It is, at least predominantly, in Obeyesekere's terms, a psychogenetic public symbol rather than a deeply transformative personal one (1981:13–18).

The Kūttāṇṭavar cult is different. It too has pan-Indian epic and ritual associations, but they are much harder to find, and have left no early echoes in the Sanskrit *Mahābhārata*. Rather, our oldest sources are from a distinctive Tamil *Mahābhārata* tradition. Kūttāṇṭavar temples are also more isolated from each other. Cult ritual and mythology vary so much that there is probably not much of which anyone can say, "Everybody knows that." Certain hair-related themes have wide currency—for instance snakelike hair. But on the level of field observation, the details are little if ever explicitly in evidence, and for the most part must be discerned in a network of associations. There is no one main metaphoric hair theme, but bits and pieces, deployed metonymically from one locale to another.

In South Arcot, however, there is a distinctive participation in the cult by Alis, Tamil-speaking transsexuals or so-called eunuchs, the wider Indian (Hindi) name for whom is *hinjra*. Here one may suspect deep motivations in appropriations of the private or personal character of the cult's mythic and ritual symbolism, which begins with the item that leads every Freudian mythologist's seemingly endless list of castration displacements: a severed head. I have not done indepth interviews of Alis that would allow me to probe the personal character of this symbolism as far as I would like. But I have interviewed enough Alis and villagers to probe two questions, each connected with hair: What happens on the level of personal participation in a cult where a presumed conventional symbolism of displaced castration is shared with Alis who have really been castrated? And, to the extent that we can trace Alis' contribution to the cult's symbolism, what is that contribution?

Aravāṉ in Sanskrit and Tamil Sources

In the Sanskrit epic, other than a brief account of Irāvat's birth in the first book, one hears nothing more about him until a single section in the sixth book tells how he died on the war's eighth day at the hands of a Rākṣasa (demon) named Alambuṣa. All the new Tamil incidents occur at the war's beginning (Hiltebeitel 1995:448–53; 1988:317–20). The earliest ninth-century telling, by the Pallava poet Peruntēvaṉār, gives the basic story. Aravāṉ agrees to sacrifice himself on the new moon night to Kālī, goddess of the battlefield, so that, with her blessing, the Pāṇḍavas will win. For his compliance, Aravāṉ obtains a succession of increasingly problematic boons that accumulate through the centuries. In Peruntēvaṉār, he asks only to stay alive to die a hero on the war's eighth day, which allows him to retain his Sanskrit exit from the story. Villipūttūr Āḻvār's fourteenth-century Tamil version of the epic adds his wish to watch the war with his severed head for a few days—which the folklore of our two cults extends to the whole eighteen-day war. The same folk traditions then add his appeal for a pre-war marriage to secure him ancestral rites that would be denied him were he to die a bachelor. Each of these boons adds something to the problematics of hair.

Hair that Stands on End

Why is Aravāṉ so specially suited for self-sacrifice before battle? Because he has thirty-two beautiful body marks. But one trait stands out among them. One first meets it in late-nineteenth-century folkloric texts: in one, Duryodhana chooses Aravāṉ because he needs a person for "battlefield sacrifice" (*kaḷappali*) who has "hair that stands on end (*etir urōmakkārarākavum*)"; in the other, Kṛṣṇa says that Aravāṉ is the ideal victim for sacrifice to Kālī because he is "handsome, truthful, observant of customs, and has hair that stands on end (*etirrōmaṉ*)."[3] What is *etirrōmaṉ*? Here we face our hermeneutical divide. Do we limit ourselves to emic interpretations specific to what people say about festivals they participate in themselves? Do we admit information from wider Kūttāṇṭavar cult circles? Do we consider Draupadī cult associations, since the two cults overlap? Do we look at other cults, some also with regional overlap, others more distant, with similar usages? Do we allow interpretative routes through other regional *Mahābhārata* folklores that appear to be variations on this one? This essay makes a case for all these lines of inquiry. Panregionally, much of the mythology that Tamils associate with Aravāṉ is associated with a virtual double of Aravāṉ in other areas of India. And regionally, participants at a particular festival include not just local villagers but performers who have intercultic and wider regional knowledgeability, and in our present case Alis who come from far and wide. But if one looks beyond participants' explanations, one must have reasons for positing some kind of selective memory or interpretative principle, which in some cases will amount to a "misrecognition" or "méconnaissance." In the case of Kūttāṇṭavar cult hair symbolism, participants' explanations seem to be most "unknowing" precisely on matters where information about similar usages from the other contexts open possibilities of psychoanalytic interpretation. If we straddle this divide, we must distinguish between what people say about festivals they participate in themselves, and what we draw from wider associations.

According to informants at his main cult center at Kūvākkam, South Arcot, Aravāṉ's *etirrōmaṉ* is a mole with hair growth. The hair surrounds the mole on the right shoulder and "stands on end." It is an auspicious beauty mark, as are all of Aravāṉ's thirty-two marks. Only a few other warriors have these features: Arjuna, Kṛṣṇa, and a Kaurava ally named Śalya. But these three are ruled out as victim for one reason or another.[4] Granted the spotty nature of our information, it is striking that Draupadī festival informants give different explanations. Locals at a Tindivanam Draupadī festival in South Arcot said that *etirrōmaṉ* denotes that Aravāṉ is "too hairy," which makes him an ideal victim because his abundant body hair (cf. Dikötter in this volume) will stand on end at the "thrill" of self-sacrifice. This trait would seem to evoke the requirement in South Indian animal sacrifices that the victim must shiver before it can be beheaded—as provoked by pouring water on its hair. On the other hand, in the folklore of Draupadī cult dance dramas, Arjuna and the god Śiva each have a "fish-shaped mark" (*maccarēkai*) on their right sides, and Śiva's wife Pārvatī and a Brahman woman named Kṛpī have them on their right thighs, which fills Śiva with lust for both of them. These moles are erotic beauty marks (Hiltebeitel 1988:191–93, 208–209, 308).

I suggest that Kūvākkam informants reject the animalian and demonic implications of excessive hair and self-sacrificial thrill, and draw upon the beauty-mark tradition to interpret Kāttāṇṭavar's *etirrōmaṉ* as a sign of their deity's handsomeness, beauty, and even erotic appeal. If Kūttāṇṭavar is often portrayed with large canine teeth (he does not have them at Kūvākkam), he is still not the grotesque with demonic facial features that he often is as Aravāṉ in Draupadī cult iconography (see plates in Hiltebeitel 1988:249; 1991a:256–60). I propose that Kūvākkam informants restrict or condense "hair that stands on end" to a beauty mark, and sublimate rather than eliminate the animalian and demonic associations of excessive and bristling hair, which reappears in other forms.

I will thus at times see hair where Kūvākkam informants see other things. The hypertrichosis of the *Mahābhārata*'s prewar victim, it turns out, is a secure folkloric motif that cannot be left as a mole, or left to Aravāṉ. In Telugu, Hindi, and Rajasthani traditions, we meet his double: Barbarīk/Barbareeka, a son of either Ghaṭotkaca (a son of Bhīma, the strongest and second oldest Pāṇḍava, and the wild demoness [Rākṣasī] Hiḍimbā), or of Bhīma himself and another "Serpent-maiden" (*Nāgakanyā*). In either case, his hairiness marks him as a typically "othered" missing link. In Sanskrit, *barbarīka*—from *barbara*, "barbarian"—means "curly hair or a particular mode of wearing the hair" (Monier-Williams 1899:722).

In Andhra folklore, where Barbareeka is Ghaṭotkaca's son, in return for his head offering to Kālī, Kṛṣṇa grants him the boon of being able to see the entire eighteen-day war from a mountain top with the severed head (Subba Rao 1976:272–73; Hiltebeitel 1988:317). One learns nothing about his hair from Subba Rao's brief account, but S. Nagaraj of the Centre for Folk Culture Studies, University of Hyderabad, tells me that it is mainly a question of head hair: to all those below the mountain top, its spread looks as vast as a cloud (personal communication, January 1995). In Rajasthan, his prewar sacrifice is known in popular *Mahābhārata* traditions (Dominique-Sila Khan, personal communication, 1993). According to a Hindi book on Kāṭ Shyām, the main village site near Jaipur of a regional *Mahābhārata* folk cult, "Barbarīk, as Ghaṭotkaca's son, had at his birth the hair naturally disheveled and standing on end, that is why he was given the name 'barbareeka.'" In certain areas of Rajasthan, his head is worshiped during the fall festival to the goddess (Navarātra or Durgā Pūjā) and immersed in a tank or well on its "tenth day of victory" (Vijayādaśamī) that celebrates the triumph of the goddess.

It is probably not incidental that in one version of the drama on "Aravāṉ's Battlefield Sacrifice," Yudhiṣṭhira (the eldest Pāṇḍava and king among them), links Aravāṉ's battlefield sacrifice with the "honoring of weapons" (*āyudha pūjā*), a subrite of the same fall festival of Dasarā (which means "tenth day"). There would seem to be a link between Aravāṉ's horripilation and the raising up of weapons for war by those who sacrifice him. Dasarā is also a festival at which buffaloes can be sacrificed to the goddess. Accordingly, Yudhiṣṭhira asks Kṛṣṇa whether it might not suffice to offer a wild buffalo, elephant, boar, horse, cock, sheep, or deer instead of Aravāṉ (Hiltebeitel 1988:321; *Aravāṉ Kaṭapali Nāṭakam* 1977:40). Here the low-status victim-hero is clearly assimilated to animal victims: especially maned ones that are supposed to shiver to signify their sacrificial consent, and ones that are hairy and tusked (Hiltebeitel 1988:327).

Aravāṉ's double, Barbarīk, is also found in parts of Uttar Pradesh,[5] including Mahoba, where I found that he is the son of Bhīma and the Serpent-maiden and has the distinctive trait that "the hair of Babrīk is like a snake."[6] I have not heard this said of Aravāṉ, but it must be considered admissable evidence in interpreting his hair, even if it is gathered far from Tamilnadu. Although they have different fathers from the Pāṇḍava faction, both Barbarīk and Aravāṉ, at least in this version, have a "Serpent Maiden" (Nākakkaṉṉi, Nāgakanyā) for their mother.[7] Yet here we have an obvious problem. In all cases, one can see how paternal "genes" could contribute to the hero's hairiness: from Ghaṭotkaca, "low" Rākṣasa genes; from Bhīma the same, with his Rākṣasic disposition; and from Arjuna, the famous trait that his body trembles and hair stands on end when he overlooks the two armies drawn up for the battle of Kurukṣetra (*Bhagavad Gītā* 1.29).[8] Like father, like son, *mutatis mutandis*. Indeed, both Arjuna and Aravāṉ's hair stands on end at the beginning of the epic's "sacrifice of battle": a trope for the *Mahābhārata* itself, since the war and the battlefield are repeatedly described as *lomaharṣaṇa*, "making the hair bristle or thrill," and one of the epic's bards is named Lomaharṣaṇa, from the hair-raising nature of the tale. It is more difficult to see how Aravāṉ or Barbarīk would derive his hairiness from an ancestry of hairless snakes. Yet clearly they have. Perhaps we may say that whereas paternal genes are dominant, maternal genes are recessive. We will thus be justified in looking for additional folkloric connections between snakes and hair.[9]

Further exploration of Aravāṉ's hair must take us into the unfolding of his boons. First and oldest is the boon that enables him to die a hero on the war's eighth day in his fight with the Rākṣasa Alambuṣa. Though there is nothing explicitly about hair in any account of this story, there is in all accounts a major role for snakes, who seek to protect their descendant, the Serpent maiden's son. This is a theme that receives rich elaboration in folkloric accounts, and deserves consideration as a bodily, and specifically hair-related, symbol. In the account of the temple icon sculptor N. Dandapani, a well-traveled expert on Kūttāṇṭavar and Draupadī cult folklores, Aravāṉ has been reduced to a skeleton in the eight days since his sacrifice. How can he best use the fifteen minutes Kṛṣṇa gives him to fight? He calls on his serpent mother, who implores her father Nākarājaṉ, "King of Snakes," to give her son strength:

> So you know all those cobras, snakes, different sizes, suiting different parts of the body—fingers, arms, thighs—they came and wound around the different parts of Aravāṉ's body. His skeleton became stiff (*viṟaippu*) now with all the snakes wound around him. He finished off one army division completely in an hour and a half. Kṛṣṇa thought, "What is this? We won't have anything left for others!" . . . So he did another trick, and called Garuḍa to appear in the sky. When even the shadow of an eagle falls, the cobras will disappear. . . . While Aravāṉ was losing all his strength with the snakes falling off, Alampucaṉ [Alambuṣa] cut off his head."

Here the hair-snakes combination relates specifically to an alternating stiffness and droopiness in Aravāṉ's combat persona.

Mustached Brides and Masquerades

Aravāṉ's second and third boons also involve his hair. The second, his war vigil, is ritualized most prominently in the Draupadī cult, in which his clay or wooden head overlooks the cult's ritual battlefield (*paṭukaḷam*) (Hiltebeitel 1991a:287–302). In the Kūttāṇṭavar cult, it is treated more variously, and usually less conspicuously, but always in conjunction with his third boon of marriage to avoid the postmortem penalties of bachelorhood. Here, whereas local villagers highlight the completion of the war vigil, Alis focus entirely on the third boon, Aravāṉ's marriage, and leave the rituals recalling the war's end—with the final death and revival of Aravāṉ's head—entirely to villagers.

In North Arcot, where Alis, at least as a group, do not participate in the Kūttāṇṭavar cult, the combination of the third and second boons presents us with a mustached bride. At Putūr village (Vellore Taluk), before dawn on the main night of his three-day festival, Kūttāṇṭavar's head is placed on a swing (*uñcil*) along with the head of "Kṛṣṇa the eunuch (*Kaṇṇaṉ pēṭi*)." This night has four main phases. First, around 9 P.M., there is a goat sacrifice (by some, identified as Aravāṉ's "battlefield sacrifice") and Kūttāṇṭavar possesses his oracles. Second, when the two heads exit the temple, they are placed on a double-bullock cart "chariot" and taken on procession late into the night. Householders make offerings—mostly vegetarian, some additional goats—as the chariot stops before their homes, and worship "Kṛṣṇa the eunuch" and Kūttāṇṭavar because, "like partners," they "created the whole *Mahābhārata* war." For Kṛṣṇa, the war "is like play (*oru viḷaiyāṭu mātiri*)." Third, before sunrise, the two heads swing from a tall stone crossbeam, and are worshiped for their favor of having "conducted the whole war like a dance" (or game: *kūttu*, as in Kūttāṇṭavar, "Lord of the Dance") and brought about justice in the end. If the sun should touch Kūttāṇṭavar, it would bring diarrhea, cholera, and other diseases. Swinging makes the pair "happy, as at a marriage" and "relaxes them," since they "must be tired after conducting the war." But the village has performed no actual marriage for them "for a hundred years," since it would cost ten thousand rupees. Male villagers, young and old, are supposed to come (none did in 1990) before the swinging heads to press swords against their chests (see Hiltebeitel 1991a:8–29, 351–523). Before daybreak, the two heads must be returned to the temple.

Clearly, the swinging ceremony suggests a condensation of Kūttāṇṭavar and "Kṛṣṇa the eunuch's" wedding. But the procession is no ordinary wedding march. The goat sacrifices and war allusions evoke a "sacrifice of battle," and the newlyweds reach the swing as disembodied heads. Rather than enjoying a marriage, they seem to dance their way through the war (in the procession) and then "watch" it (the sword feats) from the swing. Other North Arcot Kūttāṇṭavar festivals have similar swinging rites for Kūttāṇṭavar's head alone. At two such temples, the head swings facing the *Mahābhārata* reciter (*Pāratiyār*) for the eighteen days (equivalent to the war) that he sings the epic.[10] Where Kūttāṇṭavar's head is alone, the swinging thus refers to the war vigil only; where he is with "Kṛṣṇa the Eunuch" (or "Kṛṣṇa the Woman"), it seems to represent the vigil and marriage together.

What is important here is that both of the swinging heads at Putūr have mustaches (Figure 13). Despite the apparently female form he assumes to marry Kūttāṇṭavar, "Kṛṣṇa the Eunuch" has a mustache. One finds a similar pair of heads at another North Arcot Kūttāṇṭavar temple, but there the mustached female is called (at least by the priest) "Kṛṣṇa the Woman (*Kaṇṇaṉ peṇ*)."[11] This distinction may be significant. The "eunuch" identification could reflect awareness of the relatively recent publicity about Alis at Kūttāṇṭavar festivals in South Arcot, particularly Kūvākkam. But Thurston and Rangachari indicate a comparable role eunuchs might have played at swing ceremonies in small-scale south Indian village festivals: "At the annual festival of the Gadabas of Vizagapatam, thorns are set on a swing outside the shrine of the goddess. On these the priest or priestess sits without harm. If the priest is masculine, he has been made neuter. But if the village is not fortunate enough to possess a eunuch, a woman performs the ceremony" ([1904] 1965, 3:291–92; 2:250–51). Kṛṣṇa's eunuch identification at Putūr as swing partner of the soon-to-be-mutilated Kūttāṇṭavar could thus be an iconic counterpart (with the *Mahābhārata* war vigil as painful) to the swinging of eunuchs, or alternately women, on thorny swings.

Kṛṣṇa's iconography as divine eunuch or woman with a mustache has its counterpart in cases where the divinity is not just a mustached bride but a mustached goddess.[12] The goddess Yellamma-Reṇukā at her mountain temple at Saundatti (Parasgad Taluk, Belgaum District) in northern Karnataka presents the most comparable profile. For her daily decoration (*alaṃkāra*), the icon in her sanctum is fitted every morning with multiple sarees, tiara, marriage necklace (tāli), neck capsule for her "little 'phallus'" or *iṣṭa-linga* (worn by Lingāyat sectarians), and a silver mustache in the form of double lunar "croissant" (Assayag 1992b:394, 398 [plate 32]). Like Kūttāṇṭavar at Kūvākkam, this Yellamma attracts transsexuals: especially males (Jōgappas), but also, among their female counterparts (Jōgammas), some who masculinize their dress and manner (231, 234; Bradford 318; Tarachand 1991:98–100). The cult's myth is a folk version of a *Mahābhārata* story about the Brahman Jamadagni, his Kṣatriya (warrior class) wife Reṇukā (who is the same as Yellamma), and their five sons, youngest of whom is Viṣṇu's avatar Paraśurāma, "Rāma with the axe." When the four brothers refuse Jamadagni's command to slay

Figure 13. Kṛṣṇa the eunuch with mustache on left, and with Kūttāṇṭavar on right, at Putūr. Aiyaṉār, son of Śiva and Viṣṇu transformed into Mohinī, is represented on the poster in the middle. Photo by Alf Hiltebeitel.

Reṇukā for a slight lapse of marital chastity, Paraśurāma obeys the paternal command to behead both his mother and brothers, and then uses his father's boon to revive them (Assayag 1992b:42–44; Tarachand 1991:98–99, 103). Jōgammas identify with Reṇukā (Yellamma) in the status of secondary "divine brides" of Jamadagni (identified with Śiva). Jōgappas see themselves as descendants of the couple's four oldest slain and revived sons.

Jōgappas are transvestites, taking on women's dress and mannerisms, sexually impotent and indifferent to women, theoretically asexual and celibate, who display a "stereotype of aggressively erotic femininity" (Bradford 1983:316; Assayag 1992b:229–34). Only those few who have atrophied penises become eunuchs, taking it as a sign to undergo the operation from the goddess Bahuchārā, a multiform of Kālī whose Ahmedabad temple in Gujarat has pan-Indian recognition among transsexuals (Assayag 1992b:26, 229–36; cf. 1992a; Bradford 1983; Nanda 1990:145). Jōgappas dance for Yellamma more often than Jōgammas, many of whom are prostitutes. Some Jōgammas receive their sign of divine "calling" from the goddess at a very young age by the "miraculous" appearance of locks of matted hair (*jaṭē* or *jeḍi*; Assayag 1992b:217–21, plates 17 and 18). Their youth aside, this spontaneous appearance is like that of the female ascetics Obeyesekere describes in *Medusa's Hair*. The matted locks are variously explained. Assayag sees unsanitary rural and low-caste conditions as a factor (217–18). For many non-Jōgammas, it is a sign of their impurity. Jōgammas, who affect renunciation despite being prostitutes, "explain that Yellamma takes hold of their sexuality to yield back to them this extraordinary capillary vitality, a sign of their exceptional religious fecundity," and "a particle of the power of the 'Mother.'"[13] When their matted locks inevitably break, they offer them to Yellamma in a pūjā that metonymically combines them with weapons, garlands, snakes, wild vegetation, and hanging tree roots (218–21). Some Jōgappas also have matted hair, and appear together with the Jōgammas in processions (218 and plate 20).

As to this goddess's mustache, pūjārīs call it *mīsē*, "mustache." Assayag found no explanation for it (personal communication, May 1992), but contextualizes it in relation to Yellamma's royal and cosmic power (1992b:394–95) and Supreme Energy (*śakti*), which lies at the base of all gender categories and their transformation (235). Tarachand indicates that the mustache is of a type that is offered to the goddess votively by her devotees: "Those who want children vow to offer [a] miniature form of a cradle made in silver. Those who want a son offer a silver model of mustaches to the deity" (1991:90). Thus while Yellamma is the source of all children, the mustache offering generates boys from her male aspect.

Back at North Arcot Kūttāṇṭavar festivals, one finds a similar interchangeableness in the multiple identities of the second mustached head. Only at three villages were they identified as female: those already mentioned and a third.[14] But even at one of these, Virāṇantal, the priest was contradicted by other informants, who identified the second head as Mu<u>n</u>icuvara<u>n</u>, a male guardian deity. At still other North Arcot Kūttāṇṭavar temples, there were further explanations. Both heads are Kūttāṇṭavar: the smaller goes on procession, the larger stays in the temple and rides the swing to listen to *Mahābhārata* recitation.[15] Or, a red head is Aravā<u>n</u>, a gold one Kūttāṇṭavar; once someone tried to steal the original red Aravā<u>n</u>, went blind, had family problems, and left it on a hill to be recovered. To regain his eyesight, he commissioned the new gold Kūttāṇṭavar for the temple.[16] Or, a small head is Aravā<u>n</u>, a larger one Kūttāṇṭavar, while two other heads belong to Mohinī, the "Enchantress." All four fit bodies that are taken on procession on the festival's last day, celebrating Aravā<u>n</u>'s marriage, battlefield sacrifice, and the lamentation for his ordeal. Earlier in this festival, on the third day, men dress as women and put on a tāli to marry Aravāṉ like Mohinī, who is understood to be Kṛṣṇa in woman's guise; later they take off the tāli and bangles and throw them in a tank. As in South Arcot, Mohinī is the form Kṛṣṇa assumes to marry Aravāṉ as his last-minute bride.[17] But this is the only North Arcot temple where a voluntary connection was made between Kṛṣṇa's female (or eunuch) guise and the Mohinī myth. North Arcot informants who knew the story connected it with the South Arcot Kūvākkam festival. But most did not know the story. It is thus possible in this fragmented situation that North Arcot identifications of Kṛṣṇa the "woman" or "eunuch" might have originally been independent of the South Arcot myth.

Virtually all of these North Arcot Kūttāṇṭavar festivals combine their worship of Kūttāṇṭavar with that of Kenkaiyammaṉ, the river goddess Gangā (Ganges). It is again Kenkaiyammaṉ, known as Gangamma just across the North Arcot border in Andhra Pradesh, who has a big festival in Tirupati (Chittoor District) in which she is worshiped as Veshalamma, the "Mother of Costumes" or "Goddess of Disguises." Her guises reenact myths of her male transformations to seek out a vile lusting landlord who despoils budding maidens on the night before their weddings, and turns his lust on Gangamma when he sees her drying her hair after a bath. To expose and kill him, she adopts various disguises, several male, in the last of which she becomes a foreign prince (Dora) to behead him, and then momentarily revives him to show him her true supreme female form. Her transformations have their counterpart in ritual masquerades by men in women's guise during her festival, which replicate her own disguises. The landlord, in processions, has a mustached red-painted wooden head, while the goddess's terrifying image has only protruding fangs (Handelman 1995, 229-33). But her princely disguise includes a mustache (Anand Akundi, personal communication, January 1995). A eunuch also figures in the story: "her true form is also a head, lost when thrown into a deep well by a crazed eunuch." Handleman takes this to indicate "a male feminized in his loss but not made female, and therefore in disjunction, rather than in harmony, with the female" (1995:293). This is slippery territory. I would suggest that the "crazed eunuch" is an allomorph of the goddess: a joint image of what lies at the source of gender transformations, like the Supreme Śakti at Saundatti, as described by Assayag.

On the same arc but now back in western South Arcot, just southeast of the range of the North Arcot temples and west of

Kūvākkam, one finds Draupadī festivals where men dress up as women. In the village where this ceremony is said to be finest,[18] two groups of about fifty men each don both male and female guises. One represents the Pāṇḍavas and Draupadī in the "guise of low caste 'foxy gypsies'" (*narikuṟuvarvēṣam*) going to Duryodhana's court during their year incognito (cf. Hiltebeitel 1988:301–309). The other portrays Kṛṣṇa's sports with his mistress Rādhā and the cowherd women (Gopīs) in "the guise of cowherds" (*itayarvēṣam*). The sequencing of these masquerades is structurally identical to those at Kūvākkam: both occur on the night before Aravāṉ's sacrifice. In one case men don women's guise to sport with Kṛṣṇa; in the other men don a guise of Kṛṣṇa to marry Kūttāṇṭavar.

North Arcot thus lies at a crossroads of masquerading and gender-mixing rituals focused on different deities (Draupadī, Gangā, Kṛṣṇa, Aravāṉ) whose worship coincides in North Arcot Kūttāṇṭavar temples.[19] If such triangulation allows us to read behind the few accounts that identify the double-mustached heads as Kūttāṇṭavar and Kṛṣṇa as his divine bride, it is clear that our explanation is beyond our informants' horizons. Not surprisingly, the question "why a mustache?" provoked only puzzlement and amusement when asked at Putūr:

> Twenty years ago, Kṛṣṇa had no mustache. The man who painted it was a potter from Arani, an icon painter by profession.
>
> About twenty years back someone asked, why this mustache? Someone from Vaitiyanātaṉkuppam said, "No no, he must have a mustache." How do we know about such things? So it's painted once in fifteen or twenty years. We pay about one hundred and thirty rupees.
>
> How old are the images?
>
> I wouldn't know. Even my grandfather wouldn't know. Will they put another mustache on when it is repainted? It should not have a mustache. If we say no, perhaps they will leave it off.

One informant thus attributes a *new* mustache to the professional expertise of an icon painter (like Dandapani), while the other recalls a debate concluding that an *old* mustache should *not* be removed. Both, however, agree: it is twenty years since anyone had any idea as to why the mustache is there, that those who once might have known were from outside the village, and that no one living there today has a clue about it.

Perhaps the mustached companion is without a stable mythical identity because the identity derives from masquerading rituals in which identities are already multiple. Perhaps it is there because all kinds of people take the vow to marry Aravāṉ, and because Aravāṉ, given his well-known, last-minute predicament, is willing to marry all kinds of people in multiple masquerades. These are vague possibilities, but they raise precise questions. Even though the identifications of "Kṛṣṇa the woman" or "Kṛṣṇa the eunuch" may evoke the Mohinī myth, they might reflect an older stratum of the cult's ritual in which a mustached divine bride, as a symbol of this fluid state of affairs, is an intelligible incongruity.

Alis at Kūvākkam

It is in eastern South Arcot, and especially at Kūvākkam, that large numbers of visiting transsexual Alis join temporary village transvestites in donning the tāli to marry Kūttāṇṭavar. It is not clear how old this practice is. But it is intriguing that Francis, writing in 1906, mentions no Alis in attendance. He mainly describes a ceremony on the eighteenth night: "An enormous number of fowls" are sacrificed to the god while men who have vowed to marry him dress like women, pay the priest to tie tālis around their necks, and then join in laments for their "husband's" sacrifice (Francis 1906:376).

One cannot tell from this nonmention whether Alis participated ninety years ago. But some things have changed: prominence of the eighteenth day rather than the sixteenth; the massive sacrifice of cocks; the type of "sacrificial" enactment. Kūvākkam informants today differ as to whether the festival was ever without Alis, but they agree Alis came in only small numbers until the visit of an Ali named Tēvi about twenty or thirty years ago. Nārullā provides an account of Tēvi's visit (Alis refer to themselves with feminine pronouns or gender-neutral honorifics).

> Twenty years ago, this size of crowd had never come to Kūvākkam. At that time every year on the full moon of the month of Cittirai only a very small celebration occurred. The cause for this spreading is Tēvi, the ornament (*tilakam*) of the Alis' clan (*kulam*). Tēvi heard of Kūvākkam and its rites by word of mouth. She arrived on the full moon of

> Cittirai in Villupuram, went by train to Parikkal, and walked the last seven miles on foot, with the sun beating down in the middle of the road, to Kūvākkam. There she collapsed on the pyol in front of the house of a barber named Rāju, who offered her hospitality with great affection. That house, which was then a shack, is now a building.[20] And if Tēvi comes to Kūvākkam today, she stays there. When she first came, Tēvi prayed to Cāmi with fear and devotion (*payapatti*). She took part in the rites. She did all the necessary things. Within the next year, she had become a millionaire (*lakṣātipati*). She believed that it was by Kūttāṇṭavar's grace that she obtained this wealth. Therefore, the second year, she came to the festival with fifteen people. The fourth year, four hundred Alis came. Tēvi is the mother of Shanta, who is from Bombay. Through this, Alis from Bombay also began to come to Kūvākkam. . . . [Now] thousands of Alis tie their tālis at Kūvākkam village (1990:41–42)

It is intriguing that Tēvi collapsed on the pyol of the barber's shack. The story suggests an unconscious affinity between hair cutting and castration, drawing together Tēvi's initiatory journey and the barber's traditional role of performing tonsure ceremonies (and, according to Thurston, the castration operation itself for some eunuchs).[21]

Nārullā prefaces this account by saying that Tēvi felt an affinity between the festival and her own *iṉam* (kind, species, gender). Alis gather at Kūvākkam and other South Arcot Kūttāṇṭavar festivals in part to strengthen their *iṉam* (Eḻumalai 1989:57). By marrying Aravāṉ, whose battlefield sacrifice mirrors their own castration, they partake in a ritual that nourishes an iṉam that cannot reproduce itself biologically (Hiltebeitel 1995, 468–71). Affinities between Alis and this self-mutilating god are transparent, though it must be insisted that there is never a hint that Aravāṉ cuts his penis among his thirty-two cuts.[22] As the beautiful and heroic male whom the Alis impersonate Mohinī to marry, Aravāṉ evidently retains his full masculinity, but the Alis seem to have picked up on his ordeal as a theme that draws their sympathies, sadness, and lamentations.

No doubt Alis who might have preceded Tēvi to Kūvākkam would have felt the same affinity with the god as her. In Francis's time, small numbers could thus have been drawn to a masquerading type of festival more like the type encountered presently in North Arcot, where Kṛṣṇa's eunuch guise, with mustache, alternates with his more straightforward guise as a mustached woman. Today at Kūvākkam, prior to the large-scale rituals of transvestitism that reenact Aravāṉ's marriage on the fourteenth through sixteenth days, there is a second-day double ritual wedding in which two men impersonate the bride (one each from the Vaṉṉiyar and Paṟaiyar-Untouchable communities) and marry two men (from the same groups) who impersonate Aravāṉ. Kūvākkam residents consider this double wedding ancient. The Paṟaiyar playing the bride, in 1990, was surprised, albeit pleasantly, to learn that the Vaṉṉiyars—the regional landed dominant caste—regarded him as impersonating Mohinī, and did not regard himself as impersonating any woman in particular. Aside from being a regrettable instance of "interpreter effect" occasioned by fieldwork, his response looks at first like a case of forgetting the myth. But at a Salem District Kūttāṇṭavar festival where the bride is not identified as Mohinī, an Untouchable likewise dresses up as a woman to marry Aravāṉ at the festival's beginning.[23] In this temporary woman's "guise" (*vēṣam*), he marries the deity's icon, wears a tāli for eighteen days, and then removes it for the rites of battlefield sacrifice, which include public lamentation. In both situations, the bride is an Untouchable: an indication that the "guise" may not only mix genders but castes, since, on his paternal side, Aravāṉ is a Kṣatriya. Salem District informants say that Alis do not come to their festivals at all.[24] Sexual masquerading would thus seem to be an older tacit, or at least nonmythicized, *ritual* expression of marriage to Aravāṉ, in which the bride's status can be low: a category open to both Alis and Untouchables.

Whether their part in the Kūttāṇṭavar cult is foundational but originally small and only recently spectacular, or recent only, one may in any case hypothesize that since Tēvi's visit to Kūvākkam, Alis have given strong impetus to the reshaping there of earlier mythic and ritual traditions. Nowhere can their contribution be suspected to be more crucial than in their distinctive formulation of Aravāṉ's third boon: his marriage to Mohinī. The oldest known literary version of this myth refers only to Kṛṣṇa's transformation into "Mohinī as a woman (*Mōkiṉippeṇ*)." This is found in the chapbook publication of the drama "Aravāṉ's Battlefield Sacrifice," whose earliest known printing is 1897 (*Aravāṉ Kaṭapali Nāṭakam* 1967:70–71; see n. 3). Thus nine years before Francis's description of the Kūvākkam festival, which refers only to local villagers' taking on the appearance of women, the drama tells of Kṛṣṇa's transformation into Mohinī in the form of a woman, but gives no hint of Alis. The dramas in this collection seem to reflect Draupadī cult performative traditions of the mid- to late nineteenth centuries (Hiltebeitel 1988:160–62, 324).

According to Ali informants today, however, Mohinī—at least in this appearance—is not "Kṛṣṇa the Woman" or even "Kṛṣṇa the Eunuch," but Kṛṣṇa in his "Ali avatāra" (Hiltebeitel 1995:456; Nārullā 1990:43–44, 61). Rather than a temporary guise, avatar status defines a divine mode of being that the god makes permanently worshipful, and is in some sense permanent in a way that a "guise" is not. This designation reflects the Alis' own marriage to Kūttāṇṭavar, which extends beyond the festival in rites of widowhood that are unique to them, and can be renewed at the festival each year. Most Kūvākkam villagers have a different view. Like North Arcot villagers who knew some version of the story, they regard Kṛṣṇa as "Kṛṣṇa the woman." In temporarily becoming Mohinī to marry Aravāṉ, he becomes not a eunuch, but simply a woman. Both theological positions are thus found at Kūvākkam: not surprisingly, the Alis voicing the "eunuch avatāra," local villagers generally upholding the "woman" identification.

The Ali avatāra identification may, however, be older than our sources reflect, and only have surfaced with the Alis' heightened activity in the cult since the visit of Tēvi and, of course, recent fieldwork. Their increased participation in South Arcot could have encouraged them to popularize their older understanding of Mohinī. In any case, their contribution to the Mohinī-Aravāṉ marriage myth has by today taken the latent tension in the two images of Mohinī toward a "fusion of horizons" between the Alis' perceptions and those of local and regional villagers.[25] This tension and fusion provide us with a possible glimpse into the cult's deep motivational power for Alis at the personal level.

The Ali Ambiance at the One-Day Marriage

To portray the Alis' festival participation as it relates to hair, we must consider Kūttāṇṭavar's embodiment and disembodiment in three processions. First, he is carried on the heads of dancers; second, his head is carried on a portable platform (*keṭāyam*); and third, he is embodied on his full chariot (*tēr*).

The first occurs after nightfall of the opening day, and is repeated for six evenings. Kūttāṇṭavar's head is brought outside the temple to be danced through the village. Nine Vaṉṉiyars dance in relay, their bold strides said to recall medieval Vaṉṉiyar warriors. But it is Kūttāṇṭavar, "a great dancer," who is said to really be dancing.

Figure 14. Kūttāṇṭavar's head being carried on the heads of dancing Vaṉṉiyār devotees at Kūvākkam on the first night of the festival. The jasmine strings of his flowered crown fly about, looking like dreadlocks. Photo by Alf Hiltebeitel.

Dancers say they are not possessed, but they are clearly in the role of possessed god-dancers called *cāmiyāṭis*. Cut pieces of plantain stalk fixed to Kūttāṇṭavar's crown are thickly covered with jasmine flowers, while strings of jasmine hang down from the crown and fly about the dancing head. Villagers consider the ensemble a special flower-anointing (*cāttuppiṭi pū alankāram*) that has nothing to do with hair. But when the long strings fly about, they *look* like snakes or dreadlocks (see Figure 14). The god thus first appears in a mode that *looks* as if it could reflect his proverbial hairiness and his maternal snake ancestry. Alis have not yet arrived at the festival.

From the thirteenth day onward, preparations are made for the two other processions. After a secret ceremony in the sanctum, in which the god's "life" (*uyir*) is temporarily removed from his head into a vessel, the head, now "mere wood," is wrapped in red silk and taken to a shed in the back of the temple. Every year a carpenter and painter remove Kūttāṇṭavar's jewels and mustache, peel off all the paint-on-cloth that covers the head, and attach a new white cloth as the base for repainting. Aravāṉ's mustache is again important. It is one of the last signs of life removed and one of the last features restored before his life's renewal (Figure 15). As elsewhere across many cultures, hair, which continues to grow (like nails) after death, carries life of its own even beyond death. According to the sculptor Dandapani, the mustache has characteristics that make it one of Aravāṉ's thirty-two marks: "broad chest, tallness, long hands and legs; bow-shaped eyebrows; fish-like eyes; mustache twined very tightly: there is a principle that a mustache should be slightly twined and long so that you could stick a lime on the points—these principles have been handed down by our elders; wide open eyes; eyelids that should never flicker." Other than the mustache, this partial list could recall the thirty-two marks that identify the Buddha as a Mahāpuruṣa, among which is the twentieth: that "every hair on his body [is] detached, ascending upwards, and turned to the right" (Foucher 1963:258).[26] Dandapani gives fullest attention to the bristly mustache, mentioning it along with two other facial hair traits: the bow-shaped eyebrows and eyelids that never flicker. The spiking of limes on the end of the mustache evokes the conventional impalement symbol of limes on upraised weapons, and its bristling condenses, for the head, the trait of hair that stands on end. The mustache is thus another exemplar of Kūttāṇṭavar's hairiness, and, through its evocation of impalement and sacrifice, a condensation of his suitability for the "battlefield sacrifice" that, again, evokes the worship of upraised weapons at Dasarā.

Figure 15. Kūttāṇṭavar's head after it has been repainted at Kūvākkam, with the mustache, still askew, as one of the last features restored, to signify the head's revival. Photo by Alf Hiltebeitel.

On the fourteenth through sixteenth days, those who vow to marry Kūttāṇṭavar can begin to buy tālis. On the fifteenth, a festive atmosphere builds from evening on, centering on the arriving Alis. They have year-by-year arrangements to rent houses on the southern street of Kūvākkam for the nights of their stay. An overflow camps out in surrounding fields; others fill hotels in nearby towns. At the Rolex Hotel in Villupuram, before busing to Kūvākkam, Alis dress each other's hair into flowered chignons (Figure 16). At Kūvākkam, on the pyols in front of their rentals, "they put make-up on each other like cinema actresses" (Nārullā 1990:39).

After midnight, last touches are applied to the painting of the deity's head. By now it is dark on the sixteenth morning, and the sale of tālis and strings of jasmine (*malar carankaḷ*) for the hair is brisk. After an "eye-opening ceremony" restores life to the god's head, the last touches are another flower decoration and a refitting of the mustache: hair and vitality are thus restored to the icon. Meanwhile, excitement mounts outside as the faithful gather in front of the shed to await the god's emergence for his public eye opening. After a big display of fireworks in the fields, the head is brought out at about 3:40 A.M. and set onto the portable platform. It is then carried forth flanked by two additional platforms: one bearing Kūttāṇṭavar's garland-draped chestplate and epaulets, the other his "flower *karakam*," a flower-decorated pot containing his "power" or *śakti*, which has been danced—by both villagers and Alis—through the night. This procession tours the village till daybreak. As the god sets off, it is said, much as it is of the swinging heads at Putūr, that Kūttāṇṭavar's face shows him happy (*cantōsam*) and smiling.

At about 5:30 A.M. the festival then reaches its climax. Awaiting the arrival of the portable platform, a vast crowd assembles in the open area among the village temples. On top of the Kūttāṇṭavar temple, cocks are offered: no longer cut, but thrown up onto the temple roof. Officers of the Tamilnadu State-governed Hindu Religious and Charitable Endowments Board have instituted this change since the early 1980s by posting signs, even within the temple, discouraging animal sacrifice. But villagers continue to offer cocks away from the temple.[27] One will recall the "enormous number of fowls" sacrificed on the culminating day in 1906. Today, only cocks are offered: "If it doesn't crow, God (Cāmi) won't take it." As we shall see, for the Alis, at least, cock sacrifice resonates with castration.

Finally, the post on Kūttāṇṭavar's chariot stands ready for the assemblage of the god's body. The epaulets and chestplate are danced

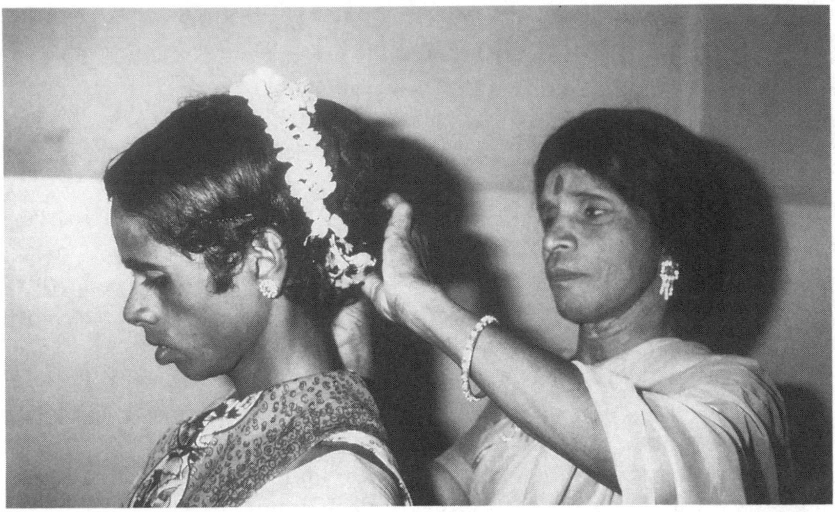

Figure 16. Alis at the Rolex Hotel in Villupuram—prior to the bus trip to Kūvākkam during the 1982 Kūttāṇṭavar festival—dress each other's hair in flowered chignons. Photo by Alf Hiltebeitel.

forward, and while the head is danced around the chariot, the epaulets are filled with flowers and the chestplate positioned. Finally the head is lifted into place. There is a grand display of firecrackers. Two hundred kilograms of camphor are lit in front of the deity, and the entire concourse flings strings of jasmine, spectacularly filling the air with two hundred thousand rupees ("two lakhs") worth of flower strings. These are gathered onto and into the deity's body by men positioned on the chariot and its scaffolding. The head is supplied by the Kūvākkam temple; the other wooden bodily parts and insignia (chestplate, flags, umbrella) come from nearby villages. But the strings of jasmine that fly snakelike through the air come from those who have vowed to marry him: in particular the Alis, who fling the flower strings that they have just removed from their hair (Nārullā 1990:40).[28] The god's temporary ritual body, made for this one-day manifestation as an epic hero, is thus the joint production of villagers, who supply solid bodily parts, and Alis, who offer snaky garlands from their hair.

Aravāṉ is thus depicted in heroic pose, prepared for battlefield sacrifice and armed to fight.[29] But he is already "looking sad, sweating, and shedding tears." No longer happy as a head, his embodiment is painful. On his body, the jasmine strings offered from the Alis' hair

Figure 17. As Kūttāṇṭavar's embodied effigy marches toward his battlefield sacrifice with jasmine strings draped from his limbs, he has an exceedingly hairy look. Photo by Alf Hiltebeitel.

now take on the position, and to me the look, of excessive body hair (see Figure 17). If so, they also remain analogous to snakes, since, as one recalls from Dandapani's account, as the god sets forth for battle, his skeleton is rigidified by snakes: snakes who, like the flowers, fill his every limb and digit. Snakes like flowers, flowers like hair, hair like snakes. As Kūttāṇṭavar marches off toward the weeping ground, the Alis now let their ungarlanded hair hang loose to begin the phase of the ritual that identifies them as his widows, and as he marches on and takes on an increasingly "dead look," his jasmine garlands fade to brown. This is a telling continuum. While the widows' hair of the Alis falls loose, the flower-strings from their hair represent Kūttāṇṭavar's loss of vigor and vitality—a theme associated, as we have seen, with hair itself.[30] Moreover, the snaky jasmine strings that the Alis have offered from their hair, which now fill Kūttāṇṭavar's body and hang from his limbs, are removed from his body, during his march, as symbols of his self-mutilation.[31] Unlike the snakes that rigidify his body and then "fall off," the jasmine strings, before they are removed, hang limp and wilt. Meanwhile, villagers still sacrifice cocks before the chariot's wheels along the march.

Most of the Alis who lament Kūttāṇṭavar go to the weeping ground long in advance of the slow procession. There they complete their weeping, and, like all the rest who have married Aravāṉ, leave their severed tālis and broken bangles at a bamboo post.[32] When the effigy arrives, entirely divested of garlands, the hanging roots of a great peepul tree behind him, the huge image looks skeletal and is said to be all but dead—his only life hovering in his eyes, which oversee the tāli and bangle offerings that continue to be made, but now only by villagers. The Alis have gone to a pond, donned white widows' sarees, and, their hair left loose, begun to head home. They should wear widows' white for thirty days before they can once again don colored sarees, bangles, forehead dot, and dress their hair with flowers.

The remainder of the day's activities primarily involves the huge regionally gathered crowd (around twenty thousand people), and then narrows to local ceremonies that concern villagers only from in and around Kūvākkam. Ultimately, the head is revived at a Kālī temple (Hiltebeitel in press), redecorated, and danced back to the Kūttāṇṭavar temple in the fashion of the first six nights with what, again, looks like snaky dreadlocks of jasmine.

Mohinī, the Ali Avatāra

Let us now consider the convergence of perceptions between Alis and local villagers that has, in the last thirty or so years, probably reanimated the symbol of Aravāṉ's head at Kūvākkam and the festival's distinctive deployments of hair. First, there is an opposition between local villagers (particularly Vaṉṉiyars) and Alis. The severed head relates to the super-male figure of Aravāṉ, the great warrior and man of thirty-two bodily perfections, a virtual equivalent of the "Great Man" (*Mahapuruṣa*) of Sanskrit lore (a title given, among others, to the Buddha with *his* thirty-two perfections), who offers his head to the goddess as the culmination of his thirty-two self-mutilations.[33] He is an embodiment of a Kṣatriya ideal that is part of the heritage and identity of his Vaṉṉiyar devotees, who consider themselves Kṣatriyas. But the symbol also relates to the involvement of the Alis, who impersonate Kṛṣṇa's Ali avatāra to marry this deity. They marry a male who shares something of their own ordeal, but evokes what they have irrevocably lost by retaining his masculinity. One cannot miss the implications of Freudian theory: the presumed displacement of castration anxiety from the penis to the severed head, which would account for the general "Kṣatriya" perception of Kūttāṇṭavar, would be reoriented for the Alis, who, having *been* castrated, would displace (or double) their formerly male identification with Kūttāṇṭavar by a feminized Ali identification with Kṛṣṇa-Mohinī.

Here one might reflect on Mohinī's wider mythology. One must first think of the classical Mohinī, who embodies the bewitching power of illusion (*māyā*) that inhabits Viṣṇu when he sleeps during the night of cosmic dissolution, and whom he projects as an "Enchantress" (*Mohinī*) to seduce demons, or Śiva, in various myths—in popular South Indian accounts, to bear their child Aiyaṉar or Hariharaputra ("Son of Viṣṇu and Śiva").[34] Yet I submit that the image of Mohinī at the genesis of the Kūttāṇṭavar cult's configuration is that of Mohinī as succubus, a seductress who appears in dreams and fantasies and lures men, especially young ones—not only Hindu and South Indian Christian (Caplan 1989:57) but Sri Lankan Buddhist ones (Obeyesekere 1981:139–40)—into debilitating activities and fantasies. Although Kūvākkam villagers do not identify Mohinī as an Ali, they speak of Kṛṣṇa's "Mohinī avatāra" as including the Mohinī who comes when a young man is sleeping to arouse sexual desires in dreams. This they distinguish from "Picācu ("Ghost" or "Demonic") Mohinī," whom they consider a "mad (*pitta*) spirit" (Ganesan and other informants, Kūvākkam, July 1994). The distinction is theological rather than psychological. According to Caplan, Mohinī mainly "appears to young bachelors, most typically on their way home from a late night film, wearing a white sari and flowers in her hair. She seeks to lure such a man in order to 'live' with him as his wife, take his strength, and finally kill him. In Madras, among both Christians and Hindus, she is generally referred to as 'Mohini-*peey*'" (1989:57).[35] In Madurai, "she is known as 'Mohinī-*picācu*'—you smell jasmine, hear anklets; a piece of charcoal or a rusty nail can keep her away" (J. Rajasekaran, personal communication, July 1994).

It is not just that Mohinī marries Aravān̠. By agreeing to marry him, she seduces him into his self-mutilation, his wasting away, his death. Similarly, it is frequently said that one mode of recruitment of Alis is for other Alis to seduce them; and several Alis interviewed at Kūvākkam said that they underwent the sexual operation and transformation because they felt they were women trapped in men's bodies. The Alis thus identify with the seducer and the seduced, with both Mohinī and Aravān̠. They are seduced by both, and identify with each as seducer.[36] It may well be that a transsexual homo-eroticism is latent in classical Mohinī myths as well,[37] but nowhere else is it combined with an allurement to self-mutilation. It is probably not possible to account for the genesis of such a symbol, and its "operative" unfoldings in South Arcot Kūttāṇṭavar festivals (cf. Obeyesekere 1981:137–39), without this "subjective imagery" of Alis as a contributing factor. And it is probably the unrecognized transsexual, if not precisely the unacknowledged Ali, in "every man," that explains the general enthusiasm among South Arcot villagers for marrying the self-mutilating god as Mohinī, even if they generally favor an identification with her as "Kṛṣṇa the [temporary] Woman" rather than the Ali avatāra. At Salem and Coimbatore Kūttāṇṭavar temples, it is still Kṛṣṇa who secures Aravān̠ a last-minute bride; but he always finds him a woman plain and simple, and never a male turned something else. We would seem to need the Alis in combination with the region's festival masquerades to understand the unique forms that Kūttāṇṭavar's marriage takes in South and North Arcot.

One should also note that in other Mohinī myths, Mohinī is a form of Viṣṇu rather than Kṛṣṇa. The Arcot mythologies thus provide the only instance I know of where the transformation into Mohinī becomes one of the "tricks" (*tantiram*) of Kṛṣṇa in the *Mahābhārata*. Here we must recognize that the story can be interpreted as "a multiform of the sort of Indian 'Oedipal' pattern" discussed by Goldman and others in which "a real or surrogate son is punished, typically by castration or impotence, for intruding on the sexual life of his 'father'"—or, in varied transpositions, by "the coercive and potentially castrating power of dominant males such as fathers, older brothers, gods, gurus, and sages" (1993:391, 395). Drawn into "the *Mahābhārata*'s ubiquitous concern with the central but often disguised triangle of father, mother, and son" (392), Aravāṉ certainly does not intrude intentionally into his fathers' sexual life, but he does provide a means to revive it. The Pāṇḍavas, who must authorize Aravāṉ's sacrifice, cannot restore marital relations with Draupadī until they have won the war and she has put up *her* hair. Aravāṉ's self-offering to mother Kālī is thus also one that satisfies mother Draupadī and his five Pāṇḍava fathers. But it is really Kṛṣṇa whose "trick" is most troubling: perhaps even more troubling than usual. He is the supreme male (*puruṣottama*), the great man (*perumāl*), who truly instigates and requires this sacrifice, and who could be the victim himself, yet becomes delusively female to guarantee it. To Aravāṉ he is both the ultimate castrating father and the surrogate—as momentary wife and lover—for the seducing, castrating mother. We should remember, however, "in defense of a devious divinity," that Kṛṣṇa is not omnipotent, that in the *Mahābhārata* "the will of God may intervene in whatever way it can" (Matilal 1991:408–15), and that here, as always, Kṛṣṇa works through the desires and fantasies of those who hear and tell his stories.

Hair, Flowers, Snakes, Cockscombs

It is, of course, problematic to ascribe the genesis of particular symbols in the Kūvākkam festival, and in South Arcot, to Alis. But the case is made more tempting by numerous symbols that reinforce this Mohinī complex. It is striking that so many of the cult's major symbols, which can be found at festivals where Alis do not regularly participate, and even, as we have seen, in rituals at Kūvākkam that anteceded their increased participation, take on deepened resonances *for* them.

Let us start with the roosters. The cock is the vehicle of Bahuchārā Mātā, the goddess of the main temple for Alis and Hinjras in Ahmedabad, Gujarat. The Tamil term *kuñcu*, "penis," also means little chick. According to Nārullā, a preliminary to the Alis' castration operation is the severing of a piece from the cockscomb of a rooster to give it to the candidate on the night of his castration (1990:61). This red piece of cockscomb is called *koṇṭai*, "hair bun" or "chignon": the term used to describe a woman's hair (for example, Draupadī's) when she puts it up, or before she loosens or dishevels it. Ali informants thus make connections between hair put up, the piece of the cockscomb, castration, and Aravāṉ's battlefield sacrifice, at which their own hair comes down. The operation, which is called *nirvāṇam*, connoting "nakedness,"[38] is "by and large conducted on the night of the full moon of the month of Cittirai, the night on which Kṛṣṇa took the Ali avatāra to marry Aravāṉ the hero" (61). When the penis is cut off, the cut piece (*tuṇṭu*) and blood are placed in a bucket of water, or a new pot. According to one account, no blood should touch the ground. The *tuṇṭu* swells up and bobs around or quivers (*tuṭi*) with a half-life (*pāti uyir*); it throbs or dances like Kūttāṇṭavar's head. Later it is taken and buried in a small pit. According to another, "The Alis . . . hold that new pot which contains the blood with the candidate's member, place it on their heads and go dancing and singing continuously in a procession. Then they go and release it in the sea" (Nārullā, 1990:63). These accounts derive from Alis who worship Kūttāṇṭavar. However momentarily, like Kūttāṇṭavar's head, the severed penis takes on a new life. At Kūvākkam and several other Kūttāṇṭavar temples, Kūttāṇṭavar's head was first discovered floating down a river, or on the sea. Happy, as a head, he floats, dances, sees, and hears. Sad, he suffers in the embodied state, however fleeting it is for him (one day's daylight in an eighteen-day festival), so that he can cut himself in thirty-two places, marry, make love, die in combat, and feel with his toes and fingers.

In Kūttāṇṭavar's worship at Kūvākkam, symbols of head and body hair alternate between hardness and softness. He is said to be the ideal person for self-sacrifice because he has *etirrōmaṉ*: a hair-circled mole on his back that concentrates into one beauty mark the theme of excessive hair that stands on end at the thrill of self-sacrifice to Kālī. His mustache bristles so sharply one can spike a lime on each end. Alis at the festival depilate or pluck out whatever trace they may have of a mustache, and wear their hair like women. But seeing them at the festival, these are matters of degree. Some have beautiful long hair and soft faces. Facial and underarm hair will cease to grow for some after their operation (Nārullā 1990:10). Others are bald (see Figure 18), or their hair hangs only from below their bald spots. Some have pancake faces and shave regularly. Nanda mentions Hinjras who nostalgically recall their former mustaches (1990:16, 60). Villagers, meanwhile, must shave their mustaches before they don the tāli to marry Aravāṉ.

If hair standing on end is an indication of Aravāṉ's predisposition toward the thrill of self-sacrifice to Kālī, it is hard not to see both

Figure 18. Artist's depiction of an Ali on the cover of Ār. Nārullā's *Alikaḷ Vāḻkkai,* "Long Live Alis," a pamphlet-sized book sold at the 1990 Kūvākkam Kūttāṇṭavar festival. Photo by Alf Hiltebeitel.

the stiff hair and stiff snakes in Dandapani's account as heightened phallic symbols of his masculinity. Alis, on the other hand, are known teasingly as "Ompōtu" (more correctly, "Oṇpatu), by which is meant the number "9," on which the lower portion of the number always dangles and never gets erect (Nārullā 1990:9); they are regarded popularly as having been males who could never get erections (cf. Nanda 1990:67). Their contribution to Kūttāṇṭavar's body and hair is not stiff snakes but dangling flower strings from their own hair.

Hair, snakes, cockscombs, and strings of jasmine thus take on a new look at Kūvākkam. Again, one can follow the chain of associations back to the Alis' castration ritual. A bobbing penis survives with a half-life that is assimilated to a decapitated dancing head: a happy head, forever revivable, that, even before the Alis arrive and after they have left, is danced through the streets with snaky dreadlocks. But while the Alis are at the festival, they are there to marry and lament a god whose embodiment is tragic and sad. The Ali life is full of regrets (Nārullā 1990:72; Nanda 1990:68–69), and their laments reflect this, referring to their situation as one of "cut hands" (*kaiyaṟu nilai*) and arms (Eḻumalai 1989:64). Kūttāṇṭavar's hair thrills for battlefield sacrifice. When the Alis let their hair down and fling their strings of jasmine onto his body, he sets forth to cut that body in thirty-two places as an offering to Kālī. When Alis are castrated, their hair must be long enough for it to muffle their cries as they hold it between their teeth (interviews, 1982, 1990; Nārullā 1990:62).

Flowers like snakes, hair like flowers, snakes like hair: all like penises, they are what Alis have had to offer.

Notes

1. See maps in Hiltebeitel 1988:24; 1991a:4; 1995:449 (the belt is wider than this indicates here, extending to Dharmapuri District and to near Trichur in Kerala. For help with various Tamil sources used in this chapter, I would like to thank Abby Ziffren, Pon Kothandaraman, J. Rajasekaran, and S. Ravindran.

2. For variants with illustrative photographs, see Hiltebeitel 1988 and 1991a. See also Hiltebeitel 1981 and 1988.

3. Respectively, Caṇmukakkavirāyar 1969:2, *Uttiyōka Paruvam,* 199 (a prose version of the eighteenth-century Tamil *Mahābhārata* of Nallāppiḷḷai), and the folk drama *Aravāṉ Kaṭapali Nāṭakam* (1977:40; Hiltebeitel 1988:321). Caṇmukakkavirāyar, active around 1890, was probably familiar with both cults, or at least their folklore (Hiltebeitel 1988:172). The drama is traceable to 1897 (ibid., 160).

4. Information from Kūvākkam July 1994, especially from Ganesan, age fifty-two.

5. Khan, personal communication 1993; William Sax, personal communication, 1995.

6. *Babrīk ke kesh nāg-saman thè*: as described in December 1995 by Baccha Singh of Mahoba, a celebrated singer of the Hindi folk epic *Ālhā* that is linked with the *Mahābhārata*.

7. The sources identifying Ghaṭotkaca as the father do not mention the mother.

8. I have not, however, found that Arjuna has *etirrōmaṉ* in this context.

9. The *Mahābhārata* opens with the story of Kadrū, mother of snakes, who orders her brood to hide in the tail of the horse Uccaiḥśravas (1.18).

10. At Cērpappaṭṭu (Chengam Taluk) and Tēvaṉūr (Tiruvannamalai Taluk).

11. At Vīrāṇantal, Chengam Taluk.

12. Beyond the cases discussed below, cf. Brückner 1987:25–26; Claus 1979:105–106: in Tulunad, the typical "family deity" of "royal" Bants, the androgynous nature-controlling goddess Jumadi, is mustached, as is her male attendant Baṇṭe.

13. Tamil Alis also consider themselves to be particles (*aṃśas*) of the same goddess Bahuchārā (Tamil Pakucāramātā; Nārullā 1990:52).

14. Pulimēṭu (Vellore Taluk, very near Putūr), where the second head belonged to Kaṇṇaṉ peṇ, Kṛṣṇa the Woman.

15. At Kilvaṉampāṭi, Chengam Taluk.

16. At Kumāramankalam, Vaniyampati Taluk.

17. At Cōḻavaram, Vellore Taluk.

18. Muṭiyaṉūr, Kallakuruchi Taluk.

19. North Arcot Kūttāṇṭavar temples may also jointly be Draupadī temples, be linked with Draupadī temples in one village (as at Vīrāṇantal), or perform "Draupadī-type" festivals (as at Pulimēṭu).

20. Kūvākkam villagers I interviewed did not know that the barber Rāju figured in Tēvi's story. When he was alive his family was well off, but is so no longer. His son is a Kūttāṇṭavar temple drummer.

21. Thurston and Rangachari [1904] 1965.3:289 mention that barbers perform the castration for south Indian Muslim eunuchs called Khōjas (apparently Nizārīs).

22. A Draupadī temple pūcāri says these are his head 1, point between brows, temple 1, nose 1, earlobes 2, lips 2, chest 1, knuckles 2, wrists 2, elbows 2, shoulders 2, stomach 1, knees 2, insteps 2, and toes 10 (Hiltebeitel 1988:327).

23. At Paṉaimatal village, Attur Taluk.

24. The same is said of Coimbatore District festivals, but one Ali conspicuously attended the 1995 Kūttāṇṭavar festival at Cinkanallūr near Coimbatore, far from South Arcot. Festival functionaries told me she had no connection with the ceremonies she attended, but that might be a matter of interpretation.

25. Although it was *defended* by the Kūvākkam pūcāri's older brother in a fraternal disagreement, the Ali avatāra explanation was *volunteered* only by Alis.

26. The Buddha has other hair-related marks (Foucher 1963:258–59), and in the Mahāyāna light rays (rather than hairs) spread from the pores of his skin.

27. "They keep saying don't cut cocks, we keep doing it. The government just takes our money. They don't do much. All the hard work is ours. Whatever they want to do they have to get permission" (June 1994 [informant's name withheld]).

28. When I saw this amazing flinging scene from the Kūttāṇṭavar temple roof, I was too stunned to take a picture.

29. The march represents both Aravāṉ's prewar *kaḷappali* and his eighth-day fight with Alambuṣa, according to different informants (see Hiltebeitel 1995, 261–62).

30. Kūvākkam informants mention this association in connection with hair and nails used in black magic (*pillicūṉiyam*), against which Kūttāṇṭavar protects people.

31. They are tossed as *prasādam* (leftovers from an offering, denoting the deity's grace) to devotees who follow the chariot.

32. Cf. Nārullā 1990:41: "A pūcāri cuts their tālis with a scythe. He snatches off the garlands of blossoms on their heads and throws them. He completely erases the red mark on their foreheads. Then they stand there and finish crying."

33. In what appears to be a northern adaptation of these themes, the legendary emperor Vikramāditya's thirty-two marks make him the ideal offering to the goddess Kāmākṣī or Kāmākhyā, who, appreciating his willing supplication, relents and fulfills his wish without the offering (Edgerton 1926.xciii:182–86).

34. On these aspects of Mohinī, see *Bhāgavata Purāṇa* 10.88:14–46; discussion and sources in O'Flaherty 1973:28–29, 32, 50–51, 228–29; 1975, 274–80; Shulman 1980:307–14; Biardeau 1991:83.

35. *Pēy*, like its more Sanskritic equivalent *picācu*, mentioned below, denotes "ghost" and/or "demon."

36. Writing of the "inner life of Alis" (*alikaḷiṉ antarankam*), Nārullā observes that many have strong "desire for men" (*āṇmītu ācai*), and may even shed seed (*vīntu*) after some time in a loving relationship (1990:24–25). Approaching the festival, some Alis even seem to be "casting a net for good-looking youths" (*aḻakāṉa vāliparkaḷai*; 46; cf. 60–61, 66).

37. Folklorists Palani and S. Rajarathinam, responding to an earlier presentation of this chapter, insisted that homosexuality is also implied in Viṣṇu's appearance as Mohinī to seduce Śiva (personal communications, 1994).

38. Nārullā 1990:61–62; cf. Nanda 1990:26–32, 66–69: "they must be as naked as the day they were born" (27). Nothing indicates whether Alis are ritually shaved for the operation, but Olivelle's mention (this volume) of the renouncer as "bearer of the form he had at birth" suggests a parallel. The new Ali's head hair is regularly attended for a forty-day period after the operation (Nanda 1990:28–29).

References

Aravāṉ Kaṭapali Nāṭakam. 1967. Madras: Irattiṉa Nāyakar and Sons.

Assayag, Jackie. 1992a. "L'un, le couple et le multiple: un complexe rituel et son pantheon dans le Sud de l'Inde (Karnataka)," *Puruṣārtha* 15 (1992):75–77.

——. 1992b. *La colère de la déesse decapitée. Traditions, cultes et pouvoir dans le Sud de l'Inde*. Paris: Presses du CNRS, 1992.

Biardeau, Madeleine. 1989. *Brahmans and Meat-Eating Gods*. In Alf Hiltebeitel, ed., *Criminal Gods and Demon Devotees: Essays on the Guardians of Popular Hinduism*. Albany: State University of New York Press, pp. 19–34.

———. 1991. Nara et Nārāyaṇa. *Wiener Zeitschrift für die Kunde Südasiens* 35:75–108.

Bradford, Nicholas. 1983. "Transgenderism and the Cult of Yellamma: Heat, Sex, and Sickness in South Indian Ritual." *Journal of Anthropological Research* 39, 3:307–22.

Brückner, Heidrun. 1987. "Bhūta-Worship in Coastal Karnāṭaka: An Oral Tuḷu Myth and Festival Ritual of Jumādi," *Studien zur Indologie und Iranistik*, 13/14:17–38.

Caṇmukakkavirāyar, T. 1969. *Śrī Mahāpāratam Cacaṉa Kāviyam* [Prose Nallāppiḷḷai]. Ed. B. A. Vallai-Pālacuppiramaṇiyam. 4 vols. Madras: B. Irattiṉa Nāyakar and Sons.

Caplan, Lionel. 1989. "The Popular Culture of Evil in Urban South India." In Caplan, *Religion and Power: Essays on the Christian Community in Madras*. Madras: Christian Literature Society.

Claus, Peter. 1979. "Mayndala: A Legend and Possession Cult of Tulunad," *Journal of Asian Folklore Studies* 38:94–129.

Edgerton, Franklin. 1926. *Vikrama's Adventures or the Thirty-Two Tales of the Throne*. Cambridge: Harvard University Press.

Eḻumalai, Kō. 1989. *Aravāṉ Tiruviḻā*. Doctoral Dissertation: University of Pondicherry, Kāraikkāl.

Foucher, Alfred. 1963. *The Life of the Buddha According to the Ancient Texts and Monuments of India*. Abridged trans. Simone Brangier Boas. Middletown, Ct.: Wesleyan University Press.

Francis, W. 1906. *Madras District Gazetteers: South Arcot*. Madras: Government Press.

Goldman, Robert P. 1993. "Transsexualism, Gender, and Anxiety in Traditional India," *Journal of the American Oriental Society* 113, 3:374–401.

Handelman, Don. 1995. "The Guises of the Goddess and the Transformation of the Male: Gangamma's Visit to Tirupati and the Continuum of Gender." In David Shulman, ed., *Syllables of Sky: Studies in South Indian Civilization in Honour of Velcheru Narayana Rao*. Delhi: Oxford University Press.

Hiltebeitel, Alf. 1980–81. "*Sītā vibhūṣitā*: The Jewels for Her Journey." Ludwik Sternbach Commemoration Volume. *Indologica Taurinensia* 8–9: 193–200.

———. 1981. "Draupadi's Hair." In Madeleine Biardeau, ed., *Autour de la déesse hindoue, Puruṣārtha* 5:179–214.

———. 1985. "Purity and Auspiciousness in the Sanskrit Epics." In *Essays on Purity and Auspiciousness*. Ed. Frédérique Appfel Marglin and John Carman. *Journal of Developing Societies* 1:41–54.

———. 1988. *The Cult of Draupadī*, vol. 1: *Mythologies, from Gingee to Kurukṣetra*. Chicago: University of Chicago Press.

———. 1991a. *The Cult of Draupadī*, vol. 2: *On Hindu Ritual and the Goddess*. Chicago: University of Chicago Press.

———. 1991b. "The Folklore of Draupadī: Sarees and Hair." In: Arjun Appadurai, Frank Corom, and Margaret Mills, eds., *Power, Gender, and Transmission: Essays on South Asian Folklore*. Philadelphia: University of Pennsylvania Press, pp. 395–427.

———. 1995. "Dying before the *Mahābhārata* War: Martial and Transsexual Body-Building for Aravāṉ," *Journal of Asian Studies* 54,2:447–73.

———. in press. "Kūttāṇṭavar: The Divine Lives of a Severed Head." To appear in Claus Peter Zoller, ed., a volume on *Death in South Asia*.

Matilal, Bimal Krishna. 1991. Kṛṣṇa: In Defence of a Devious Divinity. In Arvind Sharma, ed., *Essays on the Mahābhārata*. Leiden: E. J. Brill. pp. 401–18.

Monier-Williams, Monier. 1989. *A Sanskrit-English Dictionary*. Oxford: Clarendon Press.

Nanda, Serena. 1990. *Neither Man Nor Woman: The Hinjras of India*. Belmont, Calif.: Wadsworth.

Nārullā, Ār. 1990. *Alikaḷ Vāḻkkai*. Madras: Pūkuḻali Accakam.

Obeyesekere, Gananath. 1981. *Medusa's Hair: An Essay on Personal Symbols and Religious Experience*. Chicago: University of Chicago Press.

O'Flaherty, Wendy Doniger. 1973. *Asceticism and Eroticism in the Mythology of Śiva*. London: Oxford University Press.

———. 1975. *Hindu Myths: A Sourcebook Translated from the Sanskrit*. New York: Penguin.

Shulman, David Dean. 1980. *Tamil Temple Myths: Sacrifice and Divine Marriage in the South Indian Śaiva Tradition*. Princeton, N.J.: Princeton University Press.

Subba Rao, T. V. 1976. "Telugu Folk Additions to the Mahabharatha," *Folklore* (Calcutta) 17, 8–9:269–75.

Tarachand, K. C. 1991. *Dēvadāsi Custom: Rural Social Structure and Flesh Markets*, New Delhi: Reliance Publishing House.

Thurston and Rangachari [1904] 1965. *Castes and Tribes of Southern India*. Delhi: Cosmo Publications.

Whitehead, Henry. 1921. *The Village Gods of South India*. Calcutta: Association Press.

Winslow, M. [1862] 1979. *Winslow's Comprehensive Tamil and English Dictionary*. New Delhi: Asian Educational Services.

8 living ghosts: long-haired destitutes in colonial hong kong

james l. watson

This chapter focuses on a specific aspect of hair symbolism in China, namely long (male) hair as an expression of social and cosmological disorder. The ethnographic data for this study were collected in colonial Hong Kong during the 1960s, a period marked by dramatic social change and political uncertainty. In 1962 Hong Kong was flooded with emigres from the adjoining province of Guangdong (Vogel 1969:293–96). Most of these newcomers were fleeing what is now known as the Great Famine of 1959–1961 (see Ashton et al. 1984). In subsequent years Hong Kong's social infrastructure—housing, employment, education, welfare, and medical services—was severely strained by this influx of emigres. In 1969, when I arrived to begin field research, the future of Hong Kong was by no means certain: No one knew how long the Chinese Communist Party would allow Britain to govern this, the "last colony." The anticolonial riots of 1967, inspired by Red Guard activities across the Anglo-Chinese border, were still fresh in everyone's mind (J. Watson 1975:18). And, to further complicate matters, this period marked the height of the Cold War. The Vietnam conflict was escalating monthly and Hong Kong had become a regular port of call for American soldiers on R and R ("rest and recreation") leave. In sum, Hong Kong was a political tinderbox in the late 1960s. Many residents lived in a state of perpetual stress (see e.g., Ikels 1983:49–50), which they sometimes expressed in private fears of a Communist takeover: "I never know when I go to sleep whether I'll wake up with Red Guards holding a knife over me," a teacher volunteered one day. What prompted this statement was a seemingly unrelated discussion of a wildly disheveled young man I had seen earlier that morning.

The man in question had caused a public sensation on the streets of Mongkok, Hong Kong's most densely populated district: Pedestrians stopped dead in their tracks and gave wide berth to this stranger, no easy task on streets that resembled a crowded subway car. The young man was dressed in tattered rags that barely concealed his genitalia and had not washed for so long that his body was caked with what looked like black tar. But, what set him apart from other social marginals I had seen on Hong Kong streets was his grotesquely long fingernails and his filthy, matted hair that hung half-way down his back.

The Mongkok crowd was transfixed by this sight. Mothers clutched their children and shielded them from the man's view. Older residents recoiled and turned away, cursing under their breaths. Adolescents laughed and pointed, although they too were careful to maintain a safe distance. One young woman, aged approximately sixteen, screamed hysterically when her classmates threatened to push her into the man's path. None of these actions elicited a response; the disheveled man appeared to be totally oblivious to the social drama that had enveloped him. He made no efforts to beg for food or money and said not a word, not even to himself.

This was my first sight of what are referred to in colloquial Cantonese as *cheuhng-mouh gwai*, literally "long-haired ghosts." The term itself is revealing because *mouh* ordinarily refers to animal hair or human body hair; another completely unrelated term is used in discussions of human head hair (*tauh-faat*). Europeans were sometimes called "red-haired ghosts" (*huhng-mouh gwai*), a label that is meant to highlight their bizarre appearance and animallike nature (see also Dikötter 1992:41–47; Hibbert 1970: illust. 5). Thus, by using the gloss for animal rather than human hair these odd-looking strangers—foreign and domestic—were placed outside the realm of acceptable social life.

Long Hair in Chinese Culture

In South China human hair is a powerful symbol that conveys a variety of messages depending on context. Cantonese women are expected to have long, luxuriant hair as an indication of their good health, fecundity, and sexual energy (cf. Eberhard 1986:137). Under ordinary circumstances this hair is kept in a tightly bound bun at the back of the head, restrained by silver or gold pins that constitute an essential part of a married woman's dowry. Only at funerals did rural women unbind their hair and rub it over the coffin as an expression of grief (J. Watson 1982). Ordinarily women did not expose the full length of their hair in public.

The social management of men's hair presents an even more complex picture. For many centuries Chinese government officials have been preoccupied with hair as a visible symbol of submission to the state. Perhaps the clearest example was the imposition of the notorious queue by Manchu authorities during their rise to power in the 1640s. The queue represented a radical departure from preexisting hair styles worn by Chinese men;[1] the new code required a shaved forehead and a tightly bound, elongated braid hanging to neck level in the back (see Cheng, this volume). As Kuhn (1990:58–59) has argued, it was the shaved head—rather than the braided hair—that offended native Chinese who were loyal to the Ming dynastic court (1368–1644). Those who resisted the Manchus were warned: "Keep your head, lose your hair; keep your hair, lose your head" (see Wakeman 1975:58).[2]

Long, unruly hair on Chinese males was taken as a mark of banditry and insurrection.[3] Taiping rebels were known as "long hairs," reflecting their open defiance of state-imposed conventions (Cohen 1987:57; Shih 1967:136). From the perspective of government troops, the sight of rebels with their long hair blowing in the wind as they rode into battle was, quite literally, a vision from hell: Chinese ghosts were also portrayed (in popular iconography) with long, unruly hair (see e.g., Dore 1914: fig. 28).

More recently, during the Maoist era of the 1950s and 1960s Chinese men were expected to keep their hair close trimmed, in military style as appropriate for revolutionaries intent on building a new socialist order. Those accused of counterrevolutionary tendencies often had their heads shaved in odd patterns, creating what Red Guards referred to as "Yin-Yang" haircuts (Gao 1987:53–54). The ultimate humiliation was to be thrown into a cell and left to die while one's hair grew to abnormal lengths—as if to highlight how far one had departed from the mainstream. Such was the fate of Liu Shaoqi, the former President of the People's Republic who fell from grace during the Cultural Revolution (see Dittmer 1981:459).

In the aftermath of the 1989 Beijing massacre, Chinese youths have flirted with long hair as an emblem of protest. Male pop stars are expected to have wild, flowing hair but they have to be careful to avoid police roundups of "long hairs" and "troublemakers" who frequent the Beijing underworld of discos, bars, and concert halls. Many long haired performers have adopted a nocturnal life style and travel only under the cover of darkness (see Jones 1992:87). Communist Party officials have thus continued the Chinese tradition of equating long (male) hair with disorder and rebellion (cf. Firth 1973:274–83). Until recently the same could be said of Nationalist Party (Kuomintang) authorities in Taiwan.

Long Hair and Social Control in Colonial Hong Kong

According to a report by the Council of Social Services, there were just over one hundred long-haired destitutes living on the streets of Hong Kong in 1967.[4] Six were women, although in interviews social welfare officers made it clear that these individuals were very different from their male counterparts. Two of the six women mentioned in the Council's report had long hair knotted with rags and bits of tinsel, but they wore socially acceptable clothing and kept themselves reasonably clean. Ordinary citizens did not use the Cantonese term *long haired ghosts* when they spoke of these women.

In 1969 long-haired destitutes constituted only a tiny minority (approximately 110 people) of Hong Kong's population, which at that time was just under four million (Census 1972:9). And, yet, their impact on the colony's popular culture was far greater than these numbers might indicate. During the same period there were well over a thousand beggars and several hundred "street sleepers" in Hong Kong, but these two categories of people generated little comment from my informants (more will be said about beggars below).

It was commonly agreed among Hong Kong social workers that the majority of long-haired destitutes had entered the colony in May, 1962, when Chinese authorities stopped watching the border for a brief period (Immigration Report 1966–67:4, 11; Vogel 1969:293–96). Following that incident, senior police officers maintain, Hong Kong border patrols began to encounter long hairs who apparently had been escorted to the border and allowed to cross without hindrance. Rumors that Guangdong provincial authorities had been "dumping" their social problems in British territory circulated widely during the 1960s and 1970s.

The distinguishing characteristic of long-haired destitutes (aside from their appearance) was that they did not solicit food or money. Instead, they survived as urban scavengers, patrolling the alleys behind restaurants for food. Several restaurant workers whom I interviewed stated that they often put leftovers in designated places for these "unlucky people," but this was done in such a way to draw them away from (rather than attract them to) the restaurants. None of my informants admitted to giving these men money, although many said that they frequently gave alms to beggars.

Hong Kong government officials (European, South Asian, and Chinese) always used the English term *long-haired destitute* when referring to these disheveled strangers. In colonial discourse they were treated as a special category and were never lumped together with beggars, the latter being considered a "normal" part of the social scene. Social workers who had been assigned to monitor the street population discovered that, unlike beggars (cf. Schak 1988), the long hairs were loners. They did not congregate or sleep in the same places and did not show any evidence of cooperation among themselves. In 1969 the majority of long hairs were between the ages of twenty and thirty-five; most were (relatively) able bodied and none proved to be a drug addict, according to social workers.

Welfare officials and government psychiatrists who had worked with the long hairs classified all but a handful as "mentally ill," suffering from various forms of disorientation and depression. The professionals I spoke with expressed pity for these disheveled men but discovered there was little they could do to help.

In the early 1960s police and social workers rounded up several of the destitutes and gave them haircuts, baths, new clothes, and hot meals as part of a rehabilitation campaign—but it did not work. The men were back on the streets almost immediately and within a few months had begun to reassume their earlier appearances. To my knowledge, none of these men was ever incarcerated or detained for more than a few hours—unless implicated in a crime. On July 30, 1969, a long-haired destitute grabbed a chopper (heavy cleaver knife) from a market stall and ran down a crowded street in Wanchai, seriously wounding seven pedestrians. For the next week Hong Kong newspapers printed lurid accounts of the incident and demanded protection from these "crazed degenerates," to quote one source.[5] This appears to be the only outbreak of serious violence attributed to long-haired destitutes during the 1960s, but it was treated by many citizens as a fulfillment of their worst fears. A week after the attack, an arrest was announced and the story soon disappeared from the daily newspapers.

Senior government officials who spoke to me about the long-haired destitutes were primarily concerned about their impact on Hong

Kong's tourist industry. Interest focused specifically on the reaction of Overseas Chinese visitors (from Taiwan, Singapore, Canada, United States). One official argued Chinese tourists did not want to see dirty, long-haired people on Hong Kong streets because it reminded them of the bad times they had experienced in China during their childhood. This official, an Englishman who had lived in Hong Kong for nearly twenty years, was responding to the symbolic implications of the long hairs' physical appearance. His job was to manage and control the streets, but as is often true of colonial officers (cf. Dirks 1992; Stoler 1992), he had acquired what he took to be a deeper understanding of the problem and used this knowledge to guide social policy.

In the aftermath of the 1969 chopper attack, police began to keep long-haired destitutes away from Hong Kong's major hotel districts. Little is known about the social reproduction of this category of marginals but, by 1977 when I returned for a second round of fieldwork, the urban population of long hairs had dwindled to approximately thirty. Even fewer could be found during the 1980s and by 1995 they had almost completely disappeared from Hong Kong. It is impossible at this juncture in my research to determine whether colonial policies were responsible for this disappearance or whether improved conditions in China were major contributing factors.[6]

Reading the Body: Mourning Gone Awry

The Colonial official mentioned above was keenly aware that the disheveled appearance of long-haired destitutes brought back memories of bad times in China's recent past. He did not, however, have an explanation for the men's condition. Most of my Cantonese informants, by contrast, offered ready explanations for the bizarre appearance of the "long-haired ghosts." For ordinary citizens of Hong Kong, it was the physical attributes of the men—the overall appearance of their bodies including posture, gesture, and carriage—that supplied the clues for an explanation.

Most urbanites argued that the long hairs had collapsed into a total state of mourning and had retreated from the world. Why? Because the communists had killed their families and/or forced their remaining relatives into labor camps. These destitute young men had nothing to live for, my urban informants postulated, and the shocking state of their bodies was a sad but logical reaction to the tragedies they had experienced. This line of explanation was surprisingly consistent among city dwellers, irrespective of age, sex, and occupation; the testimonies I collected varied only in minor details (some family members were killed during Cultural Revolution struggle sessions, others were executed during land-reform campaigns or committed suicide in reeducation camps).

My urban sample did not include representatives of left-wing labor unions or supporters of the Communist Party, of whom there were thousands in Hong Kong during the late 1960s (see Johnson 1971). Given the political conditions of the time my interviews were restricted to people who were willing to talk to a foreigner: teachers, doctors, restaurant workers, shopkeepers, hawkers, and students (an urban sample of approximately thirty-five people). All but two claimed that the long-haired destitutes had come to Hong Kong from China; the two dissenters thought that they were non-Chinese, from Malaysia or India, who had jumped ship in Hong Kong. It is thus significant that the destitutes were uniformly defined as "other," outsiders from an alien and potentially threatening society.

By 1969 the most violent period of the Cultural Revolution had subsided but China was still in the throes of a massive political upheaval. Many of Hong Kong's Chinese-language newspapers (those not supported by the Communist Party) carried long articles with details of the beatings, suicides, and murders instigated by Red Guards. Perhaps as many as seventy percent of Hong Kong's 1969 population had left China in earlier decades or were the children of emigre parents. The majority of these people had (at best) ambivalent feelings toward the Communist Party. The romantic vision of the Chinese Cultural Revolution that prevailed in Western liberal circles had almost no credibility among the bulk of Hong Kong's residents, urban or rural.

Given the political circumstances, it is not surprising that ordinary citizens should have projected their own concerns for a secure future onto the disorderly bodies of the long-haired destitutes in their midst. None of my urban informants condemned these unfortunates or explained their sorry state as a consequence of personal or moral failings: They were accepted, quite simply, as victims of a political system over which they had no control. Unlike colonial officials, most of my informants were not in the least interested in helping to rehabilitate the long hairs and considered them beyond all hope.

Long Hair: Symptom or Symbol?

One of the aspects of this problem that makes it so intriguing is that the young men in question were completely *silent* about their own backgrounds. A defining characteristic of the long-haired destitutes, according to social workers and psychiatrists who had worked with them, was that they did not speak to anyone—they did not or would not communicate in speech. Most did not even talk to themselves. They generally made no efforts to engage in interpersonal interactions of any kind and appeared to be completely oblivious to the actions of others.

In other words, the long hairs were social beings only in the sense that they set off reactions among observers who interpreted these wildly disheveled bodies as a set of symbols. The young men interacted primarily through the medium of their bodies, apparently detached from all other forms of human discourse. People reacted strongly to the matted hair, long nails, and unbearable stench—attributes that begged interpretation, indeed *demanded* it.

It is unclear whether the destitutes were fully conscious of the public spectacle they were making of themselves. One government psychiatrist suspected that many of them were indeed aware of their actions and, he suggested, this might help explain their behavior. Social workers who had worked most closely with the young men were not convinced and argued that they were too dissociated to comprehend what had happened to them. Ordinary citizens were not interested in this debate. It mattered little to these informants whether or not the long hairs had consciously crafted their own bodily appearance: What was important was the physical image itself. To most urbanites the matted hair, the long nails, and the slumped posture were interpreted as symbols of extreme mourning.

Cantonese men are expected to withdraw from regular activities upon the death of a parent or grandparent. The rules of mourning call for a temporary abandonment of personal grooming: Beard, hair, and nails are left uncut; washing of body and hair is severely reduced; old clothing and special mourning garb (made of rough, natural fibers) are worn in public. The mourner is expected to avoid meetings, rituals, and banquets and must not enter temples or ancestral halls, lest these premises be polluted. Most significantly, a Cantonese male in mourning is expected to exhibit (at least in public) a detached, slightly dissociated demeanor. In Hong Kong during the late 1960s mourning lasted from seven to forty-nine days, depending on the wealth and social status of the family involved (see J. Watson 1982). Even in its most truncated form, Cantonese mourning was—especially for males—a public performance that was judged as such: There were good mourners and bad mourners, but in no case was mourning expected to become a way of life.[7] For many observers, therefore, the long-haired strangers had transgressed the boundaries of acceptable ritual behavior and voluntarily removed themselves from society.

In his study of matted hair among Sri Lankan religious specialists, Obeyesekere draws an important distinction between symptom and symbol: "A symptom is a somatic manifestation of a psychic or physical malady. In [Sri Lankan] ascetics, symptom is replaced by symbol. The symbol is generated primarily out of the unconscious; once generated, it exists on the public level as a cultural symbol. Through it the ascetics convey a public message: fear, revulsion" (Obeyesekere 1981:37).

In South Asia there is a long tradition associating long, matted hair with recognized forms of religious asceticism (see also Parry 1982). Many of Obeyesekere's ascetics offer elaborate explanations for the symbolic meaning of their own hair. Furthermore, "matted hair is a special type of symbol. It is manipulatory, that is, *used* by individuals. It is like other religious symbols that are manipulated by the worshipper" (1981:36).

Cantonese long-haired destitutes present a special problem for analysis: They played no recognized role in the religious, ritual, or social life of Hong Kong people. In this respect they were unlike beggars who were always present at religious festivals (cf. Weller 1985). Chinese beggars were conscious of themselves as public performers and played essential roles as alms recipients. Beggars converted their bodily attributes and physical symptoms into symbols in order to communicate with their audience of donors (Schak 1988), much as Sri Lankan ascetics manipulated their matted hair. The translation of physical symptom into public symbol does not appear to have happened among Hong Kong's long-haired destitutes. Although some of them may well have been aware of the aberrant appearance, they did not *use* their hair for any publicly recognized purpose (cf. Obeyesekere 1981:35-37).

Kleinman's work on "somatic amplification" is also relevant to this discussion. In China, disease and mental disorders are often explained as a malfunctioning of the body, leading to somatization: "Loss, injustice, failure, conflict—all are transformed into discourse about pain and disability. . . . The body mediates the individual's perception, experience, and interpretation of problems in social life. Mental disorder [in China] is a prime instance" (Kleinman 1986:51). Kleinman's clinical study explores the processes of somatization in people's explanations and experiences of their *own* problems.

Cantonese observers' explanations of the appearance of long-haired destitutes presents an interesting commentary on the processes of somatization, displacement, and projection: My urban informants showed no hesitation whatsoever in interpreting the bodily manifestations of the disheveled men as a consequence of internal mental anguish, expressed in extreme mourning. Biological malfunctions of the body were never offered as explanations for the bizarre behavior and appearance of the destitutes. The Cultural Revolution victims studied by Kleinman tended to deny a connection between mental distress and physical dysfunction (1986). Hong Kong residents, by contrast, appear to have developed a variation of the somatization argument to explain the actions of people who did not speak for themselves.

Living Ghosts: Visions of Bad Death?

After completing the urban phase of this research I moved to the village of San Tin in the Hong Kong New Territories, where I lived for the next seventeen months. San Tin is a single-lineage village inhabited by approximately two thousand people, all but a handful of whom are surnamed Man (Mandarin Wen). In 1969 San Tin was widely recognized as one of the most "traditional" communities in the New Territories; the Man lineage maintained a full set of ancestral rites and a lively temple cult (J. Watson 1975). An indigenous security force, composed of local men, patrolled the village every night and made sure that strangers did not linger long. Given that San Tin is located only half a mile from the Anglo-Chinese border, refugees were frequently spotted near the village in the 1960s. Much to the horror of local people, several of these strangers appeared to be visions directly from hell.

Among rural Cantonese, bad death (the result of suicide, murder, accident) is thought to produce a particularly vicious and insatiable entity known as a "hungry ghost" (*ngoh-gwai*). Ghosts of this type are also produced when people die without children or designated heirs to feed and nourish them in the afterlife (see Weller 1985). In folk art and drama, hungry ghosts are depicted as ragged beggars with filthy, matted hair and long fingernails (see e.g., Dore 1914: fig.

28). Proper ancestors, by contrast, are portrayed as well groomed elders dressed in elegant gowns.[8] Ancestors are seated on throne-chairs, center stage in the midst of ritual action; hungry ghosts are always standing, skulking on the fringe of human activity. Ancestors receive sumptuous offerings of food, clothing, and money; hungry ghosts snatch at left overs, like scavenger dogs or crows.

Cantonese villagers associated long hair and grotesque nails with another, even more horrifying vision—namely unclean, polluted corpses that had not decayed rapidly enough for secondary burial. In south China the remains of immediate ancestors were (and in the New Territories still are) exhumed after seven to ten years; the bones are then cleaned of all remaining flesh, hair, and nails. Finally, the purified bones are placed in a large urn which is buried in a permanent tomb (Ahern 1973:172–73; J. Watson 1982). Hungry ghosts, my informants explained, look exactly like these partially decayed, long-haired corpses.

It should come as no surprise, therefore, that the long-haired destitutes literally terrified some of San Tin's older residents. Even the passive presence of these strangers was considered dangerous and they were never permitted to enter the village. On the one occasion when I witnessed a group of New Territories villagers encounter a long-haired destitute, the reaction was, for me, a familiar one: Women turned their heads away and refused to open their eyes until the stranger had passed; children were hidden from view and no one uttered a word.

San Tin residents had performed similar avoidance routines during funerals. The objects of their concern on those occasions were professional corpse handlers who had come to the village to perform essential services. Corpse handlers (*ng jong lo*) were hired to dig graves, carry coffins, and prepare corpses for burial; this was a job that only the lowest of the low, men who had no families and no alternatives, would accept (J. Watson 1988). Villagers believed that the vital essence (*yeung*) of males who had touched more than seven corpses had been destroyed and that the bodies of such men were permanently corrupted by death pollution (*saat-hei*, "killing airs"). The mere glance of a corpse handler could cause illness in children (fright), nervous disorders in adults, and miscarriages among pregnant women—hence the practice of turning the head.

Long-haired destitutes elicited similar reactions, which leads me to conclude that they too were associated with the polluting influences of death. Unlike corpse handlers, however, the destitutes did not perform any services for the community. They were completely superfluous and thus constituted an unambiguous threat to the cosmological order.

Much like their urban counterparts, New Territories villagers read the physical bodies of the long-haired strangers as symbols of death, only in this case it was the stark vision of corporal decay itself that preoccupied rural observers. No one in San Tin suggested that destitutes were mourners who had lost touch with society or that these ghastly looking apparitions could have had families to lose. For most villagers the matted hair, ragged clothes, and long nails were so heavily saturated with symbolic content that no other interpretation could even be contemplated: These beings looked too much like the popular image of hungry ghosts to be anything else. Villagers did not attempt to *explain* the appearance of these strangers: All that mattered was to avoid any form of contact with them.

Conclusions

From the limited evidence available it would appear that long-haired destitutes represented, to Cantonese observers, visions of disorder—both social and cosmological disorder. For many urban residents of Hong Kong the bodies of these disheveled strangers were taken as symbols of extreme mourning. Urbanites in my sample tended to project their own concerns for a secure future onto the unfortunate men who lived on the streets. Here, but for an accident of geography, was a vision of what might have happened to the observers themselves. Revolutionary violence on an unprecedented scale had enveloped China and the prospect that it could spill over into Hong Kong was not a fantasy—indeed, this had happened in 1967 and the British had seriously considered pulling out. The body of the long-haired destitute thus had a political reading: It reminded everyone in urban Hong Kong that they were living in a borrowed place on borrowed time.[9]

Residents of San Tin had different reactions to the long-haired men who passed by their village. The Man lineage had been settled in this corner of China for nearly six hundred years by the time the British claimed the New Territories in 1898. A brief resistance against the occupying forces was organized in 1899 (see Groves 1969; Wesley-Smith 1980:45–87), but by the 1920s local lineages had reached an accommodation with the British administration (the Man were one of approximately twelve dominant lineages settled on land that had been incorporated into the New Territories). For the next seventy years the Man, and their affines in neighboring communities, were granted special privileges by colonial officers and were accepted as the original, "indigenous" (*buhn-deih*) landowners of the territory. In later decades newcomers from across the Chinese border were treated as "outsiders" (*ngoi-loih yahn*) by established villagers (R. Watson 1985:139–42). In 1969 the people of San Tin felt threatened by an influx of recent emigres who had settled near their village but colonial authorities allowed the Man lineage to maintain firm control over the local political scene (J. Watson 1975:42–48).

Thus, unlike their urban counterparts in Hong Kong's overcrowded metropolitan districts, the indigenous people of the New Territories were not living in a borrowed place; they were simply residing in their ancestral homes. Furthermore, from the local villager's point of view, if anyone was living on borrowed time it was the British.

Residents of San Tin were certainly worried about political developments across the border. But insecurity about the future was not an all-consuming preoccupation for villagers, as it clearly was for some of my urban informants. The bodies of long-haired destitutes were thus read as a different set of symbols by the two groups of informants. Urbanites may well have seen themselves, their own futures as *living* bodies, in the unfortunate strangers. They, too, might be reduced to a state of extreme mourning if the communists took control of Hong Kong. Village informants may also have seen themselves in the long-haired specters, but, if so, they were viewing their own bodies *after death*—specifically after bad death.

All of this is, of course, largely speculation on my part. Villagers were hesitant even to talk about the long-haired destitutes, let alone reveal their personal concerns about death or the precarious transition to ancestorhood that awaited them. Urban informants, although more talkative, did not state specifically that they feared a fate similar to the destitutes in their midst.

What is clear (to me at least) is that the physical attributes—the symptoms—of the long-haired destitutes had set off strong reactions in all who observed them. These symptoms (matted hair, long fingernails, dissociated demeanor) were interpreted as full-blown, unambiguous sets of symbols by both sets of informants (cf. Obeyesekere 1981:36–37).

This essay has been written exclusively from observers' points of view. One critical dimension of the story is missing, namely the testimony of the unfortunate young men who were themselves the focus of all this attention. Alas, for our purposes, these men remained silent.[10] One wonders whether anyone would have listened if they had chosen to speak.

Notes

This chapter was first presented at the panel on "Hair: Fashions and Resistance," at the 1993 Annual Meeting of the Association for Asian Studies, Los Angeles. The author thanks Eugene Cooper, Barbara Miller, Gananath Obeyesekere, and Rubie Watson for helpful comments on an earlier draft.

1. An early European visitor to China during the Ming (pre-Manchu) dynasty, Father Martin de Rada, observed that Chinese men "are proud to have a great head of hair. They let it grow long and coil it up in a knot on the crown of the head. They then put it in a hairnet parted in the center to hold and fix the hair in position . . . They take a good time each morning in combing and dressing their hair" (Boxer 1953:282, cited in Wakeman 1985:648).

2. Ming loyalists responded to these threats as follows: "To cut off my hair would be difficult. To cut off my head would be easy" (Dennerline 1981:288).

3. On July 8, 1645, the Manchu emperor issued the following command to his Han Chinese subjects: "Within ten days after this proclamation has been issued in the capital and within ten days after the [imperial] dispatch has reached each province respectively, let the hair-cutting order be completely carried out. Those who refuse will be the same as bandits rebelling against our orders and must be punished severely" (Wakeman 1975:55).

4. Mimeographed report by the Hong Kong Council of Social Services, dated 1967.

5. See *South China Morning Post* 31 July 1969, p. 1; 1 August 1969, p. 18; 2 August 1969, p. 6.

6. In 1986 and 1992 I observed long-haired destitutes walking alone along rural highways of Guangdong Province, which adjoins Hong Kong.

7. It is unclear whether this observation holds true for widows; see R. Watson (1986) on rural Cantonese women.

8. In preparing a male corpse for burial, the hair and nails were trimmed; women had their hair combed and tightly bound before burial (cf. DeGroot 1892:19).

9. This was a commonly used phrase in Hong Kong during the 1960s, and the title of a popular book (see Hughes 1968).

10. I attempted to speak to several long-haired destitutes in urban Hong Kong, but they did not respond.

Glossary

Cantonese terms in this paper follow the Yale romanization system, outlines in: *Cantonese Dictionary*, by Parker Po-fei Huang, Yale University Press (1970).

buhn-deih	本 地	(indigenous)
cheuhng-mouh gwai	長 毛 鬼	(long-haired ghost)
huhng-mouth gwai	紅 毛 鬼	(red-haired ghost)
Man	文	(surname)
mouh	毛	(animal, body hair)
ng jong lo	仵 （忤） 葬 佬	(corpse handlers)
ngoh-gwai	餓 鬼	(hungry ghost)
ngoi-loih yahn	外 來 人	(outsiders)
saat-hei	殺 氣	(killing airs)
San Tin	新 田	(place name)
tauh-faat	頭 髮	(head hair)
yeung	陽	(male essence, yang)

References

Ahern, Emily M. 1973. *The Cult of the Dead in a Chinese Village.* Stanford: Stanford University Press.

Ashton, Basil, et al. 1984. "Famine in China, 1958–61," *Population and Development Review* 10(4):613–45.

Boxer, C. R., ed. 1953. *South China in the Sixteenth Century.* London: Hakluyt Society.

Census. 1972. *Hong Kong Population and Housing Census: 1971 Main Report.* Hong Kong Government: Census and Statistics Department.

Cohen, Paul A. 1987. *Between Tradition and Modernity: Wang T'ao and Reform in Late Ch'ing China.* Cambridge: Harvard University Press.

DeGroot, J. J. M. 1892. *The Religious System of China,* vol. I. Leiden: E. J. Brill.

Dennerline, Jerry. 1981. *The Chia-ting Loyalists: Confucian Leadership and Social Change in Seventeenth Century China.* New Haven: Yale University Press.

Dikötter, Frank. 1992. *The Discourse of Race in Modern China.* Stanford: Stanford University Press.

Dirks, Nicholas B. 1992. "Castes of Mind," *Representations* 37:56–78.

Dittmer, Lowell. 1981. Death and Transfiguration: Liu Shaoqi's Rehabilitation and Contemporary Chinese Politics. *Journal of Asian Studies* 40(3):455–479.

Dore, Henry. 1914. *Researches into Chinese Superstitions,* vol. I. Shanghai: T'usewei Printing Press.

Douglas, Mary. 1966. *Purity and Danger.* London: Routledge and Kegan Paul.

Eberhard, Wolfram. 1986. *A Dictionary of Chinese Symbols.* London: Routledge and Kegan Paul.

Firth, Raymond. 1973. "Hair as Private Asset and Public Symbol." In his *Symbols: Public and Private.* London: George Allen and Unwin.

Gao Yuan. 1987. *Born Red: A Chronicle of the Cultural Revolution.* Stanford: Stanford University Press.

Groves, Robert G. 1969. "Militia, Market and Lineage: Chinese Resistance to the Occupation of Hong Kong's New Territories in 1899," *Journal of the Hong King Branch of the Royal Asiatic Society* 9:31–64.

Hallpike, C. R. 1969. "Social Hair," *Man* 4:256–64.

Hershman, P. 1974. "Hair, Sex and Dirt," *Man* 9:274–98.

Hibbert, Christopher. 1970. *The Dragon Wakes: China and the West, 1793–1911.* London: Penguin.

Hughes, Richard. 1968. *Hong Kong: Borrowed Place—Borrowed Time.* London: Andre Deutsch.

Ikels, Charlotte. 1983. *Aging and Adaptation: Chinese in Hong Kong and the United States.* Hamden, Conn.: Archon Books.

Johnson, Graham E. 1971. "From Rural Committee to Spirit Medium Cult: Voluntary Associations in the Development of a Chinese Town." *Contributions to Asian Studies* 1:123–43.

Jones, Andrew F. 1992. "Beijing Bastards," *Spin* 8(7): 80–90, 122–23 (Oct.)

Kleinman, Arthur. 1986. *Social Origins of Distress and Disease: Depression, Neurasthenia, and Pain in Modern China.* New Haven, Conn.: Yale University Press.

Kuhn, Philip A. 1990. *Soulstealers: The Chinese Sorcery Scare of 1768.* Cambridge: Harvard University Press.

Leach, Edmund R. 1958. "Magical Hair," *Journal of the Royal Anthropological Institute* 88:147–64.

Obeyesekere, Gananath. 1981. *Medusa's Hair: An Essay on Personal Symbols and Religious Experience.* Chicago: University of Chicago Press.

Parry, Jonathan. 1982. "Sacrificial Death and the Necrophagous Ascetic." In *Death and the Regeneration of Life.* Ed. Maurice Block and Jonathan Parry. Cambridge: Cambridge University Press.

Schak, David C. 1988. *A Chinese Beggar's Den: Poverty and Mobility in an Underclass Community.* Pittsburgh: University of Pittsburgh Press.

Shih, Vincent Y. C. 1967. *The Taiping Ideology: Its Sources, Interpretations, and Influences.* Seattle: University of Washington Press.

Stoler, Ann L. 1992. "Rethinking Colonial Categories: European Communities and the Boundaries of Rule." In *Colonialism and Culture.* Ed. Nicholas B. Dirks. Ann Arbor: University of Michigan Press.

Vogel, Ezra. 1969. *Canton Under Communism.* Cambridge: Harvard University Press.

Wakeman, Frederic, Jr. 1975. "Localism and Loyalism During the Ch'ing Conquest of Jiangnan: The Tragedy of Chiang-yin." In *Conflict and Control in Late Imperial China.* Ed. Frederic Wakeman, Jr., and Carolyn Grant. Berkeley: University of California Press.

———. 1985. *The Great Enterprise: The Manchu Reconstruction of Imperial Order in Seventeenth-Century China.* Berkeley: University of California Press.

Watson, James L. 1975. *Emigration and the Chinese Lineage: The Mans in Hong Kong and London.* Berkeley: University of California Press.

1982. "Of Flesh and Bones: The Management of Death Pollution in Cantonese Society." In *Death and the Regeneration of Life.* Ed. Maurice Block and Jonathan Parry. Cambridge: Cambridge University Press.

1988. "Funeral Specialists in Cantonese Society: Pollution, Performance, and Social Hierarchy." In *Death Ritual in Late Imperial and Modern China.* Ed. James L. Watson and Evelyn S. Rawski. Berkeley: University of California Press.

Watson, Rubie S. 1985. *Inequality Among Brothers: Class and Kinship in South China.* Cambridge: Cambridge University Press.

———. 1986. "The Named and the Nameless: Gender and Person in Chinese Society," *American Ethnologist* 13 (4):619–31.

Weller, Robert P. 1985. "Bandits, Beggars, and Ghosts: The Failure of State Control Over Religious Interpretation in Taiwan," *American Ethnologist* 12:46–61.

Wesley-Smith, Peter. 1980. *Unequal Treaty, 1898–1997: China, Great Britain and Hong Kong's New Territories.* Hong Kong: Oxford University Press.

9 cutting the fringes: pubic hair at the margins of japanese censorship laws

anne allison

Historical Borders/Bodily Markers

Pubic hair stands at the edges of what is legally representable in Japan. It is that which constitutes the "obscene": the site/sight at which the boundary between permissible and transgressive sexual imagery has been drawn. In a country where pictures of naked women appear in news magazines, naked breasts in public advertisements, scenes of rape and nudity on television, and sado-masochistic scenarios in comic books that are as openly read as they are sold, pubic hair is notably absent in a popular culture of constant and graphic sexual images. It is at a point of nature—the hair surrounding a woman's genitalia—that censorship laws are imposed. Or, more accurately, it is not pubic hair itself—a physical presence, after all, on the body of every woman past the age of puberty—but its representation in visual media that defines obscenity and constitutes an "offense" against the "sexual mores" of the people. Imagining a woman tied up, held down, or forcibly penetrated is acceptable, in other words, whereas revealing the reality of her pubic hair is not.

What is so offensive about the hair of women's genitalia that marks it as a sight of such public danger? Japanese children, after all, customarily enter the bath with their mothers and often until an age approaching puberty. In this context the mother does not shield her child's view and the sight the child sees is considered natural. Likewise, Japanese religion and mythology have traditionally viewed nakedness and bodily functions such as excretion, farting, sex, and burping, as a realm of nature to which no sense of shame or immorality has been attached (Schodt 1983; Kawai 1988). Images of the god Tengusan with his phallic-sized nose, for example, remain in Shinto shrines along with fertility goddesses with enlarged breasts and exposed genitalia. In mythology and such traditional arts of storytelling as *rakugo*, the exposure of body parts is commonly figured as well. One of the most popular myths surrounding Amaterasu (the sun goddess and ancestress of the emperor), in fact, features genitalic exposure as key to the plot. After Amaterasu hid herself in a cave out of anger at her brother (Susanō, the ruler of the underworld), the goddesses try to lure her out and thereby restore daylight to the earth. They dance and when one lifts her skirt exposing her genitalia to the others, the hilarity that ensues piques the curiosity of Amaterasu and she ventures outside the cave.

In Shinto-based traditions of artwork, drama, and mythology, genitalia including the pubic hair surrounding it has not been sanctioned or condemned in Japan. To the contrary, it is often included, even forefronted, as an object of obvious interest, pleasure, and joy. During the Tokugawa era, for example, the genre of erotic scroll art called *shunga* graphically and imaginatively displayed sexual bodies with all body parts intact. As is often described for this art form, penises were not only shown but commonly exaggerated into hyperbolic phalluses and female genitalia were drawn with its details of clitorises, labia, and pubic hair clearly displayed (Schodt 1988). In this period when the shogunate established civil order, outlawed the warfare that had split individual domains, and imposed a bureaucracy based on a rigid set of Confucian principles and social laws, Japan's borders were also rigidly policed. No subject of the land was allowed to leave and also return, and no one foreign to Japan was permitted entry except at the one port of Nagasaki. Domestic order, it was thought, depended on the patrolling of national borders and on ensuring that a purity of Japaneseness was upheld.

Japan did not remain isolated forever, of course. Internal pressures such as food shortages and financial collapse threatened its borders just as the demand to open up came from outside in the shape of a warship commandeered by Admiral Perry who sailed into Tokyo Bay in 1853 and "requested" that Japan become the trading partner of the United States. The shogunate accommodated this request, but the accommodation led to civil war and a reorganization of the government (Meiji Restoration of 1868) in the name of the emperor and a commitment to "ousting the barbarian." Opening up to the West was inevitable, however, and by the 1870s trade agreements with the United States and a number of West European countries had been signed. The era of Japan's modernization began: rapid industrialization; the adoption of a western-based constitution, school system, and legal structure; and a vision of becoming a world power. With two military victories at the turn of the century—one against China (the Sino-Japanese war of 1894 and 1895) and the other against Russia (the Russo-Japanese war of 1904 and 1905 which was the first defeat of a western country by a non-western one), Japan embarked upon a campaign of expansionism and colonization consistent with the imperialist trappings of modernism in the West. With military strength coupled to the economic and industrial prowess she exhibited, Japan became a figure in the international arena. Still in the eyes of many westerners, the mirror to which Japan necessarily turned for its reflection as a modern state, Japanese remained different: culturally and racially other to the model of civilization upheld in the West (Dore 1958; Rubin 1984).

Modernization and Obscenity Laws

Signs of Japan's cultural otherness were certain attitudes regarding bodies, body display, and bodily representation. Mothers nursing their babies in public, men and women entering public baths together, and graphic iconography of genitalia and/or sexual intercourse were Japanese behaviors noted by western travelers to Japan and interpreted as marks of moral laxness and social primitiveness. To counteract this negative image of its culture based not on Japanese categories of morality or social mores but Eurocentric ones stemming from Judeo-Christian ideology, the Japanese government imposed regulations on such customary practices as mixed bathing (Hane 1986; Schodt 1983; Rubin 1984). In order to gain face as a modern nation, in other words, Japan inscribed shame where it had not been located before: onto body parts and bodily functions regarded as natural by Japanese traditions. It was during this era of remarkable movement in Japan—away from a period of rigid isolationism and into one of rapid modernization conducted on the terrain of the international—that the law which prohibits the visualization of pubic hair today was first passed.

Article 175 of the Penal Code became law in 1907. It states: "A person who distributes or sells obscene writing, pictures or other objects or who publicly displays the same, shall be punished with imprisonment at forced labor, for not more than two years, or a fine. The same shall apply to a person who possesses the same for the purpose of sale" (quoted in Ihaya 1991). Obscenity as a principle was legislated by this code. Its precise definition, however, remained vague: a "form" in the Barthesian sense of a structure of meaning (1972) whose content is filled in differently at different points in time. From the beginning, censorship was imposed against explicit images of genitalia and intercourse. In earlier times, however, the definition of obscenity exceeded these sights and did not fixate so exclusively, as it does now, on the site of female pubic hair. During the war years, the period beginning in the mobilization years of the late 1920s and continuing until Japan's defeat in 1945, obscenity was categorized by any image or written commentary not in alignment with the nationalist war effort. Cartoonists who satirized the government or failed to represent the moralistic energies of the Japanese state risked penalty and imprisonment. Sex, during this time period, was a secondary concern for the censors who were far more focused on the politics of war. Significantly, however, it did become a subject that was used in propaganda against the enemy. In leaflets dropped on American troops, American wives were shown engaging in wild promiscuity as their husbands were off fighting the war as an image calculated to enrage and emasculate the GIs. For domestic audiences, however, the concentration was less on screening out specific body parts and more on the inscribing of attitudes, behaviors, and subjects devoted to the reproduction and production of the Japanese nationalist state (Hane 1986:285–86).

Following the war, democracy was officially adopted during Japan's period of enforced occupation managed primarily by the United States. Under the guidance of Occupation Forces, a democratic constitution was drafted and passed in 1947 and freedom of speech was established as a citizen's right. By the letter of the law, censorship was no longer permitted and yet article #175 of the penal code managed to survive: a survival that has been called an infraction of democratic rights in a number of court cases filed by producers or sellers of materials that have been censored or banned on grounds of their obscenity (Oshima 1981). In part because censorship is at such odds with the democratic constitution and the freedom of speech it guarantees, the language of article #175 remains as obscure today as it was when originally established in 1907 (Kimoto 1970, Ihaya 1991).

As in the United States, interpretation of obscenity falls to the hands of legislators. As Judge Stewart Potter stated while serving as a member of the Meese Commission investigating the parameters of pornography, "I know it when I see it" (on this issue, see, for example, Williams 1989 and Vance 1992), Japanese speak of obscenity in terms of its (assumed) effects rather than its (observable) content (Maeda 1980). In a 1957 court ruling, for example, which found the Japanese translator and publisher of D. H. Lawrence's *Lady Chatterley's Lover* guilty of obscenity, the concept was defined as follows: "Obscene literature is something whose contents excite and stimulate sexual desire, offend the ordinary person's normal sense of sexual shame, and go against the idea of good sexual morality" (quoted in Ihaya 1991). Invoking the aura of public morality, the injunction is against material that will produce sexual excitation and/or shame in its audience. Excitation is given a normative if nonspecific frame in this context: it is criminal when it transgresses "good sexual morality," strays from the "normal" as defined by the "ordinary" citizen, and is stimulated by a visual or written medium. Clear about its authority to both impose and police sexual boundaries, the state is nonetheless obscure here on where precisely these boundaries are to be drawn. Nonetheless, in the case of *Lady Chatterley's Lover*, twelve passages were designated "obscene" and removed from its Japanese version: passages which have yet to be reinstated more than thirty years later (Ihaya 1991).

Okudaira Yasuhiro, professor of law at International Christian University in Tokyo, has noted this gap between the state's power to regulate obscenity and its lack of a clear and uniform standard for this regulation. He writes: "The actual evil and harm caused by obscenity have never been discussed. If the grounds for controlling something are not clear, how do you control it?" (quoted in Ihaya 1991). In practice, the policing of obscenity is carried out according to two separate sets of regulations: Article 175 and local ordinances intended to check and monitor the "sound development of minors." Groups organized locally such as associations of housewives, teachers, parents, and feminists compile guidelines for the regulation of obscenity and distribute them to both producers of media such as publishers of comic books and distributors such as bookstores, convenience stores, newsstands, and video stores. Exerting pressure directly as well as eliciting the help of local politicians, producers and sellers of published materials are asked to voluntarily follow a form of censorship referred to as "self-restraint" (Kimoto 1970, Oshima 1981).

In the early 1990s, a housewives' group in Wakayama Prefecture protested the high degree of sexual imagery found in children's comic books and was extremely successful in encouraging comic book publishers to eliminate the offensive images. As Okudaira points out for another case, however, one in which a diet member agreed to assist one of his constituencies and supported her movement against obscenity in comic books, often the protest is made simply in the name of "hazardous" materials that hurt "the sound development of minors." In this case, the diet member simply declared that "things had gone too far" and as a result of the committee work that followed, 930 comic books were subsequently classified as "hazardous" in the two-month period of November and December 1990 alone.

Reacting to the label of "obscene material" now affixed literally to its cover, publishers and sellers of such materials typically engage in acts of "self-restraint": returning magazines to their manufacturers if they are sellers and destroying the stock; discontinuing the series, and recalling all copies from stores if they are publishers. While the label of obscenity may whet the appetites of consumers, it also incurs a social stigma and for this reason is bad business. Since publishers of comic books are often publishers of educational materials as well they can ill afford the charge of obscenity brought against them (Ihaya 1991).

Policing Pubic Hair

It is in the policing of obscenity through article #175 that the classification of the obscene has become so compulsively and exclusively pinned down at the site/sight of pubic hair. As if to provide concrete form to a law which otherwise would remain formless and unpoliceable, pubic hair has been reified as that which provokes sexual excitation, offends the "normal" person's sense of sexual shame, and transgresses "good" sexual morality. Those who produce or sell materials that either explicitly depict sex or include the occasional sexual depiction find this ruling random, illogical, and anachronistic. Oshima Nagisa, the director of numerous films including the sexually direct "In the Realm of the Senses" (*Ai no Korīda*), has argued that the prosecution of obscenity is more about power than anything else. In his mind, the selection of pubic hair and genitalia is arbitrary: a form randomly selected by the state to exert control over its populace. Oshima speaks from the experience of having been charged with obscenity: a charge he fought in the courts for over two years and eventually won on the basis of its unconstitutionality. The charge stemmed from a book of still photographs and the script taken from his movie *Ai no Korīda,* which was shot in Japan but edited in Paris and which was refused reentry into Japan based on Section 21 of the Fixed Tariffs Law (Oshima 1970, 1981, 1992).

The movie, based on the true story of Abe Sada who cut the penis off of her lover after strangling him to achieve a heightened sexual pleasure, is filled with scenes that show the genitalia of the two lovers, genitalic intercourse, and the pubic hair of the actress Matsui Yasuko. Oshima cut one-third of these scenes in order to pass the Japanese censors, yet the movie—which achieved cult status in the West and was viewed by over 350,000 people in Paris alone within seventeen months of its release (Oshima 1992:266)—was still refused entry. The book, not even Oshima's inspiration but masterminded by an editor Takemura Hajime for his publishing firm, San'ichi Shobō, was charged with obscenity for twelve photographs [1]—"obscene color photographs depicting poses of male-female sexual intercourse and sexual play" (269)—and nine passages in the script—"passages in which male-female sexual intercourse or sex play is described frankly" (273). Oshima, frustrated over the obfuscations of these charges and outraged that he was charged even after following the convention for obscenity in visual media and cutting pubic hair from the photographs, pursued his court case in order not only to win but also force clarification on the issue of obscenity from the authorities.

In a series of eloquently articulated questions, he demanded to know why, under what conditions, and with what parameters "male-female sexual intercourse and sex play" are constituted as "obscene." In particular, his inquiry was about representation: are there standard acts and body parts that are always "obscene" or does obscenity rest in their being represented and, if the latter, are all representations of certain acts/body parts "obscene" or are some exempt under certain conditions (Oshima 1992:269–70)? Oshima won his case, but failed to educe the clarity he sought from the government on its standards and rationale for obscenity. The question remains: Why are such sights as pubic hair and genitalic sex so prohibited when other images such as sado-masochism and anal sex circulate so freely? In a recent Japanese film exported to the States under the English title "Tokyo Decadence," for example, the entire movie is a series of vignettes featuring a prostitute with her customers where the overriding sexual trope is sado-masochism. The woman wears dog collars, chains, and a dildo in her anus and is paid to submit to the various wishes of her johns for voyeurism, dominance, humiliation, and drugging. Never is she engaged in so-called straight intercourse and the final scene ends with her penetrating the anus of a male customer with a dildo. Japanese censors passed this movie, one that structures a relationship of mastery and control where sex is conditioned by money and takes place outside the body parts of genitalia. By contrast, Oshima's film with its basic equality between the lovers and predominance of genitalic intercourse to the almost exclusion of other sexual positions or acts, was banned.

Recalling the language of the censors that obscenity is what offends the "ordinary" person's "normal" sense of sexual shame, the grounds on which these two judgments were made seems mystifying. If we use the word *perversion* to define that which transgresses a society's normative standard of/for sexuality [2] as officially determined, then it can be said that what is officially regarded as perverse is the realistic imagery of a man and woman engaging in heterosexual, consensual, and genitalic sex as shown in "In the Realm of the Senses," but what is not is the sado-masochism and commodified sexual dominance featured in "Tokyo Decadence."

Rigid Definitions/Slippery Meanings

Angela Carter has written that pornography is always in the service of a society's political and social status quo because, when it is not, the authorities ban it (Carter 1978). What, we might ask, could be so socially or politically threatening about the visualization of genitalia, particularly the pubic hair surrounding it on a woman, and genitalic intercourse that has compelled such an insistence in banning it in contemporary Japan? Observers of Japan such as the journalist, Nicholas Bornoff, note the implicit threat with an air of incredulousness as if the whole censoring of pubic hair was merely ridiculous: "Basically, current Japanese ruling amounts to an all-out war on the depictions of one singly, unruly little black anatomical detail: pubic hair. If unchecked, it seems, the very fabric of society would be severely eroded and the nation cast into untold depths of depravity (1991:401)."

Western news agencies tell the same story: of Japanese obscenity laws that are nonsensical and paradoxical. "Japanese obscenity laws are widely criticized as hypocritical" wrote a journalist in an article for Reuters in 1991, and "Japan's obscenity standards can appear quite baffling" was written in the Associated Press (quoted in Ihaya 1991). These particular remarks followed an event that inspired international attention: the impounding, by Japanese customs, of the May 1991 issue of the New York-based *ARTnews* magazine for one photo of a naked woman in which her pubic hair is visible. A Japanese reporter writing for *Japan Times International* reacted to the same event by writing of Japan's "pornographic paradox": a popular culture in which men riding to work on trains in the morning can freely read lurid sex tales in comic books and view photos and images of women whose nakedness is totally visible all except their pubic hair, which is the one thing obsessively regulated by the police (Ihaya 1991).

Those most directly affected by obscenity laws—producers and sellers of written and visual materials—find them to be similarly irrational. Most, however, simply acquiesce to the system, agreeing with Oshima that the state uses censorship as a means of exerting control over its citizens (Kimoto 1970; Maeda 1980). In this sense, pubic hair is seen as the MacGuffin, using a term from film theory to signify the object all attention is turned toward during the movie, but whose motivation is simply to spin a story (this is also closely related to Roland Barthes's term, the *alibi)* (1957). This seems to be the position taken by Suei Shoji, a writer, commentator on Japanese sexual customs, and the head of a publishing house, Byakuyosha, whose twenty magazines produced monthly are all erotic except two. He cannot explain why pubic hair has become such a sign of and for the obscene in Japan. But his energies are not turned in this direction: unlike Oshima, his interactions with the officials are not aimed toward seeking explication or changing the law but simply navigating the terrain. As he and countless others have routinely faced, the dilemma in producing sexual materials is to satisfy the market without offending the authorities. And to do this he has resorted to such tactics as shaving the pubic hair of female models and then attaching fake swatches that hang down ridiculously to their knees or drawing hair in over the photo with a magic marker. Playing with the authorities is a game, Suei admits, but in the end he knows that the offices of Byakuyosha will be raided and the offending publication banned (Bornoff 1991:400, 407).

Suei, as a player in the field of sexual media in Japan, spends more time dodging obscenity laws than trying to figure them out. Still, he wonders, perhaps the concealment of certain body parts is motivated by a Japanese aesthetic.

> Censorship is illogical, but it has something about it that is typically Japanese—the hidden is not only more titillating, but more powerful. For example, you only get to see the

> Emperor on his balcony a couple of times a year. In that way the Emperor and porno are almost the same! Also, even in daily contexts, the Japanese are vague at the best of times. They never say anything straight. (quoted in Bornoff 1991:407).

This reflection is similar to that made by Roland Barthes about a different cultural aesthetic: the Parisian striptease. In what he describes as Parisian stripteasing in the fifties, the artist starts the act of undressing by initially appearing excessively dressed. Overly adorned with multiple undergarments, layers of overgarments, and endless accessories, the stripper begins what becomes a deliciously drawn-out display of the uncovering of her body. The strip's pleasure and play is with the flirtation at the borders of each removal: allowing a brief peak, covering up again, slipping off more to the eye, covering again, and only finally removing a particular object altogether. Keeping body parts hidden, in other words, is as important to the striptease as their exposure. And at the end when the woman stands naked, the nudity of her body is anticlimactic: desexualized by a process that has sexualized not nakedness per se but the play between making visible and invisible its borders (Barthes 1972:84–87).

Eroticism establishes its identity, by this argument, in never revealing everything and in always keeping some part hidden. It is this relationship that conditions the "obscene"; it is also that without which eroticism could not proceed and whose value rests in retaining something as the unseen. To see everything produces a satisfaction that is very short lived, whereas to erect boundaries to that which is accessible makes access more difficult but also more exciting. Whereas Suei and Barthes speak as if this organization to the erotic is culturally specific,[3] Freud has argued that desire is always constructed in terms of that which is ultimately unattainable. Lacan extends this further to speak of desire as the mark of entering a symbolic order that can be conceptualized as the difference between need (located in the "real" that requires tangible objects such as milk to satisfy one's hunger) and demand (located in the imaginary, which is communicated through language and addressed to the m/other). In the imaginary stage, according to Lacan, a child demands things such as toys but is really demanding the love and attention from her mother who is not always present nor always willing to acquiesce. Hence, even when toys are received the child is never fully satisfied. So begins a stage of playing symbolically with absence and presence: the game of fort/da that Freud observed originally with his grandson who dealt with the loss of his mother when she went shopping by playing a game. He would throw and then retrieve a cotton reel and accompany the play with the words "fort"/"da": an articulation and symbolization, according to both Freud and Lacan, of the mother's absence and presence and the child's attempt to control what ultimately is out of his control—the desire to have his needs and demands met by a m/other (Grosz 1990:58–67).

The playing with the borders of presence and absence is Lacan's simplified definition of desire. The objects to which we turn to satisfy our desire ("objet a") can never be completely satisfying: where they fill a need they offer a presence, where they fail to realize a demand they encode an absence (the "excess" of demand over need which is the structure of desire). Moreover, as Lacan's example of the fort/da exemplifies, not only does desire get played out in terms of objects that both are and are not what we want, desire plays symbolically with the very categories of presence and absence themselves. Scholars such as Kaja Silverman have argued that this play is universal only in structure and that the form it takes differs according to specific cultures, histories, and economic relations. How patterns of desire are "filled in" she calls a culture's "dominant fiction," arguing as other theorists such as Fredric Jameson (1981) that groups of people share collective stories that give meaning to their lives, shape to their fantasies, and role models for their identities. Such stories not only reflect the realities within which people live but also construct them: dominant fictions, in other words, are both cultural and political. They can be and often are interwoven with the power relations of a dominant political order: the "political unconscious" in Jameson's term. The desires we see inscribed then in a movie or pornographic comicbook may seem "simply" innocuous or unimportant, yet manage to capture our imagination in ways that actually affect our behavior (Silverman 1992:1–51).

Monitoring the Borders: Customs Officials and Pubic Hair

Within such intertwinements of desire and identity, borders are critical. In this terrain of the taboo and prohibited, not only is desire put in place, but identities are formed and contested. Not surprising therefore, some of the most rigorous policing of obscenity in Japan occurs at its national borders where the boundaries of nationhood interweave with those of desire and its prohibitions. Article 21 of the Customs

Tariff Law is at the international level what article 175 of the penal Code is at the domestic, and regulates the importation of obscene materials through the Customs and Tariff Bureau of the Finance Ministry. Seated at the customs office in Yokohama is a cadre of workers, all middle-aged women it is rumored, whose job it is to scrutinize incoming media to Japan for offending sights, notably pubic hair, genitalia, and genitalic intercourse. Scrutinized are, first, such likely offenders as men's magazines—for example, *Playboy, Hustler*, and *Penthouse*—and next, artistic, fashion, and photographic publications including films. When obscenity is found, it is erased or obscured by various methods such as blotting over a spot with indelible ink or removing the ink on the page where it appears. The costs, which may be considerable, are paid entirely by the importers (Bornoff 1991; Maeda 1980).

The rigors of this process and the marks it often leaves on imported media signifies both the danger implicit in material emanating from outside the borders of Japan and the compulsiveness of the Japanese state in asserting and inserting its standards of propriety on anything moving into Japan. As protective of its national borders on the issue of obscenity as it is on trade, Japan has been highly criticized on both scores for its provincialism and hostility to international relations. In recent years there has been a string of protests from foreign artists, film makers, and publishers (often delivered from the offices of their governments) whose work has been censored by Japanese customs. In 1985 nude photos taken by the French surrealist photographer, Man Ray, were impounded by the Customs and Tariff Bureau who refused to release them until the obscene portions were blacked out to comply with local standards. In this case the French government protested and the Foreign Ministry stepped in so the Man Ray show was allowed to proceed uncensored. In the same year, at the first Tokyo International Film Festival, two foreign directors—Hector Babenco from Brazil and Michael Radford from Britain—threatened to withdraw their entries (*Kiss of the Spider Woman* and *1984* respectively) if a single frame was censored. After intense debate the films were shown untouched, but warnings were given that the films would have to be adjusted in compliance with local standards for commercial release (Bornoff 1991). Such "adjustment" befalls the fate of all imported media circulating in the market of popular culture. With their marks of excision often crudely disfiguring the text, foreign media is identified as both alien and obscene: a conflation of othernesses authorized by the state and to the stated end of protecting what are identified as

Japanese mores. Consistent with such an ideology of obscene foreignness, AIDS has been treated as a germ that entered Japan on the body of a Filipino prostitute. Consistent in this as well is the attention paid to national borders: signs are posted at the points of border crossing, such as airports, warning Japanese of the danger of AIDS as they leave and reenter Japan.

An effect of Japanese censorship laws in monitoring all incoming visual and printed media by national agents is to alter and at times mutilate the meanings intended by their foreign producers. The fixation on airbrushing out, patching over, and/or clouding the visibility of genitalia can make a particular scene, for example, appear simply ridiculous. Viewers of *Woodstock* in Japan (both Japanese and foreigners) remember it for its disfigurements: an endless de-crotching, which divested the movie of other meanings. Likewise, exposed genitalia are found where they otherwise might go unnoticed as happened in the movie *Amadeus* in which a distant sight of pubic hair was less concealed than revealed by the airbrushing wrought on it (Bornoff 1991). Scenes not intended to be sexual are consequently made both sexual and obscene by the very authorities whose job it is to patrol against obscenity. Meaning can also be lost by such a literal and rigid enforcement of censorship boundaries. Despite pleas from its American director and Japanese distributor, the pivotal scene of *The Crying Game* was shown with its exposed penis clouded over (Regelman 1993). As an example of how incomprehensible the movie thereby becomes, Donald Richie (an American scholar of Japanese film) reports overhearing two women discussing the film after watching it in Tokyo. Bewildered and unsure of what on the "woman's" body her male friend had found so disturbing, one offered her opinion that it was leprosy (personal communication, Jennifer Robertson).

It is ironic that Japan has placed herself in the role of moral arbiter, policing the standards of sexual representation on western imports when once she was the object of western censureship for exposing body parts in behavior found "primitive" by the West. Or perhaps it is only fitting given the shift in global politics. Japan's position in the world today is far different than it was in 1907, the year it established censorship laws when it was modernizing under western influence. Now Japan's position as a world power has been established and its vulnerability to a western gaze replaced by national self-assertiveness. This positioning of Japan as a nation far less secondary or subordinate to the western countries of North America and Western Europe than it was at the turn of the century is reflected in its censorship laws that erase, literally and figuratively, parts off the bodies of incoming imports.

This erasing, however, is directed not only to the sexual representations of other nations but also to those which appeared in Japan's "traditional" past. The depictions of genitalia in *shunga* (scrolls of the Tokugawa era), for example, are prohibited today under article 175 making *shunga* legally obscene and illegal to be publicly displayed or sold (Oshima 1992). Censoring the other then, Japan also censors itself. Or, to use a Lacanian metaphor of the pound of flesh that is extracted from the physical body of a person in order to socialize her into the symbolic, it could be said that what Japan has had to extract from itself in order to gain respectability in the eyes of others, it can now extract from these others as well. It is not so ironic after all then that these cuts in both directions of self and other are made on the same body parts. Also, given the censoring of pubic hair in traditional media as well as imported ones, it is not surprising that these borders inspire the similar desire to transgress them. Underground markets exist for both uncensored *shunga* as well as uncensored foreign media suggesting still another geometry to the obscene in Japan: one in which foreignness and traditionalism become connected as signifiers for the disrespectable.

Recent Transgressions: "The Hair Debate"

Borders rarely remain stable forever. And in this moment of the 1990s in Japan, obscenity standards are shifting: slipping at the site/sight of that most conventional standard of and for the obscene in recent years, pubic hair. In a controversy that has been termed "the hair debate," the public has reacted to allowances made for showing pubic hair on the grounds that the context is "artistic" (*hea ronsō*) (Heibonsha Hyakka Nenkan 1992:186–87, Imidas 1992:859-61). These moves largely began in 1991 when a number of publications appeared with photos of nude women uncharacteristically replete with their pubic hair. These included three books by the famous photographer Shinoyama Kishin (all published by Asahi Shuppansha; one entitled *Water Fruit*, another *Santa Fe*), the May issue of the journal *Geijutsu Shinchō* (published by Shinchōsha), the May issue of the magazine *An-an*, and in December, the imported book *Sex* featuring Madonna (with only four of its many nude photos censored) (Heibonsha Hyakka Nenkan 1992:186–87; Imidas 1992:859–61; Kamei 1993). The models of the photos were typically women well known in the public eye as models, actresses, or in perhaps the most publicly discussed case, an *aidoru tarento* ("idol talent," a female in her late teens or early twenties who is typically a singer and television or screen actress and whose reputation is one of social respectability). In *Sante Fe*, photographer Shinoyama Kishin shot the *aidoru tarento* Miyazawa Rie in full frontal nudity. This confusion of categories—between the obscenity of the crotch shot and the purity of her public image—was shocking enough, but even more newsworthy was the advertising of the book, accompanied by photos, in two of Japan's most respectable newspapers, the *Asahi Shinbun* (no linkage to the publishing company, Asahi Shuppansha, that published the book) and the *Yomiuri Shinbun*. Within three months sales of the book had reached a record number of 1.5 million copies and opinions were divided between finding the volume tasteful and Rie-san merely colorful in her display, and those who thought the work sensationalist and Rie-san a crude and lewd opportunist (Ihaya 1991; Schilling 1992).

The "hair debate," which has been a discursive explosion in the mass media over the issue of pubic hair representabilities, was largely set off by the apparent shift in governmental policies on censorship. Still, the borders of this law have not yet settled down into a clear and consistent position. Such was exemplified by a Japanese travel agent who, curious about the effect on the everyday labeling of obscenity by the allowances made for "artistic" nudity in 1991, traveled outside Japan with three such publications (the photo collection *Water Fruit*, and the May issues of *An-an* and *Geijutsu Shinchō* with their nude photos). When he returned he carried these materials plus a number of American magazines including *Penthouse* and *Playboy*, all of which were impounded by Japanese custom officials at Nagoya airport. Confused as to the logic of refusing reentry to a publication that had already appeared legally in Japan, Gotoh was merely told that the visibility of pubic hair was outlawed. As quoted in the Japanese press, Gotoh responded to this situation in frustration, asking for a clarity in the law that Oshima had been denied earlier. "What I want to know is the line the custom office draws between the printed materials allowed into this country and those that are not. Isn't it absurd that magazines freely obtainable in Japan cannot be allowed in once they go out the country?" (*Japan Times*, Weekly International Edition, July 1–7, 1991:20).

In such acts of questioning the authorities, the boundaries by which the law defines obscenity and the police who patrol it will perhaps be clarified over time. At the very least the whole issue is being brought into greater consciousness and debate in the 1990s. At a deeper level, however, it is also true that laws of prohibition establish patterns of desire. How have the rules against visualization of genitalia and pubic hair insinuated themselves into the images and scenarios by which desire is stimulated in popular culture and what will be the effect on popular culture if there is change in the rules? I can address this question only briefly and do so more by complicating and problematizing the question than definitively answering it.

Marking Desire by the Law

In Japanese media that explicitly or implicitly represent sex, direct shots of genitalia are replaced by both depictions and sexual positions that avoid genitalic exposure. Some scholars argue that this is the reason for what appears to be an obsession with sado-masochism, dominance, anal sex, voyeurism, and other nongenitalic dependent acts such as urination and excretion in the images that circulate as sexual in Japanese media: as mechanisms derived in large part as strategies to circumvent Japanese censorship laws (Buckley 1991; Turin 1993). It has also been argued that the trend to infantilize Japanese women in sexual imagery stems from the same source: prepubescent females are lacking, in nature, what must be shaved or erased mechanically from a postpubescent woman in order to pass the censors. To accord with the censorship laws, young girls make sense. And in order to naturalize women who are not naturally hairless, older women are often figured as young by any number of techniques including dressing them in school uniforms, tying their head hair into pigtails, and encouraging them to smile sweetly as nymphettes.

Female infantalization and sexual dominance: even if these do stem in part from legal restrictions, what effects do they have in configuring a dominant sexual or gender ideology? Commentators on sexual imagery in Japan such as Sandra Buckley and Fredrick Schodt argue that everyone can read the devices used to metaphorically inscribe what literally is prohibited by the law. At the most basic level they write of the phallic replacements for penises: the coke bottles, golf clubs, snakes, calligraphy brushes, tennis rackets, and baseball bats that stand in by magnifying that which is not permitted to be seen (Buckley 1991; Schodt 1983). What such scholars fail to point out, however, is how in suturing over the prohibited genitalia, the codes used for female and male not only differ but differ in ways that also inscribe codings of gender and power. In the case of the male he is given a phallus that exceeds and supplements a real penis and is often used in the image/text to conquer, dominate, hurt, and/or humiliate a female. Scenes of penetration into anuses, mouths, or blotched-out vaginas by objects that signify pain and domination are exceedingly common on the pages of such popular and everyday reading materials for men as erotic comic books. In the case of women, by contrast, their genitalia are simply blacked or excised out: given a less-than-real representation in which absence itself is made the sign for female. In some cases not only is pubic hair removed or fuzzed out, but also a bubble with nothing inside is put to the side to signify that the woman's pubic hair has been censored: absence representing absence which is antithetical to the move of over-representing the absent penis with a super phallus. That such females doubly marked as lacking are typically the victims in sexual scenarios is only consistent with this imaging.

Saying this, I would like to consider briefly the following scenario. It appeared in 1992 in a new genre of erotic comic books called "ladies comics," which are marketed explicitly to working women in their twenties. The story is entitled "Like a Sex Doll" and features a working woman (O. L. which stands for office lady, meaning a clerical worker) who is asked by her boss to accompany him on an "appointment" (*yakusoku*) one night. Somewhat displeased by this imposition, the woman nevertheless agrees because the man, after all, is her boss. They drive to a "mansion" (apartment building) and enter a room upon which the boss attacks her. Grabbing her head hair and telling her that even if she yells no one will hear her in the hall, the boss forces his worker to fellate him. She does so with tears running down her face and thinking to herself of the agony she is in. Once done, the boss ties her up and proceeds to perform cunnilingus on her. The woman responds despite herself and is brought to orgasm.

At this point the boss opens a razor and the woman winces, but he tells her not to be afraid. He then shaves off her pubic hair and takes a Poloroid picture of her, tied up as she is now both at her wrists and her ankles. Soon after, the session is over and the woman leaves with the photo of herself in her bag. The boss and O. L. continue to see each other usually at the mansion but also in a toilet stall of the bathroom at their office in an illicit affair depicted as dirty and obscene. The woman is compelled toward yet ashamed of this attachment and sees herself as a "sex doll," which she associates with the photo made of her, tied up with shaved pubis. This shaving of her is also an obstacle to continuing the relationship she once enjoyed with her boyfriend. It stands as a mark of her depravity, which she tries to keep hidden from him by turning down with various excuses his requests to have sex. Eventually he interprets her refusals as lack of interest and breaks up with her. Saddened, the woman nonetheless continues the affair with her boss until one day she sees her former boyfriend with a new "sweetheart." The two seem so happy and tender in their love that she is filled with nostalgia for "good romance" and yearning for her past. Resolved to turn over a new leaf, she quits her job and moves out of her apartment, leaving no forwarding address. The last page shows her sitting alone on her birthday and toasting "her future life" with a beer.

In this story, intended for a female audience, designed to stimulate feminine desires, and written by an author identified as a woman, a shaved pubis stands for female sexuality gone awry: a marker for the shape female desires should not assume in relations of heterosexuality. Ironically the symbol here inverts the law: evading the dictates of article 175 against showing pubic hair, the removal of pubic hair becomes a figuring of and for the obscene itself. But what does this mean: that clean-shaven pubises become a mark for sexual depravity rather than the reverse? What particularly does it mean in the context of material supposedly intended to represent female desires? According to a commentator who has written on this new phenomenon of "ladies erotica" in Japan, most of the stories have similar narratives of women experiencing sexual passion in a relationship that is socially transgressive. Normative borders need to be transgressed, in other words, for a woman to enjoy sex. And invariably the story ends by restoring the borders: women give up their hot lovers in order to marry or start looking to marry men who are "nice." As such the message is transmitted that a woman can't have both sex and marriage and, for a "good" woman, marriage wins out in the end (Nakano 1990).

Given that most magazines and comic books are still produced by men in Japan (Schodt 1983), and that this phenomenon of female-targeted pornography is still new, my interpretation is that these images reflect more than anything the desires of male marketers trying to capitalize on the expanding market of women in their twenties who are not yet married, work full time, and are willing and able to spend money on leisure (the audience to which these comic books are explicitly targeted). Compared with pornographic comic books for men, the ladies erotica are surprisingly similar except for the addition of the wedding scene or something comparable that signifies a return of the "good girl" at the end. The high preponderance of sado-masochistic elements compare similarly as well, which leads me to suspect that a story such as "Like a Sex Doll" is compelled far more by male than female fantasies and is placed in a comic "for women" that is little more than a transplanted male model. Still, might such a story have appeal to a woman as well as a man? From what I have read and been told about female sexuality, Japanese women often associate marriage with sexual frustration, and one out of six married women has experienced an extramarital affair (Ueno 1988; Iwao 1993). The numbers of women petitioning for divorce and doing so on the grounds of sexual dissatisfaction are increasing as well (Narabayashi, personal communication; Iwao 1993). Given the disassociation between sexual passion and marital respectability in the real lives of many women and the representation given this in the popular culture of everything from women's magazines to "home dramas" (soap operas) on television, its presence in a ladies comic book is at least consistent. And, at least, the woman gets some sex albeit in a position (bad girl, dominated woman, masochist) that confirms the dominant ideology that women should prioritize marriage; and men but not women can fool around with a partner not one's spouse.

Freud has written about the various disjunctures between desire and social constraints and the various tactics people take to navigate a course that accommodates both. One such tactic is exemplified by the masochist who experiences her pleasure only as pain. Conforming to an identity in which the subject, for whatever reason, is not supposed to enjoy sex, the masochist disguises the sexual pleasure she does receive by staging it so as to be the passive and apparent victim in its execution. The woman in "Like a Sex Doll" is similarly situated: enjoying a pleasure that is constructed in the text as forbidden. But who exactly is doing the forbidding: is it Japanese women who find the idea of sex outside of marriage so abhorrent or is it men? I have yet to read an account by a Japanese woman who claims to enjoy the so-called female erotica of ladies comics. I have found plenty of men writing, however, who acknowledge that men's erotic comics, with their images of women repeatedly victimized by men in acts of forcible sex, are stimulating and relaxing (for example, Go 1981; Ishikawa 1981). The control the boss exerts in "Like a Sex Doll" throughout the text and symbolized in such acts as removing her hair—a scene that repeats twice and is shown in the first case in an enlarged frame, razor glistening with individual hairs lining its length—pleases him and confuses her. For the duration of the story the man appears pompous and smug, as in control of the relationship as the woman feels out of control, expressed by the worried and tormented look that does not leave her face until the end. And finally, reflecting on her image in the photo—held down by rope and shaved of her pubic hair—she calls herself a "doll"—an inauthentic fake of a woman rather than the real thing. With this she decides to reform and restore her femininity: she will rid herself of the man who thinks of only sex but not marriage, find a nicer (more marriageable) man, and let, presumably, her pubic hair grow back in. The symbolism of hair is reinforced in the last three frames where the woman sits in her new apartment, nursing a beer, with her head hair flowing long and full after it has been pulled up in a ponytail the whole time she was conducting the affair.

Does a woman's pubic hair then signify marriage and motherhood and their antithetical relationship to female sexuality? Or, to put it differently, is the taboo against showing pubic hair compelled by its construction as something dirty or, rather, something clean, pure, even sacred? And, if it is at all the latter, might the sight of a woman's pubic hair be somehow threatening rather than titillating to a male viewer—a sign of a woman's feminine source that triggers feelings of weakness rather than strength, and emasculation rather than potency, in him?

The More "Terrifying Sight": A Real Penis

In the tale of Amaterasu cited in the beginning, goddesses laugh and rejoice at the sight of a woman's genitalia. In other tales such as that of the woman whose daughter has been kidnapped by an *oni* (demon), there are similar expressions of a potency inherent in female genitalia. In the latter myth, the woman has recaptured her daughter and is fleeing across a lake, when the *oni* sees them and starts drinking the lake's water so as to catch them. The woman stands up in the boat and lifts her skirt, exposing her genitals to the eyes of the *oni*. He is so stunned and taken aback that he vomits all the water he had already gulped, which thereby allows the women a safe escape (Kawai 1988). Seeing female genitalia is a stunning sight: it elicits severe reactions and grants the bearer certain powers. To cover a woman's pubic hair up is a symbolic means of denying her access to this potency. Legal restrictions against the visualization of pubic hair may not have been motivated in this ideological direction. One of their effects today, however, no matter how arbitrary, senseless, and merely illogical the law may seem on obscenity, is to construct and circulate such an ideology of male dominance. Yet, as with any ideologies or laws that articulate hegemonic forms of power, there is also the possibility of rearticulation or, as Judith Butler puts it, there are failures to "repeat loyally and, in that failure" there are opened "possibilities for resignifying the terms of violation against their violating aims" (1993:124). One such failure to "repeat loyally" the terms of a hegemonizing taboo against showing female pubic hair is the action of Japanese porn star Kaoru Kuroki, who appears on screen with the hair underneath her arms unshaved. Displacing from view that which cannot be legally shown, she displays instead another body domain with the wildness of its hair left uncut (Bornoff 1991).

Exhibiting hair, in this context, has been read as an act of female defiance: a refusal to remove or deny that which is only natural on the body of a mature woman. To think of showing bodily hair as a sign of female empowerment is a commentary on the form censorship laws take in Japan: on its configuring as obscene not acts that violate women but parts of female anatomy that mark a woman as mature. Shifts at this border of obscenity laws in Japan may indicate the beginnings of a reconfiguration of Woman in sexual imagery: filling in her symbolic wounds with the realness of the hair between her legs. And, if so, it reflects the gradual but real steps being made politically and economically by Japanese women in the 1990s.

Yet, in terms of the images used to represent sex in the media of Japanese popular culture, there remains one border whose rigidity seems even more entrenched these days than that erected against pubic hair. And that is the taboo against showing penises realistically. Rather than revealing them as they actually exist in real life—with a size that is humanlike, a potency that resembles that of an average man's, and their natural downs as well as ups—the law dictates that their portrayal must be disguised. And as disguised, the male penis assumes a "masquerade." It becomes superhumanly powerful, forceful, and big: the baseball bat used to conquer and dominate the woman. As the women in sexual imagery, however, slowly begin to emerge out of their doll-like portrayals and start, among other things, to show hair, what will the effect be on the man: both the man in the image and the man viewing the image in his pornographic comic book or on his television late at night?

From recent reports, I hear that imagery of men humiliating, victimizing, coercing, and/or raping women has become even more pervasive in the films, comic books, and videogames that people turn to for fantasy and relaxation in the Japan of the nineties than ever before. The answer to my question then may very well be that as women "come out" as gradually stronger in both the popular imagination and the social realpolitik, the trend will be for the imaginary man to be figured as ever more phallic. To project this image though, he'll have to keep his real penis in his pants.

Notes

1. This was originally designated as eight passages, a shift that confirms Oshima's suspicions of arbitrariness at work: "The mere fact that the number changed from eight to twelve clearly shows the ambiguity and haphazard nature of 'obscenity' regulation" (Oshima 1992:268).

2. This is Freud's definition of perversion (1905). Without accepting his universalist notion of what is normal sexuality, I argue that this is the structure by which Japanese censors speak of obscenity: that which offends a normal citizen's sense of sexual shame.

3. See also Ueno (1992) for a similar argument about Japan.

References

Barthes, Roland. 1972 (1957). *Mythologies*. Annette Lavers, trans. New York: Noonday Press.

Bornoff, Nicolas. 1991. *Pink Samurai: Love, Marriage and Sex in Contemporary Japan*. New York: Pocket Books.

Buckley, Sandra. 1991. "'Penguin in Bondage': A Graphic Tale of Japanese Comic Books." In *Technoculture*. Constance Penley and Andrew Ross, eds. London: Methuen.

Butler, Judith. 1993. *Bodies That Matter*. New York: Routledge.

Carter, Angela. 1978. *The Sadeian Woman: And the Ideology of Pornography*. New York: Pantheon.

Dore, Ronald P. 1958. *City Life in Japan*. Berkeley: University of California Press.

Freud, Sigmund. 1905. *The Three Essays on the Theory of Sexuality*. In *The Standard Edition of the Complete Psychological Works of Sigmund Freud* (SE). London: Hogarth Press, vol. 7.

Go, Tomohide. 1981. "Genzai Eromanga Tenbō" (View of Erotic Comic Books Today). *Bessatsu Takarajima* 13:260–62.

Grosz, Elizabeth. 1990. *Jacques Lacan: A Feminist Introduction*. New York: Routledge.

Hane, Mikio. 1986. *Modern Japan: A Historical Survey*. Boulder, Colo.: Westview.

Heibonsha. 1991. *Heibon Hyakka Nenkan*. Tokyo: *Heibonsha*.

Ihaya, Manako. September 2–8, 1991. "Obscenity and Censorship Still Flourish in Japan." In *The Japan Times Weekly* International Edition: 8.

Imidas, 1992. "Masumedia": 859–61. Tokyo: *Shueisha*.

Ishikawa, Hiroyoshi. 1981. "*Pōnogurafia*" (Pornography), *Juristo* 25: 228–33.

Iwao, Sumiko. 1993. *The Japanese Woman: Traditional Image and Changing Reality*. New York: Free Press.

Jameson, Fredric. 1981. *The Political Unconscious: Narrative as a Socially Symbolic Act.* Ithaca, N.Y.: Cornell University Press.

Kawai, Hayao. 1988. *The Japanese Psyche: Major Motifs in the Fairy Tales of Japan.* Hayao Kawai and Sachiko Reece, trans. Dallas: Spring Publications.

Kamei, Shunsuke. 1991. "Madonna Shashinshū 'Sex' o Yomu" (Reading Madonna's Photo Collection "Sex"), *Chūō Kōron* February:242–45.

Kimoto, Itaru. 1970. "Jishukisei shita no Pōnogurafia Shuppan" (The Publication of Pornography under Independent Control), in *Juristo* 25: 299–306.

Maeda, Shinjiro. 1980. "Sekkusu to Hō to Shakkai" (Sex, Law, and Society), *Juristo* 71–80.

Nakano, Tsui. 1990. "Redīsu Komikku no Yokubō o Yomu" (Reading the Desires of Ladies Comics), *Honno Zasshi* 12.

Oshima, Nagisa. 1970. "Fūzoku to Hanzai no Aida" (In-between Custom and Law), *Juristo* 25: 55–58.

———. 1981. "Bunka, Sei, Seiji: Zadankai" (Roundtable on Culture, Sex, and Politics), *Juristo* 5401:19-40.

———. 1988. *Cinema, Censorship, and the State: The Writings of Nagisa Oshima.* Ed. Annette Michelson, trans. Dawn Lawson. Cambridge: Massachusetts Institute of Technology Press.

Regelman, Karen. 1993. "Will Tokyo Tame 'Crying Game'?" *Variety,* March 22: 1, 68.

Rubin, Jay. 1984. *Injurious to Public Morals: Writers and the Meiji State.* Seattle: University of Washington Press.

Schilling, Mark. 1992. "Worshipping the Naked Goddess: The Media, Mores, and Miyazawa Rie," *Japan Quarterly* 39 (2): 218–24.

Schodt, Frederik. 1983. *Manga! Manga! The World of Japanese Comics.* New York: Kodansha International.

Silverman, Kaja. 1992. *Male Subjectivity at the Margins.* New York: Routledge.

Turin, Maureen. 1993. "The Erotic in Asian Cinema." In *Dirty Looks: Women, Pornography, Power.* Pamela Gibson and Roma Gibson, eds. London: British Film Institute.

Ueno, Chizuko. 1988. *Onnaasobi* (Women's Play). Tokyo: Gakuyō shobō.

———. 1992. *Sukākatto no shita no Gekijo* (Theater in the Skirt). Tokyo: Kawade Bunko.

Vance, Carole. 1982. "The Pleasure of Looking: The Attorney General's Commission on Pornography Versus Visual Images," *Fiction International* 22:205–38.

Williams, Linda. 1989. *Hard Core: Power, Pleasure, and the Frenzy of the Visible.* Berkeley: University of California Press.

10 cuts and culture in kathmandu

julia j. thompson

There we were in the audience of the couture shows in Paris. The Arab princess was elbow to elbow with the wife of the French politician, who cozied up to the ambassador and the socialite. Across the runway sat us working stiffs. If an alien were plopped down in the middle of the room, he'd [sic] be able to suss us out. We were the ones without hairdos (Wells 1995:60).

Introductions and Interpretations

When I walked into the back of Ritu's beauty salon in Kathmandu—where hair is cut and styled, manicures given, and henna applied—the room was abuzz. "She shaved her head?" one woman queried with her head inside a dilapidated pink hairdryer.

"All her hair is gone?" an unmarried Newār woman asked incredulously smoothing the creases out of her green *salwār kurtā* as she sat on the arm of her sister's chair.

"But why did she do that? It wasn't necessary," the first woman continued taking her head out from under the dryer to hear the response more clearly.

"It wasn't proper," the second woman decreed.

"You know Indiraji," the senior hairstylist Kumari commented, referring to Indira Rana, a prominent Chhetrī woman in her forties. "She has always worn her hair short, especially since she never married."

The second woman's sister, a married Newār woman, wore a pink sari with a flowered border and was having her nails manicured. "So when her mother died, she shaved her head. Did you hear, she even went to Pashupati and lit the funeral pyre!"

I had lifted my sari to knee height and was lowering my dirty feet into a bucket of soapy water. "Wait, wait!" I interjected in confusion.[1] "How can a woman light the pyre?" I asked, knowing that women do not even have the right to go to the cremation according to the scriptures.

Kumari's younger sister, Shima, an unmarried Chhetrī woman, who was removing large plastic rollers from a Guruṅg woman's hair, ventured, "Do you think she did it for the property? She didn't even give her brother time to come from India for the ritual."

"But what kind of woman is Indira if she shaves her head like a man and lights the pyre? She's too greedy," an older Indian Marwāri woman said as green henna powder was applied to her head by Solin, the Chinese stylist from Calcutta.

Kumari tried to clarify, having known Indira for many years, "She didn't do it for the property, but to show that women should have rights like men, that we should be equal."

The henna-slathered woman remained unconvinced. "If she had only married when she had that offer, she wouldn't need to fight for the family property; her husband would have taken care of her."

The conversation continued like this, back and forth, women leaving off as they left the back rooms to hurry home or back to work, other women picking up the tails of the conversation as they entered. Kumari tried to convince them that Indira's intentions were good and that she was not acting like a man. I listened mostly, although I interjected from time to time to ask for details about Indira's ritual mourning. This concern with hair and with a particular woman's shaven head—far from being trivial—reflects the very nature of these women's legal rights, their financial independence, gender identities, and the wide variety of reactions to radical social change in contemporary Kathmandu.[2]

These types of ongoing conversations were common during the time I spent at Ritu's as a customer and as a fictive older sister to some of the beauticians and customers. Women recounted ribald jokes while getting facials, told fortunes and misfortunes, negotiated marriages under hair dryers, phoned their lovers while paying the bill, shared copies of Hindi film tabloids and international fashion magazines such as *Vogue* and *Cosmopolitan*, and bartered and sold goods in their own version of a gray market. Ritu's beauty salon catered to women from a variety of castes, classes, and nations and included foreign development workers, diplomats, Peace Corps volunteers and other expatriates residing in Nepal. The beauticians were from lower and middle classes from many parts of South Asia. Whether they acknowledged it or not, they were embedded in longstanding historical relations to hair care and ornamentation. I witnessed how central salon life was to these women and how distinct it was from much of the rest of their lives. I also learned about beauty practices and beauty culture, most specifically about hair and hair styles.

Indira Rana's shaven head demonstrates that beauty practices may have profound impacts on individuals, families, and society. Ideas, fashions, commodities, and people now move across cultural and national boundaries in such ways that Lancôme cosmetics' tote bags are now status symbols for Beijing women (Wright 1994) and there is a clamor for Asian beauty commodities in the United States as witnessed in the rise of perfumes and cosmetics being marketed with "oriental" overtones and images. Academic writing is creating an awareness not only of the importance of understanding the impacts of "global flows of people and things" (Appadurai 1990:3) but also in locating this "postmodernity" in particular local sociohistorical contexts (e.g. Mani 1992). One particularly useful way to do this is by examining beauty culture. For example, recent research points out the links among localized beauty culture and larger global influences through an analysis of the complexities of *sari* culture and modernity in Bengal (Nag 1989, 1991). Just as beauty products travel across national boundaries, so too do theories, including western feminist ones.

Western feminists have often decried beauty practices and beauty culture as oppressive and degrading to women (e.g. Wolf 1991a, 1991b). Susan Bordo, for example, has depicted beauty culture and beauty practices—including plastic surgery, cosmetics, and media images of women—as enmeshed in historical processes, power relations, and cultural ideologies (1993). Other feminist writers argue that beauty is also "a source of gratification and pleasure for women (Davis 1991:26)"; we also see this in the works of Bartky (1982), Coward (1984), and Wilson (1985). Even further, Gina Grumke's (1993) research on women in the Mary Kay Cosmetics industry in Madison, Wisconsin, demonstrates that beauty and its associated practices may help to create and promote female autonomy, self-esteem, and sense of community.

Women's beauty culture in Kathmandu, specifically hair and hair styles, may give meaning to women's lives while simultaneously imposing control and restriction. Questions emerged during my fieldwork, and again here at home, that demonstrate that what was occurring at Ritu's was extraordinary both in local and global contexts, and yet quotidian enough to warrant sustained attention from those interested in understanding how traditions are reconfigured, resisted, or reinforced through daily practice. My concern in this chapter is to explore the ways in which women's hair styles—as a distinct set of beauty practices—projected a multitude of symbolic meanings and identities in Kathmandu. What messages were women inscribing on their bodies by wearing distinctive hair styles? In what ways have beauty salons acted as sites in which women could make connections with a world beyond Kathmandu? What claims did women—and men—make about cultural histories and systems of power through narratives of beauty salon histories by employees and customers? How might beauty culture be laden with the complexities of both historical processes and local conditions? And finally, how might women be using their hair and other beauty practices to signify cultural, national, or gendered practices, social beliefs, and identities?

One way that women place themselves and others in an urban landscape is through adornment and beauty practices. Subtle and not so subtle indicators of this relationship abound. Subtle indicators of a woman's identity can be "read" by others in the clothing and adornment a woman chooses or has chosen for her. Women told me, and demonstrated, that they could tell the class, caste, status, and often the nationality of others on the street by the particular style of dress and the details of their jewelry, hair, and other accessories.[3] Molly Myerowitz Levine, in her work on ancient Mediterranean hair (1995), describes this ability as a *grammar,*

> . . . a consistent system which accommodates, organizes, and governs the various significances of hair so as to articulate some large cultural sense. Native speakers unconsciously absorb the rules of a grammar together with its vocabulary. A grammar not only informs the way in which speakers use the elements of a language, in this case the language of hair; it also molds and limits what can and cannot be articulated. (1995:76)

In Kathmandu, people may agree on the grammar of hair, but that personal identity and deployment of hair as a symbol are not always consistent with this grammar. A woman who wears a sleeveless sari blouse is believed by many of the women at Ritu's to be more westernized, less modest, more "forward" than those who wear more covering items of apparel. A woman with a lot of makeup is said to be showy and is believed to be "loose" or improper. A woman in a short skirt may be called a "prostitute" depending on the context. How one appears to others through adornment thus marks identities or a set of social roles[4] or display group membership (Bledsoe 1984; O'Hanlon 1989:15). These identifications may be internalized, rejected, or modified to suit the positioning of individuals, and these identities may be either individually or culturally constituted (Arthur 1993). Indeed, as Mary Douglas (1970:67) and others have pointed out, the human body often stands as a symbol of the social body even though the relationship between bodily adornment and cultural ideals can be quite variable (Comaroff 1985:6–8).

This chapter first summarizes the recent history of caste relations in Nepal. Next, I show how historical Kathmandu hair styles are embedded in these historical caste identities and relationships through an elaboration of the fashion of beauty culture in Kathmandu. I then outline the history of beauty salons in Kathmandu, the connections between ideologies of the *ghar*, or house, gender-segregated space, and the kinds of innovations that occurred in these early salons. A discussion of beauty workers follows, after which I look more closely at contemporary salon life and hair practices in Kathmandu.

Caste Backgrounds and Cultural Histories

Nepal's democracy movement of 1990 brought about the downfall of the autocratic *panchayat* system, resulting in the most fundamental changes in the government since the founding of the Rana-Shah rule nearly 150 years ago. Nepal remains the only Hindu kingdom in the world, but the importance of the dominant state ideology—which reinforced Hindu traditions and legitimized monarchy—has declined with the advent of a constitutional monarchy. Caste distinctions have been banned in previous legal codes and constitutions for some time, but despite the transition to democracy, caste and ethnic heritage continue to be essential components of identity throughout Nepal.

Together with some other high-caste groups, the Bāhun and Chhetrī Hindu castes are often referred to as Parbatiyā.[5] Among the dominant families in the Chhetrī caste, the Rana and Shah families competed for rule from 1769 until the recent democracy movement. To consolidate their power, the Rana families intermarried with members of the ruling Shah dynasty and buttressed their position by fabricating a fictional past of renown emphasizing genealogical links to the Rājpūt rulers of Mewar, India, as the Shah dynasty had done before them (Bista 1991; Whelpton 1987),[6] and continuing to hinduize their practices.[7] Along with this, the rulers attempted to impose a hegemonic Brahmanical "tradition" throughout Nepal, an imposition that does not accurately reflect the great diversity of Nepalese cultures, castes, and ethnicities, nor does it recognize their influential traditions and histories.[8] Their fictional constructions—which constituted national identity and history—continue to guide behavior, attitudes, and policy at almost all levels of social life in contemporary Kathmandu even while being contested.

An important counterpoint to this process of hinduization of the Nepalese nation-state is the culture and history of the conquered Newār peoples who are among the original inhabitants of the Kathmandu valley and ruled in many of the early kingdoms (Levy and Rajopadhyaya 1990; Slusser 1982). From the Parbatiyā point of view, Newār occupy a distinct position in the middle of the hierarchy. The Newār, on the other hand, have their own culturally distinct hierarchy—also based on a division of labor, and on notions of purity and pollution—which they believe is not subsumed under the Hindu hierarchy but is instead both outside of and parallel to it. The important impact of the Newār elites, artisans, and merchants on the integration of the Nepalese state has been well documented (Lewis 1993a; Lewis and Shakya 1988; Slusser 1982). This multistranded conceptualization of culture and social organization exists throughout Nepal despite the official dominance of a Hindu ethos. These often contentious ideologies are mirrored in the competing historical frameworks within which the emergence of fashion and beauty salons as distinct phenomena in Kathmandu are situated.

The Fashion of Styles: Beauty Culture in and around Kathmandu

It is essential to distinguish between older forms and configurations of adornment and the *fashion* (an indigenized term) involved in beauty culture. The advent of foreign *fashion* beginning in the 1850s set the stage for the emergence of beauty salons in Kathmandu. Often, when *fashion* is invoked in academic literature, the prevailing view has been to speak to cloth and clothing, and to tie these to notions of modernity, capitalism, and the temporality of fashionable forms.[9] Other academic work has suggested there are culturally specific meanings of *fashion* that are in opposition to concepts of *tradition* (Nag 1989, 1991). Beyond the ideas of temporality and tradition, in South Asia, *fashion* can also imply an identification with foreign or global trends. As O. P. Joshi elaborates: "In India, 'fashion,' both as a word and as a concept, denotes a deviation from the norms of dress and in the feminine context, generally means the adoption of alien dress and the wearing of Western dress in the masculine context" (1991:220–21). In regard to clothing, some contemporary Indian fashion designers contend that "In a country where traditions are strong, there was no fashion" (Moore 1993:B1). This is patently not true in Kathmandu where there are both Nepali and Indian fashion designers who create fashionable saris, *salwār kurtā*, and clothing for both local and foreign clientele. Indian and Nepali concepts of fashion and style are quite old and are based partially on interactions with other cultures on the subcontinent and beyond and partially on the influences of the elite castes and classes.

In Kathmandu, *fashion* also included an attribution of moral qualities to the fashion wearer and nonwearer alike. For example, the Nepali word *nakkala* means *copy* or *fashion*; *nakkala* is actually a synonym for *fashion* or the Nepali *phesana* (Schmidt et al. 1993:335). The derivative *nakkali* means (1) (a) artificial, counterfeit, false, (b) forged, doctored, (c) inferior, shoddy, (d) fashionable, chic, modern; (2) (a) an imitation, fake, bootleg, copy, (b) a fashionable girl (Schmidt et al. 1993:335–36). This sense of *fashion* being associated with that which is fake, inferior, counterfeit, artificial, and false suggests also a denigrated moral character for those whom the term is used to describe. While *nakkali* is used to describe others, I never heard it used by my collaborators to describe themselves precisely because of the lack of morality implied in this. These moral qualities are not fixed but relative to a person's position in her life cycle, her class, social standing, and educational level.

Of the several Parbatiyā women who voiced an opinion to me, it was commonly believed among them that *fashionable* hair styles originated with Prime Minister Jang Bahadur Rana's trip to Europe in 1850 at the beginning of Rana rule in Nepal. Jang Bahadur's journey was historically significant; it marks the first trip made to Europe by any Hindu political leader. Among other things, Jang Bahadur brought back ideas that the Rana rulers used to build palaces that mimic European architectural designs (Sever 1993:134–35). Many critics say the Rana rulers contributed nothing to Nepal except for "a few ornate palaces, whose style reflects questionable taste" (Matthews 1986:xiii).[10] Jang Bahadur also brought ideas that effected changes in politics and military strategies (Whelpton 1986), photography (Shrestha 1986), and even women's fashions (Shrestha 1986:plate 71). As with the palaces, the Ranas copied European fashions, and, like their predecessors, imported great quantities of European fabrics and other goods that were the privilege of the elite (Liechty 1994:535ff.; 540). Liechty points out that "[F]or centuries Nepali elites have appropriated foreign clothing styles (often with accompanying sumptuary prohibitions on the general populace) in their efforts to display their distinctive power in controlling 'distant phenomena' " (Liechty 1994:305). The extensive collections of photos I examined from this period show women in clothing and hair styles that seem to be an amalgam of both older Nepali influences and the newer European trends as Liechty also corroborates (1994:541–43).[11]

Some early explorers in the Kathmandu Valley discussed how Newār women could be distinguished from other women by the way they wore their hair. Daniel Wright noted, toward the end of the nineteenth century, that Newār women wore their hair "gathered into a short thick club on the crown of the head, whereas the others have it plaited into a long tail, ornamented at the end with a tassel of red cotton or silk" (1990 [1877]:29).

Not only was caste or ethnic identity demonstrated through specific female hair styles; in addition, hair styles in ancient India were reflective of social states. For example, in his discussion of women's hair styles in classical sources, Alf Hiltebeitel (1981) documented how the *ekaveṇī* style, similar to an American ponytail, was worn by women who were separated from their husbands and thusly called *virahiṇī*. When the husband of a *virahiṇī* returned, she presented herself to her husband with her hair unbound; she was once more assumed to be sexual and her unbound hair was representative of this state. In addition to representing a social state, the bound nature of the woman's hair during her husband's absence reflected a bound or restrained sexuality. Unbound, or "open" (*kholnu*) hair, as it was described to me in Kathmandu, is sexually attractive and even has the connotation among other Bāhun and Chhetrī women of "loss of control over female sexuality" especially at moments of menstruation, new motherhood, and new widowhood (Bennett 1983:243 n.31). This relationship between a woman's unbound hair and sexuality in Nepal was corroborated by Laura M. Ahearn who did research among Hinduized Magārs in the village of Junigau in Nepal (cf. 1994). According to Ahearn, women in Junigau believe it is important for a woman who is giving birth to unbind her hair if she wants to avoid a difficult birth (personal communication 1995). While sexual attractiveness and religious pollution are very different social states, they both represent contexts when South Asian women stand outside the normative gender ideals (cf. Wadley 1980).

As noted in the debate over Indira Rana's hair at the beginning of this chapter, hair length has gendered attributes in contemporary Kathmandu and historically, for many Newār and Parbatiyā, long hair was associated with femaleness and short hair, or a bald head, is understood as male. One could distinguish between Parbatiyā and Newār women by their hair styles; presently, a more unified set of ideals was emerging partially as a result of increased interactions with a world beyond Kathmandu and partially as a result of the emergence of a significant middle class.

We can be sure that many of these trends did not filter down to the lower classes because of the sumptuary laws enforced by the Ranas. Liechty details the contacts that Nepalis in Nepal had with foreign goods and ideas (1994:493ff.). As Liechty elaborates,

> The Kathmandu valley *was* secluded to the extent that Europeans were excluded. Yet by 1950 Nepalis in the hundreds of thousands had traveled to the corners of the globe through service in the British regiments during two world wars. Foreign and especially European influences were often conspicuously present (in public architecture for example) and European goods were avidly consumed, if only by an elite class. For millennia it had important economic, political and cultural ties with Tibet, China and Central Asia to the North, and especially with the Gangetic plain to the South. . . . [Nepal's] geographic isolation, while sometimes put to strategic use, did not necessarily mean cultural isolation. (1994:493–94; original emphasis)

Other authors have noted widespread trade networks throughout the Himalayas reinforcing our understandings of the links between the Nepali elite and the influences of the outside world.[12]

The remnants of these European historical influences are still seen today in government buildings and other architecture, in political ideologies, and in contemporary hair styles among some elite women. Mrs. Pande, a Parbatiyā woman in her early fifties, told me that elite Parbatiyā Kathmandu women wore their hair in buns and braids before Jang Bahadur's trip. After his return, the maids in the elite Rana households were trained to care for their mistresses' hair and they began to copy "Victorian fashions" in hair style and clothing.[13] A "hair style" then, according to my collaborators, is a way of wearing one's hair that requires some amount of maintenance beyond buns or braids. This idea was relatively widespread; an author writing about fashionable hair styles in a Kathmandu paper referred to how women of her grandmother's generation wore plaits, or braids, to make the point that in comparison many of these newer hair styles required more maintenance (Sharma 1993).

Along with this sense of maintenance, hair styles are indeed certain kinds of cultural commodities. The concept of *fashion* can also be evoked as a cultural commodity when applied to goods, ideas, and images. Sarah Miller, who conducted research among Parbatiyā in the Kathmandu Valley, defines style as an economic standard that emphasizes "the techniques of fashion" (1992:46). As Miller notes, foreign goods and ways are termed "fashionable," and knowing how to wear them properly signifies "style" (1992:46).

In terms of the linkages of these historical practices to the lives and practices of the women at Ritu's beauty salon, these women are embedded in social relations through beauty culture and beauty practices that cross not only temporal boundaries but also class- and caste-related ones. Kumari once elaborated on some Rana *fashion* photographs from a picture book I had on my coffee table at my home in Kathmandu: *Nepal Rediscovered: The Rāna Court 1846–1951* (Shrestha 1986).

> While waiting, Kumari looked through the Rana picture book, enjoying it. She pointed out the different fashions to me including women who were wearing saris with the pleat in the back [instead of in the front as is usually done], giant ballooning salwārs [pantaloons] that acted like a stiff petticoat, the way that the Rana women would shave their eyebrows off completely and repaint them on, the long ringlets [of hair] made with a long metal rod which had been heated in a fire [and used like a curling iron], the distinctive jewels, the tiaras, etc. (Fieldnotes: 6/1/92)

While bringing my attention to some of the more remarkable aspects of Rana fashion, some of the European influences, and how particular women wore their fashion with style, Kumari was also embedding these historical photos in the social networks with which I, and most especially she, was familiar in Kathmandu. These same elite networks also led me to Shrijana Rana (see Figure 19), the first beauty salon operator in Kathmandu who opened up her salon within the courtyard of her *ghar*.

Beauty Salons in Kathmandu History

The *ghar*, or house, and the beauty salon have been intricately intertwined since the first westernized beauty salon was opened in Kathmandu in 1958.[14] Shrijana Rana, the wife of one of Jang Bahadur's descendants, told me how the ongoing influx of European ideas of fashion and style influenced her to do this. Six or eight months before this founding, she went to Calcutta, with her husband's permission, to train as a hairdresser despite the protestations of her in-laws. Upon her return to Kathmandu, Shrijana discovered that her father-in-law would not allow her to open a salon outside the house because of his concern with her potential unsupervised contact with nonkinsmen and because of the common devaluation of manual labor among many elites. She was able to convince him to let her build her salon on the family property with the outside door of the salon built into the compound wall. Technically, Shrijana never had to leave the compound to run her business; the *ghar* itself served as a mask for the relatively unconventional activities in which she was engaging. Shrijana's innovation and creativity allowed her in-laws to feel that they were upholding Parbatiyā propriety, especially in regard to women's behavior, and the families of her customers—mostly high-caste women from powerful elite families—were able to come to her salon precisely because it was enclosed within Shrijana's family's household compound. On the "public" face, all was as it should be even while what was occurring within the space of the salon, and the *ghar* compound, threatened to undermine this very set of ideologies and public impressions.

Elizabeth Enslin, in her discussion of how a mixed-caste group of women in Chitwan, Nepal, organized to create a public space for themselves, uses David Harvey's analysis of how changes in social relations in different periods of Euro-American history have entailed concomitant shifts in spatial uses and conceptions because "any struggle to reconstitute power relations is a struggle to reorganize their spatial bases" (Harvey 1989:238) (as cited in Enslin 1992:14). These beauty workers in Kathmandu were from the beginning, like Shrijana, doing just this. Shrijana was attempting to reconstitute the power relations within her family, even if only in a small way, through her struggles.

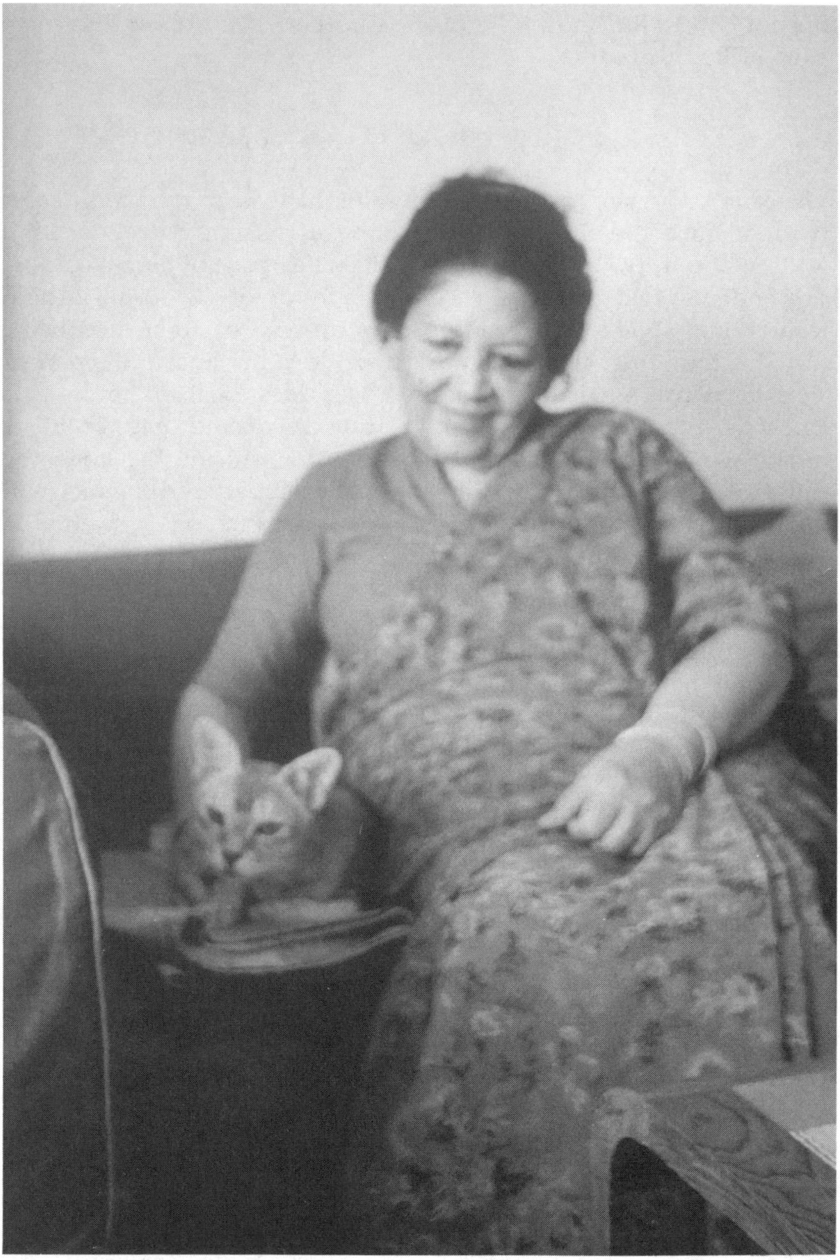

Figure 19. Shrijana Rana at her home in Kathmandu in 1993. Photo by Julia J. Thompson.

By going to beauty school in Calcutta, and setting up her salon, she was reorganizing her spatial base and the cultural ideas about business and women in the public domain. This was not a new strategy among elite women. For example, in her autobiography, Chandrakanta Malla describes her attempts to start a school for girls (1980). This "inside-the-compound" strategy for doing "public" work may have been used for a number of other activities as well, including Shrijana's beauty salon.[15]

In Shrijana's salon, as early as the late 1950s and early 1960s, women negotiated gender ideals and made changes in their lives that they could not have done in their own homes. At that time, as in India, it was customary for women in Kathmandu to wear their hair long and straight, often wrapped in a bun or plaited to keep it "closed" (*kholnu*). When Shrijana came back from training in Calcutta, she had cut her hair short, much to the consternation of her mother-in-law. In 1958, short hair on women was almost unheard of except on widows. Shrijana's mother-in-law was angry that Shrijana had cut her hair because it signaled to her mother-in-law that Shrijana was emulating more foreign ideals of womanhood that did not have much general acceptance at that time. Shrijana then told me with a twinkle in her eye, that her mother-in-law could do very little, as her hair was already cut. Shrijana proceeded to cut and style the hair of many elite women in Kathmandu; she gave many of them short cuts as well. These women, of the powerful families—descendants of royalty and the ruling elite—would never have been able to get away with cutting their hair short at home, where beauty-related activities usually took place. The lure of having a professional hairdresser cut their hair in a safe female place outside the home allowed many women to push at the limits of acceptable behavior and appearance at this time. Because the salon was physically connected to Shrijana's family compound, Shrijana was able to create a place to exercise small freedoms, earn some money, and affect the lives of other women in small ways.

For example, according to an Indian classmate of mine, the beauty parlor was one of the few outings women of a particular social class were allowed in her hometown of Delhi because it was clearly believed to be an extension of women's domestic space. The opposite movement of women also occurred. Among those groups who secluded their women to attain or maintain high status it was common to hire beauty workers to come to one's house for an afternoon or evening. As several of my collaborators told me, the hostess would invite her female friends and relatives to come drink tea, eat snacks, gossip, and have various beauty services performed.

These examples show how beauty culture lies ideologically within the realm of the domestic. The segregated nature of women's lives is not necessarily decreasing over time. As such, beauty culture has remained primarily the prerogative of women in contemporary Kathmandu. Men (and some women), therefore, believe that women workers and customers will be protected from potentially dishonorable contact with nonkinsmen—the kind of contact that can lead to unsanctioned sexual relations—precisely because it is construed as a private domestic space even while in a public setting.

I recognize, as does Shrijana, that her success as a beauty shop owner and operator was based at least partially on her elite caste, class, and status. This social positioning opened up a range of possibilities not available to women of other classes and castes at this time even while lower-caste and -class women had different types of space and urban mobility available to them. Currently, beauty salons also act as places where women—whether socially marginalized or not—may negotiate traditional gender ideals and change their lives in unorthodox ways as I illustrate below.

After this, in 1962 to be precise, salons began to make the transition from an inside-the-compound strategy for "public" or business work, to one that was intermixed in the ideologies and economies of a wider market. This transition originated with Mrs. Soi's, reputedly a Chinese woman, who opened a salon on Darbār Mārg, one of Kathmandu's main thoroughfares. Mrs. Soi's salon was more centrally located and was easier to reach than Shrijana's. Shrijana's business began to decline as her clients began to drift away to Mrs. Soi. Shrijana closed her shop not long afterward. Bolstered by her new-found skills as a salon owner and operator, Shrijana went on to other highly successful business enterprises.

After Mrs. Soi's salon opened, a woman from a Shah family operated a salon for a short period in 1963 or 1964. Then, in 1968, Mrs. Joshi, a Newār woman, opened a salon in the center of town that was still operating when I did my fieldwork. Shrijana Rana maintained that these other salons were able to flourish in Kathmandu as a result of her own initial inventiveness and incentive that begin within her own *ghar*.

In contrast with the Parbatiyā perspective on the development of the beauty salon industry, as evinced by Shrijana Rana, Newār informants related to me how it was this Mrs. Joshi, a Newāri woman, not Shrijana, who was the first trained beautician to open a beauty salon in Kathmandu. These Newār sources described the situation when Mrs. Joshi came back from her training in London in 1967: they claimed that there were only two other salons in operation (Shrijana's and Mrs. Soi's?) and none of them had trained beauticians. One Newār man, whom I met at a diplomatic dinner party, vehemently denied that the beauty parlor industry in Kathmandu is a result of Rana influence or innovation. He stated that salons burgeoned only in the 1970s as a result of what he termed "westernization" and because people were traveling outside Nepal more. He said that beauty salons are really a Newār innovation and explicitly said that beauty salons arose from the Newār history and practice of trade in the Kathmandu Valley. Rather than linking the beginning of salons in Kathmandu to the Parbatiyā ideals of women, *tradition*, and the *ghar* (in all its manifestations), this gentleman was making links to the alternative ideologies of Newār life which has, in contrast, more liberal ideals regarding female morality and conduct, and secondly to the importance of Newār merchants and businessmen and women in the expansion of the economic bases of Nepal.

A second, and corresponding, transition was also occurring at this time in Kathmandu that supports this gentleman's claims. As reported by Gopal Singh Nepali, a sociologist, beginning at least in 1965, the Newār barber caste had begun to extend their traditional ritual caste duties and "opened hair-cutting salons that are visited by all the castes, including the non-Newars" (Nepali 1965:184). At these barber shops, the barbers charged their customers money for their services rather than having their labor be considered part of ongoing patron-client relations. My other Newār informants supported this bit of history and it definitely confirms the impact that Newār merchants had on the changing economic conditions in Kathmandu. Mrs. Joshi herself, in an interview I conducted with her, declared that beauty shops are truly Newāri and that "the others" have merely copied what was first their idea.

In this particular nexus of historic transition, the above-mentioned gentleman was making a claim to Newāri status and prestige about the history of salons. By tying in the rise of salons to increasing contact with the outside world and local Newār mercantile history, he was (re)asserting the importance of the Newār peoples in Nepal's past and present configurations. This history, when read from a Newār point of view, undermines the authority of the Nepali nation-state that is built upon the hegemony of Hinduism and of the elite Parbatiyā Rana and Shah families. These alternative histories—that focused on a variety of subjects including caste, language, economics, and politics—were popular among many people at the time I was in Kathmandu. In narratives such as this Newār gentleman's, one can distinguish claims being made about the influence of these different peoples—and their respective ideologies about women, business, and the place of women in "public" life—on the rise and importance of the beauty industry and the beginning of the transition from caste-based relations to cash-based ones, in contemporary Kathmandu.

Within these divergent historical cases, we can begin to detect how having hair styles, going to beauty salons, and working as beauticians were cultural practices that signified class, caste, and ethnic demarcations through the appropriation and celebration of more western styles that lower-class people could not afford. Variform influences and divergent histories were used to account for the emergence of the beauty salons. In the movement from a social world based on traditional caste occupations and obligations toward one based more and more on class markers and privileges in Kathmandu, claims of difference of this kind reflected disparate access to limited resources and negotiated assertions of power. Each narrative of the founding of beauty salons in Kathmandu was a claim that revealed how caste and class differences were articulated and situated in frameworks of competing power systems, of histories, and cultures.

Beauty Workers in Historical Perspective

As I mentioned above, a transition occurred not only in the opening of beauty salons but also in the caste-related duties of barbers (*nau*) and barbers' wives (*nangini*). Historically, "Cutting and dressing hair are, of course, low caste occupations" (Hiltebeitel 1981:95), in much of Hindu South Asia. In both the Newār and Parbatiyā caste hierarchies, *nau* and *nangini* are also low caste, though not quite untouchable. Historically *nau* and *nangini* had caste-related duties, including critical ritual roles at weddings of many castes. I witnessed the continuity of the *nangini* and *nau* caste roles although on a much reduced scale, on several occasions. I saw *nangini*, for example, enact central roles at the mock marriage *ihi* ceremonies for young Newār girls[16] (Figure 20) and at Parbatiyā weddings *nangini* came to cut and polish the bride's nails, and rubbed turmeric on her body for beautification and protection. In other parts of South Asia, barbers and their wives have much the same roles. Paul Hershman (1974) wrote of the Punjab barber castes who participated extensively in weddings, and Charles Lindholm (1981,

Figure 20. A Newār *naunī* (female barber, left corner) cutting the toenails of a young girl at her *ihi* ceremony, a major life-cycle ritual for Newār girls. Photo by Julia J. Thompson.

1982) discussed the links between the ritual obligations of barbers at weddings and love intrigues among the Pukhtun of Swat. Pukhtun barbers acted as the go-betweens for the bride's and groom's families during the marriage negotiations and ceremonies, and were also thought to have produced love potions.

These associations between barbers and illicit liaisons, and the transition from caste obligations to cash agreements also spread to other areas of Kathmandu social life, creating the space for female-only beauty salons to emerge. At Ritu's I witnessed beauticians arranging marriages, assisting in love intrigues (including extramarital affairs, premarital affairs, and other romantic and sexual liaisons), and providing beauty services for clients for a variety of social and ritual occasions.

Currently, there is no social stigma attached to hairdressing or other beauty work; in fact, for many women it is even considered prestigious both by themselves and by others. This transformation from low-caste beauty work based on "patron-client" relationships to a modern, class-oriented business based on monetary transactions is another significant theme here. This transition has not, of course, obliterated all previous cultural configurations. Instead, ideologies become transformed, transplanted, and reimagined within and outside Ritu's beauty salon in significant ways.

The Anthropology of Hair and Hairstyles

The literature on beauty culture is sparse but there is a corpus of work that debates the symbolic meaning of hair and hair styles. Hair and hair styles are important sites of cultural meanings as previous studies have shown. Much of this earlier work has focused on either the psychological manifestations and meanings of hair (i.e., Berg 1951; Hallpike 1969; Leach 1958) or the symbolic aspects (Firth 1973; Hershman 1974; Rivière 1969). Theorists have acknowledged that hair can have both social and personal significance (i.e., Firth 1973), that the cultural context is essential in understanding hair (Uberoi 1967), and that hair can act as both a sign and a symbol (Firth 1973; Hastings 1913). It is also well documented that hair styles have symbolic meanings that vary across cultures and sometimes even within a single cultural context (i.e., Leach 1958).

More recent work includes Bodo and Baba's (1992) documentation of the manifold meanings of hair, hair styles, and hairlessness among five subcultures in the United States. Christopher Hallpike discusses hair and religion, noting "It is also quite possible for one and the same symbolic use of hair to have several different meanings simultaneously" (1987:154). Jeannette Mageo wrote that at one level of analysis (though not the only one), "As a part of local symbol systems, hair has significances that are only local" (1994:421). This is echoed in Carol Delaney's piece on the meaning of hair in Turkey (1994).

Little attention has been paid in this later research to how the symbolic and psychological aspects get worked out in the daily life of those with the specific hair styles or ways of wearing their hair. A notable exception is Obeyesekere's analysis of a Sinhalese ascetic woman's matted hair (1981). Obeyesekere demonstrates how the psychological, symbolic, and practical come together to create sets of meanings around the practice of growing and maintaining matted hair in a particular cultural context. Obeyesekere's model focuses on the multiple meanings that a single object can embody: as a *private* symbol (originating within the individual psyche), as *personal* symbols, and as *public* symbols. For Obeyesekere, as others, hair is intensely symbolic and has deeply personal meanings as well as broader cultural meanings that "are articulated to personal experience" (1981:13). While Leach, according to Obeyesekere, argues that a private symbol "ceases to have emotional meaning once it becomes publicly accepted culture" (as cited in Obeyesekere 1981:15), Obeyesekere refutes this, describing how hair can be polyvocal and deployed on a number of levels, the personal and the public, all with intensely emotional meanings (Obeyesekere 1981:15).

Another important exception is Mageo's article, "Hairdos and Don'ts: Hair Symbolism and Sexual History in Samoa" (1994). Mageo provides an excellent summary of the psycho-symbolic approaches to analyzing hair using her ethnographic data from Samoa to treat the various hypotheses. I want to set aside the debates Mageo discusses including whether head hair is symbolically representative of semen (Leach 1958), whether loose hair is associated with sexuality and a lack of hair with symbolic castration (Leach 1958), whether long hair is symbolic of freedom and short or bound hair is subordinate to social authority (Hallpike 1969), or even the argument that ritual uses of hair may convey more local significance (Hershman 1974). I am not convinced that these "one-on-one equations of symbols and meanings" (Synott 1993:123–24) are useful, especially when applied across contexts, cultures, and historical moments. Instead, I focus on how local cultural meanings around hair are not fixed but are flexible and polyvocal. Sometimes hair styles mark gender, caste, ethnic, national, or age-set identities, while at other moments, actors are positioned to reject, rework, and reconceptualize these identities and their associated meanings. In my own work in Kathmandu, I found that the symbolic message hair sends to others can change throughout the life cycle of the wearer; it can be indicative of a specific cultural state or status (nun, widow, renouncer, vow keeper); or indicate particular life circumstances (caste, class, nationality).

Beauty Salons, Hair, and Hair Styles in Contemporary Kathmandu

Ritu's, is a popular beauty salon located in a large hotel in the center of contemporary Kathmandu. As a site where claims about historical veracity, power, and authority were made, gendered identities and relations were also forged and various forms of difference were staged. Like beauty parlors in the United States, Ritu's offers a range of services including hair cutting, styling, perming, manicures, and pedicures. In addition, full-body coconut oil massages were available, as were hennas, head massages, hair threading, and facials.

The beauty parlor allowed a variety of women to express and negotiate these gender identities and interact with women in ways not possible elsewhere. Salon customers and workers had access to a realm of ideas not always available to other women. For example, Royal Nepal Airline flight attendants were frequent customers in Ritu's, dashing in and out between flights to have their hair washed, trimmed in the newest styles from London as depicted in pages torn from fashion magazines, or have their manicures renewed. These attendants told tales of the legal recourse British women have to domestic violence, of British women's place in the workforce, and of the goods available in the London shops. They related gossip surrounding western movie stars, and frequently, they shared foreign fashion and gossip magazines, discussing new clothing and popular hair styles.

The differing histories of the Parbatiyā and Newār seemed to disappear in the well-defined space of Ritu's. Even though "such handling of another's hair involves the handling of impurities" (Hiltebeitel 1981:159), it was not the case that only low-caste women were beauticians.[17] On the contrary, the majority of the beauticians at Ritu's were from middle and high castes and suffered no ritual pollution in their occupations either by their own estimations and or by the reckonings of the customers. Throughout my research, a Chhetrī woman and a middle-caste Rāi woman were the principal hairdressers. A Bāhun woman even gave pedicures, carefully soaking and scrubbing feet, massaging away tension, and clipping, filing, and painting toenails in bright reds, oranges, and pinks. The caste, ethnicity, and nationality of the customer did not seem to matter. Part of the logic in this situation lies precisely at the nexus of the ongoing contradictions that emerged in the transition from a caste-based social organization to one based on class (cf. Liddle and Joshi 1986).

Beauty practices and other cultural genres such as song (Narayan 1986; Raheja and Gold 1994; Skinner et al. 1994), myth (Bennett 1983; Harlan 1992), and weaving (March 1983) are important in contributing to South Asian female gender identity, agency, and even community. Hair styles can also be seen as expressive genres for females. In the contemporary context, beauty salons remain places where many of the newer hair styles are created and maintained. The beauty salon can, by extension, be seen as an important site of cultural production[18] where ideas regarding gender and identity can be discussed and operationalized.[19] At salons such as Ritu's there were interactions and processes responsive to wide sets of cultural and social influences contributing to women's sense of self. Scholars now recognize place as central to the construction of both national and community identities (Anderson 1991 [1983]; Gupta and Ferguson 1992); place can also be important in individual gender-identity formation.

This conceptualization of gender as finding meaning in various cultural genres and interactions is especially important when considering how women use the gendered space of Ritu's beauty salon. The hair cutters at Ritu's, despite their lack of formal training, were adept at copying what they saw from these fashion photographs. Some of the more elite customers, both Nepali and foreigners, who had access to an outside market, brought in expensive shampoos, conditioners, and styling products they obtained from Europe, Bangkok, or Hong Kong. Some brought in special formulas of hair dye or permanent solutions that were higher quality than what could be found locally or in India. These more expensive foreign products represent a class privilege and an association with what is perceived to be an exciting world beyond that found in Kathmandu.

In Kathmandu, women told me how, in the space of one generation, they were increasingly active agents in their choice of hair style, cut, color, and ornamentation (see Figure 21). At different stages in their lives, and as members of particular castes and classes, women altered their hair styles (as both *private* and *personal* symbols) to reflect and signal shifts in their various identities, whether cultural, national, or ethnic. In some ways, older symbolic associations guided contemporary women's hair styles in Kathmandu, but with social changes

Figure 21. Women who would have hairstyles: a group of Indian women at a wedding in Kathmandu. Photo by Julia J. Thompson.

occurring both locally and globally, hair styles also sent messages about personal politics thus linking their private meanings with public meanings.

By 1990, it was much more difficult to determine caste, or even ethnicity, through hair styles—even with these important historical antecedents—since both women and men were making choices based more and more on individual proclivities rather than being guided by older, more idealized forms (see Figure 22). In addition, people may have been attempting to camouflage or downplay ethnicity-, class-, or caste-identified hair styles in order to signal associations with the emerging modernity, a sense of national identity, and some kind of a global identity. The contemporary stories I collected from both Newār and Parbatiyā women regarding the symbolic meanings embedded in contemporary hair styles tended to be similar despite the divergent caste histories. For example, the portions of the wedding ceremonies of both Newār and Parbatiyā that focus on the bride's hair contain explicitly sexual symbolism, according to my informants, ethnographic sources, and as related by other ethnographers (personal communica-

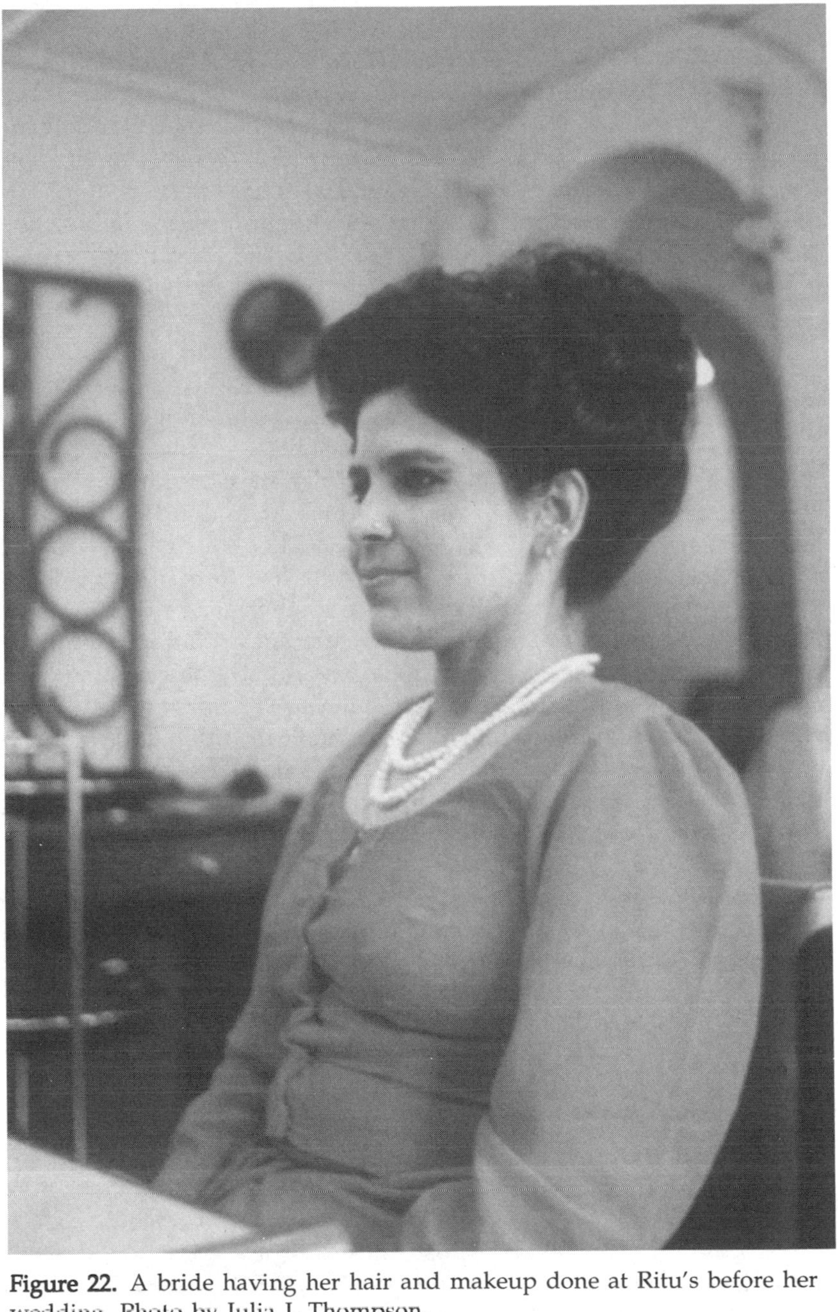

Figure 22. A bride having her hair and makeup done at Ritu's before her wedding. Photo by Julia J. Thompson.

tions: Laura Ahearn 1994; Todd Lewis 1994). Bennett documents the Parbatiyā Chhetrī *sídur hālne* ceremony during which the groom ritually deflorates the bride by rubbing a line of vermilion *tikā* powder in the bride's hair part (1983:86, 89) and this is evidenced in a more recent work as well (Ahearn 1994). None of the bride's family (her consanguineal kin) witnesses this especially traumatic portion of the wedding; women reported to me (as did Ahearn) that watching the *sídur hālne* is like watching the bride be raped. The Newār counterpart to this ceremony is the *sōn pyake* that in contrast is a more light-hearted event for all but the bride (Lewis 1985:293, 1993b:146).

My collaborators also reported recognizable differences in the past in hair styles based on ethnicity and nationality. For example, Tibetan men historically wore their hair long. Kathmandu women and Rajasthani Rājpūt women made distinctions between the ways Nepali and Indian women wear their hair. Several elite Rajasthan-born women, who were either living in or visiting Kathmandu, told me stories about their marriages to Nepali men. Kamala and her cousin Bina, Rājpūt women who had arranged marriages with elite Nepali families, cut their hair after their marriage ceremonies on their way from the wedding celebrations in Rajasthan to their new *maiti* in Kathmandu. Both women had heard from their female relatives (both their natal and inmarried kinswomen) that Kathmandu high-class and high-caste women have "hair styles." Kamala, in her attempt to fit in with her new Nepali female relatives, went to a male hairdresser in one of the larger hotels in Delhi; he was famous for cutting the long hair off unsuspecting female customers. Kamala then related to Bina and me, while touching her dark shoulder-length locks, that her hair used to be very long, thick, and the envy of everyone. Kamala told us that she went to get her hair cut into a "style" and came out with short permed hair. She was horrified at the results. With measurable sadness in her voice, she told of how when her new husband came to pick her up at the hotel he told her she looked like a man.

In order to appear suitably attractive and fashionable and to feel as though she belonged, Bina also decided to cut her hair after her marriage. After innocently visiting the same hairdresser, she too emerged with cropped hair. Bina's husband, Ram, told me later that when Bina had her hair short that she also looked like a man to him. Bina was devastated because she was afraid her in-laws would dislike her hair as much as her new husband did. These examples demonstrate the cultural entanglement of Parbatiyā ideals of femininity with long hair and also hint at widespread beliefs about how national differences are reflected in the ways that elite Rājpūt and Parbatiyā women wore their hair.

According to both my Nepali and Indian informants, another difference between Nepali and Indian women was that urban Nepali women rarely covered their heads with the ends of their sari or shawls—a custom popular in parts of India. One forty-five-year-old Chhetrī woman reported to me that she suspects this is why Nepali women have hair styles; since Nepali women don't usually cover their heads, they probably needed to pay more attention to their hair. This transition, from being an Indian woman with covered hair to a Nepali woman with uncovered (and perhaps even styled) hair is exemplified in the life experiences of Jiji, whom you met earlier. Jiji told me that when she first came to Nepal as a new Rājpūt bride to live with her Chhetrī in-laws, her mother-in-law continually scolded her to uncover her hair to signify Jiji's new identification as a Nepali wife and daughter-in-law. It took Jiji a long time to lose her shyness at exposing both her face and her hair to her in-laws, a practice of showing modesty and respect to those above one in the caste and gendered hierarchies that had become an unconscious habit while she was growing up in India. Jiji related that, even with the changes in how women are wearing their hair, such displays were still thought to be disrespectful and sometimes even a sign of hostility or aggression in northern India where she grew up.

Not only can beauty products, hair lengths, and hair coverings send messages about a woman's status, hair styles also marked stages in a Kathmandu woman's life. Young women—when they are called *tarunī*—sometimes experimented with various hair styles, often shorter, more westernized cuts.[20] These young unmarried women often came into Ritu's in groups of two, three, or four, giggling shyly and clutching magazine photographs, or they hauled in a friend whose hair style they wanted to emulate. One popular style was the *ashiki,* which is permed on top and has "a deep inward curve at the back of the head," as a recent article about popular hair styles in a Kathmandu English-language publication attested (Sharma 1993). Some *tarunī* wore asymmetrical hair styles where one side of the head was cut shorter than the other. Also popular were the newly imported spiral permanents, layered cuts (also called "step cuts") and interesting fringes, or bangs.

Tarunī may be both undermining and reinforcing the various systems of power to that which changing hair styles refer. These young women may feel independent, attractive, and modern as a result of their hair styles (and dress) and want to be international fashion models, rock stars, or video-disc jockeys on MTV. I heard parents say that such associations made arranging desired hypergamous marriages for their daughters with grooms in Kathmandu or India difficult. Does the globalizing culture of capitalism offer more true "choice" for these *tarunī*? As Lila Abu-Lughod (1990) wrote of young Bedouin women of the Western Desert of Egypt, co-opting the enticements and excitements of a wider global economy may subject these young women to new alternatives that they are helpless to either resist or understand. With their more radical haircuts, these *tarunī* might well be considered unmarriagable precisely because of the association between these haircuts and the outside world with its perceived loose sexual mores and aggressive women. In Kathmandu, it is still extremely difficult for women to remain unmarried and not become socially outcaste in one form or another. Unless these young women are exceedingly wealthy, or come from highly esteemed families, they risk their social standing, their familial membership, and the reputations of their parents if they are not able to, or do not, marry.

When women approach marriageable age, sometimes as early as fifteen or sixteen, *tarunī* find themselves pressured to grow their hair long. Their mothers, grandmothers, aunts, and cousins do this in order to make the best marriage match through the young woman's conformity to more conservative ideals of appearance.[21] In addition, they hope a more "traditional" hair style will please a potential mother-in-law thereby softening the difficulty of the transition from the *maiti* to the *ghar*. In Nepal, as in India, many women told me that their mother-in-law had the ability to control many aspects of a new bride's life, including how she will wear her hair. Instead of experimenting with hair styles as they once might have done, these young marriageable women gratify themselves with applications of henna, head massages thought to stimulate hair growth, and occasional trims to even up lengthening hair. They might have fringes, and tend to choose simpler styles compared with those a younger woman may choose. Sulochana is a nineteen-year-old Chhetrī woman enrolled at a local all-woman's college who worked part time as one of my research assistants. She has been growing her hair long for the past couple of years, and except for some subtle layering in the lengths, she has not cut it. Her two younger sisters aged thirteen and fifteen, in contrast, cut their hair every couple of months. These younger girls often pored over the American fashion magazines I hoarded while in Nepal, discussing the relative merits of all manner of hair styles they wanted to try next.

Mrs. Shrestha, a Newār woman in her forties who was born in the Kathmandu Valley, said that when the prospect of her own marriage had approached, she too had begun to grow her hair long; it was about shoulder length when she married. She did this because she was told by her family that her mother-in-law probably preferred it long. After marriage, Mrs. Shrestha was going out to an evening party with her new husband and was putting her hair back in a bun. Her mother-in-law intervened, telling her that since she was still so youthful, she should wear her hair unbound instead of pulled back so harshly. The younger Mrs. Shrestha was relieved and happy because this demonstrated that her mother-in-law was a liberal woman and would be easy to get along with in the future. This concern by a mother-in-law with her daughter-in-law's hair may be interpreted as a reflection of the culturally held beliefs about the tensions between a mother-in-law and a new in-marrying bride and the control of the younger woman's appearance by the older. For a newly married woman to wear her hair open is seen as taunting to her mother-in-law—an obvious display of sexuality. Mrs. Shrestha was happy that her mother-in-law dispelled these potential tensions.

A married Newār or Parbatiyā woman may cut her hair short, especially after children have grown, just as young unmarried women may wear shorter hair. Both of these are life-cycle moments when a woman stands outside the ideals of appropriately fecund womanhood with a living husband. On an older woman, shorter hair can signal a transition into menopause and a lack of sexuality. An older woman may also have permanent waves to give her hair body and apply henna more frequently to cover the newly emerging gray hair. Mrs. Pande—a woman of Rājpūt origin in her late forties—had cropped hair. One evening while dining at a mutual friend's house, we were discussing when Mrs. Pande first had cut her hair short. She said that until a few years ago she kept it very long and back in a bun or braid, even though she has always preferred short hair. In a reversal in the usual relationship between brides and mothers-in-law, Mrs. Pande cut off her mother-in-law's hair about six or seven years ago when her mother-in-law got ill. Mrs. Pande encouraged her mother-in-law by telling her how much easier it was to have short hair, especially now that she was older and was ill so often. Mrs. Pande told me with a laugh that she cut her hair short at the same time, since her mother-in-law could not then really argue.

Reinterpretations

There is another potential significance to women wearing short hair in contemporary Kathmandu: it may be a rejection of more traditional Nepalese values. As a self-proclaimed radical feminist in her mid-thirties, Jamuna was very politically active. Her hair came just to the bottom of her ears and she wore it unstyled and disheveled. For Jamuna, as she once told me amid conversation about feminism in Kathmandu, this was a conscious lack of effort. In addition to her short unkempt hair, although Jamuna is considered to be Chhetrī through marriage, she refused to wear any ornamentation at all, especially those items associated with a wedded Parbatiyā woman: not glass bangles (*churā*), nor a gold ornament (*tilhari*) on a necklace of glass beads (*pote*), no vermilion powder (*sídur*) for her hair part, nor a sari. In doing so, Jamuna overtly rejected the associations of long hair and ornamentation with older Hindu ideals of adult femininity. Jamuna's radical politics were, in a sense, inscribed on her body in her lack of conformity to these particular gender ideals that she perceived to be at work in her cultural environment. Instead, she had self-consciously taken her cues from her impressions of what western feminists look like.

The women I have described thus far have tended to have hair styles that matched—or were an attempt to match—their own sense of self and changing cultural identities. Women sometimes had hair styles that did not match their internal identity—wearing long hair could detract from associating the wearer with more radical sets of beliefs. One of Jamuna's friends, Bharati, had very long straight hair; although she did braid it in fancy ways and put it up in a variety of coils and buns, she had never visited a beauty salon and did not believe that she had a "hair style" as such. Bharati wore the traditional jewelry of a married Parbatiyā woman and wore either sari or *salwār kurtā* depending on the occasion. While Bharati may have looked conservative—and took great pride and pain with her appearance—she was actually considered very radical in her political beliefs and activities. Bharati's more conservative appearance actually gave her some amount of respectability in her social world, which then allowed her to be more radical in her actions. Jamuna, in contrast, had no desire for respectability and saw her appearance as an important step in social revolution.

Irena also reinterpreted traditional hair symbolism to suit her own life choices. Irena was an elite Parbatiyā woman who held an important position in the new democratic government. Irena wore her hair long, open, permed or curled, and often decorated, in an unruly frame around her head and shoulders. Irena did not bind her hair back or restrain it in any way as was expected by others at this stage in her life cycle, married with one grown daughter. She was scolded by women her own age and older about her hair. They described how Irena should wear her hair pulled back, braided, or in a bun, saying Irena shouldn't wear it so "open" and "wild"—it just didn't suit someone of her age and social position. Irena ignored these pressures and continued to wear her hair loose. In some ways, despite the inappropriateness of her hair style at this phase of her life, Irena also reinforced ideals of youthful feminine beauty both for herself and perhaps for other younger women. These ideals were contested by women like Jamuna and Indira Rana, whom we met briefly at the beginning of this chapter.

Indira Rana's shaven head is an extreme example of how women may use their hair style, or complete lack of hair, to make social statements (figure 23). Indira, also a Chhetrī woman, is a high-level government official whose life and work are centered on her efforts to bring about social change beneficial to all Nepalese women. At Indira's wish, I have not disguised her identity because as she says, the story is true, and because the amount of publicity this incident received in the local press makes anonymity difficult. At her mother's funeral (*kāj-kriyā*), Indira made a public and courageous statement about her role as a daughter and her position as a woman in Nepalese society. Indira is an exceptional woman by many cultural standards. She has never married, despite strong social pressures to do so, and has led an independent and public life. Indira has two brothers, but because she has supported, cared for, and lived with her mother throughout her life, Indira took the virtually unprecedented responsibility of performing the necessary thirteen-day funeral rituals and duties when her mother died before either brother could make the trip to Kathmandu from India; traditionally, it is the son or other male relative who performs these duties.

As the local newspapers reported, Indira's performance of her mother's *kāj-kriyā* was one that contested traditional gender ideals while conforming to traditional requirements through her performance of the rituals. It was a defiant move, which in some ways negated Indira's gender identity as a female because she acted as if she was a male and therefore has a valid claim to her parent's property. By Parbatiyā tradition and by Nepalese law, women generally share no part in the family property even though by law women may claim a portion of

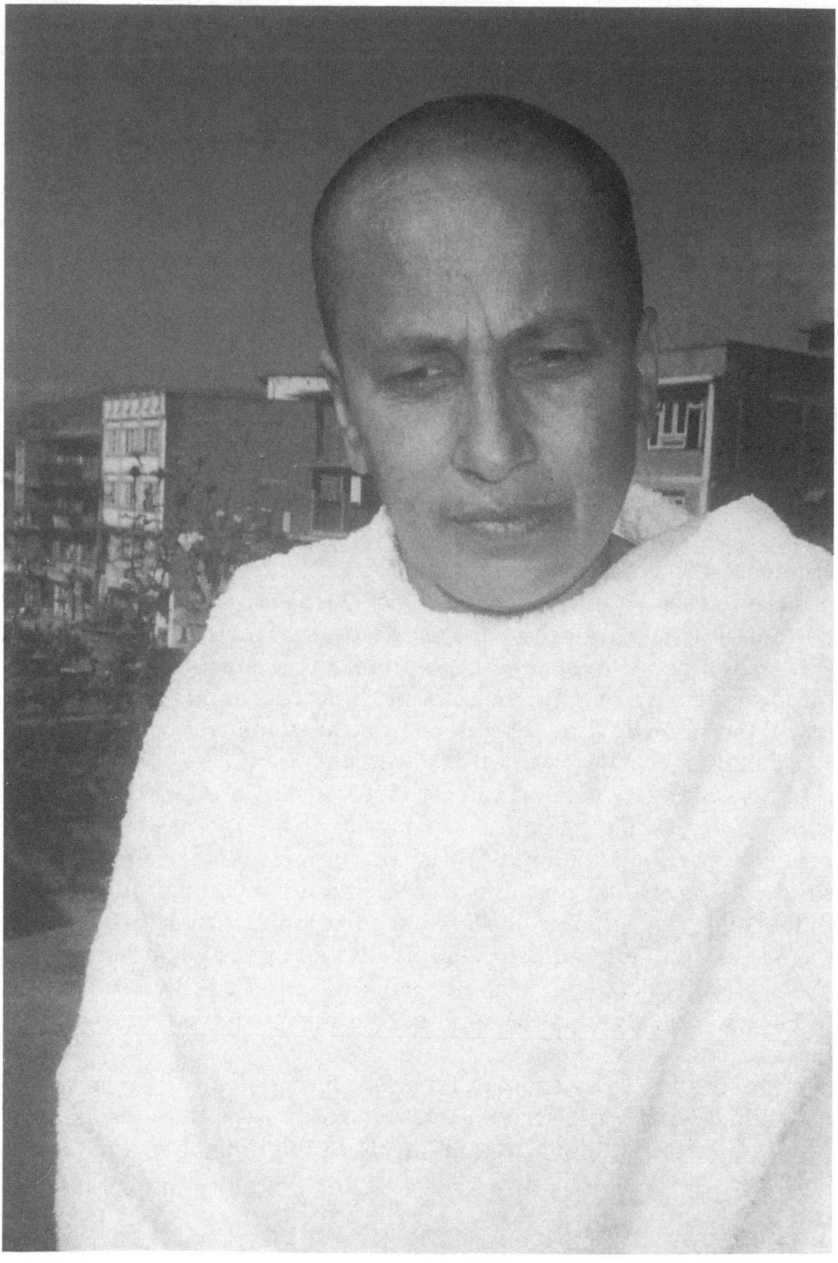

Figure 23. Indira Rana after her mother's *kāj-kriyā*. Photo by Indira Rana.

their father's property if they remain unmarried and are over the age of thirty-five (Bennett and Singh 1979; Gilbert 1992). Unfortunately, there are "significant factors affecting women's ability to pursue their legal rights" (Gilbert 1992:731), the very factors that prompted Indira to "act like a man." Indira's biological sex could not be denied and became the focus of her brother's refutation of her claims. Indira's shaven head, in a world full of women with hair, stood as a statement to her personal commitment to women's rights and social change in Nepal. This commitment continues, as I discovered in a letter I received from Indira dated March, 1994. "Last November was my mother's first anniversary [of her death], so I cut my hair [off] again, now [it is] growing nicely" (personal communication 1994).

As these examples show, women who are positioned outside ideals of womanhood may wear shorter hair. Hair styles have been—and continue to be—markers of gender, caste, ethnicity, nationality, and class. The question arises whether these women were merely appropriating western or foreign identities through their manipulation of hair styles or creating new identities in relation to their cultural world. There is a small but burgeoning critical literature which argues that even if a phenomenon appears western, it doesn't necessarily mean that the ideologies or practices are a complete adoption of western ideals and values. In Japan, for example, American-style wedding cakes are now popular additions to weddings. Walter Edwards (1982) demonstrated that the American marriage symbolism of these cakes is not wholeheartedly incorporated into Japanese weddings. Instead, Japanese have imbued these white-frosted cakes with their own culturally distinct sets of meanings.

In Korea, "double eyelid" (*ssangkkop'ul*) plastic surgery, where creases are sewn into women's eyelids to make their eyes look rounder, bigger, and more Eurasian is increasingly popular. According to Hannah Yang, this surgery "is more popular among teenage girls in Korea than dental braces are in the United States. Forty percent of young Korean women undergo the surgery" (1993:55). Yang argues that "The link between *ssangkkop'ul* and the Korean standard of attractiveness is so strong that the surgery has become embedded in the country's customs. Double eyelids are no longer even considered an emulation of Western features" (1993:55), but a distinctly Korean cultural practice.

As early as 1970 in India, Rama Mehta was investigating how Hindu women with western educations dealt with incorporating new, more "western" values with "traditional" attitudes (1970). These women were shown to be very innovative in blending these often conflicting sets of values. We can see, in these examples from Kathmandu, how the local sociohistorical context interacts with the influences of a broader global culture to produce new hair styles such as the *ashiki*. Although Kathmandu women often looked to the outside world for new gender models and identities, these new forms are incorporated into their lives in a distinctly Nepalese way. Universalizing symbolic associations of hair with sexuality, morality, constraint, or control do not hold up under scrutiny and application to real-life situations in Kathmandu; hair styles are reflective of cultural identities and of how individual and collective gendered identities are continually reworked and reimagined.

Cultural traditions in South Asia, and throughout the world, are not static but are constantly being reinvented in innovative ways (i.e., Hobsbawm and Ranger 1983; Narayan 1993). Hairstyles are not timeless although we may have an impression of what a Hindu woman looks like, or how a Tibetan woman wears her hair. There is no easy singular model that can account for the different types of meanings associated with hair. Like Obeyesekere's findings relating to the matted hair of Sinhalese ascetics, I found in Kathmandu that the symbolic message hair sends to others can change throughout the life cycle of the wearer; it can be indicative of a specific cultural state or status (nun, widow, renouncer, vow keeper); or indicative of particular life circumstances (caste, class, nationality). Moreover, it might be different now than ten years ago, or perhaps even ten years hence.

Notes

This chapter emerges from dissertation fieldwork conducted from October 1990 through June 1993, supported by a Grant-in-Aid of Research from Sigma Xi, The Scientific Research Society, and a Fulbright-Hays Award. Earlier versions were presented at the annual meeting of the American Anthropological Association (1993), a Department of Anthropology Colloquium at the University of Wisconsin–Madison (1993), and at the Politics and Poetics of the Body: Pacific Rim Triangulations Conference at the University of California, Santa Barbara (1994). I use pseudonyms, and occasional composite characters, and have changed minor details to protect the privacy of almost all those people portrayed here.

1. My explorations of beauty culture in Kathmandu were carried out in a combination of the Nepali and English languages. Conversations at Ritu's, while primarily in Nepali, English, and Hindi were also interspersed with Tibetan, Newāri, German, French, Spanish, and other regional languages and dialects.

2. I also interviewed Indira Rana during this period; for more on this incident see Thompson (1993).

3. Liechty (1994) corroborates this ability of people to "read" others appearance as well in his research in Kathmandu.

4. For example, Arthur (1993), Reynolds (1980), Roach and Eicher (1979), and Wadley (1994).

5. I use the designation Parbatiyā for the high-caste Hindus of Indo-Aryan origin (Bāhun and Chhetrī) to distinguish them from the Newār peoples (both Hindu and Buddhist) whose historical origins are in the Kathmandu valley. As is well documented, the Nepalese Parbatiyā caste system is a derivative of the classical Hindu *varna* system although there are some important distinctions. For more on caste relations in Nepal, see Gaborieau (1982), Höfer (1979), and Levine (1987).

6. The city of Udaipur, in the state of Rajasthan, is the former capital of Mewar, "a princely state whose royal line ranks first among the various households of Rajasthan" (Harlan 1992:2). Most of the rulers of contemporary Rajasthan come from the Rājpūt caste who are, by tradition, fighters and rulers (Harlan 1992:1). Contemporary Rāṇā and Shāh families in Kathmandu have a tradition of marrying their daughters into Rājpūt families and taking daughters-in-law from these same families. As such, Rana and Shah families believe themselves to be the caste equivalents of Rājpūt. But Rājpūts have reported to me that they do not see these relationships in the same way.

7. Some recent work on the invention of culture, history, and tradition includes Clifford (1988), Hobsbawm and Ranger (1983), Lepowsky (1991), and Wagner (1981).

8. For example, see Des Chene's (1991) historiography of Guruṅg Gurkha soldiers, and Lewis's (1993a) and Lewis and Shakya's (1988) work on Newār influence on the Nepalese state.

9. See Schneider and Weiner (1989) for an overview of these issues.

10. Many of these palaces are still standing today. While many now house government offices, a few are still in the hands of private Nepali owners. I visited several of these homes—one of which the main palace had been confiscated by the government and the family now lives in what used to be the gardener's residence—and they were indeed evocative of a European sense of power and prestige even in their often ramshackle state.

11. The Gladys Gilbert Collection; Smithsonian National Anthropology Archives, Washington, D.C.

12. Cf. Lewis 1993a; Lewis and Shakya 1988; March 1992, and Mikesell 1988.

13. Although I attempted to find out, I was never able to discover how, where, or by whom these maids were trained.

14. In the urban worldview, the marital household (*ghar*) is described as a woman's place and her occupation. It is usually the nexus of her personal and social obligations and one of the major sites in which her *dharma* may be expressed. The word *ghar* has a multitude of meanings, all of which reflect the complex of ideologies related to women, gender, domesticity, and family in contemporary Kathmandu. *Ghar* can mean: (a) house, building; (b) home; (c) family; (d) a woman's marital home; or (e) marriage (Schmidt et al. 1993:169–70). It can

also mean *family group*. Anthropologist Sarah Miller astutely describes the multiple meanings of the word *ghar* as it is used in Kathmandu and the narrative constructions that define it: "*ghar* is more than just a physical plant: the word also refers to a family's identity; it means a group defined by place and historical continuity" (1992a:46; cf. 1992b). And of course, there are essential ideological links between honor, which Miller also elucidates, and a woman's place in maintaining the prestige and honor (*ijjat*) of the *ghar*. Miller further writes, "family identity or *ghar* is symbolically constructed; it is not just a collection of names linked by birth and marriage, but a genealogy of related stories. These stories focus almost exclusively on marriage and on geographic movements" (1992a:46)

15. I thank Mary Des Chene for bringing this reference and its implications to my attention.

16. For information on the Newār *ihi* see Allen (1990 [1981]) and Vergati (1982).

17. There are mythic examples of queens and elite women acting as hairdressers under exceptional circumstances; on this point, see Shulman's (1994) discussion of the tale of Nala and Damayantī. The earliest records of hairdressers at work come not from South Asia but from North Africa. On a false door, dated to the sixth Egyptian Dynasty (2225 B.C.) in Giza, "a hairdresser named (?)Nefer is shown arranging the locks of a lady, Mi-nfrt" (Riefstahl 1956:16, n.27). Another early example is a small limestone statuette dated from about 2000 to 1800 B.C. depicting "An Egyptian lady nurses her baby while a slave hairdresser attends to her hair" (Cooper 1971:152).

18. Holland and Skinner (1995) also discuss cultural production among Nepalese women through an analysis of Tīj songs.

19. In the United States, barber shops provide the same kind of setting of cultural production for black males (cf. Brown 1994; Franklin 1985; Milloy 1994).

20. This is also documented in other cultural contexts. See, for example, McAlexander and Schouten's (1989) study of the links between changing hair styles and life-cycle transitions among American youth. Hershman (1974:281) mentions this phenomenon among Punjabi women and it also occurs in the Jewish tradition.

21. Of course, this assumes that these young women have arranged marriages.

References

Abu-Lughod, Lila. 1990. "The Romance of Resistance: Tracing Transformations of Power Through Bedouin Women." *American Ethnologist* 17.1:41–55.

Ahearn, Laura M. 1994. "Consent and Coercion: Changing Marriage Practices Among Magars in Nepal." Ph.D. Dissertation. University of Michigan, Ann Arbor.

Alkazi, Roshen. 1983. *Ancient Indian Costume*. New Delhi: Art Heritage Books.

Allen, Michael. 1990[1981]. "Girl's Pre-Puberty Rites Amongst the Newars of Kathmandu Valley." In Michael Allen and S. N. Mukherjee, eds., *Women in India and Nepal*. Delhi: Sterling Publishers, pp. 179–210.

Anand, Mulk Raj. 1993. *The Book of Indian Beauty*. (Reprint of the 1981 Anand and Hutheesing volume, which is a reprint of the original 1947 Anand and Hutheesing.) New Delhi: Rupa and Co.

Anand, Mulk Raj, and Krishna Nehru Hutheesing. 1981. *The Book of Indian Beauty*. Rutland, Vt.: Charles E. Tuttle.

Anderson, Benedict. 1991[1983]. *Imagined Communities: Reflections on the Origin and Spread of Nationalism*, 2nd ed.. London: Verso.

Appadurai, Arjun. 1990. "Disjuncture and Difference in the Global Cultural Economy." *Public Culture* 2.2:1–24.

Arthur, Linda Boynton. 1993. "Clothing, Control, and Women's Agency: The Mitigation of Patriarchal Power." In Sue Fisher and Kathy Davis, eds., *Negotiating at the Margins: The Gendered Discourses of Power and Resistance*. New Brunswick, N.J.: Rutgers University Press, pp. 66–84.

Balakrishnan, Padmini. 1967. *Sundaramāya Talamuṭi*. Kottayma, Kerala, India: Sahitya Pravarthaka Cooperative Society, Ltd.

Bartky, Sandra Lee. 1982. "Narcissism, Femininity, and Alienation." *Social Theory and Practice* 8.2:127–44.

Bennett, Lynn. 1983. *Dangerous Wives and Sacred Sisters: Social and Symbolic Roles of High-Caste Women in Nepal*. New York: Columbia University Press.

Bennett, Lynn, and Shilu Singh. 1979. *Tradition and Change in the Legal Status of Nepalese Women*, vol. 1, part 2, "The Status of Women in Nepal." Kathmandu: CEDA.

Berg, Charles. 1951. *The Unconscious Significance of Hair*. London.

Bista, Dor Bahadur. 1991. *Fatalism and Development: Nepal's Struggle for Modernization*. Calcutta: Orient Longman Limited.

Bledsoe, Bronwen. 1984. "Jewelry and Personal Adornment among the Newars." Unpublished manuscript. College Year in Nepal Program, University of Wisconsin-Madison.

Bodo, Dawn, and Marietta Baba. 1992. "Hair Routes: An Anthropological Look at Hair and Hair Loss in Diverse American Cultures." A study sponsored by The Upjohn Company. New York: Manning, Selvage, and Lee.

Bordo, Susan. 1993. *Unbearable Weight: Feminism, Western Culture, and the Body*. Berkeley: University of California Press.

Brody, Jane E.. 1994. "Notions of Beauty Transcend Culture, New Study Suggests." *The New York Times* (Monday, March 21):14.

Brown, Cecil. 1994. "How to Read Black Hair." *Reader (San Diego's Weekly)* 23.15 (April 14):1, 16–26.

Clifford, James. 1988. *The Predicament of Culture: Twentieth-Century Ethnography, Literature, and Art*. Cambridge, Mass.: Harvard University Press.

Comaroff, Jean. 1985. *Body of Power, Spirit of Resistance: The Culture and History of a South African People*. Chicago: Chicago University Press.

Cooper, Wendy. 1971. *Hair: Sex, Society, Symbolism.* London: Aldus Books.

Coward, Rosalind. 1984. *Female Desire.* London: Paladin. Also reprinted in 1985 *Female Desires: How They are Sought, Bought, and Packaged.* New York: Grove Press.

Davis, Kathy. 1991. "Remaking the She-Devil: A Critical Look at Feminist Approaches to Beauty." *Hypatia* 6.2:21–43.

Delaney, Carol. 1994. "Untangling the Meanings of Hair in Turkish Society." *Anthropological Quarterly* 67.4:159–72.

Des Chene, Mary. 1991. "Relics of Empire: A Cultural History of the Gurkhas, 1815–1987." Ph.D. Diss., Stanford University.

Douglas, Mary. 1970. *Natural Symbols: Explorations in Cosmology.* New York: Vintage Books.

Edwards, Walter. 1982. "Something Borrowed: Wedding Cakes as Symbols in Modern Japan." *American Ethnologist* 9.4:699–711.

Enslin, Elizabeth. 1992. "Collective Powers in Common Places: The Politics of Gender and Space in a Women's Struggle for a Meeting Center in Chitwan, Nepal." *Himalayan Research Bulletin* 12.1–2:11–26.

Fabri, Charles. (1960)1993. *Indian Dress: A Brief History.* Hyderabad, India: Disha Books, a Division of Orient Longman.

Firth, Raymond. 1973. "Hair as Private Asset and Public Symbol." In *Symbols: Public and Private.* Ithaca, N.Y.: Cornell University Press, pp. 262–98.

Franklin, Clyde W., II. 1985. "The Black Male Urban Barbershop as a Sex-Role Socialization Setting." *Sex Roles* 12.9/10:965–79.

Gaborieau, Marc. 1982. "Les Rapports de Classe dans L'idéologie Officielle du Népal." *Collection Puruṣārtha* 6:251–90.

Gaswami, Rama. 1981. *The Book of Beauty—Some Aspects of Ancient Cosmetics and Perfumery with Particular Reference to Assam* (in Assamese). Gauhati, Assam: Sahitya-Prakash.

Gilbert, Kate. 1992. "Women and Family Law in Modern Nepal: Statutory Rights and Social Implications." *New York University Journal of International Law and Politics* 24.2:729–58.

Giri, Kamal. 1987. *Bhāratiya Sṛṅgāra.* Barānasi, India: Motilal Banarsidas.

Grumke, Gina. 1993. "Anti Anti-Feminism: Tales from Mary Kay." Presented at the American Folklore Society Meetings; Eugene, Oregon.

Gupta, Akhil and James Ferguson. 1992. "Beyond 'Culture': Space, Identity, and the Politics of Difference." *Cultural Anthropology* 7.1:6–23.

Hallpike, Christopher R. 1969. "Social Hair," *Man* (n.s.) 9.2:274–98.

———. 1987. "Hair." In Mircea Eliade, ed., *The Encyclopedia of Religion*, vol. 6. New York: Macmillan, pp. 154–57.

Harlan, Lindsey. 1992. *Religion and Rajput Women: The Ethic of Protection in Contemporary Narratives.* Berkeley: University of California Press.

Harlan, Lindsey, and Paul B. Courtright, eds. 1995. *From the Margins of Hindu Marriage: Essays on Gender, Religion, and Culture.* New York: Oxford University Press.

Harvey, David. 1989. *The Condition of Postmodernity.* Cambridge, Mass.: Basil Blackwell.

Hastings, James, ed. 1913. "Hair and Nails." *Encyclopedia of Religion and Ethics* VI:474–77. Ficton-Hyksos, Edinburgh: T & T Clark.

Hershman, Paul. 1974. "Hair, Sex and Dirt." *Man* (n.s.) 9:274–98.

Hiltebeitel, Alf. 1981. "Draupadī's Hair." *Puruṣartha* 5:179–214.

Hobsbawm, Eric, and Terence Ranger, eds. 1983. *The Invention of Tradition.* Cambridge: Cambridge University Press.

Höfer, András. 1979. *Caste and State in Nepal.* Innsbruck: Universitṣtsverlag Wagner.

Holland, Dorothy, and Debra Skinner. 1995. "Contested Ritual, Contested Femininities: Appropriations of a Hindu Women's Festival in Nepal," *American Ethnologist* 22.2

Joṣhi, O. P. 1991. "Continuity and Change in Hindu Women's Dress." In Ruth Barnes and Joanne B. Eicher, eds., *Dress and Gender: Making and Meaning. Cross-Cultural Perspectives on Women.* New York: Berg, pp. 214–31.

Leach, Edmund R. 1958. "Magical Hair." *Journal of the Royal Anthropological Institute* 88:147–64.

Lepowsky, Maria. 1991. "The Way of the Ancestors: Custom, Innovation, and Resistance." *Ethnology* 30.3:217–35.

Levine, Molly Myerowitz. 1995. "The Gendered Grammar of Ancient Mediterranean Hair." In Howard Eilberg-Schwartz and Wendy Doniger, *Off With Her Head!: The Denial of Women's Identity in Myth, Religion, and Culture.* Berkeley: University of California Press, pp. 77–130.

Levine, Nancy. 1987. "Caste, State, and Ethnic Boundaries in Nepal." *Journal of Asian Studies* 46.1:71–88.

Levy, Robert I., and Kedar Raj Rajopadhyaya. 1990. *Mesocosm: Hinduism and the Organization of a Traditional Newār City in Nepal.* Berkeley: University of California Press.

Lewis, Todd T. 1985. "The Tuladhars of Kathmandu: A Study of Buddhist Tradition in a Newār Merchant Community." Ph.D. Diss., Columbia University.

_____. 1993a. "Himalayan Frontier Trade: Newār Diaspora Merchants and Buddhism." In Charles Ramble and Martin Brauen, eds., *Anthropology of Tibet and the Himalaya: Proceedings of the International Seminar.* Zürich: Ethnological Museum of the University of Zürich, pp. 165–78.

_____. 1993b. "A Modern Guide for Mahāyāna Buddhist Life-Cycle Rites: The *Nepāl Jana Jīvan Kriyā Paddhati,*" *Indo-Iranian Journal* 36:135–81.

Lewis, Todd T., and Daya Ratna Shakya. 1988. "Contributions to the History of Nepal: Eastern Newār Diaspora Settlements." *Contributions to Nepalese Studies* 15.1:25–65.

Liddle, Joanna, and Rama Joshi. 1986. *Daughters of Independence: Gender, Caste and Class in India.* Delhi: Kali for Women/Zed Books.

Liechty, Mark. 1994. "Fashioning Modernity in Kathmandu: Mass Media, Consumer Culture, and the Middle Class in Nepal." Ph.D. dissertation, University of Pennsylvania.

Lindholm, Charles. 1981. "Leatherworkers and Love Potions." *American Ethnologist* 8.3:512–25.

———. 1982. *Generosity and Jealousy: The Swat Pukhtun of Northern Pakistan.* New York: Columbia University Press.

McAlexander, James H., and John W. Schouten. 1989. "Hair Style Changes as Transition Markers." *Sociology and Social Research* 74.1:58–62.

Mageo, Jeannette Marie. 1994. "Hairdos and Don'ts: Hair Symbolism and Sexual History in Samoa." *Man* (n.s.) 29.2:407–23.

Malla, Chandrakanta. 1980. *Mero Ãthma-Kathā.* Kathmandu: Lekhikā Swayam.

Mani, Lata. 1992. "Cultural Theory, Colonial Texts: Reading Eyewitness Accounts of Widow Burning." In Lawrence Grossberg, Cary Nelson, and Paula Treichler, eds., *Cultural Studies.* New York: Routledge, pp. 392–405.

March, Kathryn S. 1983. "Weaving, Writing and Gender." *Man* (n.s.) 18.4: 729–44.

Matthews, David J. 1986. "Foreword." In Padma Prakash Shrestha, ed., *Nepal Rediscovered: The Rana Court 1846–1951 (Photographs from the Archives of the Nepal Kingdom Foundation).* London: Serindia Publications, pp. xi–xiv.

Mehta, Rama. 1970. *The Western Educated Hindu Woman.* New York: Asia Publishing House.

Miller, Sarah E. 1992. "Structures of a Lived-In Discourse." *Himalayan Research Bulletin* 12(1–2):45–50.

Milloy, Courtland. 1994. "Brother Jake." *The Washington Post Magazine* (Washington, D.C.) (January 9):12–15, 29.

Moore, Molly. 1993. "Altering India's Sari State: Designers Try to Make Traditional Garb Old Hat." *The Washington Post* (Style Section) (August 18):B1, B4.

Murthy, K. Krishna. 1982. *Hair Styles in Ancient Indian Art.* Delhi: Sundeep Prakashan.

Nag, Dulali. 1989. "The Social Construction of Handwoven Tangail Sari in the Market of Calcutta." Ph.D. Diss., Michigan State University.

———. 1991. "Fashion, Gender and the Bengali Middle Class." *Public Culture* 3.2:93–115.

Napolitan, M. Louis. 1939. *Six Thousand Years of Hair Styling.* Polygraphic Company of America.

Narayan, Kirin. 1986. "Birds on a Branch: Girlfriends and Wedding Songs in Kangra." *Ethos* 14:47–75.

———. 1993. "Refractions of the Field at Home: American Representations of Hindu Holy Men in the Nineteenth and Twentieth Centuries." *Cultural Anthropology* 8.4:476–509.

Nepali, Gopal Singh. 1988 [1965]. *The Newār: An Ethnosociological Study of a Himalayan Community.* Kathmandu: Himalayan Booksellers.

Obeyesekere, Gananath. 1981. *Medusa's Hair: An Essay on Personal Symbols and Religious Experience.* Chicago: University of Chicago Press.

O'Hanlon, Michael. 1989. *Reading the Skin: Adornment, Display and Society among the Wahgi.* London: British Museum Publications.

Palchoudhuri, Ila. 1974. *Ancient Hairstyles of India.* Calcutta: Rupa and Company.

Postel, M. 1989. *Ear Ornaments of Ancient India.* Project for Indian Cultural Studies, Publication II. Bombay: Franco-American Pharmaceuticals.

Raheja, Gloria Goodwin, and Ann Grodzins Gold. 1994. *Listen to the Heron's Words: Reimagining Gender and Kinship in North India.* Berkeley: University of California Press.

Reynolds, Holly Baker. 1980. "The Auspicious Married Woman." In Susan S. Wadley, ed., *The Powers of Tamil Women.* Foreign and Comparative Studies/South Asian Series, No. 6. Syracuse, N.Y.: Maxwell School of Citizenship and Public Affairs, Syracuse University, pp. 35–57.

Riefstahl, Elizabeth. 1956. "Two Hairdressers of the Eleventh Dynasty." *Journal of Near Eastern Studies* 15.1:10–17.

Rivière, Peter G. 1969. "Myth and Material Culture: Some Symbolic Interrelationships." In R. F. Spencer, ed., *Forms of Symbolic Action.* Seattle: American Ethnological Society, pp. 151–66.

Roach, Mary Ellen, and Joanne Bubolz Eicher. 1979. *The Fabrics of Culture: The Anthropology of Clothing and Adornment.* Justine M. Cordwell and Ronald A. Schwarz, eds. The Hague: Mouton, pp. 7–21.

Roshen, Alkazi. 1983. *Ancient Indian Costume.* New Delhi: Art Heritage.

Schmidt, Ruth Laila, Ballabh Mani Dahal, Krishna Bhai Pradhan, and Gautam Vajracharya, eds. 1993. *A Practical Dictionary of Modern Nepali.* New Delhi: Ratna Sagar.

Schneider, Jane, and Annette B. Weiner. 1989. "Introduction." In Annette B. Weiner and Jane Schneider, eds., *Cloth and Human Experience.* Washington, D.C.: Smithsonian Institution Press, pp. 1–29.

Sever, Adrian. 1993. *Nepal Under the Ranas.* New Delhi: Oxford and Ibh Publishing.

Sharma, Namarata. 1993. "Spiral, Loose, Tight Perms, and *Ashikis.*" *The Independent* (Kathmandu) (March 24):2.

Shrestha, Padma Prakash, ed. 1986. *Nepal Rediscovered: The Rana Court 1846–1951 (Photographs from the Archives of the Nepal Kingdom Foundation).* London: Serindia Publications.

Shulman, David. 1994. "On Being Human in the Sanskrit Epic: The Riddle of Nala." *Journal of Indian Philosophy* 22:1–29.

Skinner, Debra, Dorothy Holland, and G. B. Adhikari. 1994. "The Songs of Tij: A Genre of Critical Commentary for Women in Nepal." *Asian Folklore Studies* 53.2:257–303.

Slusser, Mary Shepherd. 1982. *Nepal Mandala: A Cultural Study of the Kathmandu Valley,* 2 vols. Princeton, N.J.: Princeton University Press.

Synott, A. 1993. *The Body Social.* London: Routledge.

Thompson, Julia J. 1993. "Speaking of Dissent, Speaking of Consent: Ritual and Resistance Among High-Caste Hindu Women in Kathmandu." *Contributions to Nepalese Studies* 20.1:1–27.

Uberoi, J. B. Singh. 1967. "On Being Unshorn." *Transactions of the Indian Institute of Advanced Study* (Simla) 4:87–100.

Vergati, Anne. 1982. "Social Consequences of Marrying Vishṇu Nārāyaṇa: Primary Marriage among the Newars of Kathmandu." *Contributions to Indian Sociology (n.s.)* 4.2:271–87.

Wadley, Susan S., ed. 1980. *The Powers of Tamil Women*. Foreign and Comparative Studies/South Asian Series, No. 6. Syracuse, N.Y.: Maxwell School of Citizenship and Public Affairs, Syracuse University.

Wadley, Susan S. 1994. *Struggling with Destiny in Karimpur, 1925–1984*. Berkeley: University of California Press.

Wagner, Roy. 1981. *The Invention of Culture*. Chicago: Chicago University Press.

Wells, Linda. 1995. "The Ones With Hairdos." *Allure* (September):60.

Whelpton, John. 1986. "Rana Nepal: A Political History." In Padma Prakash Shrestha ed., *Nepal Rediscovered: The Rana Court 1846–1951 (Photographs from the Archives of the Nepal Kingdom Foundation)*. London: Serindia Publications, pp. 1–17.

_____. 1987. "The Ancestors of Jang Bahadur Rana: History, Propaganda and Legend," *Contributions to Nepalese Studies* 14.3:161–90.

Wilson, Elizabeth. 1985. *Adorned in Dreams*. Berkeley: University of California Press.

Wolf, Naomi. 1991a. *The Beauty Myth: How Images of Beauty are Used Against Women*. New York: Anchor Books.

_____. 1991b. "Faith Healers, Holy Oil: Inside the Cosmetics Industry." *Ms.* May/June:64–67.

Wright, Christian. 1994. "Worldly Goods." *Allure* (July):30.

Wright, Daniel. 1990 [1877]. *History of Nepal with an Introductory Sketch of the Country and People of Nepal.* Translated from the Parbatiyā by Munshī Shew Shunker Singh and Pandit Shrī Gunānand. New Delhi: Asian Educational Services.

Yang, Hannah. 1993. "An Eye-Opening Account." *Mirabella* 55 (December): 34–35.

11 the disappearance of the oiled braid: indian adolescent female hairstyles in north america

barbara d. miller

"The quality of life depends on the quality of your hair" is the straightforward equation broadcast in a radio advertisement for a women's hair salon in Pittsburgh, Pennsylvania, in 1992. A strong case can be made that women's hair in the United States is highly commercialized and commoditized, along with many other aspects of female beauty.[1] Among nonelite, so-called traditional populations of India, the formula would be the opposite—"the quality of your hair depends on the quality of your life"—since long, black, and thick hair is primarily thought of as resulting from good health.

Cultural constructions of female beauty and guidelines about how to achieve or enhance it, however, are not new or confined to the Western capitalist world. They are ancient and pervasive, if not universal to all cultures. The contents of a particular cultural beauty complex, including people's preferences and perceptions, how styles are disseminated and how they change, are highly variable. Well-known variations in ideal female beauty include preferences concerning body size and weight, particular shades of skin color, hair length and style, and practices that alter the body via piercing, tattooing, and surgery.

Within the dazzling array of contemporary variation, dominating trends are discernible especially in the transnational world of upper-class populations in large urban centers from Buenos Aires to Tokyo (see Thompson, this volume). Key questions concern how certain styles become dominant, why some people opt for particular styles and others do not, what cultural strains might be involved in such choices, and if and why oppositional styles emerge. A look at how young members of diaspora South Asian culture change their perceptions and practices related to female beauty provides some idea of the choices being made, the conflicts that may ensue, and the re-creation and manipulation of forms in the culture of origin and the culture of immigration. In this study of Hindu youth culture in the eastern United States, we see most clearly the demise of the oiled female braid as a norm and the widespread adoption of "loose and fluffy" Euro-American female hair styles.

I first review three theoretical approaches that could be used to pursue further analysis related to "Westernization" of Indian female looks: political economy, feminist theory, and theories related to racism. I then compare certain aspects of female beauty in India and the United States. Next I present sketches of Hindu youth hair culture in urban areas of the eastern United States. The conclusion reconsiders the disappearance of the oiled braid.

Theoretical Perspectives on Female Beauty

The political economy approach prompts us to examine critically the question of who benefits from current definitions of female beauty and ways to attain it. Looking at the United States, one cannot avoid seeing the immense profiteering involved from direct "providers" such as diet centers, exercise and health spas, hair-styling salons, tanning salons, and the whole host of medical and quasi-medical practitioners including surgeons who do facial tucks, tummy tucks, breast implants, liposuction, and eyelid tattooing. Innumerable beauty-related products line department stores and drug stores: cosmetics, perfumes, false eyelashes and fingernails, skin creams and lotions. The clothing and jewelry industries thrive on a market driven by need created by the style industry to look good in a different way each season every year. Psychiatrists, psychologists, and medical doctors are increasingly called on to treat body-related disorders such as bulimia and anorexia.

Western capitalist beauty culture has compartmentalized women into breasts, teeth, hair, eyes, and legs, which the beauty seeker must deal with separately (Freedman 1988:27). Compartmentalization further contributes to the growth and profitability of various aspects of the beauty industry. Orthodontics constitutes a major area of expenditures for parents of teenagers in the United States. Both getting braces and then getting rid of them have become parts of a pervasive rite of passage for those whose parents can afford to pay the price. Surgery to reshape the nose to create a more "little girl" look is not an uncommon rite of passage for teenage girls. Increasingly eyelid surgery is being undertaken by girls and women of East Asian descent (Kaw 1993). Good looks and a positive self-image can be purchased, but only part by part. The costs—in both time and money—for achieving the right look have increased substantially in recent decades.

Significant class differences exist in the coding of dress and grooming (Bourdieu 1984), including hair style. Marjorie Lord's analysis of the class standing of the popular doll, Barbie, reveals that Barbie's "mountains" of hair, flashy polyester clothes, and vapid face combine to place her in the middle class (Lord 1994:183–85). An analysis of class differences in female looks in the United States echoes this association of big fluffy hair with the middle/working class: the professional woman's look of flat heels, simple clothes, little or no makeup, and "classic bob" contrasts with the "working girl" presentation of "high heels, too-short skirt . . . exaggerated make-up, and Big Hair" (Kron, quoted in Lord 1994:185). Women's styles in the professional upper class appear to downplay sexuality, while middle-class styles that include Big Hair tend to amplify it.

In sum, political economy theories argue that the beauty culture significantly benefits industries and health professions of many sorts. It victimizes women in the name of the beauty cult by placing them at risk of body-related afflictions. It perpetuates and accentuates class differences, promoting competitive, status-marking consumption patterns.

Feminist theories can be summarized as arguing that the contemporary United States beauty cult exploits women to men's benefit. A study in the United States reveals that respondents thought that "preoccupation with appearance" was normal for healthy women but it was thought not normal for healthy *people* (Freedman 1988:26). Important points in the feminist argument are that ideals of female beauty are means of social control of females by males—whether or not men are conscious of this, as a "conspiracy theory" model would suggest. Naomi Wolf, in *The Beauty Myth*, equates the beauty cult with racism (1991:3). She argues that the beauty myth keeps women "down," contributes to their "political paralysis," keeps them psychologically weak, and therefore maintains male dominance. Linking this view to the comment above about class differences between professional upper-class women and middle-class women suggests the hypothesis that middle-class women tend to be more male dominated in their lives than professional, upper-class women, and their dependence is expressed in a more sexualized, male-oriented style (this question merits future research).

In America, the widespread female preoccupation with appearance demands so much time and energy that it functions materially to keep women from devoting their time and energy to what feminists consider more autonomous pursuits. A longitudinal anthropological study of women attending two American southern colleges demonstrates how the romance myth derails women students from career paths, while allowing males to proceed apace (Holland and Eisenhart 1990). A difference emerged, however, between students at the predominantly white college and students at the predominantly black college. The white students were characteristically more entrapped in the romance culture of male dependency and far more likely to be derailed from the career paths than the black women. This research reveals an important difference within the broad category of the "middle class" based on the fact that African American women have a stronger sense of economic independence and autonomy from men than Euro-American women. They therefore are less likely to becomes victims of the beauty myth.

Race and ethnic differentiation certainly play a major role in American beauty culture. Cultural critic bell hooks goes to the heart of the matter, linking political economy, feminism, and racism. She states that "within commodity culture, ethnicity becomes spice, seasoning that can liven up the dull dish that is mainstream white culture" (1992:21). According to hooks, the old maxim that blondes have more fun has evolved into a maxim that white men can have more fun with "ethnic" women because of their latent desires about "the primitive" and the assumed correlations between ethnicity and animalistic sexuality. She cites the Tina Turner look that is dominated by a lionlike mane of hair.

Ethnic "differences" in looks are fabricated in the interests of both social control and commodity innovation (Hal Foster, cited in hooks 1992:25). They often blend features of "white" and "black looks": a beautiful black and anorectic female with a mountain of hair (artificially straightened or a wig), exemplified in a famous photograph of singer Diana Ross lying nude, wrapped only in a white sheet but draped with streams of very long hair. Biracial women, says hooks, have "crossover" appeal. This concept provides direct insight into how Indian females in the United States are viewed by white males—as crossovers, not quite black, but exotic nonetheless. Indian females' looks combine many of the desired "natural" physical features such as generally long and thick hair, brownish but not black skin, relatively delicate bone frames (a "natural" anorectic look), and a tendency to having smaller body size and being shorter than many American females.

Female Beauty and Hair in India

Contemporary perceptions of female beauty in India, as in the United States, are not monolithic. Variations reflect the fact that Indian society is socially and regionally diversified. International elites add another dimension. But in spite of local and historic variations, certain generalities can be perceived. Hair should be black, not lightened by malnutrition or albinism, or whitened by age. Females' hair should be long, preferably never cut, and thick. In rural areas and among nonelite urban women, head hair is oiled with coconut oil, creating a smooth shiny appearance and enhancing control of flyaway ends. Adult women maintain their hair bound in either a single braid or a bun at the back of the head (see Olivelle, this volume). Traditional meanings of women's hair still hold throughout much of India: unbound and unkempt hair on a woman may indicate either that she is in mourning, in an "impure" state due to menstruation, or sexually "loose."

Color is an important marker of health and sexuality, and dark color has positive implications (see Ebersole, this volume). When I first went to India during 1969 and 1970, I lived in the conservative North Indian city of Banaras. Although I was in my early twenties, a significant amount of gray had appeared in my dark brown hair. People often asked me: "How old *are* you?" "What happened to you?" "Were you ill as a child?" "How much will your father have to give for your marriage?" I learned that the emerging gray in my hair was an obvious "defect" that would—if I were an Indian female—put me at serious risk in the Indian marriage market. I tried to explain something about how "premature graying" ran in my family and that it would not affect a woman's potential marital arrangements in the United States.

The length of my hair (it was chin length at that time) was also a cause for questioning: had I had some illness as a child? An Indian girl's hair, ideally, is never cut. Affliction with head lice is one reason for cutting off a girls hair. If a child gets very ill and then recovers, his or her head hair may be cut off and offered to a temple deity in gratitude; in North India this is more often done for boys than girls, while in the South it is common for girls and women. I explained that the short length of my hair was due to neither of these but was simply a matter of style and convenience.

The predominant hair style of young girls in nonelite Indian populations is still long hair worn loose or in double braids. Braiding or binding up the hair into a knot does not usually begin until puberty and/or marriage, although regional and social variations exist. In contrast, college and university students and urban women choose from hair styles ranging from the traditional centered single braid to cropped, curled, and even permed hair of any length. Oiling is less apparent in the elites.

In India, short hair on girls and women is associated with a more "Western" than "traditional Indian" look. Bharati Mukherjee's novel, *The Tiger's Daughter*, contains several revealing references about "looks" and hair (1990). Tara, the leading character, was born in Calcutta, attends Vassar College, and marries a Euro-American male named David. After graduating from college, she returns to Calcutta. On her arrival, people are struck by how thin she is and how much more glamorous she is with "her short hair and all" (1990:42). Family members and friends study and discuss her, especially "her hair, the shades of her lipstick, her sunglasses." (42). Mukherjee writes that, in sum, "hair and deportment" are "an Indian woman's inner index."

Short hair on girls and women as a statement of "modernity" along Western lines is clearly marked in Anjana Appachana's short story "Her Mother" (1990).[2] In this story a young girl cuts off her long, thick hair right before migrating to the United States. The effects on her parents are stunning: "The abruptness and sacrilege of this act still haunted the mother, while the girl's father feels like a limb has been amputated" (182). The parents interpret the hair cutting as an act of liberation from Indian tradition and from the family. Notably, the daughter's act is viewed as cultural "sacrilege" by the mother but as self-"amputation" by the father. The mother's view is the more "moral" one while the father's is personally—if not psychoanalytically—painful.

Short hair on Indian females can also indicate defiance. In *The Tiger's Daughter*, a minor character named Arupa had been chronically nervous from childhood and was abandoned by her husband early in her marriage:

> In time the young woman lost her beauty and her strength. In time she became a legend in Pachapara, an eerie shape beneath the red cotton quilt of her bridal four-poster, her

> hair cropped close as a gesture of defiance, her limbs bare of all ornaments, her eyes cold and accusing (Mukherjie 1990:8).

Not all hair, of course, is on the head. In India, having abundant and cared-for hair on the head is a positive social and psychological statement, but certain hair elsewhere on the body is unwanted. In North India, pubic hair is especially unwanted, while underarm hair and leg hair are not a traditional focus of concern. Owen Lynch reports that among the Chaubes of western Uttar Pradesh, female pubic hair is thought of as *ganda* (dirty) and is considered by males to be an impediment during intercourse (personal communication, 1987). Erin Moore confirms, on the basis of fieldwork in rural Rajasthan, that village women use a special soap about once a month that completely removes their pubic hair (personal communication 1987). She also conveys an anecdote about a female American friend of hers who went to a hospital in Delhi for an appendectomy. The nurse who prepped her before the surgery was appalled at the woman's full pubic hair: "she looked at my friend as if she were a barbarian." Before a marriage in North India and Pakistan, a preparatory ritual for the new bride is removal of her pubic hair (cf. Olivelle's comments on the treatment of male head hair).[3]

Thus a formula for a "normal" North Indian woman in everyday life is:

> *auspicious and sexual = WIFE = head hair[+] hair care[+] pubic hair[-]*

A married woman who is in mourning, in contrast, would be characterized differently, assuming that she lets her head hair go uncared for as well as not indulging in pubic hair care (the latter is sheer supposition at this point):

> *inauspicious and asexual = WIDOW = head hair[+] hair care[-] pubic hair[+]*

This formula contrasts with that for a widow whose head hair is completely shaved off and—since she no longer has a husband for whom body grooming would be done—whose pubic hair would be left to grow

> *inauspicious and asexual = WOMAN IN MOURNING = head hair[-] pubic hair[+]*

Female beauty, including long and luxuriant black head hair, is marital currency in India since the bride's beauty, like her level of education, translates into her dowry; the marriage of a beautiful daughter will cost her family less than if she is unattractive. Amounts of dowry have been escalating dramatically in India since the 1960s. A question arises as to whether standards of female beauty may be becoming more competitive, too.

An important area of change in elite populations of India is in the meaning of body weight. Traditionally, slenderness in a girl was valued because it signified that the girl is controlled in her eating, that she will not eat too much in her in-laws' house. Girls learn to fast from a young age, and to live with hunger. This is done not primarily to gain beauty but to exhibit self-control, to maintain a nonthreatening demeanor in relation to the wellbeing and continuation of the husband's family. Thinness relates to the pervasive Indian ethic of female self-control and self-sacrifice, the socialization of daughters for "secondary status" (Papanek 1990). But indications now are that female thinness is taking on the Western dimension of a beauty feature rather than a moral characteristic. Considering but one reference group, women cabin attendants on Indian flights are thinner than they were twenty years ago. An obsession with thinness in India is beginning to result in cases of anorexia nervosa that resemble those in the West (Adityanjee, Raju, and Khandelwal 1989).

Another "looks" factor for Indian girls is height, though it is not one that appears to be pursued excessively. Many middle- and upper-class urban parents want their children, especially sons, to be tall. The commercial economy is tapping into and feeding that desire. During a visit to India in 1992, I saw an ad for a health spa in a Delhi newspaper claiming that one of its fitness results is increased height. At a conference on adolescence in Pune, many of the experts in child growth and development (medical researchers and biologists) who presented papers emphasized height as a positive value. True, height is a good indicator of health status: other factors being equal, well-nourished children tend to gain more height than malnourished children. But there appeared to be more than just a "normal growth" interest. Rather, it is possible that this positive evaluation of tallness may be based on a reference-group standard determined by Euro-Americans who tend to be taller than Indians, on average.

Female Beauty in American Popular Culture

Studies conducted in the United States reveal some of the ways that perceived looks affect the way a person is treated (Freedman 1986:28; Driskell 1983). "Cute" babies are held and cuddled more than other babies (Hildebrandt and Fitzgerald 1978). "Good-looking" children get more attention from their teachers (Adams and Cohen 1974). "Pretty" women date more and tend to marry earlier (Krebs and Adinolfi 1975). "Attractive" women are more readily hired for jobs deemed appropriate for females, so-called pink-collar jobs (Heilman and Stopeck 1985). A downside to all of this for the favored attractive ones is that they may be more likely to be derailed from intellectual and professional advancement by the romance game and the "sexual auction block" at college (Holland and Eisenhart 1990). In addition, physically attractive females may know that their success is due to their looks and not to some inner quality or achievement. And, in this cultural construction, attractiveness inevitably fades with age. The negative valence of aging in Western beauty culture also supports tremendously lucrative industries and enterprises including cosmetics such as antiwrinkle creams and "remedial" surgery to "lift" the face, breasts, and buttocks.

The contemporary beauty canon for females in the United States is largely a Caucasian model of "thin nose, lips, and limbs" (hooks 1992:72) with some space for non-Caucasian features such as fuller lips, fuller breasts, and a more prominent rear end. A glance at any fashion magazine or catalogue for the "general" audience (dominantly white) reveals that the majority of the female models are white, but that a notable number of near-white or lightly "ethnic" female models are now displayed. These "ethnic" models appear to be either biracial (usually white mixed with nonwhite) or from some population (such as Malaysian) among whom skin tones tend to be brownish but not black and hair curly and lush but not "kinky." Their hair is usually straightened, wild and loose, or done up in rasta-inspired braids with wispy flyaways.[4]

Weight is the most frequently mentioned concern of Euro-American girls and women when they are asked about their looks (Freedman 1988:84). Over the years, *Playboy* centerfold models, like female Indian airline attendants, have become progressively taller and thinner. Desired thinness has reached a level that is nearly impossible for most people to achieve. In America, one woman in two is dieting most of her life (Freedman 1988:3). This aspect of Euro-America's beauty culture is related to the significant increase since 1970 in the rate of anorexia nervosa and bulimia predominantly among Euro-American females (Brumberg 1989; Fabrega and Miller 1995; Gremillion 1992), while the diet and exercise industries are multi-million dollar successes. Recent studies document that females of South Asian immigrant populations in the United States and elsewhere are also becoming afflicted with these disorders that are extremely difficult to cure and even fatal (Bhadrinath 1990; Khandelwal and Saxena 1990).

Being taller does not seem to be a major concern of Euro-American females. This fact may relate to the widespread preference for "height hypergamous" pairings in which the preferred pattern is that the male is taller than the female. A student-conducted survey of a small number of undergraduates at Cornell University in the late 1980s revealed that no woman was interested in dating a male shorter than herself. I asked the females in my class of three hundred undergraduates at the University of Pittsburgh if they would be willing to date a male shorter than they, and a scattering of hands was raised; when I asked the males if they would want to date a woman taller than they, no one raised his hand.

What about hair? A rule on many college campuses in the early 1990s concerning desirable female hair was that there should be a lot of it—the Barbie doll image of "big hair" (Lord 1994). A term for looking good—"looking high"— meant, in part, having big fluffy hair. Length of hair always conveys important messages, dependant on cultural context. In popular American culture, long hair on females is associated with heterosexuality, youth, and sexiness. Beautiful hair, like beauty in general, can be sexually alluring. A college survey cited by Freedman (1988:xx) found that "good-looking" students have more liberal attitudes about sex and start having intercourse earlier than their less attractive classmates. But, she notes, this could be a self-fulfilling prophecy: "If pretty women are expected to be more sexually responsive, they may get more offers and thus engage in more sex" (1988:139).

On the other hand, uncared-for long hair can be a sign of not caring about either "looks" or men, as documented in a brief personal statement by feminist linguist Robin Lakoff (1984:8-12). When she was ten years old, she faced the realization that she was not a beautiful princess and "claimed homeliness as my own choice. . . . I let my hair grow long, but stopped brushing it or combing it, so that it finally matted into a tangle that no comb could penetrate" (p. 9). At her college, appearance was downplayed, but she "did less" with her hair than her classmates. Her subsequent marriage of eleven years was not happy: "I cut my hair for my wedding; then not again for eleven years (I cut it again about a month before my husband announced he was leaving me)" (12). For Robin Lakoff, cutting and caring for her hair is "playing the game." Letting it go uncut and uncared for instrumentally and symbolically removes her from playing the game. Long but neglected hair is not sexually alluring in "mainstream" terms because it signals rejection of the love/romance/attractiveness game.[5]

Long and cared-for hair is quite the opposite. It conveys a message that the girl or woman seeks and appreciates heterosexual admiration and involvement. Cared-for long hair requires different amounts of time and money, depending on the aspired-for look. Very long hair that is regularly colored or permed probably requires the most upkeep. Such hair also makes the strongest statement of heterosexual interest and availability. Shaving underarm hair and leg hair is a widespread practice among heterosexual women in the United States, but is rejected by many feminists and lesbians. Susan Basow's questionnaire sent to over two hundred professional women in the United States revealed that about one-third of the self-identified "strong feminists" do not shave their legs and underarms, while about 40 percent of lesbian and bisexual women do not.[6] So, we might generate the following codes for Euro-American female identity and hair:

> *conforming heterosexual/sexy female BABE = head hair[+] hair care[+] leg and underarm hair[-]*
>
> *nonconforming nonheterosexual female LESBIAN = head hair[-] hair care[+] leg and underarm hair[+]*
>
> *nonconforming politically resistant female FEMINIST = head hair[=] hair care[-] body hair[+]*

These categories are crude, but they capture some of the key differences in head and body hair treatment. Too little is known about pubic hair treatment in the United States to say much on that subject, but my hunch is that a much smaller minority of Euro-American women pay it as much attention as they do to leg hair and underarm hair. In the United States, shaved or otherwise removed female pubic hair is seen in photographs in *Playboy* and similar magazines and is more generally associated with pornographic images of women.

Hindu Youth Culture in the United States

The children and young adults discussed in this chapter were born to parents who immigrated to the United States after the 1967 change in the immigration law, which opened immigration to professionals and other highly educated people.[7] This large influx of relatively well-off migrants was followed in subsequent migration flows from India characterized by lower education and income levels. Families of these first-generation youths live mainly in large urban centers in New York, New Jersey, Texas, California (Bhardwaj and Rao 1990; Helweg and Helweg 1990). But many are more isolated, for example, a family headed by a physician who may have taken a position in a small town in West Virginia (the state with the highest proportion of "foreign" physicians), or those families who own motels in small towns or rural areas as depicted in the film "Mississippi Masala." Location, and by implication, density and wealth of the Indian immigrant community affect the degree of exposure of Hindu adolescents to "traditional" Indian/Hindu culture as a source of identity in competition with Euro-American stylistic trends.

Class position affects identity formation and choices about appearance. Most of the adolescents being discussed here are from well-off families. In many families, both parents work and both are professionals drawing good salaries, and their adolescent children attended expensive private high schools and universities. This picture does not characterize all the youths in the study. There are individuals in families struggling to make ends meet. In one case a family business failed and the parents returned to India leaving a college-aged child behind to attend school on his own. In areas outside this study, especially New Jersey where the density of working-class Indians is high, income levels are low and declining in the early 1990s.

In larger cities with more Indian immigrant families, one finds, increasingly, Hindu temples and "ethnic" associations such as special groups of Gujaratis, Bengalis, or Punjabis. Two periodicals are especially widely read: *India Abroad*, which along with news offers information on activities and events related to ethnically specialized organizations, and *Hinduism Today* which contains articles on such matters as proper dress in Hindu temples, the value of vegetarianism, and "marriage is forever."

Pittsburgh is a major center of Hindu cultural strength where youths are actively involved in learning about their religious and cultural heritage. The first major Hindu temple in the United States, the Sri Venkateswara Temple in Penn Hills (a suburb of Pittsburgh), is an internationally known pilgrimage site for Hindus. In another suburb of Pittsburgh is a smaller temple formed after a split from the Sri Venkateswara temple: the Hindu-Jain Temple that houses both Jain and Hindu deities and celebrates rituals in each tradition.

In many large American cities, Sunday schools for children are held in temples or in neighborhood centers. Nationwide, annual summer camps are increasingly popular, where children are further enculturated into "Hindu values" along with being able to participate in secular activities like hiking and swimming. The temples sponsor cultural events such as concerts and dance performances. They may provide extracurricular classes in Sanskrit and other Indian languages, music lessons (vocal, instrumental), dance, and yoga.

My fieldwork was conducted in several locations in the eastern United States, mainly with children and adolescents of Hindu heritage, but with a few Muslims and Sikhs as well. I conducted participant observation at several Hindu temples (including regular and irregular ritual occasions and monthly youth meetings), at summer camps for children and teenagers, at special youth events like temple overnights, and at special events organized by east coast college students including the first Conference of the National Hindu Students Council held in Pittsburgh, the annual South Asia Society Meeting of college students, and several student-organized events at colleges involving "cultural performances" such as *bhangra* dancing and fashion shows. I have also conducted informal interviews, in person and over the telephone, with several youths. I have had informal discussions with many adults.

The young people whom I have met and with whom I have talked range from being quiet, studious, exemplars of "Hindu values" as espoused by the more conservative parents (these are usually the younger kids) to outspoken campus radicals who reject the bourgeois values of their double-doctor parental configurations. I have heard carefully prepared enunciations on the value of premarital chastity and comments such as the one from a college student that "nobody really takes that [premarital chastity] seriously anymore." This is not, in other words, a population evidencing a high degree of consensus on some key issues. On the other hand, they all face some similar questions as children of immigrant Indians/Hindus, and these questions are deep and potentially troubling ones that concern problems of identity (which all children and adolescents face, but immigrant children more so) and problems of meaning in their lives. They concern the multiple and often conflicting scripts about their potential identity that are being handed to them by parents, grandparents, schools, temples, friends, the media, summer camp, college peers, and potential partners.

Some features of Hinduism receive special emphasis because of the immigrant context. Parental anxiety about dating and premarital sex no doubt drives the emphasis I have heard in some contexts placed upon gender segregation (this was at a summer camp—one adult counsellor did not want boys and girls to sit in mixed groups during discussion sessions). Debates and discussions at temples, and in homes, about dating are often heated. According to Indian psychoanalyst Sudhir Kakar, who has spent a substantial amount of time in the United States, dating, and the unspoken fear of premarital sexual relationships, pervades conversations between Indian parents living in America:

> In sexual terms, the West is perceived as a gigantic brothel, whereas the "good" Indian woman is idealized nostalgically in all her purity, modesty and chastity. For Indians living in the West, this idealization and the splitting that underlies it are more emotionally charged and more intense than would be the case in India itself. The inevitable Westernization of wives and daughters is, therefore, the cause of deep emotional stress in men, and of explosive conflicts in the family. (1986:39)

It must cause deep emotional stress in the wives and daughters, too.

Indian standards of female modesty are challenged in the context of the United States. While young women would not wear shorts to a temple in India, they do at some Hindu temples in the United States. The dress of female youths varies considerably, depending on the season and the event. At the Hindu-Jain Temple in Murrysville, most of the young girls wear completely Westernized clothing most of the time, donning Indian-style clothing at very special events like a sacred thread ceremony. Boys wear completely Western clothing, unless they themselves are taking part in a ceremony. Members of the youth group are notably unmarked by any Indian clothing or ornaments with one exception—a high-school-aged girl had a tiny gold nose stud. Adult women at the temples are always modestly dressed, with their legs completely covered either with a sari or a "punjabi" outfit (loose-fitting, long shirt-dress and matching ankle-length pants). Female attire, in this case and cross-culturally, is more often a signal of ethnic loyalty than males', although parents are also displeased when boys wear shorts to the temple. In contrast to the Hindu-Jain temple teen-age girls, young females at the predominantly South Indian temple near Pittsburgh (which many say is less "acculturated" than the North Indian temple) more often wear Indian clothing such as punjabis, and they wear bindis (forehead dots). During my fieldwork, I rarely saw adult women wear a bindi at the Hindu-

Jain temple, but, with great delight, one woman outfitted me with one when I appeared at a summer camp event wearing a sari (she carries a supply in her purse).

The 1992 South Asia Society student conference drew together several hundred college students, mainly from eastern universities, for three days at a university in Washington, D.C. Only a few students wore overtly South Asian clothing: one male Sikh wearing a turban, one Bangladeshi female with her hair covered by a scarf, and two older females in punjabis. There were no bindis, no nose pins, no saris, and very few of the young women wore their hair in a braid and the braid was always loose and not oiled.

Another "American" arena in which Indians participate in a seemingly acculturated way is the beauty pageant. An article in *India Today* (Malhotra 1993) describes this growing interest as a "fever." In 1993 there were twenty-two city or state competitions, three independent national pageants, one international pageant with twelve "feeder" pageants, and many minor "Miss Indias." The range extends from Miss Marwari and Miss India-Sind to Miss India-Texas and Miss India-Worldwide. Along with this growth is the development of a professional industry of pageant trainers who charge between $250 and $350 per day. The pageants serve several functions—they may help give the girl an entry into professional careers in modeling and film, they give various communities a chance to get together, and they serve as showcases for daughters as prospective brides. Anu Bagal Deshpande, 1987 Miss India-USA says, "It's a way for upmarket Indians to display their daughters to eligible bachelors" (Malhotra 1993:52h). The expenses involved in putting a daughter in a pageant are high, including professional training in posture, dance, and interviewing, entry fees, and dress for the sari, gown, and regional dress segments.

For Indian teenage girls, this high-level competition may have more negative consequences than for their non-Indian counterparts. Comments one psychologist, "In cultures where daughters are considered burdens, the pressure to be saleable is enormous. A pageant becomes an auction block . . . losers are instantly traumatized, and winners self-destruct twenty years later, when their 'glory' has faded" (Malhotra 1993:52h). Several competitors agree, commenting on their subsequent bouts of depression and hysteria. The time and energy devoted to beauty competitions is another factor in derailment of young women from other pursuits that might earn them greater self-esteem and autonomy.

Beauty and Hair Practices

Indian girls' beauty and hair practices change as they move from childhood to adolescence. My observations at two summer camps reveal that many of the youngest girls (aged eight–ten years) begin practicing beauty and hair routines every day. A telltale sign is the omnipresent "kaboodle," a plastic box with an upper and lower level and a mirror in the lid.[8] The kaboodle contains makeup, combs and brushes, hair clips and pins, and maybe even a blow dryer. Kaboodles are opened and fiddled with by some girls in this age group several times a day. Frequent interactions between the girls center around playing with and fixing one another's hair, perhaps very much like what one would see in a camp of Euro-American children.

"Family cultures of hair" appear in the frequent similarity of hair styles between mothers and young daughters. One of the more active women leaders in a summer camp had very short hair, and so did her daughter. One mother with a traditional (but unoiled) braid had a daughter with hair done just like hers. Once the daughter gets to high school age, though, the mother-daughter pattern begins to break down. Concerning hair length, occasional comments of girls revealed that their father's preferences play a role in keeping it long. I once complemented a little girl on her long hair, and asked her if she liked it better than short hair. She said yes, and that her father "hates" short hair.

In the high-school-age category, one sees hair that is more obviously managed. There is hair in the lion-mane/sexy category, hair with a side part instead of the traditional center part, hair that changes its style in the course of a day. One girl with very long and loose hair and drapey bangs that cover an eye had to hold her hair with one hand when she ate so that she could put food into her mouth. I have not often seen either single or double braids worn by high school girls. They frequently wear their hair pulled up into a high "clinch" or pony tail, or pulled back into a loose bun with a cloth crimp, or achieving a look at attractive but relaxed containment.

Chin-length hair is more common among high-school girls than among the younger set, even very short pixie-style cuts. In the latter, I know of one case in which a very outspoken and critical-thinking young woman combined that behavior with extremely striking facial beauty and short hair. In her case, the short hair may be one sign of possible "rebellion" against her father who is very strict.

Changing the color of a girl's hair is uncommon among high school-aged Indian students. Two high school girls in my fieldwork experience obviously lightened their hair, and they tended to sit together at meetings and other events. Permed hair also is not much in evidence in the high school category, although I have heard of parent-child conflicts because the daughter wants a perm and the parents say no.

At summer camp, high school girls would rarely appear at the first morning event (prayers) with wet hair, although some of the younger ones would. It is a matter of quiet amusement among the adults about how early the high school girls will get up in order to shower, shampoo their hair, style their hair, and apply makeup. One summer, a new rule was promulgated by the adult camp committee that in each of the girls' cabins no more than three blow dryers could be used at one time because there had been several electrical outages due to circuit overloads.[9]

In college, Indian female students (meaning American-born or permanently immigrated as opposed to "international" students who come to the United States only for a few years to study and then return home) tend to follow the high school trends. Very few dye their hair, though I have seen a few "punk" style hair cuts on Indian college women, and one with a swatch of burgundy dye on the top and side. Hair styles are varied with length ranging from medium (chin to shoulder) to very long, but they do not include braids, especially oiled braids.

Changing Hair Styles and Women's Status

The single oiled braid has been largely abandoned by all but the most traditional members of Indian culture in America. It is nonexistent among college age women and is not likely to be adopted by them after marriage. Indian women's braid styles in classical texts (see Hiltebeitel, this volume and 1981, 1988) operated as a clear code, indicating a woman's marital and moral state, even whether or not her husband was out of town. Traditional braid symbolism is as complex and rich as that of kimono sleeve styles as described by Dalby for Japan that convey similar messages about the wearer (1993). Like kimono sleeve styles, the meaning of a woman's hair style in India is largely referential in terms of patriarchal connections: Is she under the control of a father or husband? If her hair is properly uncut, groomed, and braided, the answer is likely to be yes. If not, it may mean several different things: she is "out of bounds" due to the ascription of pollution either through her own menstruation or a relative's death, she is rebellious, she is sexually loose or a prostitute, she is a religious renunciate, or her husband is away from home.

It would be tempting to say that Indian girls and women in America who have abandoned the meaningful braid are thus liberated from patriarchal control and from using their hair to convey public messages about their marital status, sexual identity, or menstrual cycle. Does the demise of the oiled braid and its symbolism mean that Indian women in America have more individual autonomy? hooks, Wolf, and other cultural theorists would argue that the medium may have changed but the message has not. Contemporary American hair styles are also codes for age, sexual orientation, and "interest" in being approached sexually. The Big Hair look says, "I like guys and I am willing to spend time and money to communicate that." One outstanding difference between traditional Indian and contemporary American styles is in menstrual messages. I cannot think of any way that an American hair style can encode whether or not a woman in America is menstruating. In contrast to India, what is amplified in America is the content of sexual messages among high school aged females. In "traditional" and rural India, unmarried girls wear their hair in nearly the same style, and they change their hair in similar ways after marriage. In America, a range of "sex messages" can be conveyed through hair styles among unmarried girls from "I am not interested" to "I am very interested," and these messages vary by class. Many Indian high school girls are economically members of the upper class, but they tend to opt for the more middle-class, Big Hair style. It is possible, and an important matter for further study, that the traditional female dependency cultivated in (especially North) India more firmly tracks Indian girls in America (perhaps especially North Indian girls) into the beauty cult than other girls who may be in the same socioeconomic class but are from less male-dominated ethnic backgrounds.

The culture of hair is no trivial matter. When Euro-American college students go to the south Indian city of Madurai to study for a semester, the first things they learn how to do is wear a sari and oil and braid their hair. These are key elements of proper female deportment, of conveying a moral message of propriety. Wearing loose and wild hair will surely put an American female student at greater risk of being harassed by men on the street than if she employs "signs" that say "I am not a loose Western woman." Head hair is one of the most powerful signs. Culturally constructed hair messages are ubiquitous. Whether or not you have hair, whether or not it is black or white, long or short, cared for or disheveled, it all means something. In traditional India, contemporary Euro-American culture, and Indian immigrant culture, female hair styles convey different messages about class, sexuality, and interpersonal politics. There is no way to avoid the message power of hair. Even if you cover it with a hat or scarf, it still talks.

Notes

My thanks to the many Indian people who have allowed me to learn about their culture in India and the United States over the past years. They all remain unnamed in order to protect their anonymity. Discussions with several scholars about hair practices have also contributed to this chapter: Gerald Berreman, the late Agehananda Bharati, Wendy Doniger, Alf Hiltebeitel, Owen Lynch, Robin Moore, Kenneth X. Robbins, H. Daniel Smith, and Melford Spiro.

1. A lesser industry is hard at work selling "male looks" as well, but is not of concern in this chapter.

2. Marie Norman, doctoral student in the Department of Anthropology at the University of Pittsburgh, brought this passage to my attention (1992).

3. Werbner's research among Pakistani immigrants in England reveals the same practice (1986).

4. On college students' images of beauty and related matters see Berscheid et al. 1971; Haug 1986; Patzer 1985; Lakoff and Scherr 1984; and Freedman 1986.

5. This pattern parallels that of some Hindu male ascetics who, as discussed by Leach (1958), signal nonsexuality by their matted and long hair. Obeyesekere offers a more complicated interpretation of some women ascetics' matted locks in Sri Lanka which also, however, links their hair to sexuality diverted from the everyday and unsatisfying secular world including marriage to a satisfying sexualized association with a deity.

6. It must be noted, however, that the majority of professional women in all categories of the analysis—including strong feminists and nonfeminists, lesbians, bisexuals, and heterosexuals—conform to the "hairless norm" in American culture within which shaving of underarm and leg hair is prescribed.

7. Some parts of the following description are taken from an earlier publication (Miller 1996).

8. See the informative discussion on mirrors in Freedman (1988:23-25, 33-37) and Hatfield and Sprecher (1986).

9. I know little about grooming among the boys. While there are variations in hair cut—from brush cuts to longer more drapey looks—the prevailing "look" for males tends to be more uniform than for females.

References

Adams, G. R., and A. S. Cohen. 1974. "Children's Physical and Interpersonal Characteristics that Affect Student-Teacher Interaction." *Journal of Experimental Education* 43:1–5.

Adityanjee, G. S., P. Raju, and S. K. Khandelwal. 1989. "Current Status of Multiple Personality Disorders in India." *American Journal of Psychiatry* 146:1607–1610.

Appachana, Anjana. 1990. "Her Mother." In *The Inner Courtyard*, ed. Lakshmi Holmstrom. London: Virago Press.

Basow, Susan A. 1991. "The Hairless Ideal: Women and Their Body Hair." *Psychology of Women Quarterly* 15:83–96.

Berscheid, E., K. K. Dion, E. Walster, and G. W. Walster. 1971. "Physical Attractiveness and Dating Choice: A Test of the Matching Hypothesis." *Journal of Experimental Social Psychology* 7:173–89.

Bhadrinath, B. R. 1990. "Anorexia Nervosa in Adolescents of Asian Extraction." *British Journal of Psychiatry* 156:565–68.

Bhardwaj, Surinder M., and N. Madhusudana Rao. 1990. "Asian Indians in the United States: A Geographic Appraisal." In Colin Clarke, Ceri Peach, and Steven Vertovec, eds., *South Asians Overseas: Migration and Ethnicity*. New York: Cambridge University Press, pp. 197–217.

Bourdieu, Pierre. 1984. *Distinction: A Social Critique of the Judgment of Taste*. Translated by Richard Nice. London: Routledge and Kegan Paul.

Brumberg, Joan Jacobs. 1989. *Fasting Girls: The History of Anorexia Nervosa*. New York: Plume/Penguin.

Dalby, Liza Crihfield. 1993. *Kimono: Fashioning Culture*. New Haven, Conn.: Yale University Press.

Driskell, J. E. 1983. "Beauty as Status." *American Journal of Sociology* 89(1):140–165.

Dworkin, S. H. 1989. "Not in Man's Image: Lesbians and the Cultural Oppression of Body Image." *Women and Therapy* 8(1/2):27–39.

Ewan, Stuart. 1990. *All Consuming Images: The Politics of Style in Contemporary Culture*. New York: Basic.

Fabrega, Horacio, Jr., and Barbara D. Miller. 1995. "Toward a More Comprehensive Medical Anthropology: The Case of Adolescent Psychopathology." *Medical Anthropology Quarterly* 9(4):431–461.

Freedman, Rita. 1986. *Beauty Bound*. Lexington, Mass.: Lexington Books.

———. 1988. *Bodylove: Learning to Like Our Looks and Ourselves*. New York: Harper & Row, Publishers.

Gibson, Margaret. 1988. *Accommodation without Assimilation: Sikh Immigrants in an American High School*. Ithaca, N.Y.: Cornell University Press.

Gremillion, Helen. 1992. "Psychiatry as Social Ordering: Anorexia Nervosa, a Paradigm." *Social Science and Medicine* 35(1):57–71.

Hatfield, E. and S. Sprecher. 1986. *Mirror, Mirror*. Albany, NY: State University of New York Press.

Haug, Wolfgang Fritz. 1986. *Critique of Commodity Aesthetics: Appearance, Sexuality and Advertising in Capitalist Society*. Trans. Robert Bock. Minneapolis: University of Minnesota Press.

Heilman, M., and M. Stopeck. 1985. "Attractiveness and Corporate Success: Different Causal Attributions for Males and Females." *Journal of Applied Psychology* 70(2):379–388.

Helweg, Arthur W., and Usha M. Helweg. 1990. *An Immigrant Success Story: East Indians in America*. Philadelphia: University of Pennsylvania Press.

Hildebrandt, K. A., and H. E. Fitzgerald. 1978. "Adults' Responses to Infants Varying in Perceived Cuteness." *Behavioral Processes* 3:159–172.

Hiltebeitel, Alf. 1981. "Draupadī's Hair." In *Autour de la déesse hindoue*. Madeleine Biardeau, ed., *Puruṣārtha* 5:179–214.

———. 1988. *The Cult of Draupadī: Mythologies from Gingee to Kuruksetra*. Chicago: University of Chicago Press.

Holland, Dorothy C., and Margaret A. Eisenhart. 1990. *Educated in Romance: Women, Achievement, and College Culture*. Chicago: University of Chicago Press.

hooks, bell. 1992. *Black Looks: Race and Representation*. Boston: South End.

Kakar, Sudhir. 1986. "Male and Female in India: Identity Formation and Its Effects on Cultural Adaptation." In *Tradition and Transformation: Asian Indians in America*. Richard H. Brown and George V. Coelho, eds. Williamsburg, Va.: College of William and Mary.

Kaw, Eugenia. 1993. "Medicalization of Racial Features: Asian American Women and Cosmetic Surgery." *Medical Anthropology Quarterly* 7(1):74–89.

Khandelwal, S. K., and S. Saxena. 1990. "Anorexia Nervosa in Adolescents of Asian Extraction." *British Journal of Psychiatry* 157:784.

Krebs, D., and A. Aldinolfi. 1975. "Physical Attractiveness, Social Relations, and Personality Style." *Journal of Personality and Social Psychology* 31:245–253.

Kroker, Arthur, and Marilouise Kroker. 1988. *Body Invaders*. Canada: New World Perspectives.

Kuhn, Annette. 1985. *Power of the Image: Essays on Representation and Sexuality*. New York: Routledge.

Lakoff, Robin Tomach, and Raquel L. Scherr. 1984. *Face Value: The Politics of Beauty*. Boston: Routledge and Kegan Paul.

Leach, Edmund R. 1958. "Magical Hair." *Journal of the Royal Anthropological Institute* 88(2):147–164.

Lord, Marjorie G. 1994. *Forever Barbie: The Unauthorized Autobiography of a Real Doll*. New York: William Morrow.

Malhotra, Angelina. 1993. "Hardselling Glamour." *India Today*, September 30.

Miller, Barbara D. 1996. "Precepts and Practice: Researching Identity Formation among Indian Hindu Adolescents in the United States." In *New Directions for Child Development*. Jacqueline Goodnow and Peggy Miller, eds. No. 67. San Francisco: Jossey-Bass.

Mukherjee, Bharati. 1990. *The Tiger's Daughter*. New York: Penguin Books.

Norman, Marie. 1992. "Between Two Worlds: The Literature of Indian Immigrant Women." Unpublished paper prepared for course on

Migration and Mental Health, Department of Anthropology, University of Pittsburgh.

Obeyesekere, Gananath. 1981. *Medusa's Hair: An Essay on Personal Symbols and Religious Experience*. Chicago: University of Chicago Press.

Papanek, Hanna. 1990. "To Each Less Than She Needs, From Each More Than She Can Do: Allocations, Entitlements, and Value." In Irene Tinker, ed., *Persistent Inequalities: Women and World Development*. New York: Oxford University Press, pp. 162–181.

Patzer, Gordon L. 1985. *The Physical Attractiveness Phenomena*. New York: Plenum Press.

Werbner, Pnina. 1986. "The Virgin and the Clown: Ritual Elaboration in Pakistani Migrants' Weddings." *Man* 21:227–50.

Wilson, Deirdre. 1978. "Sexual Codes and Conduct: A Study of Teenage Girls." In *Women, Sexuality, and Social Control*. C. Smart and B. Smart, eds., London: Routledge and Kegan Paul, pp. 65–73.

Wolf, Naomi. 1991. *The Beauty Myth: How Images of Beauty are Used Against Women*. New York: Anchor.

12 afterword: hair power

barbara d. miller

Power involves the ability of a person or group to control another person or group of people. Control may be implicit and subtle, explicit and brutal. What does hair have to do with power and control? This flimsy, fragile, delicate but very material stuff is related to power in complex and culturally varied ways as the chapters in this volume demonstrate. By taking a look at a range of hair contexts in Asian populations, these studies establish a field of inquiry that has long been neglected as serious. They provide a basis from which further theorizing and research about the links between power and particular parts of the body can be generated cross culturally.

In a ground-breaking conceptual article on the body, cultural anthropologists Nancy Scheper-Hughes and Margaret Lock define and consider the interrelations between the "three bodies:" the individual body, the social body, and the body politic (1987:7). The first is "understood in the phenomenonological sense of the lived experience of the body-self," while the second refers to "the representational uses of the body as a natural symbol" (deriving from work by Mary Douglas), and the third concerns "the regulation, surveillance, and control of bodies" (derived from Foucault). We may conceptualize hair, similarly, from these three angles: individually experienced hair, socially symbolic hair, and political hair. Alf Hiltebeitel's Introduction mainly addresses the first two categories; this Afterword considers the last.

State Power and Hair

Several examples in this book fit a Foucauldian model of state control of, or discipline of, individuals and groups through hair practices. One could find no clearer case than the Manchu government's 1644 decree on hair style and its extensive campaigns among the Han as analyzed in Weikun Cheng's chapter. The Qing government was serious about having its new subjects adhere to hair prescriptions that involved men's shaving of the forehead and braiding their hair into a queue. A Manchu slogan equated "keeping one's head" with changing one's hair to the Manchu style. Many who did not obey, in fact, were killed. In the early twentieth century, hair politics erupts again in the anti-Manchu resistance movement and growing nationalism: This time, queues were cut as a public statement of separation from Manchu control, and in 1912, Sun Yat-sen issued a formal decree requiring men to abandon the queue.

Sarah Nelson's excursion through several centuries of Korean history and hair practices reveals political and religious structuring of hair and dress practices from very early times. During the Silla kingdoms (from about the seventh century B.C. to the tenth century A.D.), elaborate codes of hair style and dress were used to define intrasocietal hierarchies. Clearly defined social ranks of people were either permitted or forbidden the use of particular hats, hair styles, hair ornaments, and clothing. These sumptuary laws were gender differentiated, reflecting the high degree of compartmentalization and regulation of male and female "looks." Commoner women were allowed to wear only brass hairpins, while queens did not wear hairpins at all but wore gold crowns.

Social and political order thus asserts its claims through "codes for and social scripts for the domestication of the individual body" (Scheper-Hughes and Lock 1987:26). James Watson's anthropological analysis of the silent, long-haired destitutes of Hong Kong reveals a contemporary case of marginalized individuals who do not follow the code. These young men, between the ages of twenty-five and thirty years, appeared on the streets of Hong Kong from China in the early 1960s. Watson describes his first sight of one of these men: "What set him apart from other marginals I had seen on Hong Kong streets was his grotesquely-long fingernails and his filthy, matted hair that hung halfway down his back." Hong Kong residents who see these men on the streets express fear or disdain, and they keep their distance. Senior officials told Watson they worry that the destitutes will harm the tourist industry. One time, the destitutes were rounded up and given baths and haircuts. On his last visit, the destitutes were nowhere to be seen.

Hair and Identity

Hair may be used to define group identity and to mark status differentials. Frank Dikötter's historical study exposes how hair was the primary biological marker of race used in China over many centuries and up to the present. The theory held that the superior race is marked by less body hair. Hairy people are uncivilized barbarians. The Chinese first applied this theory to Western missionaries among whom males often had beards. The negative valence of hairiness was later attributed to the Japanese invaders during the 1930s who were caricatured as stubbly and furry dwarfs intent on raping "virginal Chinese girls." Contemporary rumors about the existence of hairy "wild men" maintains the boundary between civilization and barbarism. Such enduring definitions support and maintain political and social solidarity in the face of continuing intrusions and perceived threats from "outside" forces.

Hair, Gender, and Sexuality

Gender identity, inequality, and male fear and censorship of female sexuality is at the center of Anne Allison's chapter. She asks why the censorship laws of the Japanese state draw the line at showing female pubic hair in popular cultural representations when they allow all sorts of clearly pornographic and violent scenes to be published. Her theory implicates patriarchal control: by censoring female pubic hair, the male-dominated media censors protect themselves and the wider society of males from the potential power of female sexuality.

Gary Ebersole's chapter takes us to the level of personal power and identity through its consideration of classic Japanese poetry. Here we find links between a woman's long black head hair and themes of sexuality and life, between the spirits in her hair and her personal power. The poetry contains implicit social messages, too, since the poetic conventions indicate that power vested in head hair defines and stratifies people according to gender, social position, and the sacred.

Alf Hiltebeitel's study of the worship of a hairy deity in South India involves multiple power relationships: between men and women, temporary male transsexuals and permanent transsexuals, kings and subjects, fathers and sons, mothers and sons, humans and animals, humans and demons, humans and barbarians, gods and humans, and dominant landed castes and Untouchables. His material indicates that the worship of the god Kūttāṇṭavar can be seen as a ritual statement of the nonpowerful and marginalized, with its few brahmans and the pervasive presence of hinjras.

Hair and Resistance

Understanding how powerful forces manipulate people through hair practices is only one side of the power relationship, because the very enforcing of political hair codes may foster resistance to such control. Hair itself may act as an aggressive statement. "Rebellious" hair practices function as statements of individual resistance to family, group, or state control. "Punk" hair styles of young men and women in the West are clear messages of antifamilism and identification with a larger, resistant cultural code.

Weikun Cheng's description of queue cutting is a case of hair resistance in history. A contemporary example from China involves the act of a single person who used his hair to express dissatisfaction with state policies. This incident erupted around the issue of artistic censorship in China. In August 1991, Chinese artist Song Shuangsong learned that an exhibition scheduled to open at the National Gallery in Beijing had been edited. According to a report, artists who "failed to show the positive side of life in the People's Republic . . . were unacceptable" and therefore the artists were allowed to show only a fraction of their work (Solomon 1993:44). Song Shuangsong went to the gallery with a professional barber and sat, having his long hair cut in protest, in the exhibition room. Soon officials entered the room and removed Song; subsequently the exhibition was permanently closed. His haircut stopped the show.

Hair Power in the Household

Scattered evidence of husbands controlling wives' hair and parents controlling children's hair appears in fiction, memoirs, and the news. In a recent Australian novel, Bob, the family patriarch, is presented as peculiarly oppressive (Glaister 1993). Two signs of his oppressiveness are that he does not allow a television in the house because of its ostensibly dangerous gamma rays, and he refuses to let his wife or his thirteen-year-old daughter cut their hair. In an article in *Parents* magazine, a father describes the time when his daughter, Beatrice, cut her long hair and how he had to "come to terms with the loss of his daughter's gorgeous curls" (Rodin 1995). What supports parental (especially father's) emotional connections with their children's (especially daughter's) hair? In many cultures, the physical appearance—especially their hair—of family members is an important sign to the wider social world of family status. This point appears in my chapter on Indian girls' hairstyles in the United States in regard to fathers' wishes that their daughters would not cut their hair. This paternal interest surely extends beyond Indian culture, but its boundaries and deeper meanings remain unexplored. In the immigrant context, ethnic anxieties about group identity may accentuate the psychological underweave.

Contemporary Change

Another important avenue of inquiry is contemporary change in power relations acted out through hair. Hair styles and fashion that premier in Paris have long been important status symbols in North America, and now they are increasingly pervasive in Asian cities. Julia Thompson's chapter on elite women's hair styles in Kathmandu, Nepal, documents the powerful cultural force of the West on women's changing hair styles and some tendencies for local "remaking" of Western styles within the Nepali context.

Thompson's material on Kathmandu hair styles does not contain examples of outright rejection or remaking of Western styles, or resistance to Western fashion norms as are recently apparent in Japanese high fashion (Kondo 1992). The question arises as to the relationship between a nation's economic and political autonomy and its reactions to Western fashions and hair style. And how do changes in hair style or clothing relate to other changes such as new definitions of sexuality, identity, and efficacy? Is the decision by a Nepali upper-caste woman to adopt a Parisian hair style testimony to her individuality and agency or does it mean she is simply a structural victim of Western stylistic hegemony?

There is much material in the changing cultures of Asian populations for a deeper examination of this question. My chapter on Indian youth culture and female hair in the eastern United States considers a normative Indian female hair style that is abandoned, and others that are adopted, suggesting implications about why styles change the way they do. I propose that the power of the multifaceted beauty industry to determine style (and to promote styles that are costly to achieve and maintain) has to be included in any explanation, along with the gender-specific codes that many young women strive to follow in their pursuit of romance. Accepting or resisting dominant hair codes not only characterizes heterosexual populations, but is also found in gay culture as humorously described in an article about hair styles among aging gay men (Cohen 1995). Many gay American men who lose their hair as they age tend to cut it shorter and start working on their bodies. Given this trend, the author points out that eventually all aged gay men will look like Mr. Clean. He proposes instead to be "glad to be gray."

Once one becomes aware of hair themes, they appear everywhere. And they are constantly changing in shape and meaning. As the world economy continues to expand, as centers of fashion and style grow and diversify, as Asian people migrate to non-Asian cultures and adopt and adapt local styles, Asian hair styles and meanings will change. Forces of globalization and localization will interplay, with varying outcomes. Personal hair symbols, as first outlined by Gananath Obeyesekere in *Medusa's Hair* need to be examined throughout Asia, as do the politics of hair styles and meanings. The theoretical impetus provided by the South Asian models has a rich field of inquiry ahead because hair will always remain a focal point of power, identity, and expression, as it long (perhaps always) has been.

References

Cohen, Jaffe. 1995. "Glad to Be Gray." *10 Percent* 3(13):44–45.

Glaister, Lesley. 1993. *Digging to Australia*. New York: Atheneum.

Kondo, Dorinne. 1992. "The Aesthetics and Politics of Japanese Identity in the Fashion Industry." In Joseph J. Tobin, ed., *Re-Made in Japan: Everyday Life and Consumer Taste in a Changing Society*. New Haven, Conn.: Yale University Press, pp. 176–203.

Rodin, Bob. 1995. "Bea's New 'Do." *Parents* 70(1):24–25.

Scheper-Hughes, Nancy, and Margaret M. Lock. 1987. "The Mindful Body: A Prolegomenon to Future Work in Medical Anthropology." *Medical Anthropology Quarterly* 1(1):1–36.

Solomon, Andrew. 1993. "Their Irony, Humor (And Art) Can Save China." *New York Times Magazine*, December 19, 1993, pp. 42ff.

contributors

Anne Allison is Associate Professor of Anthropology at Duke University. She has published *Nightwork: Sexuality, Pleasure, and Corporate Masculinity in a Tokyo Hostess Club* (University of Chicago Press, 1994) and *Permitted and Prohibited Desires: Mothers, Comics and Censorship in Japan* (Westview/HarperCollins, 1996). Her recent and current research is on Japanese superheroes in animated television cartoon shows and *manga* (comic books) as they are exported globally.

Weikun Cheng received his doctorate in history from the Johns Hopkins University, completing his dissertation in 1995, titled "Nationalists, Feminists, and Petty Urbanites." He has taught in the Department of History at the State University of New York at Oswego and now teaches at California State University, Chico.

Frank Dikötter teaches history at the School of Oriental and African Studies. His publications include books on *The Discourse of Race in Modern China* (Stanford University Press, 1992) and *Sex, Culture, and Modernity in China* (University of Hawaii Press, 1995), and an edited volume, *The Construction of Racial Identities in China and Japan* (University of Hawaii Press, 1997).

Gary L. Ebersole is Associate Professor of History and Religious Studies at the University of Missouri-Kansas City. His books include *Ritual Poetry and the Politics of Death in Early Japan* (Princeton University Press, 1989) and *Captured by Texts: Puritan to Post-Modern Images of Indian Captivity* (University of Virginia Press, 1995). He has a forthcoming article in *History of Religions* on "The Function of Ritual Weeping Revisited: Affective Expression and Moral Discourse" and is currently working on a book entitled *Telling Tears: A Comparative Study of Ritual Weeping*.

Alf Hiltebeitel is Professor of Religion and Director of the Human Sciences Program at the George Washington University. He has authored *The Ritual of Battle: Krishna and the Mahābhārata* ([1976] State University of New York Press, 1990), *The Cult of Draupadī*, Vol. 1: *Mythologies, From Gingee to Kurukṣetra* (University of Chicago Press, 1988) and *The Cult of Draupadī*, Vol. 2: *On Hindu Ritual and the Goddess* (University of Chicago Press, 1991), and, in press, *Rethinking India's Oral and Classical Epics: Draupadī among Rajputs, Afghans, and Dalits* (University of Chicago Press). He is finishing a book on "The Education of Yudhiṣṭhira" in the *Mahābhārata* and working on one about Aravāṉ-Kūttāṇṭavar.

Barbara D. Miller is Associate Professor of Anthropology and International Affairs and Director of the Women's Studies Program at the George Washington University. Her books include an edited volume, *Sex and Gender Hierarchies* (Cambridge University Press, 1993), and an updated version of her first book, *The Endangered Sex: Neglect of Female Children in Rural North India* (Oxford University Press, 1997). A textbook on *Cultural Anthropology* (Allyn & Bacon) will appear in 1998. She continues to study the social causes and policy issues related to unbalanced juvenile sex ratios in India and is now also researching the effects of economic development in the Andaman Islands.

Sarah M. Nelson is John Evans Professor of Archaeology in the Anthropology Department at the University of Denver. She is currently working on a joint archaeology project with Liaoning Provincial Archaeological Research Institute in northeastern China. She has published *The Archaeology of Korea* (Cambridge University Press, 1993), *Equity Issues for Women in Archeology* (American Anthropological Association, 1994), *The Archaeology of Northeast China* (Routledge 1995), and *Gender in Archaeology: Analyzing Power and Prestige* (AltaMira Press, 1996).

Gananath Obeyesekere is Professor of Anthropology at Princeton University. His books include *Medusa's Hair: An Essay on Personal Symbols and Religious Experience* (University of Chicago Press, 1982), *The Cult of the Goddess Pattini* (University of Chicago Press, 1984), *The Work of Culture: Symbolic Transformation in Psychoanalysis and Anthropology* (University of Chicago Press, 1990), *The Apotheosis of Captain Cook: European Mythmaking in the Pacific* (Princeton University Press, 1992), and he has co-authored with Richard F. Gombrich *Buddhism Transformed: Religious Change in Sri Lanka* (Princeton University Press, 1988). His latest book manuscript is on "Imagining Karma: Ethical

Transformations in Amerindian, Buddhist and Greek Rebirth." He is now working on a book about the discourses of cannibalism developed on board ships and islands in the wake of Cook's "discovery" of Polynesia.

Patrick Olivelle is Professor of Sanskrit and Indian Religions, Chair of the Department of Asian Studies, and Director of the Center for Asian Studies at the University of Texas at Austin. Among his recent publications are *The Saṃnyāsa Upaniṣads: Hindu Scriptures on Asceticism and Renunciation* (Oxford University Press, 1992), *The Āśrama System: History and Hermeneutics of a Religious Institution* (Oxford University Press, 1993), *Rules and Regulations of Brāhmanical Asceticism* (State University of New York Press, 1994), *The Upaniṣads* (Oxford University Press, 1996), and *Pañcatantra: The Book of India's Folk Wisdom* (Oxford University Press, 1997). His current research is on the human body in ancient Indian society and on a critical edition of the *Laws of Manu*.

Julia J. Thompson earned her doctorate in anthropology from the University of Wisconsin-Madison. She has written several academic articles and book reviews and is currently working on a book based on her dissertation, "Unmasking Culture: Women and Beauty Salons in Kathmandu, Nepal." She has taught at the University of Wisconsin-Madison and Williams College and now works as a free-lance writer and journalist in Colorado.

James L. Watson is Fairbank Professor of Chinese Society and Professor of Anthropology at Harvard University. His publications include *Emigration and the Chinese Lineage: The Mans in Hong Kong and London* (University of California Press, 1975), *Asian and African Systems of Slavery* (University of California Press, 1980), and *Death Ritual in Late Imperial and Modern China* (University of California Press, 1988). His most recent book is *Golden Arches East: McDonald's in East Asia* (Stanford University Press, 1997). In 1997 he conducted fieldwork on the decolonization process in Hong Kong and, together with Rubie S. Watson, he is writing a book about the transition to communist rule.

index

magatama (crescent-shaped bead)
worn in women' hair in Japan, 86–87, 89, 102n. 13
Mageo, Jeannette, 237
Manchu queue-cutting campaign, 128ff
marriage and female hair style, 108–109, 149, 265
matted hair, 23–24, 40, 152–153, 185–186, 280
Mauss, Marcel, 11
Medusa, 6
menstruation and hair style, 144, 226
modernization
and attitudes toward depictions of hair and the body in Japan, 197
and hair styles in China, xiv, 129–131
and hair styles in Korea, 118
and men's topknot in Korea, 111
see also globalization and westernization
moles, hair on, 145–147
mourning and hair style
dishevelment as sign of suffering in China, 182, 184, 187–188
of widows in India, 20, 144, 219–220, 247, 265
moustaches, of Westerners, as viewed by Chinese, 54–55
moustached goddess, South India, 149–156, 161

nationalism
and queue-cutting in China, 129
and Japanese censorship of hair and body images, 196–197, 205–208
"natural" symbolism of hair (vegetativeness), 29–30, 36–37, 77–78, 79, 99
neglected (wild) hair, 13, 15, 40
see also disheveled hair and matted hair
neo-Lamarckism in China, 55
Obeyesekere, Gananath, 3, 27, 31, 34–35, 144, 153, 185, 237, 250, 286
obscenity laws
about pubic hair depiction in Japan, 198–202
occupation and hair style, 105
Orientalism, xii
ornaments in the hair, female
beads, in Japan, 89
flowers and leaves, in Japan, 89–90
see also combs and hairpins

penis (phallus), 37, 151–152, 157, 167, 169–172, 207, 211, 215
personal symbols, 31, 144, 237, 239
phallic symbolism related to hair
and death and rejuvenation, 149
and stiffness of hair, 172
policy on hair
Japanese policy of censoring pubic hair images, 202–206
Manchu policy against Han queue, 125
Sun Yat Sen's decree concerning tonsure of, 1912
political economy approach, 260
pornography
and depiction of female public hair in Japan, 202
poverty and hair style
matted hair in India, 23–24
dishevelment in China, 179–180
psychoanalytic theory, 33–34, 145, 167
pubic hair
in Chinese thinking on race and female sexuality, 61
in Japan, 99n. 3, 195, 200–202, 208, 214, 265, 269
removal of by females in India, 265
public symbols, 12, 144, 237
punk hair styles, 275, 282

race
and beauty practices of females in the United States, 262–263